D1566208

On Henry James

On Henry James

The Best from *American Literature*

Edited by Louis J. Budd and Edwin H. Cady

Duke University Press   Durham and London 1990

© 1990 Duke University Press
All rights reserved.
Printed in the United States of America
on acid-free paper ∞
Library of Congress Cataloging-in-Publication Data
appear on the last printed page of this book.

Contents

Series Introduction

From Vol. 1, no. 1, in March 1929 to the latest issue, the front cover of *American Literature* has proclaimed that it is published "with the Cooperation of the American Literature Section [earlier Group] of the Modern Language Association." Though not easy to explain simply, the facts behind that statement have deeply influenced the conduct and contents of the journal for five decades and more. The journal has never been the "official" or "authorized" organ of any professional organization. Neither, however, has it been an independent expression of the tastes or ideas of Jay B. Hubbell, Clarence Gohdes, or Arlin Turner, for example. Historically, it was first in its field, designedly so. But its character has been unique, too.

Part of the tradition of the journal says that Hubbell in founding it intended a journal that should "hold the mirror up to the profession"—reflecting steadily its current interests and (ideally) at least sampling the best work being done by historians, critics, and bibliographers of American literature during any given year. Such remains the intent of the editors based at Duke University; such also through the decades has been the intent of the Board of Editors elected by the vote of members of the professional association—"Group" or "Section."

The operative point lies in the provisions of the constitutional "Agreements" between the now "Section" and the journal. One of these provides that the journal shall publish no article not approved by two readers from the elected Board. Another provides that the Chairman of the Board or, if one has been appointed and is acting in the editorial capacity at Duke, the Managing Editor need publish no article not judged worthy of the journal. Historically, again, the members of the successive Boards and the Duke editor have seen eye-to-eye. The Board has tended to approve fewer than one out of every ten submissions. The tradition of the journal dictates that it keep a slim back-log. With however much revision, therefore, the journal publishes practically everything the Board approves.

Founder Hubbell set an example from the start by achieving the almost total participation of the profession in the first five numbers of *American Literature*. Cairns, Murdock, Pattee, and Rusk were involved in Vol. 1, no. 1, along with Boynton, Killis Campbell, Foerster, George Philip Krapp, Leisy, Mabbott, Parrington, Bliss Perry, Louise Pound, Quinn, Spiller, Frederick Jackson Turner, and Stanley Williams on the editorial side. Spiller, Tremaine McDowell, Gohdes, and George B. Stewart contributed essays. Canby, George McLean Harper, Gregory Paine, and Howard Mumford Jones appeared as reviewers. Harry Hayden Clark and Allan Gilbert entered in Vol. 1, no. 2. Frederic I. Carpenter, Napier Wilt, Merle Curti, and Grant C. Knight in Vol. 1, no. 3; Clarence Faust, Granville Hicks, and Robert Morss Lovett in Vol. 1, no. 4; Walter Fuller Taylor, Orians, and Paul Shorey in Vol. 2, no. 1.

Who, among the founders of the profession, was missing? On the other hand, if the reader belongs to the profession and does not know those present, she or he probably does not know enough. With very few notable exceptions, the movers and shakers of the profession have since the beginning joined in cooperating to create and sustain the journal.

The foregoing facts lend a special distinction to the best articles in *American Literature*. They represent the many, often tumultuous winds of doctrine which have blown from the beginnings through the years of the decade next to last in this century. Those articles often became the firm footings upon which present structures of understanding rest. Looking backward, one finds that the argonauts were doughty. Though we know a great deal more than they, they are a great deal of what we know. Typically, the old best authors wrote well—better than most of us. Conceptually, even ideologically, we still wrestle with ideas they created. And every now and again one finds of course that certain of the latest work has reinvented the wheel one time more. Every now and again one finds a sunburst idea which present scholarship has forgotten. Then it appears that we have receded into mist or darkness by comparison.

Historical change, not always for the better, also shows itself in methods (and their implied theories) of how to present evidence, structure an argument, craft a scholarly article. The old masters were far from agreed—much to the contrary—about these matters.

But they are worth knowing in their own variety as well as in their instructive differences from us.

On the other hand, the majority of *American Literature*'s authors of the best remain among us, working, teaching, writing. One testimony to the quality of their masterliness is the frequency with which the journal gets requests from the makers of textbooks or collections of commentary to reprint from its pages. Now the opportunity presents itself to select without concern for permissions fees what seems the best about a number of authors and topics from the whole sweep of *American Literature*.

The fundamental reason for this series, in other words, lies in the intrinsic, enduring value of articles that have appeared in *American Literature* since 1929. The compilers, with humility, have accepted the challenge of choosing the best from well over a thousand articles and notes. By "best" is meant original yet sound, interesting, and useful for the study and teaching of an author, intellectual movement, motif, or genre.

The articles chosen for each volume of this series are given simply in the order of their first publication, thus speaking for themselves and entirely making their own points rather than serving the compilers' view of literary or philosophical or historical patterns. Happily, a chronological order has the virtues of displaying both the development of insight into a particular author, text, or motif and the shifts of scholarly and critical emphasis since 1929. But comparisons or trend-watching or a genetic approach should not blur the individual excellence of the articles reprinted. Each has opened a fresh line of inquiry, established a major perspective on a familiar problem, or settled a question that had bedeviled the experts. The compilers aim neither to demonstrate nor undermine any orthodoxy, still less to justify a preference for research over explication, for instance. In the original and still current subtitle, *American Literature* honors literary history and criticism equally—along with bibliography. To the compilers this series does demonstrate that any worthwhile author or text or problem can generate a variety of challenging perspectives. Collectively, the articles in its volumes have helped to raise contemporary standards of scholarship and criticism.

This series is planned to serve as a live resource, not as a homage to once vibrant but petrifying achievements in the past. For several sound reasons, its volumes prove to be weighted toward the more recent articles, but none of those reasons includes a presumed superiority of insight or of guiding doctrine among the most recent generations. Some of the older articles could benefit now from a minor revision, but the compilers have decided to reprint all of them exactly as they first appeared. In their time they met fully the standards of first-class research and judgment. Today's scholar and critic, their fortunate heir, should hope that rising generations will esteem his or her work so highly.

Many of the articles published in *American Literature* have actually come (and continue to come) from younger, even new members of the profession. Because many of those authors climb on to prominence in the field, the fact is worth emphasizing. Brief notes on the contributors in the volumes of their series may help readers to discover other biographical or cultural patterns.

Edwin H. Cady
Louis J. Budd

On Henry James

Young Henry James, Critic

Laurence Barrett

THE REVIVAL of interest in the critical work of Henry James, evident in the recent publication of two discriminating selections from his reviews and essays,[1] has been long overdue. Heretofore, too few of us have been familiar with the great body of criticism which came from his prolific pen, particularly in his earlier years[2] Even fewer of us have taken the time to give it the study and analysis it deserves.[3]

In the failure to do so we have been guilty of an oversight, for James's earlier critical writings are important. For the student of James they have a value beyond weighing. In embryonic form they hold the theories which produced James's later narrative techniques. The idea of the "germ," for instance, makes its first appearance something more than forty years before the *Prefaces;*[4]

---

[1] Morris Roberts, *The Art of Fiction and Other Essays by Henry James* (New York, 1948), and Allan Wade, *The Scenic Art* (New Brunswick, N. J., 1948).

[2] The complete list is to be found in LeRoy Phillips, *A Bibliography of the Writings of Henry James* (New York, 1930).

[3] But three or four valuable studies must be acknowledged. The broadest in scope is Morris Roberts, *Henry James's Criticism* (Cambridge, Mass., 1929). A more detailed study of the earlier criticism alone is available in Cornelia Pulsifer Kelley, *The Early Development of Henry James,* University of Illinois Studies in Language and Literature, XV (1930). Although Miss Kelley's primary interest is not in James as a critic, she looks to the books he reviewed for signs of influence upon him, and turns to the reviews he wrote for evidence of his own changing theories. Léon Edel, *The Prefaces of Henry James* (Paris, 1931), is a useful general study, and there is much of value in the more analytical introduction to Richard Blackmur, *The Art of the Novel: Critical Prefaces by Henry James* (New York, 1947); this introduction was also printed as an article in *Hound and Horn,* VII, 444–477 (April–May, 1943).

Less valuable, but still necessary to the serious student are the following: Van Wyck Brooks, "Henry James as a Reviewer," *Sketches in Criticism* (New York, 1932); George E. DeMille, "Henry James," *Literary Criticism in America* (New York, 1931); M. Sturges Gretton, "Mr. Henry James and His Prefaces," *Contemporary Review,* CI, 68–78 (Jan., 1918); Philip Littell, "Henry James as Critic," *New Republic,* I, 26–28 (Nov. 21, 1914); Edward Clark Marsh, "James: Auto-Critic," *Bookman* (N. Y.), XXX, 138–43 (Oct., 1909); Brander Matthews, "Henry James, Book Reviewer," *New York Times Book Review,* June 12, 1921; John G. Palache, "The Critical Faculty of Henry James," *University of California Chronicle,* XXVI, 399–410 (Oct., 1924); William Lyon Phelps, "Henry James, Reviewer," *Literary Review,* I, 4 (June 4, 1921); LeRoy Phillips, *Views and Reviews by Henry James* (Boston, 1908), Introduction; Pierre la Rose, *Notes and Reviews* (New York, 1921), Introduction.

[4] "Goethe loved her, seduced her, left her, and carried away the germ of the story of Margaret . . . ." ("Dumas and Goethe," *Nation,* XVII, 293, Oct. 30, 1873).

the principle of a central intelligence is clearly expressed in 1868, only three years after James had begun writing reviews;[5] and, as Morris Roberts has pointed out, the concept of Romance expressed in them is essentially the same as that which appears much later in the Preface to *The American*.[6]

But it is not only to the student of James that these essays are important. They are of equal value to the student of American literature as a whole. For a decade and a half they must have been a powerful influence on American taste. Time and again the editors of the highly respected and widely read periodicals for which he wrote—the *North American Review*, the *Atlantic Monthly*, and the *Nation*—assigned him the most important review of the issue, the one to which their readers would turn first. He reviewed as they came fresh from the presses the most recent novels of George Eliot, Victor Hugo, Trollope, Kingsley, and Dickens; the poetry of William Morris, Browning, and Tennyson; and the critical writings of Matthew Arnold, Scherer, and Swinburne. His readers would not have known whom they had to thank, for these early reviews went unsigned, but they could hardly have avoided the deep influence of his persuasive arguments.

Because of the very fact that the young James was important as a critic, I have examined his earlier criticism here, not in relation to his art, but simply as criticism. I have arbitrarily chosen a period beginning with his first published review in 1864 and terminating with the publication of *French Poets and Novelists* in 1878, and I have studied the reviews and essays he wrote in that period with the one intent of trying to understand what some of his basic critical principles were.

In the course of those fourteen years, James published more than 250 critical articles, the greater part of them reviews In them he showed himself to be a most assured young critic.[7] He sometimes

[5] "In every human imbroglio, be it of a comic or a tragic nature, it is good to think of an observer standing aloof, the critic, the idle commentator of it all, taking notes, as we may say, in the interest of truth. The exercise of this function is the chief ground of our interest in Juan" ("The Spanish Gypsy, A Poem," *North American Review*, CVII, 633, Oct., 1868).

[6] *The Art of Fiction*, p. x.

[7] He said that Swinburne's critical writing was "simply ghastly—ghastly in its poverty of insight and its pretension to make mere lurid imagery do duty as thought" ("Swinburne's Essays," *Nation*, XXI, 74, July 29, 1875). As a result of this assurance, when James was wrong he was very wrong indeed. He said that the new author of *Far from the Madding Crowd* was only an imitator of George Eliot, and a poor one at that. He believed that *Linda Tressel* and *Nina Baletka, the Story of a Maiden of Prague* were anonymous works by Trollope, and the best he had yet written.

showed himself to be provincial.[8] He wrote in a style direct, easy, and rapid, yet lucid and powerfully expressive—the style of a man whose ideas are clear-cut and integrated. Indeed, the most pronounced characteristic of these early essays is their unity of thought. The standards by which James judges have been carefully worked out; they fit together. He has taken his job seriously, and he has not come to it unprepared.

If anything, his system is too tight. It restricts him and makes him a narrow critic—a specialist in prose fiction and, to limit it still further, in the prose fiction of his own time. By far the greater part of his reviews and articles deals with novels of the mid-nineteenth century, and when he comes to poetry he is out of his element. He judged the sowing of the dragon's teeth at Colchis as "too complex and recondite a scene"[9] for graceful poetic expression. Yet he liked it when he found it in Morris, and honestly said so, though he could not tell why. But when he dealt with Dickens, George Eliot, or contemporary French novelists, he spoke with an assurance which makes it very clear that he had thought out the problems of the critic and of his own function as a member of that brotherhood.

Direct statements of James's critical tenets come up again and again in these essays, most frequently, interesting enough, in reviews of the least successful and the dullest dooks, where he seems to have felt free to leave the book behind and to fill the required space with his own speculations.[10] One review which seems to have suggested much in this way was that of "Dallas Galbraith,"[11] in which he states his critical manifesto clearly and uncompromisingly. Even more valuable are his reviews of the works of other critics—Matthew Arnold, Sainte-Beuve, Scherer, and Swinburne—

8 "What California was, socially, fifteen years ago, we cannot say; but it certainly was not the headquarters of politeness, and we accordingly leave it to Mr. Sedley's tender mercies. But we are better qualified to judge of New York and Boston" ("Marian Rooke," *Nation*, II, 248, Feb. 22, 1866).

". . . when a poet has secured for a hero a veritable prophet, with the bloom not yet rubbed off by literature, he has our heartiest congratulations. It perturbs our faith a little to learn that the prophet is Mr. Joe Smith, and the *dénouement* is to be the founding of Salt Lake City by Mr. Brigham Young; we reflect that there is a magic in association, and we are afraid we scent vulgarity in these . . . Mormonism we know to be a humbug, and rather a nasty one . . ." ("The Prophet, A Tragedy by Bayard Taylor," *North American Review*, CXX, 189, Jan., 1875).

9 "The Life and Death of Jason," *North American Review*, CV, 690 (Oct., 1867).

10 "We may frankly say that it strikes us as a ponderous failure; but it is an interesting failure as well, and it suggests a number of profitable reflections" ("Flaubert's Temptation of St. Anthony," *Nation*, XVIII, 365, June 4, 1874).

11 *Nation*, VII, 330–331 (Oct. 22, 1868).

for not only do they lead him into revealing discussions of criticism and critical problems, but what he approves and disapproves in them is clear sign of what his own standards are.

The first of these evaluations of a brother critic is his review of Matthew Arnold's *Essays in Criticism,* which appeared in the *North American Review* of July, 1865. That date puts it very early in James's critical career, his eighth publication, to be exact, and the first in which he dealt directly with the problems of the critic. It is, further, one of the most important, for in these early years the critic James owed more to Matthew Arnold than to any other.

The most basic of the ideas to appear in this essay is one which springs, in part at least, from James's own provincialism and his hatred of the vulgar, and which finds welcome support in Arnold's doctrine that the only salvation for the Philistine lies in learning to see life steadily and see it whole. It is the principle that the function of criticism is to exalt the importance of the ideal. Criticism deals with facts of course, must deal with them of necessity, but it deals with them disinterestedly, as Arnold said, and not for their sake alone. It deals with them for the sake of the truth in them, for it is only for the expression of truth that these facts exist.

. . . the great beauty of the critical movement advocated by Mr. Arnold is that in either direction its range of action is unlimited. It deals with plain facts as well as with the most exalted fancies; but it deals with them only for the sake of the truth which is in them, and not for *your* sake, reader, and that of your party. It takes *high ground,* which is the ground of theory. . . . We said just now that its duty was, among other things, to exalt, if possible, the importance of the ideal. We should, perhaps, have said the intellectual; that is, of the principle of understanding things. Its business is to urge the claims of all things to be understood. If this is its function in England, as Mr. Arnold represents, it seems to us that it is doubly its function in this country.[12]

It is obvious to anyone reading this early criticism that James did not always act upon this principle, but when he failed to do so the reason was simply that he found himself reviewing books which had very little in them to be understood, very little that admitted the critic to high ground; and when he found himself dealing with this kind of thing he simply gave up, and talked wearily to the Philistines in their own language.

[12] "Arnold's Essays in Criticism," *North American Review,* CI, 211 (July, 1865).

We do not open his [Trollope's] books with the expectation of being thrilled, or convinced, or deeply moved in any way, and, accordingly, when we find one to be as flat as a Dutch landscape, we remind ourselves that we have wittingly travelled into Holland, and that we have no right to abuse the scenery for being in character. We reflect, moreover, that there are a vast number of excellent Dutchmen for whom this low-lying horizon has infinite charms. If we are passionate and egotistical, we turn our backs on them for a nation of irreclaimable dullards; but if we are critical and disinterested, we will endeavor to view the prospect from a Dutch stand-point.[13]

Whatever it might become in practice, ideally the primary function of the critic was for James, as it was for Arnold, to perceive truth. But James differed from Arnold as to how that truth was to be apprehended. For him it was far less a matter of touchstones and far more a matter of intellect, and he perceived this difference and expressed it. Arnold, he said, unquestionably had feeling and observation, but these alone are not enough, and they may even be secondary.

He has these qualities, at any rate, of a good critic, whether or not he have the others,—the science and the logic. It is hard to say whether the literary critic is more called upon to understand or to feel. It is certain he will accomplish little unless he can feel acutely; although it is perhaps equally certain that he will become weak the moment he begins to "work," as we may say, his natural sensibilities. The best critic is probably he who leaves his feelings out of account, and relies upon reason for success.[14]

The admission here that feeling might challenge understanding as the primary faculty of the critic and the statement that it is a hard choice between them are, I think, largely the rhetorical device of minor concessions. James seems to present them only to assert more strongly the importance of the understanding. He has no trouble in deciding against feeling elsewhere. For him criticism is a rational process, and he cannot easily think of it otherwise. When he finds himself reviewing something which has moved him, yet which he does not fully understand, he is at a loss. Both Kipling and Morris leave him saying that he has been deeply stirred but does not know why, and it is obvious that this is a critical position

---

[13] "The Belton Estate," *Nation*, II, 22 (Jan. 4, 1866).
[14] "Arnold's Essays in Criticism," p. 208.

which James finds most uncomfortable. Indeed, a lack of reasonable understanding is the most severe charge he can bring against a
critic, and ten years after the Arnold review he brings it against
Swinburne:

His book is not at all a book of judgement; it is a book of pure imagination. His genius is for style simply, and not in the least for thought nor
for real analysis; he goes through the motions of criticism, and makes a
considerable show of logic and philosophy, but with deep appreciation
his writing seems to us to have very little to do. . . . He is an imaginative commentator, often a very splendid guide, but he is never a real
interpreter, and rarely a trustworthy guide.[15]

In charging it against Swinburne that he was no real interpreter
and hardly a trustworthy guide, James would seem to imply that
he thought it a primary function of the critic to interpret a work of
art to those of less perception and less ability to understand than he.
Perhaps; but James feels so pronounced a hatred of the vulgar and
expresses it so strongly that he gives the impression that this understanding which the critic seeks is more his own understanding than
teaching of his readers. If they do not follow him, if they do not
learn from him, that is hardly his fault. For James the critic is not
a zealot, not a crusader, not a missionary.

When you lay down a proposition which is forthwith controverted, it is
of course optional with you to take up the cudgels in its defense. If you
are deeply convinced of its truth, you will perhaps be content to leave
it to take care of itself; or, at all events, you will not go out of your way
to push its fortunes; for you will reflect that in the long run an opinion
often borrows credit from the forbearance of its patrons. In the long
run, we say; it will meanwhile cost you an occasional pang to see your
cherished theory turned into a football by the critics. . . . Unless, therefore, you are very confident of your ability to rescue it from the chaos of
kicks, you will best consult its interest by not mingling in the game.[16]

This idea that truth will make its own way, that it will succeed
without favoritism or assistance, is no mere escapism on James's
part. It is, instead, another facet of the disinterestedness he had
learned from Matthew Arnold, and he stresses its importance again
and again.

15 "Swinburne's Essays," *Nation*, XXI, 73 (July 29, 1875).
16 "Arnold's Essays in Criticism," p. 207.

Of all men who deal with ideas, the critic is essentially the least independent; it behooves him, therefore, to claim the utmost possible incidental or extrinsic freedom. His subject and his stand-point are limited beforehand. He is in the nature of his function *opposed* to his author, and his position, therefore, depends upon that which his author has taken. If, in addition to his natural and proper servitude to his subject, he is shackled with a further servitude, outside of his subject, he works at a ridiculous disadvantage. This outer servitude may either be to a principle, a theory, a doctrine, a dogma, or it may be to a party. . . .[17]

Only with this disinterestedness is the critic left free to practice that even-handed, almost ruthless justice which we see James himself administering in the reviews of this early period. Unfortunately, at the same time that it liberates him, this concept also reduces the critic's importance; for if truth will make its own way regardless of the opposition against it, there would seem to be no necessity for the critic to exist in order to preach and support it.

It is this very circumstance, we think—the fact that when a book is of decided ability it gets a fair hearing and pushes its own fortune—that makes it natural and proper to criticise it freely and impartially. The day of dogmatic criticism is over, and with it the ancient infallibility and tyranny of the critic. No critic lays down the law, because no reader receives the law ready made. The critic is simply a reader like all the others—a reader who prints his impressions.[18]

One is led, of course, to this admission that the critic is nothing but a printing reader, if one makes the critic, as James did, largely an individual searcher after understanding, rather than an interpreter and a teacher. The premise can lead only to a negative evaluation of criticism. Ten years later he wrote: "Art is one of the necessities of life; but even the critics themselves would probably not assert that criticism is anything more than an agreeable luxury—something like printed talk."[19]

But James's view of the critic is not purely negative; he does not mean that the critic serves only his own function, that his only purpose is to reach understanding within and for himself. True, that is for James one of the reasons why a man engages in the critical process, but beyond that is the fact that truth is a sum of many

[17] "A French Critic," *Nation*, I, 469 (Oct. 12, 1865).
[18] "Dallas Galbraith," *Nation*, VII, 331 (Oct. 22, 1868).
[19] "Notes on Whistler and Ruskin," *Nation*, XXVIII, 119 (Feb. 13, 1879).

opinions, of which his is one. The critic may no longer be dictator, but he is a contributor, and as such it is his responsibility to make his contribution clearly and emphatically.

Public opinion and public taste are silently distilled from a thousand private affirmations and convictions. No writer pretends that he tells us the whole truth; he knows that the whole truth is a great synthesis of the great body of small partial truths. But if the whole truth is to be pure and incontrovertible, it is needful that the various contributions to it be thoroughly firm and uncompromising. The critic reminds himself, then, that he must be before all things clear and emphatic.[20]

Singularly, it is here that feeling and sentiment, heretofore so rigorously excluded, do come in and fill their places. For though, in the process of evaluation, sentiment is dangerous and feeling only a substitute for reasonable understanding, yet once that understanding has been achieved sentiment is of inestimable value in expressing it. Sentiment can "seize upon a shade of truth and convey it with a directness which is not at the command of logical demonstration." Sentiment and feeling, in short, should be used sparingly by the critic, if at all, in evaluating a work; but they are invaluable aids when it comes to contributing his share to that great body of partial truths which is the whole truth.

We come full circle, then, to the idea with which we began, the idea that the function of the critic is to understand truth. That, obviously, is the keystone of James's whole theory, and what he meant by truth determines to a large extent the soundness of his entire critical doctrine. What he meant by it is, if not defined, at least further limited in his essay on Scherer:

The philosopher's function is to compare a work with an abstract principle of truth; the critic's is to compare a work with itself, with its own concrete standard of truth. The critic deals, therefore, with parts, the philosopher with wholes.[21]

And, since the function of the critic is to compare a work with itself, with its own standard of truth, "The critic's first duty in the presence of an author's collective works is to seek out some key to his method, some utterance of his literary convictions, some indi-

20 "Dallas Galbraith," p. 330.
21 "A French Critic," p. 469.

cation of his ruling theory."[22] The *Prefaces* are clear testimony that this critical tenet remained with James to the end; for their purpose is manifestly to give to the reader "some key to his method, some utterance of his literary convictions, some indication of his ruling theory" and then to leave it to the reader to act as his own judge of the extent to which the author has succeeded or failed.

It is, of course, sound criticism to watch the author's intent, but James does not take the position that the only truth which the critic must understand is the author's truth. He does not reduce the critic to a mere mathematician, subtracting the writer's achievement from his intent, and announcing, mechanically, the result. When we remember that in his essay on Matthew Arnold, James had equated, in the same breath, the principle of understanding things with that of exalting the ideal, it is obvious that there was for him some standard outside the work of art by which the critic is to judge. That standard he found, as did his fellow critics of his time, in an appeal to the critic's moral sense—to his conscience.

But as a critic, quite as much as any other writer, must have what M. Scherer calls an inspiration of his own, must possess a *unit* of sincerity and consistency, he finds it in his conscience. It is on this basis that he preserves his individuality, or, if you like, his self-respect. It is from this moral sense, and, we may add, from their religious convictions, that writers like Scherer derive that steadfast and delicate spiritual force which animates, coordinates, and harmonizes the mass of brief opinions, of undeveloped assertions, of conjectures, of fancies, of sentiments, which are the substance of this work.[23]

This concept of the moral response on the part of the critic, this appeal to conscience, is no mumbled creed with the early James; on the contrary, it is a living standard for his own judgments. His highest praise is cast in these terms. Mrs. Gaskell's *Wives and Daughters* is destined to attain the immortality of a classic because of "her social and moral knowledge" for which, so deep it runs, he feels his praise is all too little thanks. To our time George Sand seems a little less at home in the garb, but he assigns it to her as easily as to Mrs. Gaskell. Among her great virtues is "a moral maturity." And of Scherer, who he said in 1865 was "a solid embodi-

[22] "The Novels of George Eliot," *Atlantic Monthly*, XVIII, 479 (Oct., 1866).
[23] "A French Critic," p. 469.

ment of Mr. Arnold's ideal critic" (and, we might add, a solid
embodiment of young Mr. James's as well), he said:

But we prefer him [to Sainte-Beuve] because his morality is positive
without being obtrusive; and because, besides the distinction of beauty
and ugliness, the aesthetic distinction of right and wrong, there constantly occurs in his pages the moral distinction between good and evil;
because, in short, we salute in this fact that wisdom which, after having
made the journey round the whole sphere of knowledge, returns at last
with a melancholy joy to morality.[24]

The assumption of world-weariness in this last sentence may pro-
voke a smile when we remember it was written by a young man
of twenty-two, but that in no wise negates the fact that for this
young man the moral judgment was the final, the most important
judgment that the critic passed.

But James's concept of the moral in art was nothing so broad
as simply the ethically good opposed to the ethically bad. It was,
instead, a very precise concept, so carefully limited that he seldom
found it to his satisfaction in the books he reviewed, so precise that
we can best understand what he meant by a process of elimination—
by looking at some of the many cases of what he thought was
clearly not morality.

Morality was, for one thing, not sentimentality or didacticism.
There was nothing James disliked so much as the book with an
obvious moral, the kind of thing God-fearing parents picked out
for their children.

They offer neither the best history, the best piety, nor the best fiction,
but they appeal to a public which has long since become reconciled to
compromise—that extensive public, so respectable in everything but its
literary taste, which patronizes what is called "Sunday reading."[25]

Reviewing one book in which a very wise and very good and very
unreal little girl served as a continual mouthpiece for the pious
thoughts of her author, James chalked the whole off as "sentimental
in cold blood." What he objected to in this kind of thing was the
patent untruthfulness of it.

There is something almost awful in the thought of a writer undertaking
to give a detailed picture of the actions of a perfectly virtuous being. . . .

24 *Ibid.*
25 "The Schönberg-Cotta Family," *Nation,* I, 344–345 (Sept. 14, 1865).

Miss Muloch . . . gives us the impression of having always looked at men and women through a curtain of rose-colored gauze. This impediment to a clear and natural vision is nothing more, we conceive, than her excessive sentimentality. Such a defect may be but the exaggeration of a virtue, but it makes sad work in Miss Muloch's tales. It destroys their most vital property—their appearance of reality; it falsifies every fact and every truth it touches; and, by reaction, it inevitably impugns the writer's sincerity.[26]

But if sentiment and didacticism fail of moral depth because they are untrue, it does not for a minute follow that moral depth is to be found in their converse—realistic fiction. On the contrary, James brought an unrelenting charge of moral superficiality against the French realists.

The common aim of French *littérateurs* at the present moment seems to be to out-do Juvenal on his own line, and M. Feydeau has bent his bow last, and, we may say, shot furthest. It is hardly needful to say that his story is a tale of the seventh commandment, as that injunction is handled in French fictitious literature. It is filled with all manner of indecent episodes, and it terminates in an incident so monstrous that its exact nature is not even hinted to us. . . .
. . . to the average French mind the sentimental portions of M. Feydeau's narrative will doubtless seem very natural and touching. Even to such a reader, however, they must yield in reality and interest to the more repulsive portions. So long as the exploits of vice are so clearly described, so long will books of this class continue to be read for their pictures of vice.[27]

Morality, then, is neither sentiment nor realism. Neither is it history.

If there is one thing that history does not teach, it seems to us, it is just this very lesson. What strikes an attentive student of the past is the indifference of events to man's moral worth or worthlessness. What strikes him, indeed, is the vast difficulty there is in deciding upon men's goodness and their turpitude. . . . In history it is impossible to view individuals singly. . . . To judge them morally we are obliged to push our enquiry through a concatenation of causes and effects in which, from their delicate nature, enquiry very soon becomes impracticable, and thus we are reduced to talking sentiment. Nothing is more surprising than the alertness with which writers like Mr. Froude are ready to pronounce

[26] "A Noble Life," *Nation*, II, 276 (March 1, 1866).
[27] " 'The Manners of the Day' in Paris," *Nation*, VI, 73 (Jan. 23, 1866).

upon the moral character of historical persons, and their readiness to make vague moral epithets stand in lieu of real psychological facts.[28]

Our clue to a positive understanding of what James meant by moral depth in fiction lies in that last suggestion that too often "vague moral epithets stand in lieu of real psychological facts." In a review of another of those French novelists he expressed more clearly still this idea that the only morality in fiction is to be found in psychological realism and in the study of the human personality in all its complexity:

The author, indeed, has aimed at making it something more—at writing a work with a high moral bearing. In this we think he has signally failed. To stir the reader's moral nature, and to write with truth and eloquence the moral history of superior men and women, demand more freedom and generosity of mind than M. Feuillet seems to us to possess. Like those of most of the best of the French romancers, his works wear, morally, to American eyes, a decidedly thin and superficial look. Men and women, in our conception, are deeper, more substantial, more self-directing; they have, if not more virtue, at least more conscience; and when conscience comes into the game, human history ceases to be a perfectly simple tale. M. Feuillet is not in the smallest degree a moralist, and, as a logical consequence, M. de Camors is a most unreal and un-substantial character.[29]

Morality in fiction, then, is the morality of intelligent, complex characters clearly portrayed. Saints, as James says when discussing good Boston men and woman in a review of Eugénie de Guérin's *Letters,* are innocent but complex. They are not ignorant, and they cannot well be, for if ignorant they are not moral characters, but pious ones. Even Mlle de Guérin is such an empty, pious figure. "There is something very pathetic in the intellectual penury with which [she] had to struggle."[30]

It is evident to readers of the *Prefaces* that, although James never abandoned the belief that the clear portrayal of complex character is the primary function of the novelist, he ceased to speak of it as morality. There is obviously a shift in emphasis, and that shift begins to be evident in the reviews of the mid-1870's. It may have risen in part from James's constant reaching for more precise prin-

28 "Mr. Froude's Short Studies," *Nation,* V, 351 (Oct. 31, 1867).
29 "Camors," *Nation,* VII, 92–93 (July 30, 1868).
30 "The Letters of Eugenie de Guerin," *Nation,* III, 206 (Sept. 13, 1866).

ciples than contented many of his contemporaries. Certainly it also rose from the fact that as James wrote more and more fiction and less and less criticism, he found his principles being tested, and considerably tempered, in the fire of his own practice.

This mutual modification of practice by principle and of principle by practice is clearly evident in *Roderick Hudson*. Written in 1875, *Roderick Hudson* was, if we exclude *Watch and Ward* as James would have us, his first full-fledged novel. The story of an artist, it reflects, both in what it does and in what it says directly, much of James's thinking about the problems of the artist, and particularly about the problem of morality.

The idea that saints are complex, that mere virtue if linked with intellectual penury is nothing more than a pathetic piety, comes clear early in the book when Rowland Mallet and Roderick Hudson discuss Miss Garland. Rowland is obviously speaking for James.

"Why, she's a stern moralist [says Hudson], and she would infer from my appearance that I have become a gilded profligate. . . ."

"Shall you think I take a liberty," asked Rowland, "if I say you judge her superficially?"

"For heaven's sake," cried Roderick laughing, "don't tell me she's not a moralist! It was for that I fell in love with her—and with rigid virtue in her person."

"She is a moralist, but not, as you imply, a narrow one. That's more than a difference in degree; it's a difference in kind. I don't know whether I ever mentioned it, but I have a great notion of Miss Garland. There is nothing narrow about her but her experience; everything else is large. My impression is that she is very intelligent, but that she has never had a chance to prove it. Some day or other I am sure she will judge fairly and wisely of everything."

"Stay a bit!" cried Roderick; "you are a better Catholic than the Pope. I shall be content if she judges fairly of me—of my merits, that is. The rest she must not judge at all. . . ."[31]

This misconception of morality in Roderick Hudson is an essential part of his failure. It leads to the prophetic irony of his remark when he first sees Christina Light: "If beauty is immoral, as people

[31] *Roderick Hudson* (London, 1883), I, 66. When James prepared *Roderick Hudson* for the New York Edition, he made many pronounced changes in such passages as this. Those changes reveal much of the older James, but we are dealing with the young James here, and my quotations are, therefore, from the most easily available of the earlier editions.

think at Northampton," said Roderick, "she is the incarnation of evil."[32] And it leads to his rebellious theory that the artist should be a law unto himself, to his insistence that he is free of moral standards, even when judged by Mary Garland and Rowland Mallett. In so far as Hudson has freed himself from the Northampton idea of beauty, he has his author's sympathies. Certainly when he completely shocks Mr. Leavenworth, a rather heavily drawn Philistine, by doing a statue of a drunken lazzarone, he has James behind him. But when he expresses his doctrine of moral irresponsibility, James is not behind him:

"I think that when you expect a man to produce beautiful and wondeful works of art you ought to allow him a certain freedom of action, you ought to give him a long rope, you ought to let him follow his fancy and look for his material wherever he thinks he may find it! . . . You demand of us to be imaginative, and you deny us the things that feed the imagination. In labour we must be as passionate as the inspired; in life we must be mere machines. It won't do! When you have got an artist to deal with, you must take him as he is, good and bad together."[33]

Actually, James cannot help betraying doubts in this book. That is natural enough, for he wrote it while many of these basic ideas were in transition. Often he seems to be not quite sure. Even Rowland Mallett suspects that the artist should enjoy a certain moral exemption.

He wondered gloomily, at any rate, whether for men of his companion's large easy power there was not a larger moral law than for narrow mediocrities like himself, who, yielding Nature a meagre interest on her investment (such as it was), had no reason to expect from her this affectionate laxity as to their accounts.[34]

But in spite of Rowland Mallett's doubts, James's strong sense of the importance of morality in art forces the book to become essentially a story of moral degeneration. The important point is that it is not a moral degeneration in the Philistine sense. Roderick Hudson breaks none of the ten commandments; he commits not so much as a single act for which he could be tried in any court of law. He is simply unstable and irresponsible. His personality is unintegrated; it does not fit together as an intelligent, complex

32 *Roderick Hudson,* p. 73.
33 *Roderick Hudson,* p. 167.
34 *Roderick Hudson,* I, 142.

whole. That he should be so portrayed is natural enough, for by the mid-seventies morality was coming to be for James more and more a matter of complex, refined personality.

Hints of the change are evident, even before *Roderick Hudson,* in the reviews of 1874 and 1875. The review of "School for Scandal" which appeared in the *Atlantic Monthly* in December of 1874, is, if it is by James,[35] one of the most direct early expressions of this dissatisfaction with the conventional critical standard of morality.

> We are inclined to think . . . that it does seriously matter whether even uncultivated minds are entertained in good taste or in bad. Our point would be simply that it matters rather less than many of the people interested in the moral mission of art are inclined to admit. We are by no means sure that art is very intimately connected with a moral mission. . . .[36]

And the clearest expression of it, if we may step twelve years ahead, appears in "The Art of Fiction." There, more precisely than ever before, James expresses the doubts and questions to which this principle of morality has led him. And, faced with them, he comes back to that principle which, as we have seen before, he never doubted, the principle of the author's achievement and his intent:

> The most interesting part of Mr. Besant's lecture is unfortunately the briefest passage—his very cursory allusion to the "conscious moral purpose" of the novel. . . . It is a question surrounded with difficulties, as witness the very first that meets us, in the form of a definite question, on the threshold. Vagueness, in such a discussion, is fatal, and what is the meaning of your morality and your conscious moral purpose? Will you not define your terms and explain how (a novel being a picture) a picture can be either moral or immoral? You wish to paint a moral picture or carve a moral statue: will you tell us how you would set about it? We are discussing the Art of Fiction: questions of art are questions

35 Authorship has been challenged by Edna Kenton. See Wade, *op. cit.,* p. 20 n. Wade believes there is not sufficient evidence to throw it out of the canon. The reader of James's reviews of 1874, '75, and '76 will find the same tone, sometimes less positively expressed, running through them. James is saying much less of morality and much more of technical skill. "In fact, we suspect that moralizing too rigidly here is a waste of ingenuity . . ." ("Notes on the Theatres," *Nation,* XXI, 178–179, March 11, 1875). And he no longer feels that morality is essential to success in a novel: ". . . not to be sentimental, not to be moral, not to be rhetorical, but to have simply a sort of gentlemanly, epicurean relish for the bitterness of the general human lot, and to distil it into little polished silver cups—this was Merimee's conscious effort, and this was his rare success" ("Prosper Merimee," *Nation,* XVIII, 111, Feb. 12, 1874).
36 "The Drama," *Atlantic Monthly,* XXXIV, 755 (Dec., 1874).

(in the widest sense) of execution; questions of morality are quite another affair, and will you not let us see how it is that you find it so easy to mix them up? . . . To what degree a purpose in a work of art is a source of corruption I shall not attempt to inquire. The one that seems to me least dangerous is the purpose of making a perfect work. . . .

There is one point at which the moral sense and the artistic sense lie very near together; that is in the light of the very obvious truth that the deepest quality of a work of art will always be the quality of the mind of the producer. In proportion as that intelligence is fine will the novel, the picture, the statue partake of the substance of beauty and truth. To be constituted of such elements is, to my vision, to have purpose enough.[37]

The young Henry James was, then, primarily a critic, and there is reason to believe he was a much more influential one than we have hitherto suspected. Long before his name as author gave weight to his opinions as judge, he was quietly evaluating great writers in the most widely read and most respected literary periodicals of his time. He was certainly a careful and systematic critic. Although he borrowed much from Matthew Arnold, he did not borrow without qualifying nor without reaching for a greater precision of thought. He perceived a sharp distinction between judging a work within itself and judging it against an absolute standard, and in his need for such an absolute he accepted, for a time, the contemporary yardstick of morality. Then, as he labored to make this concept, too, more precise, and as he faced the problem of applying it in his own writing, he found himself thinking of morality as intellect; and the basic purpose of the artist, as he conceived it, became essentially the portrayal of complex, refined personality. James's whole history is a process of clarification of thought, a story of increasingly precise principles. He would never have been the novelist he was without the schooling of the earlier criticism, and without the novels he would never have been the critic he showed himself to be in the *Prefaces*.

[37] "The Art of Fiction," *Partial Portraits* (London and New York, 1894), pp. 404–406.

Henry James, Lecturer

Marie P. Harris

A N EARLY WRITER on Henry James as a lecturer commented that, literally speaking, there was no occasion for
consideration of the subject inasmuch as James was not a " 'lecturer,'
in our popular sense, and can scarcely be made into one by placing
him next a high table and inviting him to speak from nine until
ten o'clock in the evening."[1] If one adopts such a strict interpretation of the term, then obviously Henry James was not a lecturer.
Both the lectures he gave during the early months of 1905 are the
"orally delivered" essays Miss Dunbar tagged them. Nevertheless,
however "semi-publicly" or even privately he did so, James did
address more than a dozen different groups from Cambridge to
Los Angeles during the latter part of his 1904-1905 stay in America.
Hence, miscast as he at first may seem in the role, James was a
lecturer for a few months. But, one wonders, why did James become a lecturer? And what sort of a lecturer was he? What was
the audience reaction to his lectures? Since the answers to these
questions are not precisely what one might expect them to be,
a study of this relatively little known aspect of Henry James's career
makes an illuminating excursion into James biography as well as
furnishes a picture of James slightly different from the usual one.

Unlike other famous writers (for instance, Thackeray and
Dickens) James had not come to America in 1904 in order to lecture. He had, in fact, months before sailing from England, refused
the invitation to lecture which he had received from the Lowell
Institute, one of the oldest and most influential lecture-sponsoring
institutions in the United States. At the time, James recognized
the honor done him by the Institute but felt that the small amount
of money offered could not compensate for the time and trouble
lecturing would cost him. He had more important business—the
gathering of material—in America. Once he was in this country,
however, he did lecture—for more money than the Lowell Institute
had been able to offer him. He had had, as a commentator put it,

[1] Olivia Howard Dunbar, "Henry James as a Lecturer," *Critic*, XLVII, 24 (July, 1905).

"indeed, a lecture in his pocket, but rather as though it were part of his luggage than as the motive of his enterprise."[2] Still it actually was the money James earned from his lecturing which enabled him to extend his American visit from the originally contemplated six or eight months to ten months and possibly even permitted him to make a more comprehensive tour of America than he might otherwise have been able to do. For he lectured, as he put it, "to pay the Piper, as I go—for high fees (of course). . . ." It was "a public development on [his] desperate part" which paid his traveling expenses.

James took the "leap" (in his phrase) for the first time on January 9, 1905, before the Contemporary Club of Philadelphia. He was introduced by the president of the Club, Miss Agnes Repplier,[3] the well-known Philadelphia essayist, to a large audience. The Clover Room of the Bellevue-Stratford was crowded, the Philadelphia *Public Ledger* said, with an audience including, "apart from members of the club, some of Philadelphia's most distinguished representatives of letters, art, the learned professions and public life." All apparently felt, as many later audiences were to do, that the man who was sometimes called[4] the dean of his particular department of American letters was well worth hearing— even if one had to stand, as "fully a hundred persons" did this time.

James's second lecture, at Bryn Mawr, supposedly to a "small" group, was attended by over seven hundred persons. He read his "The Lesson of Balzac" lecture again—as he was to do many more times in the Midwest, the West, and later in the East once more. Since both these lectures were much written about, the accounts of them furnish a reasonably complete answer to the question as to what sort of lecturer Henry James was, an answer which the reports of his later lectures confirm rather than alter.

James was past sixty at this time, a heavily built, vigorous-looking man, who preferred to dress in comfortable rather than modish clothes.[5] Those American correspondents who had already formed

[2] Wilmer Cave France, "Mr. Henry James as a Lecturer," *Bookman*, XXI, 71 (March, 1905).

[3] One of Miss Repplier's friends heard that her introductory speech "eclipsed Henry James's, whereof the delivery was almost irredeemably bad" (*The Letters of Horace Howard Furness*, Boston, 1922, II, 122). However, see below on James's delivery.

[4] With "doubtful wisdom," the *Book News* thought (XXIII, 485, Feb., 1905).

[5] "He looked like a gentleman who had dressed in the dark," Hamlin Garland com-

their own picture of Henry James were naïvely surprised, when they saw him, at his energy and size. The New York *Sun* reporter who met James at the boat is representative: the "immensely robust" James seemed, to this reporter, "anything but the man one is inclined to fancy from reading his delicate tales."[6] Others thought James wore "the aspect of a prosperous man of affairs engaged in projects of haute finance, rather than the guise of a dazzling literary lion."[7] While audiences "expected to see merely an agreeable man, with an irrepressible 'literary' earmark or two," another critic added, most of them must have been surprised to find themselves in "the presence of a man of tremendous power, even, perhaps, of greatness."[8] Further, James had, it was noticed, an unexpectedly genial and kindly presence[9] as well as a faintly "clerical" aspect.[10] Just prior to sailing for America James had had the beard and mustache which had characterized his middle years removed,[11] and his conventionalized, impassive exterior was a younger version of the clean-shaven, thoughtful[12] one now familiar as his seventieth birthday Sargent portrait. In 1905 James's face was said to be still "unwrinkled," with "sharp and clear" features and "piercing" gray eyes; his profile was considered striking, his jaw "powerful," his head "dome-like."[13]

Even during his first lecture, his actual debut on the platform,

---

mented on James's appearance one evening in Chicago. "His hat of the 'bowler' type was a little askew on his head and a little too large for him. His black tie always at an angle was of a piece with the long-suffering evening suit. His vest was black and cut in the fashion of 1898, and his trousers needed pressing" (*Companions on the Trail*, New York, 1931, pp. 259-260).

[6] Aug. 30, 1904.

[7] Philadelphia *North American*, Jan. 10, 1905. See also "Mr. Henry James on Balzac," *Book News*, XXIII, 487 (Feb., 1905) and *Reader*, V, 360 (Feb., 1905).

[8] "Henry James as a Lecturer," *loc. cit.*

[9] James's not generally recognized geniality and kindliness are well represented in Witter Bynner's account (*Saturday Review of Literature*, XXVI, 23, May 22, 1943) of how James approved the young Bynner's apocryphal "interview" (*Critic*, XLVI, 146-148, Feb., 1905).

[10] This vanished, however, Miss Dunbar observed, when James left the platform. Still, James "bodied forth almost precisely my notion of a bishop of the Episcopal Church," Hamlin Garland noted about this time (*op. cit.*, p. 256).

[11] The removal made him "much handsomer," some thought. See *Reader*, V, 360 (Feb., 1905).

[12] Garland found James's "conversation, though lively (almost vivacious) . . . lacking in humor. There was no chuckle in his voice, no lines of fun lurking about the corners of his mouth. Without being solemn or portentous he was serious" (*op. cit.*, p. 257).

[13] Philadelphia *North American*, Jan. 10, 1905; *Reader*, V, 360 (Feb., 1905); and others.

James was quite at ease, no "trace of embarrassment" appearing in his manner.[14]   He read his lecture with "one hand holding the manuscript, the other resting for the most part in a pocket, save where, two or three times, there came an involuntary gesture. . . ." His utterance was said to be distinct, slow, and deliberate, and he was always "ready to acknowledge any little ripple of laughter occasioned by his numerous small witticisms, prepared though they were, with a slight nod and a pleasant smile." He read from loose sheets of manuscript, and, for the most part, without expression— "whether he was praising or blaming," the Philadelphia *Public Ledger* disapprovingly noted, "making a point or carrying the audience to a change of viewpoint."[15]   The *Nation* correspondent, however, thought James's "complete absence of emphasis and gesture [gave the] agreeable impression that there [was] no effort on the part of the speaker."[16]   James's voice, "low in key" and "evenly modulated," with "the peculiar falling inflection at the close of sentences so often heard in pulpit delivery,"[17] was also "rhythmic and in accordance with the rhythm his body swayed slowly back and forth."[18] The *Public Ledger* reporter thought James's stammer "frequently" sent the novelist back to the beginning of his sentences.[19]   Other reporters, either more kindly or less observant, merely noted the tardiloquence which, a result of an only partial victory over his boyhood stammer, was sometimes mistaken, according to a friend, "for affectation—or, more quaintly, for an artless form of Anglomania. . . ."[20]

On the whole, public reaction to James's carefully written, orally delivered study of Balzac, the "master," was favorable. Wilmer Cave France, an unfriendly critic of James, said that as "the pleasant even voice of [James] uttered strings of images . . . his audience almost seemed to breathe, 'O still delay, thou art so fair!' and still

[14] *Book News*, XXIII, 487 (Feb., 1905).   The two succeeding comments on James's delivery and manner are from this account also.

[15] Jan. 10, 1905.

[16] *Nation*, LXXX, 53 (Jan. 19, 1905).

[17] Philadelphia *North American*, Jan. 10, 1905.

[18] *Book News*, XXIII, 487 (Feb., 1905).

[19] Philadelphia *Public Ledger*, Jan. 10, 1905.

[20] Edith Wharton, "Henry James in His Letters," *Quarterly Review*, CCXXXIV, 188 (July, 1920).   Garland found James's *conversational* manner "maddeningly hesitant," but thought James's "pauses were in no sense those of a stammerer. . . . He appeared to grope for the exact, exquisite, ultimate adjective until, at times, I ached with his effort. But the word came—and the halt was justified!" (*op. cit.*, p. 258).

Mr. James delayed."[21]   Certainly the Balzac lecture as printed is
long, and as given it must still have been intricate, at least. Garland
said that it was "austerely literary."[22]   Still, possibly because of
James's careful organization and articulation and his reviewers'
conscientious attention, fairly coherent accounts of it were given
during the first part of 1905.[23]   For "The Lesson of Balzac" is
another essay on the art of fiction, an art about which James had
thought long and intelligently. Balzac, "the father of us all," is
commended for his many great qualities but not very specifically
and always for the somewhat extrinsic reason of his "lesson." The
contrasts which James makes in this lecture—between earlier novels
(eminently Balzac's and Thackeray's) and the "object of easy manufacture . . . produced in quantity" which the contemporary novel was
—are illuminating to the student of James; they were probably
puzzling, however, to many in his audience. James later was to
feel that the lecture was too special and critical for at least the
"primitive propensities" of his Midwestern audiences. The lecture
is technical—as Elizabeth Luther Cary said, James's hearers had
been taken "frankly into the workroom of art. . . ."[24]—and does not
have what would seem to be the wider appeal of his second lecture
on the question of American speech.

But the fact that Henry James was lecturing was the important
thing, not what he was lecturing about; and when, after the Bryn
Mawr lecture, he resumed his tour through the Atlantic states,
journeying as far south as Palm Beach, Florida, before returning
briefly to New York and Cambridge, James received a number of
invitations to lecture from "private," "literary," and "ladies'" clubs
as well as from a few prominent individuals. James judiciously
accepted those offers which were most advantageous to him both as
regards place and payment. He had very soon become conscious,
he wrote Howells at this time, "that I couldn't at all face the prospect of [lecturing] in many smaller places, on minor terms."[25] As

[21] *Op. cit.* Throughout James's lecture tour the enthusiastic approval he received from
women was heavily weighted against him by such critics as France. France thought that
James's audiences, predominantly feminine, were necessarily so, since nine out of ten *men*
could not read Henry James.

[22] *Op. cit.*, p. 259.

[23] While the lecture was still unpublished. This was not true of his second lecture,
but there his hearers seem at fault. See below.

[24] New York *Times*, May 27, 1905, p. 338.

[25] Unpublished letter, James to Howells, March 1, 1905, in Howells collection in the
Houghton Library at Harvard.

a consequence, when he did lecture, it was for high fees—usually, he said, as much as a pound (about five dollars) a minute, and sometimes twice that. From his six Midwest "recitals" in March, 1905, he made, he estimated, $1350. In the space of ten days he lectured before the Contemporary Club of St. Louis (March 7); before the Twentieth Century Club of Chicago (March 10); before the Fortnightly Club of Chicago (March 11); before a group at Notre Dame University in Indiana (March 14); as well as before the Indiana Literary and Contemporary Clubs and the Irvington Athenaeum in Indianapolis (March 17). The latter Indianapolis clubs, while James was still in Florida, through Booth Tarkington had offered him four or five hundred dollars to make one lecture under their combined sponsorship while other groups such as the Fortnightly in Chicago offered as much as $250.

In addition to these cheerful financial results, James felt that his lecturing was improving. He thought he did better, for instance, his second time, at Bryn Mawr, than his first, at Philadelphia, and even felt that he had perhaps "discovered [his] vocation"; then he thought he got through "honorably" at St. Louis; and in Chicago, he lectured, he said, with unmistakable success.[26] His lectures in the Midwest, like all his others, were popular. There was, for instance, a capacity crowd at his afternoon lecture in Chicago even though he was competing with such an attraction as Paderewski (who, however, played to an audience of about three thousand; James, to three hundred). The newspapers, in Chicago particularly, made much of James's visit, one reporter amusing himself the afternoon of James's arrival in that city by essaying a description of James's "too, too analytical imagination" embroidering on (among other things) "the wonderful element in the astonishing redundance of the [Pullman porter's] gratitude" (the porter supposedly said, "Thank you, sah, thank you"). After getting off at the North Shore suburb of Winnetka, according to this reporter, James

looked about him helplessly as if it would have been a relief to discover Maria Gostrey waiting to offer her inestimable services as cicerone. He was to recall later that he had noticed a face in the crowd that was remarkably reminiscent of Daisy Miller's, but he was not sure—it was so

[26] Garland attended one of the Chicago lectures and thought James read "well" from his manuscript: "His voice was resonant and his utterance quite free from hesitations" (*op. cit.*, p. 259).

long since he had seen her. One other face arrested his attention—the countenance of a girl who looked as if she might know all that Maisie knew and volumes more. . . .[27]

Daisy Miller, the best known of James's heroines, was featured again that evening when James was introduced to the Twentieth Century Club.

"Twenty or twenty-five years ago [it was said then] Mr. James published 'Daisy Miller,' and Boston immediately declared that 'Daisy' was a Chicago girl. We claim her, therefore; and we have good right. Twenty-five years ago Daisy Miller was the impulsive, frank Chicago girl drawn by Mr. James, but to-night she is in this audience, an intellectual, charming diplomatic Chicago woman. The prototype of Daisy Miller is with us now, and after his address we are privileged to ask Mr. James who she is."[28]

The novelist listened to this announcement with "wide-eyed amazement," and then registered good-humoured resignation. Attention, however, was inevitably directed more toward this identification of Daisy Miller than toward anything James said during his two-hour lecture on Balzac. Afterwards to "each and every one" of the three hundred who quizzed him James had to say that there was no real Daisy Miller:

"These creations [he is quoted as adding] are the crystallization of many impressions, the final product of much observation. Daisy Miller is a type, not a portrait drawn with slavish realism to one model. There may be one hundred Daisy Millers for all I know. Perhaps every woman here is a Daisy Miller."

Despite his gallantry[29] James quite possibly did not completely enjoy this joke, which must have come close to rendering his lecture ineffective. The *Record-Herald* reporter himself was more concerned with the hoax than with anything the lion of the evening had had to say. Unlike the reporters of James's earlier lectures, he only briefly remarked that James's paper "glowed" with "keen critical insight" and "sparkled" with "high-polished phrases."

[27] Chicago *Daily Tribune*, March 10, 1905.

[28] This joke "threatened . . . to become as famous a hoax as Stockton's 'The Lady, or the Tiger?'" according to the Chicago *Record-Herald*, March 11, 1905, from which this account of the evening is taken.

[29] James, in turn, might have pointed out with some justification that Daisy Miller was from Schenectady, New York.

When James lectured the next afternoon, the unfriendly *Tribune* writer commented that the novelist who wrote like a psychologist[30] lectured to an audience of over three hundred made up of the Fortnightly and Friday Clubs "and a few men" who were also invited.

When Mr. James had turned the last pages of his manuscript [the writer continued] only two men remained. As George Ade would have said, one had gone to sleep and the other was penned in. But the 300 women were greatly interested from first to last.

A little later when William James was in the Midwest, he wrote Henry that he had been hearing "the most extravagant opinions about the charm of your lectures,"[31] so that the sarcastic reports of James in the papers do not represent all phases of the Chicago reaction to his lectures. But it is improbable that James, despite his continued improvement and continued popularity as a lecturer, was any more an unqualified success as a lecturer in the Midwest than he had been in Pennsylvania. In Indianapolis the next week, for instance, his reading was still reported as being "without color . . . except in few places and briefly."[32] Another Indianapolis reporter, however, did feel that James was "in a peculiarly happy vein" and reported that "he held the attention of his audience without interruption." There were even (again) at times ripples of applause following "the recital of particularly effective parts of the narrative."[33] The same reporter added, noncommittally but still not favorably, that James's effort was "an ambitious one" and that it "taxed the mentalities of his hearers at times to follow the deductions of the reader." The Indianapolis *News* writer more explicitly thought James's lecture a mere

panorama of word pictures requiring an hour to unroll. Looking over his audience and realizing that he was in Indiana [the reporter added], he apparently assumed that all the brilliant assemblage were authors, novelists, or shortly to become so, and in describing Balzac's methods, very properly referred to the great Frenchman as our model—meaning his model and the model of all of us—in the art of story writing.

[30] " 'You say he writes like a novelist?' asked one before the lecturer appeared. 'No. That is his brother,' said another. 'This one writes like a psychologist' " (Chicago *Tribune*, March 12, 1905).

[31] Unpublished letter, William James to Henry James, July 12, 1905, in the James collection in the Houghton Library at Harvard.

[32] Indianapolis *News*, March 18, 1905.   [33] Indianapolis *Sentinel*, March 18, 1905.

This somewhat ill-natured tone, scarcely warranted by anything James says in his lecture, probably is the result of the ever-present American resentment of England and the English which more than one patriotic reporter in 1905 took out on Henry James.[34]   James's kindly meant remarks to an Indianapolis reporter about the people of the United States having "advanced in civilization" during his stay abroad, for example, made an Indianapolis editor wish

To remove any possible misapprehension that may exist in his mind . . . the progress made is not due to reading Mr. James's inane books.[35]

James had also urbanely but untactfully said that one might "find in the far West many beauties that are wanting in the middle parts of the country,"[36] which made him a target for this additional shot:

Evidently the middle country doesn't impress Henry James. He hopes, or thinks he hopes, or believes that he may reasonably share an expectation that he may hope, or at least for thinking that he may hope, to see something between Indiana and the coast that will look or that has the appearance of looking better to his eyes.

After such a reception James, in Chicago once more, between trains, declared himself in a letter to a friend "weary of motion and chatter," and once on the coast although liking California he commented that he still did not like "the way one must go to get here. Forty-eight hours of desert, two days of parching wind and dry sand. . . ."[37]   In Los Angeles he made what he called "the obvious trips," and then, "shrinking from ostentatious publicity," he retired to Coronado Beach for over a week. He worked on a new lecture there, the one for his return in June to Bryn Mawr, and returned to Los Angeles to lecture (April 7, 10:00 A.M.) only after being "pounced" on by what he called a "female culture club of 900 members" who wanted him to deliver his "famous 'address.'"
From Los Angeles he proceeded northward through San Fran-

---

[34] Many of the reportorial jibes would seem to be in the nature of what the genial Chicago *Record-Herald* writer said the victimization of James before the Twentieth Century Club (the Daisy Miller "hoax") was: punishment for James's "having expatriated himself from this, his native land, wooed away by the literary seductions of London. . . ." The general subject of the American journalistic reaction to James, although it will be taken up briefly in reference to James's other lecture, "The Question of Our Speech," might well be a paper by itself.

[35] Indianapolis *Sentinel*, March 18, 1905.   [36] Indianapolis *News*, March 17, 1905.

[37] Los Angeles *Sunday Times*, March 26, 1905.

cisco, Portland, Seattle, and Vancouver, British Columbia, to return
East over the Canadian Pacific Railroad. In the East once again he
lectured the latter part of April in New York City and Washington,
the early part of May at Smith College and Brooklyn,[38] and later
the same month in Cambridge. An audience of over a thousand
crowded into Sanders Theatre in Harvard's Memorial Hall to hear
this lecture of James's; it was reported that "several ladies from
professorial households were obliged to sit on the floor. . . ."[39]

James reserved his new lecture, "The Question of Our Speech,"
for his return to Bryn Mawr. There, at commencement time, he
considered, good-naturedly but seriously, the currently popular
question of American speech—although not precisely in the way
other commentators of the time did. He did see the English language as an "unrescued Andromeda," "distracted, dishevelled, despoiled, divested of [the] beautiful and becoming drapery of native
atmosphere and circumstance"; but he devoted less than a quarter
of his lecture to this phase of the problem. He was principally
concerned instead with the slovenly way most Americans spoke,
attributing American carelessness[40] in speech to the lack of a "tone
standard"; newspapers and common schools were open to criticism,
James said, because in so greatly a "newspapered" and "schooled"
country they were used as a standard while they were actually
"below the mark" for discrimination.

In reporting James's lecture the newspapers, naturally enough
perhaps, concentrated on the more sensational aspects of James's
digressive pointing out of the adverse influences on American
speech. James's remark that the newspapers ("black eruptions of
print") and the common schools were influences which kept our
speech crude, untidy, and careless was widely quoted. The Philadelphia *Public Ledger* sarcastically commented, in reporting James's
address, that of course James spoke " 'tidily' [but] many persons

[38] His early perceptive critic Elizabeth Luther Cary who, like many of her contemporaries, considered it a great privilege to hear James, had arranged the Brooklyn lecture
(May 10) at the Packer Collegiate Institute.

[39] *Reader,* VI, 336 (Aug., 1905).

[40] James called attention particularly to the American lopping off of syllables, the
slurring of *o's* and *e's,* and the American attempt to restore certain missed values by insertion of consonants between vowels. "Vanilla-r-ice-cream," "California-r-oranges,"
"Cuba-r-and-Porto Rico," and "Atalanta-r-in Calydon" were some of his examples of this
latter tendency.

quaked, and wondered how long his 'black eruption' was going to last." Both the *Ledger* and the *Inquirer* also sourly commented on what, in the light of James's "attack," was conceived of as the irony of President Carey Thomas's introduction. She had said that they were about to have "the privilege of hearing from his own lips what is thought of our matchless English speech by one of the greatest living masters of written English." "Mr. James told them what he thought of it, sure enough," the *Inquirer* said.[41]

As was probably the case with the questions of James's "obscurity" and the general public reaction to his lectures, the controversial question of James on "Our Speech" more than likely had its roots in at least two misunderstandings: one, of what James was actually saying and the other, of the complex problem of James's relation to America. In regard to the latter, it was inconceivable to many Americans in 1905 (as it is even today for that matter) that anyone could be a loyal American and live abroad. Actually, James was quite as loyal an American as any who felt that the feathers of the American eagle were ruffled by the slightest wind of adverse criticism. *The American Scene* (1907), James's record of a portion of his 1904-1905 impressions of America, "throbs," as Edmund Wilson has justly observed, with "old-fashioned American patriotism." Warmly attached to America, James was usually eminently fair about it, pointing out but not condemning what he did not like, always making an effort (in his words) to "do justice" even to what he did not like. A ready-to-take-offense attitude can always find much in little. A Portland, Oregon, paper even aggrievedly resented James's registering at his hotel as "Henry James, London," feeling that he thereby showed that "he did not consider this country his home"[42]—disregarding the fact that James had been making his home abroad for over thirty years.

A concomitant of this unjust view of James's expatriation is the climate of opinion about his literary effort. James's last important novel, *The Golden Bowl,* had come out in November of the year (1904) he returned to America. Not well-liked in general, it was usually thought to be abysmally obscure.[43] From the perspective

[41] Philadelphia *Public Ledger*, June 9, 1905; Philadelphia *Inquirer*, June 9, 1905.

[42] Portland *Morning Oregonian*, April 18, 1905.

[43] It was also considered decadent and enjoyed, according to H. G. Dwight, "a *succès de scandale*,' selling as James's novels seldom did ("Henry James—'In His Own Country,'" *Putnam's Monthly*, II, 165, May, 1907).

of forty years the controversy which occupied the public prints through the fall and winter of 1904-1905 about the real or assumed obscurity of both *The Golden Bowl* and its author's style has amusing resemblances to the one about the elliptical obscurity of Browning a few years before or to the more recent one about the obscurity of modern poetry. The letter page of the New York *Times* book section almost regularly had some enthusiastic or irate comment on James.[44]   Indeed, the joke of the season[45] was a variation on the story about the woman who knew "several languages which she could speak fluently—French, New Thought, and Henry James," or the one about a lady who boasted that she could read Henry James in the original.

It was James's own "English," tortured and incomprehensible as it was believed to be, according to most of those who "answered" his Bryn Mawr speech, which put him in the glass-house position of one who should not throw stones.   When questioned by a New York *Herald* reporter, for instance, Dr. Woodrow Wilson, then president of Princeton, thinking that James was sneering at "newspaper English" commented that critics

should look at home before committing themselves, and remedy their own shortcomings and their laboriously correct style of writing. I think the English used in newspaper articles is remarkably good. It is generally terse and clear and right to the point, and tells in a simple way exactly what the writer wants to say. . . . None need be afraid of spoiling their taste for good English by reading newspapers. The articles are almost always delightfully free from stiltedness and trite conventionality. . . .[46]

The average newspaper reporter, another commentator said, "writes better English than Henry [James], if good English means clear,

[44] One other interesting defense of James's lecture style, while not favorable to the whole James, is a letter by Charles Battell Loomis, a fellow craftsman (although one of a more popular stamp), who liked James's humor and thought James's sentences "Evartsian" in length but "perfectly parsable" (New York *Sun*, May 19, 1905). Loomis's letter answers a gratuitous attack on James in the *Sun's* "Books and Authors" column of May 17, 1905.

[45] It was popular enough to be occasionally reported in the newspapers and, finally, even to "make" the old *Life*. The cited versions are from *Life* and a New York *Sun* report of a publisher's dinner at which Hamilton Wright Mabie, the toastmaster, used the second version. See also *Current Literature*, XXXIX, 97-99 (July, 1905).

[46] "Henry James on 'Newspaper English,'" *Current Literature*, XXXIX, 155 (Aug., 1905). See also *Outlook*, LXXXIII, 17 (May 5, 1906), for another comment.

comprehensible English."[47]   Still another admitted that "We are a sensitive people, and we do not like to be accused of 'untidiness' in our use of English . . ." and thought that it was really American voices rather than American English that James objected to.[48]   All this, a careful reading of James's lecture shows, was beside the point. At the Bryn Mawr commencement, addressing the American girl whom he had always seen as the carrier of culture, he had merely asked her to carry that indication of manners, speech, a little less loosely, a little more carefully.   It was not her voice that he criticized, but her carelessness in pronunciation, her lamentable lack of a tone standard.   The lecture, another of James's mild-mannered, urbane pleas for "discrimination," for form, was not taken for what it was; and, as an "attack" on America, it was referred to widely and considered repeatedly as an ungratefully bitter fruit for James to gather in his first return to his native land in over twenty years.

As a lecturer James had shown himself always modest, agreeable, even witty, and the farthest removed from pomposity;[49] yet when he sailed back to England in July, 1905, after ten months, over a dozen lectures, and considerable publicity, he was not only misunderstood but also abused for what he had not said and disliked for what he had not been.   From the standpoint of becoming widely though inaccurately known, Henry James, Lecturer, had been a success; the irony, by then probably familiar to the long-unpopular James, is almost Jamesian.

[47] Quoted in *Current Literature*, XXXIX, 156.   Was James's own English beyond suspicion? the Baltimore *Herald* asked.   Wasn't it " 'crude, untidy, careless,' bedraggled, loose, frowsy, disorderly, unkempt, uncombed, uncurried, unbrushed, unscrubbed?" (Quoted in *ibid.*, p. 155.)
Herald asked.   Wasn't it " 'crude, untidy, careless,' bedraggled, loose, frowsy, disorderly, unkempt, uncombed, uncurried, unbrushed, unscrubbed?" (Quoted in *ibid.*, p. 155.)

[48] Albert Henry Smyth, "Henry James on American Speech," *Book News*, XXIII, 856 (July, 1905).

[49] One early reviewer had found James the lecturer *far* "more human and likeable than . . . James the novelist. . . . the rare glimpses that we have had of . . . Henry James [he added], glimpses dependent chiefly upon his books, have not revealed him with so agreeable an effect as has this address of an hour and a half" (*Book News*, XXIII, 487, Feb., 1905).

James's Portrait of the Southerner

Charles R. Anderson

T HE PROTAGONIST of *The Bostonians* is an unreconstructed rebel
from Mississippi who literally steals the show from a group of
New England reformers. Henry James succeeded in making Basil
Ransom one of his most complex male characterizations, but in
attempting to create him as the embodiment of chivalry and a traditional society he reveals a certain ambivalence that raises some interesting problems in technique. When James wrote the novel in
1886 he had never visited the South, and he even feared that his
long residence in Europe had thrown him out of touch with the
America he had known in his youth. But during a trip to Boston
and New York a few years before, he had determined to prove that
he could produce an important novel about his own country. In
his first exploration of the theme in his *Notebooks* he recorded:

I wished to write a very *American* tale, a tale characteristic of our social
conditions, and I asked myself what was the most salient and peculiar
point in our social life. The answer was: the situation of women, the
decline of the sentiment of sex, the agitation on their behalf. . . . The
subject is strong and good, with a large rich interest.[1]

This purpose led him inevitably to select one set of his characters
from among the modern agitators for women's rights and to develop them into extreme examples of an idea of social justice abstracted from the basic needs of society.

Nor did he need to invent a fountainhead of radical reform in
America. Legend, growing about a core of demonstrable facts, had
fixed it by common consent as the region around Boston. This
world in its heyday had included the utopian experiments at Brook
Farm and Fruitlands, Alcott the Swedenborgian mystic, Thoreau
the lone striker, Margaret Fuller the *avant-gardiste,* Emerson the

[1] *The Notebooks of Henry James,* ed. F. O. Matthiessen and K. B. Murdock (New
York, 1947), p. 47. James, who had made his home in Europe since 1875, spent more
than fifteen months in Boston, New York, and Washington during two visits, 1881-1883.
The first entry in the *Notebooks* for *The Bostonians* occurs in the middle of the latter
visit.

spiritual anarchist—who could nevertheless describe with some show of humor the Disciples of the Newness at the Chardon Street convention of 1840 as: "Madmen, madwomen, men with beards, Dunkers, Muggletonians, Come-outers, Groaners, Agrarians, Seventh-day Baptists, Quakers, Abolitionists."[2] The elder Henry James had been a friend of many of these reformers, with progressive ideas and millennial schemes of his own, and had finally settled his nomadic family there in the 1860's. This was the last home the novelist had known in America and the one to which he had just returned on a visit in 1883. In his letters of this period Cambridge is described as "dry, flat, hot, stale, and odious," Boston intellectuals as arid and filled with spiritual pride. For James, New England highmindedness had now degenerated into a grotesque comedy.

Since the theme of his new novel was to show the decline of the sentiment of sex, its outward embodiment occurred to him quite naturally as a Boston bluestocking, as he sketched her in the *Notebooks,* a wealthy young woman active in the feminist movement and sponsor of a beautiful girl with a prodigious gift for public speaking. The psychological motivation for Olive Chancellor's agitation on behalf of her own sex he astutely conceived as hatred or at least fear of the opposite sex—in a word, incipient Lesbianism—though he phrased it indirectly as "one of those friendships between women that are so common in New England." As a foil to Boston's latter-day saints he knew he needed a young man "who, being of a hard-headed and conservative disposition, is resolutely opposed to female suffrage and all such alterations." Also, as the opposition to this unnatural friendship between the two young women he was to be the embodiment of the sentiment of sex, in love with the heroine Verena and determined to snatch her from the clutches of her reformer friend. The choice of a Southern gentleman was indicated had James only bethought himself of the legend: the South is reactionary in social doctrine but chivalric towards women. The *Notebooks* go no further than to remove him from the scene by making him a distant cousin of Miss Chancellor's just returned from ten years in the West. When the novel was completed, however, he was given not only a name, Basil Ransom, but a local

[2] *The Complete Works of Ralph Waldo Emerson,* Centenary Edition (Boston, 1904), X, 374.

habitation in the unreconstructed South, which increased his dramatic contrast with New England radicalism. Likewise, in the process of composition James reversed his emphasis and made his main theme affirmative: a vindication of the sentiment of sex. Ransom became properly speaking the hero, for what began as a satire of Bostonians ended by being the triumph of a Mississippian in more than just plot.

On the surface this seems like a mere romance in the late Victorian fashion. (James normally kept his story within the traditional framework of love, courtship, and marriage.) Read closely, however, it has more serious import as a fable—the word he habitually used to describe his later fictions—a fable championing the institution of marriage and reaffirming the values of a traditional society in which the family is central. This purpose dictated the method for controlling his materials. It led him in the first place to select as his protagonist a gentleman from the South, since he could count on the popular notions of that region—what I am tempted to call the collective myth of the South—to furnish almost automatically the appropriate background for his theme. Southern conservatism had been a byword throughout the century, enhanced rather than diminished after the collapse of the Confederacy by nostalgia for a vanished past. One of the most "feudal" aspects of this, symbolized in tournaments where the most valiant knight crowned the Queen of Love and Beauty, was the cult of woman worship. Always skeptical that change makes for progress, Southerners became increasingly resistant to further reforms. When Northern radicals turned from abolition to feminism, chivalry and traditionalism united in the South to offer the chief opposition to the movement.[3] Thus fact and legend made credible James's development of his hero by heightening these special qualities until he became the quintessential cavalier of the old regime.

Though we learn many things about Ransom, they revolve mostly around two poles: his chivalry and his conservatism. Rather, these are the words the New England opposition uses of him, but the author in his sympathetic analysis of these concepts brings out

[3] Virginius Dabney, "The Emancipation of Women," *Contemporary Southern Prose,* ed. Beatty and Fidler (Boston, 1940), pp. 67-77. Even though an amendment to the Constitution granting suffrage to women became law in 1920, it was never ratified by Virginia, North Carolina, South Carolina, Georgia, Florida, Mississippi, and Louisiana— partly because of the opposition of prominent Southern women.

other and far more favorable aspects of them than are implied in the collective myth of the South. Using the terms in their broadest coverage, we may group under "chivalry" all that we learn of his theory and form of behavior; under "conservatism," his principles and modes of thought. Both words, and the associations clustered around them, appear continually in the text with meanings as varied as the characters who utter them. It is a commonplace of James criticism to say that his characters exist largely in terms of their relations to each other. In a letter to his brother he insisted specifically of *The Bostonians* that his title referred to Olive and Verena only "as they appeared to the mind of Ransom, the Southerner and outsider,"[4] and we can assume that he would have made the same claim in reverse. So it is of the essence to discriminate whose ideas about the South, or New England, are being presented in a given passage.

Basil Ransom's background is presented in some detail. The son of a Mississippi planter, once wealthy but ruined by the Civil War, he has come to New York in the early 1870's to seek his fortune as a struggling young lawyer. In spite of the cruelty of defeat he has accepted the idea of reunion in the form of an invitation to visit his distant cousin Olive Chancellor in Boston. The novel opens on this scene rich in sectional contrasts. Ransom is plunged headlong into a gathering of Bostonians who are involved in varying degrees in the feminist movement. Being mostly women they have constantly on their lips, but with differing intonations, references to his gallantry, his Southern flourish, his fondness for elegant phrases. In what they think of him, and especially in his reaction to them, is his chivalry defined.

It is a minor character, the woman doctor Prance, who puzzles him most at first. He mistakes her for the typical Yankee female, the product of the Puritan code, the uncongenial climate, the absence of chivalry: "Spare, dry, hard, without a curve, an inflection or a grace" (pp. 33-34).[5] But as soon as he divines her as the completely unsexed woman he accepts her as he would any professional companion. In fact he comes to like her so well that when he goes

---

[4] F. O. Matthiessen, *The James Family* (New York, 1947), p. 329.

[5] All page numbers for quotations from the novel, given in parentheses in the text, refer to the recent reprint of *The Bostonians* (New York, 1945).

fishing with her later on Cape Cod, he "would greatly have enjoyed being at liberty to offer her a cigar" (p. 295). Ransom is
not a man to scatter the seed of his gallantry on stony soil.

With Mrs. Luna, the rich and pretty widow, it is a different
matter. At first he plays the game, the ritual, in all his dealings
with her, which are purely social. He is lonely, enjoys feminine
company, and even indulges momentarily in the whim of marrying her to secure the leisure for his secret ambition of doing some
good in the world. But she is a sentimental, posturing fool "who
loved the landed gentry even when landless, who adored a Southerner under any circumstances" (p. 164). Overwhelmed by Ransom's charm, she thinks of him as one of the fallen aristocracy, an
old monarchist, a *gentilhomme de province* who had emigrated to
America after the French Revolution. "She could see by the way
he talked that he was a conservative, and this was the motto inscribed upon her own silken banner" (p. 175). In her view of Chevalier Basil, uniting the chivalric and the old-fashioned, James made
use of the most romantic threads in the collective myth of the Southern gentleman to heighten his color in contrast with the plainness of
New England but refused to subscribe himself, declaring her to be
the dupe of illusions. So does Ransom, who finds her snobbish notions about the state of the republic highly comical. As he gradually
discovers that she has serious designs on him, he uses his Southern
gallantry as a weapon to spar with her. He is not such a formalist
as to be trapped in a code of manners by a predatory flirt.

When Ransom's chivalry and conservatism come in conflict with
the leaders of the feminist movement, they have the added significance of taking us deep into the plot. From the first meeting with
his bluestocking cousin their incompatibility is marked. He deplores the fact that she is a roaring radical. In her strenuous hu-
manitarian zeal and her personal coldness she strikes him as morbid, the very opposite of the women he has known in his own soft
clime. He thought most reform movements misguided, and as
for the emancipation of Olive Chancellor's sex—"what sex was it,
great heaven? he used profanely to ask himself" (p. 280). Such
a woman can only fill with dismay the chivalric embodiment of
the masculine principle. For her part she is horrified at the way
he blames the Civil War on female abolitionists and makes fun of
women's rights even while he praises their beauty. Fearing both

personally and as a feminist any surrender to masculine power, she suspects that his gallantry is only a pretty front for his brutality. To her the chevalier masks the slave-driver, as she phrases it, "a man who, no doubt, desired to treat women with the lash and manacles, as he and his people had formerly treated the wretched coloured race." Miss Chancellor clings to one of the most lurid abolitionist versions of the collective Southern myth. Convinced that chivalry is also the sure sign of a reactionary, she begins to probe. When she asks if he believes in human progress, he replies: "I don't know—I never saw any." When she asks if he cares for the new truths, he replies that he has no idea what they are: "I have never yet encountered in the world any but old truths—as old as the sun and moon" (pp. 16, 17). The clash between them, of personalities and of two distinct ways of life, supplies the staple of the plot—their tug-of-war for the beautiful titian-haired Verena, the heroine who is loved possessively by both Basil Ransom and Olive Chancellor. Such a man is not only an enemy to the feminist cause but a menace to all women, especially lovely maidens, and Olive tries to warn her young protegée of the danger.

In a theatrical way Verena Tarrant is the embodiment of the feminine principle, lovely of face, charming in manner, desiring only to please. This pliability puts her at once under the sway of Olive's ideas, but it leaves her equally vulnerable to Ransom's masculine will. Superficially she subscribes to her sponsor's definition of him, yet finds herself from the beginning flattered by his gallant attentions. His campaign of conquest is a frontal assault with no concealment of his conviction, and the author's, that their agitation for the equality of the sexes is absurd. As his power over her grows so does his eloquent praise of her and his abomination of her Cause as an immense quackery. He utterly loathes the idea of her making a spectacle of herself ranting on a platform; as he puts it: "she was meant for something divinely different—for privacy, for him, for love" (p. 227). When he finally proposes marriage he makes as a condition her complete abandonment of the feminist movement.

Miss Chancellor tries to bolster her for the final stand, arguing that he does not really love her but wants to crush the Cause by making his victory over her consummate proof of the servility of women. She considers his courtship a covert persecution of herself and hence a blot on his chivalry. When Verena relays this to Ransom it makes him laugh, but it also prompts him to give an explicit definition of his code as a Southern gentleman: "Chivalry had to do with one's relation with people one hated. . . . He didn't hate poor Miss Olive, though she might make him yet; and even if he did, any chivalry was all moonshine which should require him to give up the girl he adored in order that his third cousin should see he could be gallant. Chivalry was [also] forbearance and generosity with regard to the weak," and Olive is not weak (p. 329). But Verena is, and in the end it is his "chivalry" that sweeps her off her feet. Outwardly it reaches a climax in the romance of the rescue: he snatches her from the enchanted castle of Boston's Music Hall just as she is about to be sacrificed on the lecture platform, and escapes with her into the night (a horse-car presumably serving as his fiery charger). What really won her was his old-fashioned notion about the relation between the sexes: his ideal of the yielding beauty, his masculine will to dominate. Chivalry means that the strong are not only willing to protect the weak but may insist on doing it when they are also fair and beloved.

This quality of fable is effectively enhanced by James's symbolic playing with names. Ransom's rival suitors, weakly named Pardon and Burrage, are too enfeebled by compromise with feminism to be taken seriously by a true hero. He quickly sees through the pale charms of Mrs. Luna, who tries to distract him from his proper star. Nor does he find a formidable opponent in Miss Chancellor, who sits in the judgment seat prating of justice to women. Although the heroine is at first overawed by the eminence of her position, there is never any real danger that a spinster christened Olive will be able to supply the emotional needs of her wholly feminine nature. But what of Verena? The name has an odor of verbena about it, but we need only turn as James probably did to the theatrical page at the time the novel was written to find Rita Lawrence, Elita Otis, and in our own day Rhonda Fleming, Veronica Lake, or any of the other exotic names concocted by prima donnas. Verena is simply the name for the glamorous if somewhat stagey young lady who is the modern equivalent of the princess, for whom any valiant knight would break a lance. And who more appropriate than the royal Basil (*basilicus*) to rescue her from captivity and servitude in a fatuous Cause and crown her with his own surname, Ransom.

In the text of the novel the words most constantly associated with the hero are "home," "family," "wife," and "love." Those on the lips of the formidable array of feminists are "lecture platform," "the cause," "reformers," and "justice." The choice and arrangement of scenes makes this conflict vividly concrete. The heroine's parents camp in a little rented suburban shanty from which the father, a mesmeric healer, sallies forth to Chautauqua auditoriums and séances. One such performance of father and daughter, where Ransom first meets Verena, is held in a large bare edifice which houses transient radicals including the owner Miss Birdseye, a famous old abolitionist who confesses that she is mostly to be found on the streets of Boston. The heroine's sponsor lives in a fine old Back Bay mansion which has all the accoutrements of a home, but has ceased to be one since it no longer houses a family. Of the two masculine rivals Ransom has to cope with, one is a Boston journalist, offering his hand as joint husband and publicity agent, who promises to lodge her in the best hotels while promoting her speaking tours. The other, a wealthy New Yorker, promises to launch her on a more fashionable career, performing in salons such as the spacious music room in his mother's apartments, complete with marble busts and gilded chairs. What is common to these residences is the total absence of a family circle, of hearth and home.

All this is heightened by the ironic contrast of Ransom's present modest lodgings in New York's East Side, yet he is the only one who stands for all the familial values. This point he continually presses home in the sociological discussions that make up their strange courtship. When he outlines his conservative theory of society—woman's place is in the home, and so on—Verena counters by declaring that for modern women "marriage isn't their career, as a matter of course, any more." To this he replies that the feminists can't pervert "a truth as old as the human race. . . . What is most agreeable to women is to be agreeable to men!" As the argument rises to a climax she breaks out:

"I am to understand, then, as your last word that you regard us as quite inferior?"

"For public, civic uses, absolutely—perfectly weak and second-rate.
. . . But privately, personally, it's another affair. In the realm of family
life and the domestic affections—" (pp. 284-287)

The champion of love and marriage, Ransom makes no compromise with what James calls the great modern pestilence. He denies
Verena the career of a suffragette though he is able to offer her
in compensation only the simplest of prospective homes and the
promise of a family. This is sufficient to win her. James implies
that their marriage will fall short of the ideal, but she is satisfied
that all will be well.

All is not well with *The Bostonians* artistically, however. The
author was one of the first to point this out. In a letter to his
brother, William James, he gave his *post mortem* on the weaknesses
in the method of his novel: "The whole thing is too long and
dawdling. This came from the fact (partly) that I had the sense
of knowing terribly little about the kind of life I had attempted to
describe—and felt a constant pressure to make the picture substantial by thinking it out—pencilling and 'shading.' "[6] Some of these
strokes are excellent in themselves but they tend to distract the
reader's attention from the main theme of the novel. James's great
problem was to secure credibility for his fable without letting the
sociological interest overshadow the transcendent value he aimed to
illustrate. So it is necessary to examine his confessed excess of
"pencilling and shading" in his effort to make the picture substantial. It is not a question of degree so much as of method.
The term "chivalry" comprises the hero's whole theory and form
of behavior. In rounding out this aspect of his character James
was largely successful, for he kept it minimal and made it all suggestive of Ransom's eminent qualifications for his role as champion
of the sentiment of sex. The illustrations already given of his
gallantry towards women and his general social conduct prove
sufficiently that he is no formalist, but a gentleman living by a code
that is vital. He knows how to relax as well as how to bow from
the waist. To him there is a time and a place for everything. He
is appalled by such unmitigated strenuousness as that of his New
England cousin; he himself "takes things easy" and knows how to

[6] Matthiessen, *The James Family,* p. 329.

enjoy leisure. In his bachelor poverty in New York he does not disdain to drink beer in German cellars and amuse himself with a little variety actress. In Boston he offers to debate not on the subject of Feminism but of Temperance, "his conviction being strong that civilization itself would be in danger if it should fall into the power of a herd of vociferating women . . . to prevent a gentleman from taking his glass." But he declines to make a speech about the stricken South: "He had a compassionate tenderness for his own country," like his chivalric attitude towards a lady in distress, that made it seem as vulgar to talk about it before an audience of Northern fanatics "as to read aloud his mother's or his mistress's letters" (p. 42). But he is no stereotyped sentimental-ist, and in private he talks amusingly about his native region, "its social peculiarities, the ruin wrought by the war, the dilapidated gentry, the queer types of superannuated fire-eaters, ragged and unreconciled, all the pathos and comedy of it." After a long discourse of this sort Mrs. Luna concludes, "there was no one who could make a lady's evening pass so pleasantly" (p. 175). All this serves to make Ransom attractive to women as a romantic hero, even while it suggests the three-dimensional roundness needed to make him credible as a human being.

Another facet of his variety is his ready wit, usually allied to his sensitive pride. In the very opening scene, when he apolo-gizes for not being properly dressed to accept an unexpected dinner invitation, the Boston lady asks condescendingly of her poor rela-tion from the South if he is ever really different from this. His quick reply explodes her preconception of Southern violence by borrowing its terms: "Oh yes; when I dine out I usually carry a six-shooter and a bowie knife" (pp. 2-3). Pride is proper to an aristocrat but it must combine pride of function with pride of status. Though Basil Ransom cherishes his long and distinguished lineage, he never mentions it. But of his ambition to do something as well as be something, he is vocal. He admits to Verena that he would like to be President of the United States, or at least a Sena-tor: "He had always had a desire for public life; to cause one's ideals to be embodied in national conduct appeared to him the highest form of human enjoyment" (p. 160). There being no place for a conservative Southerner in the radical reconstruction govern-ment of the 1870's, he is determined to fulfil his public function by becoming an essayist and publishing "much salutary criticism" to reform the reformers.

It is in trying to make substantial the picture of Ransom's conservative principles and modes of thinking that James lost the thread that could have served his purpose, the evocation of a traditional society in which the institution of marriage could be vindicated. He simply became engrossed in his hero's ideas for their own sake. He probably justified this excessive exposition on the grounds that contemporary progressive Bostonians needed to be instructed in the difference between conservatism and mere reaction. Verena, for example, thought that "conservatives were only smug and stubborn and self-complacent, satisfied with what actually existed" (p. 277), and she is amazed that Ransom has his own private vision of reform. He does not want to revive such old Southern ideas as slavery; on the other hand he does not subscribe to the new positivism, the religion of humanity—he had read Auguste Comte, "he had read everything."

In New York he does an immense amount of study at the Astor Library, authors like De Tocqueville being his favorites, for his chief interest is in economic, social, and political theory. He is a great admirer of Carlyle and like him suspicious of the encroachments of democracy. "He was sick of all the modern cant about freedom and had no sympathy with those who wanted an extension of it." What the human race needs is to make better use of the liberty it already has, and for the rest learn to bear its troubles. He denounces the spread of education as "a gigantic farce—people stuffing their heads with a lot of empty catchwords that prevented them from doing their work quietly and honestly" (p. 277). Verena thinks of herself as one who admires new ideas and approves of reforming society, but she has never heard of such a wholesale criticism of the *status quo*. As we read page after page of this we get the feeling we are reading an essay rather than participating in a courtship. As a matter of fact, we are given to understand that the ideas Ransom expresses in his conversations are the very ones he has worked up into critical essays and submitted to the magazines. They are all rejected at first, one with the suggestion that it might have been acceptable to an editor of the sixteenth century. The author admits he is out of date; only he is convinced that his ideas are not too old but too new. When near the end of the novel his first article is accepted, and others are requested, it is significantly by the *Rational Review*.

It was too late at that point for James to try to relate all this to the plot by making Ransom's initial success as a critic sufficient promise of a career so that he felt free to propose marriage. The reader cannot let go his interest in the sociological argument even when James attempts to tie his hero's conservatism to his proper role as champion of the traditional sentiment of sex, as in his peroration to convince Verena that her feminist movement is the very opposite of what is needed to redeem the times:

The whole generation is womanised; the masculine tone is passing out of the world; it's feminine, a nervous, hysterical, chattering, canting age, an age of hollow phrases and false delicacy and exaggerated solicitudes and coddling sensibilities, which, if we don't soon look out, will usher in the reign of mediocrity, of the feeblest and flattest and the most pretentious that has ever been. The masculine character, the ability to dare and endure, to know and yet not fear reality, to look the world in the face and take it for what it is—a very queer and partly very base mixture—that is what I want to preserve, or rather, I may say, recover; and I must tell you that I don't in the least care what becomes of you ladies [the suffragettes] while I make the attempt. (p. 283)

This eloquent castigation of the watery idealisms of Boston is not without interest and significance. In fact, that is its very trouble. Ransom's ideas have won the center of critical interest in the novel all along, though commentators have usually taken a dim view of them because they are conservative.

The most favorable interpretation of James's protagonist is by Philip Rahv in the latest edition of *The Bostonians:* "In the figure of Basil Ransom he created with remarkable prescience a type of intellectual . . . like the school of Southern agrarians, whose criticism of modern civilization is rooted in traditionalist principles. Thus James anticipated, in the content and shading of Basil Ransom's ideas, one of the major tendencies in twentieth-century thinking."[7] This has some point to it but it unnecessarily forces the novelist into the role of prophet. The twentieth-century school is more of a revival than an innovation. Ransom is simply an intellectual in the general Southern tradition that found its chief

[7] *The Bostonians* (New York, 1945), p. ix. This is the only reprinting since the original edition in 1886.

spokesman in Calhoun, his essay rejected as three hundred years out-of-date sounding like an echo of Calhoun's doctrine of the concurrent majority. It is a school based on reason and experience, with an emphasis on the stable traditions of an agrarian society, opposed to utopian reforms and faith in progress.

All critics whether favorable or unfavorable have taken *The Bostonians* to be a novel of ideas, a social history in the Balzacian sense, which I hold to be a sign of its partial failure. For James says explicitly in his *donnée* that his theme is "the decline of the sentiment of sex," and the main drift of the story itself proves that he did not change his intentions. So, if Ransom is the protagonist, as all agree, then he should engage our interest primarily as the champion of that sentiment. The author should have confined his treatment of Southern conservatism to suggesting that the stability of Southern society was due to its emphasis on family, and that it provided a clearly defined civilization in which his hero could operate as a man of principle. This would have explained his pride by endowing him with moral certainty of self—that quality Henry Adams found, disconcertingly, at the heart of the Southern system, "the life of it all—the vigor—the poetry." And it would have fortified the conviction with which he vindicated the primary worth of marriage in the face of a hostile modern world. As the novel is written, however, its overemphasis on conservative versus radical ideas in all their economic and political particularity serves only to distract the reader's attention from the fable intended. Besides, all this central matter is presented by expository rather than dramatic methods. It is clearly what the author was referring to when he put his finger on the flaw in this novel: "All the middle part is too diffuse and insistent—far too describing and explaining and expatiating."[8]

The tendency of *The Bostonians* to fall between two stools is evidenced by this conflict of interest between Ransom as polemicist and Ransom as the natural representative of the sentiment of sex. Part of the difficulty can be illuminated by reference to his place in the history of James's struggles with male characterizations. In the earlier fictions there had been a temptation to divide them too neatly into categories, the rationalists and the men of imagination. The novels of his middle period show this struggle continuing. In *Con-*

[8] See note 4.

fidence (1880) everything is so built around a conflict between the two types as to give the effect of plot by formula. They reappear strikingly in *The Tragic Muse* (1890), where they threaten to break an otherwise fine novel in halves, though the two main characters have a redeeming degree of roundness. Peter Sherringham seeks compensation for the limited rationality of a diplomat's mind by yielding to the fascination of the Bohemian world of the theater; Nick Dormer defines for himself the true meaning of the life of the imagination only after his devotion to art has won a long-drawn battle against the practical career in Parliament that was his by birth and a prospective wealthy marriage. And the two plots are dextrously united in the glowing figure of the actress who is the focal point at which the worlds of the two young men meet. She warms the former into life by the headlong passion she inspires; she sits for the latter's masterpiece as the tragic muse.

The two most successful novels of the decade solve the problem largely by the skilful use of point of view. In *The Portrait of a Lady* (1881) the cynical, even mercenary, realist and the man of intuition are seen only through the consciousness of Isabel Archer. They are given a saving ambiguity by her romantic vision which persists through half the book in seeing them in reverse, Gilbert Osmond as the embodiment of art and Ralph Touchett as the simple homely man. And the final meaning of her pilgrimage from innocence to experience is spelled out in terms of her gradual recognition of their true natures. *The Princess Casamassima* (1886), published in the same year as *The Bostonians,* is an even more interesting treatment of the problem. For there the viewing consciousness, one of James's most convincing male characters, is literally split between two ways of life as symbolized by his ambiguous heritage. Hyacinth Robinson is equally drawn to the world of art created by a hierarchical civilization and to the revolution against that order. The logic of his depressed position, economically and socially, makes him cast his lot with the latter; but since he has no capacity for ideologies, that potential half of him is gradually objectified in his *alter ego* Paul Muniment, the names again being suggestive of a fable. Pre-eminently a man of imagination, Hyacinth has a brief flowering in art appreciation. But even this is snatched from him by the inadequacies of his situation, just as his actual tragedy is brought on by his entanglement in the anarchist conspiracy.

The dramatic possibilities of the man divided against himself led James to a number of experiments in a third kind of male characterization, one who combined something of the realist and the idealist, the man of imagination who was also a rationalist. Such an ambivalence lends interest to Morris Townshend, a secondary figure in *Washington Square* (1881), because the inconsistency is pinned to his character rather than stated in the characterization. But the real triumph in this kind did not come until many years later, in *The Ambassadors* (1903). Lambert Strether is not so much a man actually torn between two natures as he is one who develops from a false notion of himself to a full realization of his true nature. Until the age of fifty-five almost the whole of his life had been dictated by the conviction that he was a logical and practical man of affairs. At that point his "ambassadorial" mission to Paris, for which he was chosen because of these supposed qualifications, gradually reveals to him an increasing awareness of the possibilities for living which he had missed by suppressing his imagination. Through a masterful handling of point of view there is unfolded to the reader layer by layer an evaluation of this complex character that James, free of ambivalence himself, had firmly in control all the time.

The elements are likewise mixed in Basil Ransom in such degree as to make him potentially one of James's most significant male characterizations. He is the only one in *The Bostonians* with any awareness of the rich possibilities of life, yet his is also the practical mind that sees through the unrealities of the current New England idealisms. He is as imaginative as an artist in his quest of beauty, yet restrains himself from proposing until he has launched his writing career with a critical essay on public affairs in the *Rational Review*. In a word he is sufficiently complex to engage our interest deeply, but the ambiguity is not so much worked into his character as stated in the characterization. Rather, the fault lies in James's equivocal attitude towards his creation, for his moral vision was never more unstable than in this novel. The difficulty, I suspect, came from James's inadequate understanding of the Southerner and his consequent personal involvement in those popular generalizations and preconceptions which I can only describe, for lack of a better term, as the collective myth of the South. Collective myths have elements of truth in them but they are also partial truths, in the sense of being oversimplifications based on prejudice, self-justification, a penchant for romance, and the like. They should be used to suggest the welter of appearance and reality that make up the societies of men, to complicate the issues and create the desired ambiguity through multiple interpretations— but they should never confuse the author himself.

In James's novels of international and intersectional contrasts, these collective myths are most successfully presented as the attitudes of characters who have only partial views which limit their understanding and help to precipitate the dramatic conflict. The core of reality in each of them may well become the starting point of the author's own vision, but this must emerge in the end as a whole way of envisaging the inner truth and of reorienting all the materials so as to illuminate it. When James accepted a collective myth at face value and adopted it literally as his own view, he produced a stereotype that was essentially false, as with the Southerner in his short story "Pandora." When he failed to discriminate clearly between collective myths and his own final vision, as in *The Bostonians,* his uncertainty confuses the reader and damages his full acceptance of the value which the author's fable was created to affirm.

Technically, in this novel at least, it boils down to the always troublesome matter of point of view. With considerable success James manipulated the collective myths by letting us see the Bostonians through Ransom's eyes and the Southerner through varying degrees of New England astigmatism. These partial views are somewhat corrected by the characters' own revelation of themselves in dialogue, action, and unspoken soliloquy—all of which results in a satisfactory complication of the issues. But since the author denied himself the advantages, and the hazards, of a single viewing consciousness, the problem remains as to how the reader may get at the whole truth. For the subordinate theme, what the Boston reformers really stand for, James simply adopted Ransom's vision, which though increasingly perceptive remains one-sided. The result is a satire of New England that is good-humored enough to be acceptable to most, yet it has been objected to as "a personal animus raised to the level of a general observation." With the elucidation of his Southern hero he took more pains. The most prejudiced New England views of him—he is stiff-necked and exotic, his principles are bound to be as strange as his speech, "a person from Mississippi is sure to be all wrong"—are soon discounted by the reader because of their extravagance and because they are corrected by everything Ransom says and does. A full and affirmative understanding of his values could have come with Verena's developing love had James endowed her with intelligence, but all we get is the implication of his worth from her abject and romantic surrender.

Instead, the author resorted to a desperate remedy, as he confessed many years later: "I 'go behind' right and left . . . in *The Bostonians.*"[9] That is, he violated the dramatic method by explaining to the reader in his own voice. Much of this exposition bolsters the reader's acceptance of Ransom's chivalry and conservatism as desirable values since they lead to marriage, family, and traditional society, but James's belief in his hero wavered at several crucial points. For example, though very little blood from English titled nobility actually flowed in Southern veins, the cavalier tradition was cherished as an ideal and literally molded the outlook of the ruling class in the South, so that it furnished an appropriate imagery for the author of this particular fable. But in what should have been the central image of Ransom as an aristocrat who naturally held conservative views, the author's equivocalness is disconcerting: "I know not exactly how these queer heresies had planted themselves, but he had a longish pedigree (it had flowered at one time with English royalists and cavaliers), and he seemed at moments to be inhabited by some transmitted spirit of a robust but narrow ancestor, some broad-faced wig-wearer or sword-bearer." Here James took away with his left hand what he had given with his right, "queer heresies" being reinforced by a judgment of his social and political opinions as "ill-starred" and "reactionary." In the same context he added that Ransom has "a more primitive conception of manhood than our modern temperament appears to require," and that his attitude towards women is one of the provincial superstitions of Mississippi, representing "a state of mind which will doubtless strike many readers as painfully crude" (pp. 161-164). Again and most devastating of all is his comment on Ransom's

[9] *The Letters of Henry James,* ed. Percy Lubbock (New York, 1920), II, 324-325.

principle that a gentleman should not propose marriage when he can only support a wife in sordid conditions: "His scruples were doubtless begotten of a false pride, a sentiment in which there was a thread of moral tinsel, as there was in the Southern idea of chivalry" (p. 271). Even the hero of a fable should be flawed with some human weaknesses, but if the author has misgivings on such fundamental issues how can we accept Ransom in his proper heroic role? How can he vindicate the institution of marriage if his conception of it is obsolete and false in coloring?

Most of the disparagements of the South clearly represent the Boston point of view, and they create effective irony when put in Ransom's own mouth, such as his reference to himself as "barbaric" and as coming "out of the darkness of Mississippi." Perhaps in the whole context of the book even those made by the author himself are intended to be ironical, but if so James certainly overdoes in reverse the romanticized legend of the South's baronial manors, formal society, and the grand style. Ransom, though the son of a wealthy planter, is described as overwhelmed by the elegance of Miss Chancellor's house, the architectural wonder of Harvard's Memorial Hall, the fashionable salon at Mrs. Burrage's. The people he knew at home had no taste, there were no paintings or brilliant society in Mississippi, and his own idea of material comfort was a cane-bottom chair, a box of cigars, and a bottle of brandy. On his first meeting with his Boston cousin, "Even the young Mississippian had culture enough to see that she was refined" (p. 15). All this from the author's own mouth. If this is meant for irony it can only mislead the reader who knows nothing of the social life of the Delta country and the plush splendor of Natchez, not to mention the civilization of nearby New Orleans. Unsupported by any material panoply, how could Ransom's cavalier pride, his aristocratic conservatism, his cult of chivalry, be anything but tinsel and pretension?

A character made complex by controlled ambiguity is certainly more credible than an oversimplified one. And the author who frankly admits there are dark areas in his fictional creation that he will never understand is more convincing than one who pretends to omniscience. But all this is quite different from shifting evaluations, equivocalness of attitude, on the part of the author. The available external evidence corroborates my conjecture as to the root of Henry James's trouble in this novel, that he knew precious little about the South. This in itself would not have prevented him from creating a hero sufficiently consistent and coherent to serve the purposes of his fable. But it resulted in an ambivalent attitude towards the South, lasting throughout his life, that troubled his imagination. Indeed at the time of writing *The Bostonians* his knowledge was so slight as to make one wonder how he created Ransom at all.

In the whole published record there is only one extended account of his acquaintance with a Southerner. When James was ten years old, in 1853, a family named Norcom moved from Kentucky to Washington Square and became neighbors and close friends for two years. The first volume of his autobiography, *A Small Boy and Others,* makes clear the impact they had on his sensitive young imagination: "We were provided by their presence with as happy a foil as we could have wished to the plainness and dryness of the Wards," former friends in New England whose image paled "in the Southern glow of the Norcoms." The "higher intensity" of their impression on him he attributed to their speech, their grace, their large and easy hospitality, and the exotic note they struck, especially in the "pictorial lustre" of their domestic slaves. There are some unfavorable strokes in the picture—"I doubt whether their house contained a printed volume," the father was "a large bald political-looking man, very loose and ungirt," the mother "a desiccated, depressed lady"—but the main effect was of their vivid difference. In later years he came to feel, quite "absurdly and disproportionately, that they had helped one to 'know Southerners.' The slim, the sallow, the straight-haired and dark-eyed Eugene in particular haunted my imagination. . . . I cherished the thought of the fine fearless young fire-eater he would have become." This is strikingly like the initial description of Basil Ransom, who was lean and bronzed, had "thick black hair, perfectly straight and glossy" and magnificent eyes, "dark, deep, and glowing . . . with their smouldering fire" (p. 2), which suggested, at least to Miss Olive Chancellor, a man of potential violence. When one considers the similarity of surnames, the fact that Norcom as well as Ransom was a lawyer who had come to New York from the South, and that his Kentucky friends loomed also as the antithesis of New Englanders, there can scarcely be any doubt that the hero of *The Bostonians* sprang from this Southern family intimately known in James's boyhood.[10]

By the time he recorded his memories of the Norcoms over half a century later, however, they seem to have been strongly colored with the collective myth of the Southerner as both noble and ignoble, for along with the semiaristocratic aura surrounding them there is more than a hint of the slovenly, the uncultured, even the barbaric. At about the same time, in 1905, James visited the South for the first time in his life. Though he did not go to Mississippi, or Kentucky, it is possible to cite chapter and verse for this coloration of the Southerner in several revealing passages on Virginia and Carolina in his *American Scene*.[11] What met his outward eye frequently puzzled him, but he kept adjusting the kaleidoscope until it produced the picture he came to see. As a young man, he recalled, it had been Europe that held out for him impressions of the "highest intensity." Returning to America as an expatriate in his sixties he found this reversed. As he approached Richmond he realized "how much I had staked on my theory of the latent poetry of the South, . . . of vivid images, mainly beautiful and sad" (pp. 365-368). At the Confederate Museum there he was charmed by the provincial good manners, the inimitable felicity, of the lady in charge: "No little old lady of the North could, for the high tone and the right manner, have touched her." But as for the contents of the museum, it made him reflect: "It was impossible to imagine a community, of equal size, more disinherited of art or letters. . . . The illiteracy seemed to hover like a queer smell" (p. 385). Richmond had never been important as a literary center, yet at the time of James's visit both James Branch Cabell and Ellen Glasgow had established themselves as novelists of some distinction. But the sponsor of the young Edith Wharton had apparently never heard of them.

James was looking for a different kind of latent poetry in the South. He confessed that forty years earlier to his young imagination "the Confederate capital had grown lurid, fuliginous, vividly

[10] Henry James, *A Small Boy and Others* (London, 1913), pp. 259-265.

[11] Henry James, *The American Scene* (New York, 1907). In the recent Scribner reprint (1946), ed. W. H. Auden, the account of Richmond and Charleston is found on pp. 365-435. Page numbers, in parentheses, for the following quotations refer to this edition.

tragic," but the Richmond of 1905 he found "simply blank and void." This quite baffled him until he worked himself around to the conclusion that this blankness was itself the essence of the old Southern idea: "I was tasting of the very bitterness of the immense, grotesque, defeated project—the project, extravagant, fantastic, and today pathetic in its folly, of a vast Slave State" (pp. 369-371). Not finding in this staid Southern town the requisite violence and folly, he had to supply it from his reading. He named specifically as his authority James Ford Rhodes's *History* dealing with the pre-liminaries to the Civil War, which he said "shows us, all lucidly and humanely, the Southern mind of the mid-century in all the convulsions of its perversity" (p. 373). Though previous Northern historians had been much more denunciatory of the South, Rhodes's volumes provided James with a source book for the collective myth he levied on to fill out the blanks in his tourist's picture. Here the Southerner is described as superior in manners but greatly inferior in culture to the Northerner, aristocatic in bearing but violent in behavior, and so on. As for the huge fallacy of slavery and the headlong vanity that produced secession and war, two sample quotations will suffice. Referring to the conduct of Southern leaders in the controversies of the 1850's, Rhodes declared: "This was the beginning of the madness that the gods send upon men whom they wish to destroy." At the capture of Fort Sumter in 1861, he attributed the enthusiasm in the Confederacy to "the martial ardor which lay constantly in the Southern breast," and quoted with approval an English journalist in Charleston at the time: "Crowds of armed men singing and promenading the streets, the battle-blood running through their veins."[12] The tourist of 1905, in his desperate search for a living fire-eater, happily created one out of a gallant and very handsome young Virginia farmer who, after recounting his father's heroic deeds during the Civil War, admitted that he would be ready to do them all over again himself. "I could but thank him," James cried, "for being the kind of Southerner I had wanted" (pp. 387-388).

Charleston presented him with the same paradox of quiet charm awaiting him at every turn in the very citadel of the Great Rebel-

[12] J. F. Rhodes, *History of the United States from 1850 to 1877* (New York, 1892-95), I, 70; III, 355, 381, and *passim*. The English travel book quoted by him was that of W. H. Russell, *My Diary North and South* (New York, 1863).

lion. Having just read Owen Wister's new novel, James made a pilgrimage to the Woman's Exchange, where he tasted not only the famous Lady Baltimore cake but "the exact *nuance* of oddity, of bravery, of reduced gentility, of irreducible superiority" in the bearing with which the proud daughters of old Southern families waited on him. But there was something disturbingly wrong in this Charleston that met his eye, a city of gardens like some "little old-world quarter of quiet convents," with its prevailing feminine air, as if the war were still raging and all the men at the front. "The puzzlement," he told himself, "is in the sense that the 'old South' could have had no such unmitigated mildness. . . . The ancient order was masculine, fierce, mustachioed" (pp. 415-417). Surely the Battery would correct the picture and bring it in line with the militaristic violence his reading had led him to expect. As he stood on the water's edge he bolstered his preconceptions with a recent speech by a friend. "Filled as I am, in general, while there, with the sadness and sorrow of the South," he recalled the friend's words, "I never, at Charleston, look out to the old betrayed Forts without feeling my heart harden again to steel." With this text echoing in his mind, James tried for some time to make the scene before him come alive with the proper bellicosity, probably remembering also the lurid engravings in *Harper's Weekly* of the rebels bombarding Fort Sumter, the shot heard round the world of Concord and Boston in 1861. But the Battery was so peaceful, the little fort in the harbor so dim and remote, "It was a blow even to one's faded vision of Charleston viciously firing on the Flag" (pp. 412-413). He shook off the insidious charm by reflecting, "The South is in the predicament of having to be tragic, as it were, in order to beguile . . . ; since it appears the only way by which they can be interesting" (pp. 419-420).

This determined search for images of pride and violence in the South sounds like an attempt to corroborate the preconceptions of Miss Chancellor (and James himself?) some twenty years before. When he put aside his authorities and allowed his own imagination to soar, "to the highest Carolinian pitch," he caught another series of impressions. The high-walled gardens gave him a sense of privacy he had felt nowhere else in the American scene. The quiet closed mansions suggested the provincial *palazzini* he had seen in Italy, the sea islands and waterways a "Venice that had never mustered," and even his hotel took on "a certain romantic grandeur of scale, the scale positively of 'Latin' construction." He persisted in this search through the deep South for a Mediterranean atmosphere, "almost as absurdly . . . as if he had expected Charleston and Savannah to betray the moral accent of Naples or Seville" (p. 405). These images of the aristocratic and exotic might be attributed solely to the blurred vision of Mrs. Luna had not James adopted them as his own in *The Reverberator* (1888), where they transfigure a Carolina family that has migrated to Paris and become irrevocably absorbed into the French nobility.[13]

A final point must be discriminated, in favor of *The American Scene*. Here, as in James's best travel books, ambivalence and multiplicity of view are stylistically sustained. But in the novel, at least as he best wrote it, style usually subserves a simple, as opposed to a complex, moral vision. In *The Bostonians* there is an odd tourist's skepticism and reserve in James's attitude. And almost every version of the collective myth of the South that had so colored his vision as to hurt the effectiveness of this novel is reflected in the ambivalent impressions of the traveler in 1905. Though the demonstration is *ex post facto,* his equipment was even less adequate twenty years earlier. Not knowing enough of the reality, he could not create a Southerner as hero in whom he could altogether believe nor an entirely credible fable of the traditional society that produced him.[14]

In all fairness it should be remarked in conclusion that James was much more successful in his subordinate theme, his satire of the Boston reformers. In none of his other fictions did he achieve such high comedy, and rarely such fullness of actuality in his backgrounds, as in this evocation of New England's Indian Summer. But all this is another matter and beyond the province of the present study.

[13] See my article, "Henry James's Fable of Carolina," *South Atlantic Quarterly*, LIV, 249-257 (April, 1955).

[14] I am grateful to W. S. Worden for a number of critical suggestions in connection with this article, and to Leon Edel for calling my attention to James's boyhood acquaintance with the Norcom family.

The Triple Quest of James: Fame, Art, and Fortune

Alfred R. Ferguson

R ECENT criticism upon Henry James has emphasized his special position: an absorbed artist springing from a family "simply never to be preoccupied with money,"[1] detached from the market place and from ordinary conditions by his quality of observer dedicated to his difficult craft.   Yet he did confess to his brother William, "Like you, with all my heart, I have 'finance on the brain.' At least I try to have it—with a woeful lack of natural talent for the same."[2]   He was, as Leon Edel demonstrates, tremendously concerned with the economics of his trade; he was a professional writer who "made his way by his pen" until he was past fifty, turned over his inheritance to his sister, and scrupulously repaid his parents most of the funds he drew from them.[3]   And finally, he longed, as F. W. Dupee has pointed out, for recognition or at least for "simple gross success,"[4] and admitted that he was impelled by an "extreme ambition."[5]   Such qualifications in the legend of James as pure symbol of "that queer monster, the artist"[6] deserve examination.

James himself provided an explicit statement of the major motives behind his efforts.   In a diary entry recalling his "old, valued, long cherished dream of doing something for the stage," he glori-

---

[1] Katherine Anne Porter, "The Days Before," *Kenyon Review*, V, 490 (Autumn, 1943). See also Desmond MacCarthy's remark, quoted in Simon Nowell-Smith, *The Legend of the Master: Henry James* (New York, 1948), p. 25: "No array of terms can do justice to [James's] lack of interest in the making of money."

[2] HJ to WJ, April 20, 1898, in Percy Lubbock, *The Letters of Henry James* (New York, 1920), I, 282. This important source will hereafter be referred to as *LHJ*.   In the pattern made familiar by Leon Edel I shall refer in notes by initials only to the members of the James family and to William Dean Howells.

[3] *Henry James: The Untried Years, 1843-1870* (Philadelphia, 1953), p. 16.

[4] *Henry James* (American Men of Letters Series, New York, 1951), p. 167.

[5] HJ to WJ, Oct. 1, 1887, in R. B. Perry, *The Thought and Character of William James* (Boston, 1935), I, 399.

[6] HJ to Henry Adams, March 21, 1914, in *LHJ*, II, 361.

fied success "for fame's sake, and art's, and fortune's."[7] The phrase
is significant for the critic who is, like James, "harassed by [the]
necessity to weave into [his] general tapestry every thread that
would conduce to a pattern."[8] Here is James's design of success,[9]
and though the lines shifted slightly as he failed to achieve his pattern, his triple quest for fame, art, and fortune must be understood
as a part of his personal life and of his artistic creativity.

Ideally, or perhaps in fairy tale and fable, success should be at-
tainable by a simple progression. If one were to work devotedly
for art's sake, with talent and endless care, fame ought to follow
and just as inevitably fortune should accrue. Most important is
consecration to art; then, as James described the pattern in the
phrase of the narrator of "Collaboration," "Art protects her children in the long run—She only asks them to trust her. She is like
the Catholic Church—she guarantees paradise to the faithful."[10]
But the life of the artist does not always follow the design of the
fairy tale; as James discovered with increasing anxiety, devotion
to art did not necessarily lead to fame and to fortune. Yet a constant dedication to his craft remained the central as well as the most
easily distinguished element of his ambition. His vision was of
the "solid, the honourable . . . the absolute and interesting success."[11] Such triumph was the reward of intense absorption in the
"luminous paradise of art," which alone was free from "depres-
sions and darknesses."[12] When frustrations in his effort to attain
fame and fortune vexed James in his later years, he turned for
refuge to the "great good place" of art, rejoiced more in difficulty
and technique for their own sake, and comforted himself with the
kind of success which he described through the voice of Gabriel
Nash in *The Tragic Muse:* learning to play to perfection a controlled and mastered instrument. At moments, indeed, he affirmed

[7] *The Notebooks of Henry James,* ed. F. O. Matthiessen and Kenneth Murdock (New
York, 1947), p. 99: May 12, 1889.
[8] HJ, *The Middle Years* (New York, 1917), p. 33.
[9] See HJ to Theodora Sedgewick, Oct. 9, 1890 (H), for an explicit statement: "Of
course, after all, one writes for success." I wish to express my thanks to the Houghton
Library of Harvard University for permission to quote from unpublished letters of
Henry James. Citations from unpublished letters are indicated by (H).
[10] *The Novels and Stories of Henry James* (London, 1923, 36 vols.), XXVII, 158.
All citations to James's work, unless otherwise indicated, refer to this edition, which
will hereinafter be abbreviated as *Novels.*
[11] *Notebooks,* p. 111: Oct. 22, 1891.
[12] *Ibid.*

that this mastery alone represented "what I call duty, what I call conduct, what I call success."[13] Devotion to art, the most familiar side of James, has been so emphasized that it needs the least attention here. Whatever the discouragements, he was always convinced that his sacred craft would bring its justification in time if he were left free "To keep at it—to strive toward the perfect, the ripe, the only best; to go on, by one's own clear light, with patience, courage and continuity, to live with the high vision and effort, to justify one's self—and oh, so greatly!"[14]

In this dream of self-justification James's operative word is *greatly*. Springing as he did from a society in which all things were considered possible, he shared the American feeling that partial triumph was equivalent to defeat. At the age of forty, for example, when he reviewed his apparently successful career he set down his own warning: "I must make some great efforts during the next few years, however, if I wish not to have been on the whole a failure. I shall have been a failure unless I do something *great!*"[15] To do something great meant in American terms to realize also a great reward. Hence the triumph of art alone could hardly satisfy one who was, as Edel has noted, marked by the "impulse . . .—had his Albany grandfather not demonstrated its truth?—that to be worth one's salt in the world one had to elbow one's way to achievement by solid worldly enterprise!"[16] Nor could a success unaccompanied by recognition and financial independence alleviate James's deep-seated personal frustrations. Too often in his odd boyhood he had seen himself "only as an obscure, a deeply hushed failure."[17] Too often he had hidden away his early attempts at writing or had been oppressed by a "buried sense of his subordinate position alike to father and brother."[18] His permanent longing was for a relief from dependence, for assurance of identity, and for an end to the haunting fear that his call to destiny was as empty as John Marcher's obsession in "The Beast in the Jungle."

Moreover, though the world of "downtown" and of business was

[13] *Novels*, XIII, 23. Cf. the similar comment by St. George in *ibid.*, XX, 60.
[14] *Notebooks*, p. 111: Oct. 22, 1891.
[15] *Ibid.*, p. 45: Nov. 11, 1882.
[16] *The Complete Plays of Henry James* (Philadelphia, 1949), p. 51.
[17] *Notes of a Son and Brother* (New York, 1914), p. 4.
[18] Edel, *Henry James*, p. 61.

closed to James, he was incurably money-conscious. As Newton Arvin has demonstrated, one of James's most important themes of fiction and many of his most impressive symbols evolved from a Balzacian vision of the preoccupation of society with wealth.[19] But the "almighty dollar" was more than a matter of fiction or of social interest; it was a personal problem, for wealth meant freedom and the chance to triumph or to fail greatly. Poverty was equivalent to the total failure of the human being and its appurtenances were "the merciless signs of mere mean stale feelings."[20]

Though James's correspondence is carefully modified to its audience, frequently conceals intense longings under a surface jest, and in peculiarly American fashion often justifies an ambition by explaining it on acceptable economic grounds, again and again the letters unite fame and fortune as twin concepts. Obviously he longed for both: one as a seal of success, the other as its necessary concomitant. On receiving the news of the sale of the *Atlantic Monthly,* he wrote to William Dean Howells, "All prosperity to the new dispensation and fame and fortune to both of us."[21] When his parents showed signs of worry about their income after the depression of 1877, he assured them of his ability to stand alone and perhaps in good time to offer them his support: "I have only to keep quietly working," he wrote, "to arrive at fame and fortune."[22] Earlier in the same year he had written, half-jokingly as was his custom when he spoke of his most permanent ambitions, that though they might be troubled now by his drafts upon them they need only to wait for their reward:

Have a little patience & believe that you will be very promptly reimbursed, not only in coin, but in reflected glory: of which latter article I propose to furnish myself with a very considerable amount. It is time I should rend the veil from the ferocious ambition . . . which enabled me to support unrecorded physical misery in my younger years; and which is perfectly confident of accomplishing considerable things![23]

To Macmillan he indicated gracefully his hope for *The Europeans:* it should be, he wrote, "a beginning of my appearance before the

[19] "The Almighty Dollar," *Hound and Horn,* VII, 434-443 (April-June, 1934).
[20] Quoted in Dupee, *Henry James,* p. 142.
[21] Jan. 9, 1874 (H).
[22] HJ to Mrs. HJ Sr., Oct. 27, 1878 (H).
[23] HJ to Mrs. HJ Sr., Feb. 17, 1878 (H).

British public as *the* novelist of the future, destined to extract from the B.P. eventually . . . a colossal fortune."[24] The comment concealed a serious hope under its humor, for he confided to William James during the next year his belief that "no reasonable share of fame & no decent literary competence" were out of his reach.[25] With less optimism he confessed to Howells at about the same time that though he rejoiced at the progress of his fame in America he was disappointed that the rewards of fortune there left so much to be desired.[26]

Such assurance of attaining fame and fortune strikes one as curiously American, reminiscent of the neat conclusion of the Horatio Alger version of success. Yet it is characteristic of the early James. In spite of his diffidence and detachment he was the first of the James brothers to fix upon his career. Throughout his fifteen-year apprenticeship with its ceaseless justifications for the tardiness of his genius, he saw his way clearly, even though success actually came slowly and incompletely. When his studies of the American abroad had made him a figure of importance, he looked back on his beginnings and recalled his mood:

The feeling of that younger time comes back to me in which I sat here scribbling, dreaming, planning, gazing out upon the world in which my fortune was to seek, and suffering tortures from my damnable state of health. . . . What strikes me is the definiteness, the unerringness of those longings. I wanted to do very much what I have done, and success, if I may say so, now stretches back a tender hand to its younger brother, desire.[27]

At first he described his dreams humbly, although even then there may have been in his mind that boyhood vision from the Louvre, in which, according to Edel, he experienced "the sense of triumph and glory and conquest and power."[28] Yet there is no reflection of the apocalyptic nightmare in his remark to Thomas Sergeant Perry after four years of seeing his work in print that he wrote little and mainly only tales which he would probably con-

[24] 1878, in Charles Morgan, *The House of Macmillan, 1843-1943* (London, 1944), p. 115.
[25] June 15, 1879 (H).
[26] June 17, 1879, in *The James Family*, ed. F. O. Matthiessen (New York, 1947), p. 501.
[27] *Notebooks*, pp. 35-36: Dec. 26, 1881.
[28] *Henry James*, p. 75.

tinue "to manufacture in a hackish manner, for that which is bread. They *cannot* of necessity be very good; but they *shall not* be very bad."[29] The workman determined to earn a living by the best work he is able to do was less modest three years later when he outlined his projected career to Charles Eliot Norton: "To write a series of good little tales I deem ample work for a life-time. I dream that my life-time shall have done it."[30] Actually his ambitions were more expansive than he admitted to Norton, for in 1870 he had informed William James that he meant to rival Hawthorne as an American novelist—"to write as good a novel one of these days (perhaps) as *The House of the Seven Gables*,"[31]—and in 1873 he told Grace Norton that he was determined to produce "some little exemplary works of art" which might be less cerebral than George Eliot's *Middlemarch* but which would "have more *form*."[32] To challenge Hawthorne and George Eliot, to write tales perfect in form, to be a great American novelist, and to earn his bread at the same time: these ambitions may have induced the implicit comparison which he drew between himself and Howells even before he had escaped the family hearth to independence:

[Howells] has little intellectual curiosity, so here he stands with his admirable organ of style, like a poor man holding a diamond & wondering how he can wear it. It's rather sad, I think, to see Americans of the younger sort so unconscious and unambitious of the commission to do the best. . . . For myself, the love of art and letters grows steadily with my growth.[33]

Some day he would possess the diamond of style and know perfectly how to display it; until then he would wait for his abilities to catch up with his ambitions.[34] In the meantime he would gather impressions, turn over the treasures of Europe, alleviate his illness by travel, and generally expand his life in preparation for the future. But such a program cost money which, until he could make his own way, must come from the generosity of his family. The flood of ink from his pen in the early 1870's, much of it almost purely

[29] March 27, 1868, in Virginia Harlow, *Thomas Sergeant Perry* (Durham, N. C., 1951), p. 288.
[30] Jan. 16, 1871, in *James Family*, p. 499.
[31] Feb. 13, 1870, in *ibid.*, p. 320.
[32] March 5, 1873 (H).
[33] HJ to C. E. Norton, Aug. 9, 1871 (H).
[34] HJ to WJ, May 19, 1873, in R. B. Perry, *William James*, I, 345.

journalistic, was his response to the challenge of self-support and his means of self-justification. Whenever he considered his economic condition he had reason to long for the success which would bring fortune. Though his parents were indulgent, he was never unaware that the funds supplied him could have been used elsewhere. Hence in explaining to his family that his costs would be repaid in coin and glory, he wrote extensively of "plans and expenses" (sometimes in reply to obvious warnings against extravagance). Early in 1870 he was impelled to take stock of his position:

> I have been careering along, drawing money which has seemed furnished by some mysterious magic on which I have been almost afraid to reflect— lest in following the golden stream to its source I should find it flow from the great parental lap in obedience to something of a cruel pressure. But it has been gushing forth in noble abundance & still it gushes.

Then after reporting in detail on his expenditures, he wondered if they might seem excessive to his parents and confessed, "I feel a most palpable weight of responsibility & gratitude."[35] It was this burden which made him fret over money, castigate himself for errors in practical economy, and justify his course of action by an appeal to a bright future. It was this responsibility which made him yearn inevitably and compulsively for fortune.

In reading James's correspondence, or indeed his creative work, one recognizes an obvious ambivalence in his attitude toward the relation of money and fame to art. By the conventions of his family, making money or even talking too seriously of it verged on vulgarity. To accept this convention, to agree heartily that an art must be disassociated from its by-products, and yet to be seriously concerned with those by-products as a satisfaction and a symbol of achievement created inevitable ambiguities. James often concealed practical concern, therefore, under external flippancy. Early in the seventies he was worried about his expenses. He excused his cost to the family by the jest that future savings in the budget for entertainment would far outweigh present burdens, for when he returned to his parents his polished European conversation would charm guests away from their food and thus make catering a trivial matter. But the joke was followed by the serious

[35] HJ to Mrs. HJ Sr., Feb. 5, 1870 (H). See also HJ to Mrs. HJ Sr., June 28, 1869, in *James Family*, p. 257.

comment that he would yet make the family's fortune and reappear, if not as a prodigy, certainly not as a prodigal.[36] With Miltonic overtones he insists again and again that his slow seed time precedes a bountiful harvest. Consider the assurance of this comment, over-emphasized though it may be, to reassure anxious parents:

I have had too little time to write, to lay up any great treasure to commence with; but I shall need but little to start with & shall be able to add to it fast enough for comfort. . . . My improvement is going on now at so very rapid a ratio that I feel an almost unbounded confidence in my powers to do & dare. In short, I am really well, & confident of being able to work quite enough to support myself in affluence.[37]

James's correspondence with his family in 1873 indicates clearly his preoccupation with finances and the potential rewards of a literary career. At intervals throughout the year[38] he discussed his prospects for self-support, assuring his parents that he should make at least three thousand dollars by his pen. Obviously he feared being regarded as a threat to the family purse, as an idler diverting funds from his brothers, or as a dilettante unable to settle on serious pursuits. Late in the year he summed up his prospects optimistically to his father:

I have it at heart to say more about this matter of my writings & their getting published & paid for. I am better & better in health. . . . I feel more & more apt for writing, & more active and ambitious. At the same rate of improvement for the next year I shall be able to do really a great deal. Meanwhile I am able to do amply enough to secure a comfortable—an easy—monthly income. . . . I'm afraid I have been rather heavily testing your powers of letting me draw on you while waiting for my own efforts to produce something. Their doing so— I can answer for it—their producing enough to completely cover all my expenses—is only a question of time.[39]

A comfortable income was one measure of success at this time; but as his reputation grew so did the vision of an adequate reward. Five years later when he was being sought after by publishers he envisaged a future cornucopia of fortune opening up to pour out gold enough not only for him "to live very comfortably" but for

[36] HJ to Mrs. HJ Sr., Feb. 5, 1870 (H).
[37] HJ to Mrs. HJ Sr., Sept. 9, 1872 (H).
[38] HJ to his parents, Jan. 8, Feb. 17, and Oct. 26, 1873 (H).
[39] Oct. 26, 1873 (H).

him "to 'put by,' & to make an allowance to each member of the family." This, he confessed was his dream; and this he clung to even though the absorption by the *Atlantic Monthly* of the *Galaxy* cost him an outlet worth twelve hundred dollars to him in 1877.[40]

In pursuit of his dream he became very much the artist in the market place, turning his hand to many kinds of literary production and publishing in every available periodical. Travel sketches, comments on manners, and criticisms of art, literature, the drama, and even the political scene abroad served him as matter for the magazines. This was not the writing of an artist limited to that pure creativity which ignores the demands of the pocketbook. His letters provide a running commentary on his recognition of the problems involved in the quest for fame and for corresponding payment from his writing. For years he balanced the richness of Europe as a source of stimulation and material against its possible poverty as a place for publication. In 1873 he debated the need for living in the United States in close touch with the magazines from which he was drawing his support. Such a decision might, he thought, be required to establish himself "on a remunerative & perfectly practical literary basis," since in America he would have, as he phrased it in most mundane terms, "a better market for my wares and more definite work to do (especially in the way of reviewing books) than in this far away region."[41] In the next year, still wavering between two worlds, he wrote to his parents, "You will see that I perfectly perceive the propriety of getting home promptly to heat my literary irons & get myself financially & reputationally on my legs."[42] Indeed, practical, financial considerations of copyright laws may have been an added inducement to his final decision to remain in Europe. When he at last obtained a foothold in the English magazines he was perfectly aware that as an English resident he could acquire copyright there at the same time that as an American citizen he could obtain copyright in his own country. Periodical publication in both countries offered him the opportunity, as he phrased it, of "doubling my profits."[43]

James's longing for fame and fortune was perhaps even a factor

---

[40] HJ to WJ, July 23, 1878 (H); and HJ to Mrs. HJ Sr., Feb. 17, 1878 (H).
[41] HJ to HJ Sr., Dec. 22, 1873 (H).
[42] Feb. 15, 1874 (H).
[43] HJ to WJ, July 23, 1878 (H).

in his relationship with his native land. As early as 1872 he begged
his friend Norton, who was returning from Europe to Cambridge,
"to interpret my absence to our fellow citizens as eloquently as you
may feel moved to. I ought, myself, to justify it by doing more
than I have done this winter."[44] This concern for what his fellow
citizens thought of him was visible again in 1880 when he was
firmly settled in England. With both eagerness and trepidation
he discussed a visit to his native shores, but he delayed his proposed return for a year, using as one excuse—possibly a valid one—
his wish to arrive impressively under the best circumstances of
fame and wealth:

If by waiting a while I become able to return with more leisure, fame,
& money in my hands, & the prospect & desire of remaining at home
longer, it will be better for me to do so; & this is very possible. When
I *do* come, I wish to come solidly.[45]

Throughout the year he repeated and expanded upon his reasons
for postponement. One significant excuse was his desire to complete an American novel and so arrange for its sale that it might
"redound to [his] profit, glory, & general felicity."[46] He hoped
to receive six thousand dollars from the publication in two countries of *The Portrait of a Lady;* and his expectation that it would
also increase his American reputation is implicit in his remark concerning it three years earlier: "The 'great novel' you ask about is
only begun; I am doing other things just now. It is the history
of an Americana[?]—a female counterpart to Newman."[47] Even
while he delayed he insisted that his longing to return was immense and that soon he would arrive trailing clouds of glory:
"I wish to go keenly, & see a thousand uses and satisfactions in it;
but I wish to do it in the best conditions & return in a word with
a little accumulation of opulence & honour."[48] His desire for
personal success had been heightened by his years in England with
their opportunity to "go in for genius & fame even at breakfast &
lunch."[49] The impact upon James of being in constant association
with wealthy and famous personages is evident in a revealing re-

[44] March 13, 1872 (H).
[45] HJ to Mrs. HJ Sr., July 4, 1880 (H).
[46] HJ to Mrs. HJ Sr., July 20, 1880 (H).
[47] HJ to WJ, July 23, 1878 (H). See also HJ to Mrs. HJ Sr., July 20, 1880 (H).
[48] *Ibid.*
[49] HJ to Grace Norton, April 6, 1869 (H).

mark he made after a visit to a particularly splendid English country house. He found that the chief effect of his experience had been "to sharpen my desire to distinguish myself by personal achievement, of however limited a character."[50]

Before his return to the United States in 1881, he had become a personage himself. *The American* had established him as a coming novelist; *Daisy Miller* and "An International Episode" had made his reputation. Unfortunately he had received only two cents per copy on the large sales of *Daisy Miller,* and as he noted ruefully the check for two hundred dollars represented "but meanly so great a vogue." "An International Episode" he had to his later disappointment sold outright for "a very moderate sum" of ready money paid for its use in *Harper's Magazine.*[51] But the future appeared propitious; perhaps with *The Portrait of a Lady* he had at last learned to combine artistic achievement with fame and reward. His apprenticeship seemed complete; his eternal need to place a long serial pressed him less; and he had reached a point where he could report with some satisfaction to his brother William:

If I keep along here patiently for a certain time I rather think I shall become a (sufficiently) great man. I . . . mean to do some [work] this year which will make a mark. I am, as you suppose, weary of writing articles about places, & mere potboilers of all kinds; but shall probably, after the next six months, be able to forswear it altogether, & give myself up seriously to "creative" writing. Then, & not till then, my real career will begin.[52]

Swept up for a moment on a high tide of popularity, James caught a glimpse of success, like an ever-expanding horizon. He had, he thought, shaped his course wisely with his eyes always on his native land.[53] There were great experiments still to be made. He dreamed of the theater in which he might "astound the world";[54] he thought of audiences still unreached and wrote his

[50] HJ to Mrs. HJ Sr., Nov. 28, 1880, in Dupee, *Henry James,* p. 138.
[51] HJ to WJ, June 15, 1879 (H); and HJ to WDH, June 17, 1879, in *James Family,* p. 501.
[52] Jan. 28, 1878 (H).
[53] HJ to WJ, May 1, 1878, in *LHJ,* I, 60.
[54] *Ibid.* See also HJ to WJ, July 23, 1878 (H): "I am very impatient to get at work writing for the stage—a project I have long had. I am morally certain I should succeed, & it would be an open gate to money-making."

sister Alice that he was publishing in *Scribner's* in spite of his dislike of the magazine, because there "one's things are read by the
g[rea]t American people—the circulation, I believe, is enormous.
Last not least, I am to be very well paid—$1500 for a thing not
much longer than the *Europeans*."[55] To William he confided with
mingled complacency and guilt:

I shall have made by the end of this year very much more money than
I have ever made before; & next year I shall make as much as that again.
As for the years after that,—"vous verrons voici." . . . What strikes me,
in everything of this kind is the absurd, the grotesque facility of success. What have I done, juste ciel? It humiliates me to the earth, &
I can only right myself by thinking of all the excellent things I mean
to do in the future.[56]

Even his mistakes in dealing with publishers seemed to point
to a more triumphant future. When an American firm brought out
an unauthorized edition of "A Bundle of Letters," James discovered
that because he had failed to take out copyright he had no re-
course against the piracy. It was a costly lesson in his trade, but
as he wrote his mother in extenuation for his concern: "Excuse
my appearance of vulgar greed; I am getting to perceive that I
can make money, very considerably, if I only set about it right, and
the idea has an undeniable fascination."[57] There were clouds on
the horizon even in this moment of sunlight. Though his fame
had expanded through two hemispheres, its "pecuniary equivalent"
appeared "almost grotesquely small."[58] His vision of a popular
audience might well be a mirage, for he remembered the reverse
he had suffered in 1872 when his travel letters to the *Nation* had
been discontinued for overrefinement and the ghost which was to
haunt his career had materialized. "My only question," he had
written then, "is how to dispose of my wares. But in this, too,
I shall not fail."[59] Both his brother and Howells had urged him
not to ignore the tastes of his audience. He had not forgot their

[55] March 26, 1879 (H).
[56] June, 15, 1879 (H). See also the sharp indication of the complex and often un-
acknowledged rivalry with WJ in HJ to WJ, Nov. 10, 1879 (H): "I am much ashamed
that my frivolous efforts sh[ou]ld be acclaimed while your much more valuable lucu-
brations go a-begging; but such, apparently, is the taste of a light-minded generation."
[57] Feb. 2, 1880 (H). The matter is explained further in HJ to HJ Sr., Feb. 15,
1880 (H).
[58] HJ to WDH, June 17, 1879, in *James Family,* p. 501.
[59] HJ to WJ, Sept. 22, 1872 (H).

admonitions, but he had decided that if art and the public taste conflicted he must hold fast to his conscience and if necessary "give up the ambition of ever being a free-going and light-paced enough writer to please the multitude." Even then, though he desired the rewards of popularity, he had felt sure that it was no criterion of excellence: "The multitude, I am more and more convinced, has absolutely no taste—none at least that a thinking man is bound to defer to. To write for the few who have is doubtless to lose money—but I am not afraid of starving."[60] The question was less that of starvation than of the degree of fortune to which he might aspire. Driven though he was by inner compulsions "always to keep the pot a-boiling,"[61] he made a comfortable living by his immense productivity. But as Edel has said, financial insecurity afflicted him with a permanent anxiety "so that even larger earnings would have seemed to him to be insufficient," and he was American enough to insist upon his freedom from the pressure of the multitude and yet to long for "a roaring success in the market place of literature."[62] His later years were darkened by an unfounded terror of an impecunious old age and a sense of the injustice of a society which rewarded the efforts of lesser men more munificently than his own. Hamlin Garland was impressed by James's amazement when he heard an account of American writers attaining enormous sales and consequent fortunes[63] and James himself revealed his own reaction to the ironies of fortune during a period of later depression:

When I look round me at the splendour of so many of the "literary" fry my confrères . . . & I feel that I may strike the world as still, at 56, with my long labour & my genius, reckless, presumptuous & unwarranted in curling up (for more assured peaceful production,) in a poor little $10,000 shelter—once for all, for all time—*then* I do feel the bitterness of humiliation, the iron enters into my soul, & (I blush to confess it,) I *weep*.[64]

Such economic humiliation was the mark of James's last years, but it was even then accompanied by an optimism as incorrigible

---

[60] *Ibid.*, in *James Family*, p. 320.
[61] HJ to WDH, June 17, 1879, in *James Family*, p. 501.
[62] *Complete Plays of Henry James*, p. 42; and introduction to *The Ghostly Tales of Henry James* (New Brunswick, 1948), p. xvi.
[63] *Roadside Meetings* (New York, 1930), p. 459.
[64] HJ to WJ, Aug. 9, 1899 (H).

as the despondency was bleak. In spite of all appearances he always clung to the fairy tale of success; it was unthinkable that genius should go unrewarded, even though its audience was often incurably dense. In the middle years, his mind was, as he wrote, "full of plans, of ambitions; they crowd upon me, for these are the productive years of life."[65] He is reported to have announced once to W. W. Jacobs, "I should so much have loved to be popular!"[66] To attain that desire in the 1880's he courted the reading public as assiduously as he could without being false to his ideal of art. Dupee refers to *The Bostonians* and *The Princess Casamassima* as attempts to captivate the public with "timely novels full of arresting incidents and character."[67] And the editors of James's *Notebooks* consider the stories in *The Tales of Three Cities* (1884) as deliberate efforts to capitalize on the international scene, with conclusions softened in each case to appeal to public taste, demonstrating that both James and his publisher had "no doubt, an eye for the ingredients which might make a popular success."[68] He was still convinced that he could write for the multitude (as he had been earlier in his dealing with *Scribner's* and would be again in writing expressly to capture the readers of the London *Illustrated News* with his melodrama *The Outcry*). He was experimenting with Dana's *Sun* for reasons which he outlined to his sister Alice: "The die is cast—but I don't in the least repent of it—as I see no shame in offering my productions to the widest public, & in their being 'brought home,' as it were, to the great American people."[69]

Ironically, James's efforts to attract a great, well-paying audience led only to years of ever-deepening frustration. Both his long novels fell flat, although he spoke of *The Bostonians* as the "best fiction I have written."[70] He confessed to William that he had suffered a double disappointment in receiving no returns either in money or in glory,[71] and to Howells he spoke even more despairingly:

I have lately published 2 long-winded serials—lasting between them for more than 2 years—of which in all that time no audible echo or rever-

[65] *Notebooks*, p. 37: Dec. 26, 1881.
[66] Nowell-Smith, *The Legend of the Master*, p. 135.
[67] *Henry James*, p. 162.   [68] P. 53.
[69] Feb. 5, 1884 (H).
[70] HJ to WJ, Feb. 14, 1885, in *LHJ*, I, 117.
[71] HJ to WJ, Oct. 9, 1885, in *James Family*. p. 32ᵀ

beration of any kind, either in America or here, has come back to me. If I had not my bread & butter to earn I should lay down my pen to-morrow—hard as it is, at my age, to confess one's self a rather offensive fiasco.[72]

For years shifting uneasily on his own "bench of desolation," James faced his earlier visions of fame and fortune and watched them fade. From the moment of the comparative failure of his two great novels of the mid-eighties he began to depend more upon the achievements of art than upon its tangible returns to his pocket and reputation. In self-extenuation he stressed more heavily than before the stupidity of his audience, deriding the "vulgar-minded-ness of the public to which one offers the fruits of one's brains," and insisting that dependence upon such readers

would chill the artist's heart if those fruits were not so sweet to his own palate! One mustn't think of the public *at all,* I find—or one would be nowhere & do nothing. It is everywhere the same—the form & pro-fession of dulness and density are different; but the [?] hatred (it is not too much to say) of any independent evolution is equal.[73]

Though James characterized his own nature as always prepared for the worst and expecting the least,[74] one of his remarkable quali-ties was a constant resilience. There was always a pot of gold at the end of the rainbow. He could not lay down his pen for he had his bread to earn, and if fame would not come in his lifetime, posthumous glory was always possible with a future audience better trained than his own. He was seldom blind to dismal facts, but he could not believe that his early portent of glory could diminish into darkness and silence. In 1888 when *The Princess Casamassima* and *The Bostonians* had apparently reduced the demand for his work to zero, when editors left him "irremediably unpublished," or kept back the stories they did accept "for months and years, as if they were ashamed of them," he was still certain of his future. He sketched the grim picture of editorial neglect and then added his own unquenchable response:

However, I don't despair, for I think I am now really in better form than I have ever been in my life, and I propose yet to do many things.

[72] Oct. 19, 1886 (H).
[73] HJ to WDH, Feb. 25, 1887 (H).
[74] HJ to WJ, April 20, 1898, in *LHJ*, I, 282.

Very likely too, some day, all my buried prose will kick off its various tombstones at once.[75]

Whenever the discouragements seemed unbearable he reminded himself, "courage, courage, and forward, forward. . . . There is an immensity to be done, and, without vain presumption—I shall at the worst do a part of it."[76] It was possible to redefine the concept of success, to heighten the significance of artistry, and to lessen the importance of fame or fortune. If the novels were failures, other forms beckoned. With the publication of *The Tragic Muse* (1890) he divorced himself for the time being from the long novel, remarking, "For the rest of my life I hope to do lots of short things with irresponsible spaces between. I see even a great future (ten years) of such. But they won't make money."[77] To abandon the novel meant for him the elimination of long cherished visions of circulation and popularity but no real diminution of the desire for ultimate fame or for the highest artistic accomplishment. The future still beckoned, though in a new guise: "One must go one's way and know what one's about and have a general plan and a private religion. . . . I shall never make my fortune—nor anything like it; but—I know what I shall do, and it won't be bad."[78]

The short story and the drama were in the forefront of his general plan. Through them he could expand his treatment of life, leave behind him a multitude of finely etched pictures of human relationships, or, as he summed up his reasons: "By doing short things I can do so many, touch so many subjects, break out in so many places, handle so many of the threads of life."[79] After twenty-five years of literary effort he had begun to feel that the dimensions of his work mattered less than its quality and multiplicity, and he was inclined to believe that his literary monument ought to consist of a number of little blocks of form rather than the great masses of a few novels.[80]

"To do many," James wrote, "and do them perfect: that is the refuge, the asylum."[81] His ambition to make an imperishable mark

[75] HJ to WDH, Jan. 2, 1888, in *LHJ*, I, 135.
[76] *Notebooks*, pp. 87-88: March 11, 1888.
[77] HJ to WJ, May 16, 1890, in *LHJ*, I, 163.
[78] HJ to WJ, July 23, 1890, in *LHJ*, I, 170.
[79] *Notebooks*, p. 106: July 13, 1891.
[80] See *ibid.*, p. 101: May 19, 1889, and p. 134: May 7, 1893.
[81] *Ibid.*

in short fiction was renewed and intensified by a conversation with Taine on Turgenev and by memories of the genius of de Maupassant.[82] Moreover practicality governed the new emphasis; he could create a multitude of stories in the time required for one novel and obviously he could publish most easily "very short tales—things of from 7,000 to 10,000 words."[83] Harking back to his earlier image of the diamond of success he thought now of leaving a literary heritage of multiple facets, each "fine, rare, strong, wise—eventually perhaps even recognized."[84]

More fully than the novel, moreover, short fiction permitted James to objectify his increasing personal anxieties and, by transmuting them into art, diminish their impact upon him. Lack of immediate success, failure of popular recognition, the vulgarity or stupidity of his audience, even the nightmare of death were anxieties that could be relieved by expression.[85] According to James's own admission he mined his private experiences for subjects for his short fiction: the man of letters, for example, trying to make a living, longing to "take the measure of the huge, flat foot of the public," even if only by doing something successful and vulgar, had been suggested by what he referred to as "all the little backward memories of one's own frustrated ambition."[86] When in a moment of dismay he felt himself to be "perishing in [his] pride or rotting ungathered like an old maid against the wall & on her lonely bench,"[87] he drew from his own situation the general subject of the artist as he might become if he were to sell his birthright of genius for the lesser advantages of popularity:

The little tragedy of the man who has renounced his ambition, the dream of his youth, his genius, talent, vocation—with all the honour and glory it might have brought him: sold it, bartered it, exchanged it for something very different and inferior, but mercenary and worldly.[88]

All the nuances of the artist's life, especially in its renunciations and failures so uncomfortably close to his own fears, all the threats

[82] See ibid., pp. 89, 92, 101, 102, and 104.

[83] Ibid., p. 102: Feb. 22, 1891. Much to James's dismay, magazine requirements later limited him to 5000 words.

[84] Ibid., p. 101: May 19, 1889.

[85] See especially, Edel, Complete Plays of Henry James, pp. 60-61, and Dupee, Henry James, pp. 175-180.

[86] Notebooks, p. 180: Jan. 26, 1895. Cf. Novels, XX, xvi.

[87] HJ to WDH, Nov. 27, 1897 (H).

[88] Notebooks, p. 183: Feb. 5, 1895.

to poor, sensitive gentlemen provided a multitude of windows from which could be described what he called

the drama, the tragedy, the general situation of disappointed ambition— and more particularly that of the artist, the man of letters: I mean of the ambition, the pride, the passion, the idea of greatness, that has been smothered and defeated by circumstances. . . .[89]

In this period James was further attracted to the short story because of the neatness with which it dovetailed into his project of a dramatic career. The account of James and the theater has been so lucidly treated by Leon Edel that it warrants only passing consideration here. It is evident, however, that his experiment offered fulfilment to his triple desires. The play possessed an "intrinsic solicitation,"[90] offered a challenge to his art, and promised fame to the writer who could brighten the shoddy English stage.[91] Last, and always most emphasized in his correspondence, playwriting gleamed with the lure of a tremendous remuneration which would permanently assure him of "real freedom for . . . [his] general artistic life."[92] He wrote hopefully that a successful play would make him £350 in England alone and a much larger sum if there were an American run,[93] and declared that he "simply *must* try, and try seriously, to produce half a dozen—a dozen, five dozen— plays for the sake of . . . [his] pocket, . . . [his] material future."[94] Indeed, he went so far as to explain to Howells that he embraced the "sordid profession of the playwright" on purely economic grounds: "It isn't the love of art and the pursuit of truth that have goaded me into such miry ways; it is the definite necessity of making for my palsied old age, more money than literature has ever consented, or evidently *will* ever consent, to yield me."[95] Entranced by his visions he warned himself to concentrate on short fiction for his pleasure and on the drama for his pocketbook: "I must absolutely *not* tie my hands with promised novels if I wish to keep them free for a genuine and sustained attack on the theatre."[96]

His constant insistence that he wrote plays "all & *only* for the dream of gold—*much* gold"[97] was, as Edel has indicated, an over-

[89] *Ibid.*, p. 143: Jan. 9, 1894.
[91] See HJ to WDH, Jan. 10, 1891 (H).
[93] HJ to AJ, June 6, 1890 (H).
[95] Jan. 10, 1891 (H).
[97] HJ to WJ, Nov. 7, 1890 (H).
[90] HJ to WDH, July 23, 1909 (H).
[92] *Notebooks*, p. 99: May 12, 1889.
[94] *Notebooks*, p. 99: May 12, 1889.
[96] *Notebooks*, p. 106: July 13, 1891.

simplification.[98] As early as 1878 he had said that for a long time he had harbored a "most earnest and definite intention to commence at play-wrighting";[99] he had briefly attempted the form in the eighties and had flirted with the theater so long that it finally became "the focus of anxiety, fear, insecurity, conflicting emotions,"[100] to which he turned as a last resort in his desperation. Though his resources were not so seriously reduced as he complained (*The Tragic Muse,* for example, had brought in $15 a page or about $300 monthly),[101] the theater became a symbol of fortune for him as well as a new outlet for those accumulated resources of talent which would yet, he felt, permit him "to do something more—to do much more—than I *have* done." All that was necessary was for him to "try everything, do everything, render everything—be an artist, be distinguished, to the last."[102]

In 1895, the year that F. O. Matthiessen referred to as the "great turning point of James's career,"[103] *Guy Domville* failed, leaving its author sick with personal humiliation, anxious over years spent on drama without financial return, and aghast at his folly in trying to appeal to the clumsy public's taste. "And yet," he remarked, "I had tried so to meet them! But you can't make a sow's ear out of a silk purse."[104] But even in this moment of despair he rallied as he always did. The short story still remained no matter how badly the drama had failed. Less than three weeks after the disaster of *Guy Domville* James set down his unshaken belief in his call to destiny: "I take up my *own* old pen again—the pen of all my old unforgettable efforts and sacred struggles. To myself— today—I need say no more. Large and full and high the future still opens. It is now indeed that I may do the work of my life. And I will."[105] Writing to Howells a day earlier he had been more fearful of the future but still determined to make an undying name for himself in short fiction. For a long time he had felt uneasy:

I have fallen upon evil days—every sign or symbol of one's being in the least *wanted,* anywhere or by any one, having so utterly failed. A

[98] See Edel, *Complete Plays of Henry James,* pp. 42, 49-52.
[99] HJ to WJ, May 1, 1878, in *LHJ,* I, 60. See also note 54 above.
[100] Edel, *Complete Plays of Henry James,* p. 44.
[101] See *ibid.,* p. 51.
[102] *Notebooks,* p. 106: July 13, 1891.
[103] *The Major Phase* (New York, 1944), p. 1.
[104] HJ to WJ, Jan. 9, 1895, in *LHJ,* I, 229.
[105] *Notebooks,* p. 179: Jan. 23, 1895.

new generation, that I know not, and mainly prize not, has taken universal possession. The sense of being utterly out of it weighed me down. . . .

But at the end of his complaint, though he feared that the door to fortune was closed to him, he could add his inevitable coda of optimism. In spite of all outward circumstances he could and would write "six immortal short . . . [novels]—and some tales of the same quality." One thing alone was necessary: " 'Produce again—produce; produce better than ever, and all will yet be well.' "[106]

Stubbornness and a refusal to admit defeat were deeply engrained in James. Hence, though he said with scorn, "I have always hated the magazine form, magazine conditions and manners, and much of the magazine company,"[107] he continued to write prolifically and with his eye on the audience and upon the demands of editors. He sold *The Other House* to the London *Illustrated News,* willingly meeting the requirements of a "love story" in his effort to captivate a large audience.[108] When the book showed symptoms of success he was delighted, saying cheerfully, "If *that's* what the idiots want, I can give them their bellyfull."[109] He made a concentrated effort to place his work and worried endlessly over his payments from publishers and editors. How his sense of economic insecurity sharpened as his dream of fortune dimmed is illustrated by his comment on the twelve articles concerning literature which he published in *Harper's Magazine.* He had, he wrote, "succumbed, in that matter, *purely* to the pecuniary argument.... It means £40 a month, which I simply couldn't afford not to accept." In the same letter he confessed to Howells that it had been the argument of cash and popular notice that had led him to create the horrors of "The Turn of the Screw." If the tale was good so much the better; yet it remained in James's mind "the most abject, down-on-all-fours potboiler, pure & simple, that a proud man brought low ever perpetrated." If the publishers would pay for such inanity, he would, he added, "do it again & again, too, even for the same scant fee: it's only a question of a chance."[110]

Actually James wooed the magazines so assiduously that in his

[106] Jan. 22, 1895, in *LHJ,* I, 230-232.   [107] *Ibid.*
[108] HJ to Clement Shorter, Feb. 24, 1896, in *Letters to an Editor* (1916), p. 5.
[109] HJ to WJ, Oct. 30, 1896 (H).   [110] HJ to WDH, May 4, 1898 (H).

long career only nine of his shorter fictions failed to achieve original publication in a periodical.[111] Yet his success was more apparent than real and for years he was tormented by his inability to manage the problems of placement and payment. At a moment of high popularity he had complained to William James that his fortune suffered because of his failure as a "grasping businessman," and he had developed his grievance further in a remark to Howells: "The truth is I am a very bad bargainer and was born to be victimized by the pitiless race of publishers."[112] He had been warned then that he worked his reputation too little and needed a lawyer-agent to relieve him of details and assure him of the most advantageous terms.[113] Ten years later his young American friend Wolcott Balestier had emphasized the enormous rewards and the freedom from painful detail possible through the efforts of a skilful agent.[114] Finally in 1898 after what he characterized as years of "such abject depression on my part as to disposing of my work, that I scarce cared what I did with it,"[115] James turned to a competent professional agent, J. B. Pinker, so that he might have all the aids of the business world in managing his literary affairs.

Not even Pinker's assistance could simplify James's long struggle with the compressed short story. The quest for brevity—interrupted by *What Maisie Knew, The Awkward Age,* the three great productions of the major phase, and notable excursions into the form of the "beautiful and blessed *nouvelle*,"[116]—obsessed James from the end of the eighties until the publication of "The Bench of Desolation" in 1909. Then, abandoning another path to fame, art, and fortune, he remarked, "But clearly I have written the last short story of my life."[117] For twenty years he had deliberately endured "the cramp of the *too* intensely short"[118] in his effort to meet the challenge of an art form, the demands of public taste, and the requirements of the magazines from which his income was

---

[111] See A. R. Ferguson, "Some Bibliographical Notes on the Short Stories of Henry James," *American Literature*, XXI, 292 (Nov., 1949).

[112] June 15, 1879 (H), and June 17, 1879, in *James Family*, p. 502.

[113] See HJ to HJ Sr., Feb. 15, 1880 (H).

[114] See Edel, *Complete Plays of Henry James*, p. 51.

[115] HJ to J. B. Pinker, March 27, 1906. The unpublished letters from HJ to his agent Pinker may be found in the Yale University Library. I am grateful to the University for permission to quote from these letters.

[116] *Novels*, XX, viii.

[117] HJ to J. B. Pinker, July 21, 1909 (Yale).

[118] *Notebooks*, p. 135: Aug. 30, 1893.

derived. Sometimes he succeeded brilliantly; more often he watched his short tales grow by a "rank force" of their own into works as expansive as *The Sacred Fount* and *The Spoils of Poynton*.[119] His correspondence and notebooks express a frequent revulsion against squeezing his talent into "a fixed and beggarly number of words," against the pursuit of brevity, which was ultimately "a poor and a vain undertaking—a waste of time," and against the compulsion "to be mature in 5000 words [which] is rather, *for* the mature, . . . a sickening effort."[120] Yet no matter how he agonized he would not give up the "anecdotal," for there lay his most favorable opportunity for publication and payment.

He reminded himself of the practical necessity of his exertions: "I can *place* 5000 words—that is the coercive fact, and I require, obviously, to be able to do this."[121] To attain conciseness involved a second apprenticeship in his trade and a "more scientific trial of the form,"[122] but this too could be endured if it rescued him from silence. Too often he had winced at the effects of his expansive richness on the public. *The Awkward Age,* for example, planned as a seventy-thousand word novel, had grown and rounded itself; but its final perfection had merely "awakened the disgust, thereby, of Editor & Publishers" and had left its author "under the dreadful sense of having failed (as if I were 25 again)."[123] At times he feared that even skilful compression could hardly save him, that for some unknown reason he had "ceased to be serially placeable."[124]

His endless efforts to "conciliate the fastidious editor"[125] drove him into immense productivity. In 1908 Alden of *Harper's* asked him for a five-thousand word story. Eager for publication, James accepted the offer with the wry comment to his agent, "I shall have to do two or three—too irreducibly and irredeemably long—in order to pull off the really short enough." He understated the difficulty, for a month later he wrote in dismay that he now had on hand five stories: "A most ridiculous commentary on my

[119] HJ to WDH, Dec. 11, 1902, in *James Family*, p. 513.
[120] *Notebooks*, p. 135: Aug. 30, 1893, and HJ to WDH, Sept. 25, 1899 (H). See also the discussion in the introduction to *Notebooks*, pp. xvi-xvii.
[121] *Ibid.*, p. 232: Dec. 21, 1895.
[122] *Ibid.*
[123] HJ to WDH, Sept. 25, 1899 (H).
[124] HJ to J. B. Pinker, Oct. 23, 1898 (Yale).
[125] HJ to WDH, Jan. 25, 1902 (H).

ruinously expensive mode of work & the annoyance of his asking me for things of a form that I can't but assent to for the money's sake."[126] He was appalled by the expansion of his germinal ideas; he despaired of publication; he mourned over its tardiness and the inadequate payments which it brought. Yet both as artist and as economist he felt it necessary to master the short story and for two decades he experimented with the "innumerable repeated chemical reductions and condensations" which made the compressed tale seem to him "one of the costliest, even if, like the hard shining sonnet, one of the most indestructible, forms of composition."[127]

Two other experiences in James's later career represent in concentrated form the triple motivations behind his creative activity. In 1904-1905 America once more had become a land of romance and usable material stimulating to his artistic imagination. Travel in his native land appealed to James as a chance to revitalize his treatment of the American scene and American character. By it he hoped also to increase his reputation and to replenish his fortune. Hence he explained: "It is more & more important I should go, to look after my material (literary) interests in person, & quicken & improve them, after so endless an absence—of that I am authentically assured, & *see* it, above all, for myself."[128] He shrugged off all deterrents with the remark that he was being urged on by "absolutely economic" motives: the lure of a book of impressions that would make him large sums and his expectation of paying his way through lecturing.[129] As he later described his journey in one of his inveterate symbols of wealth, it laid up for him memories which in the quiet of Lamb House would "begin to gleam and glitter and take form like the gold and jewels of a mine."[130]

Yet neither the American journey nor James's later cherished project of solidifying his success by a definitive edition established any real equilibrium of fame, art, and fortune. The twenty-four plum-colored volumes of the New York edition were a triumph of revision, criticism, and selection. In them, as Dupee points out, James offered his final "gesture in defiance of oblivion."[131] The

[126] HJ to J. B. Pinker, Dec. 3, 1908, and Jan. 3, 1909 (Yale).
[127] *Novels,* XXI, xiii.
[128] HJ to WJ, April 10, 1903 (H).
[129] See *ibid.,* and HJ to WJ, May 24, 1903, in *LHJ,* I, 416-421.
[130] *Notebooks,* p. 318: March 29, 1905.
[131] *Henry James,* p. 277.

careful, loving prefaces provide a clear record of long devotion to art; the mass and density of the volumes themselves recall his constant ambition for fame. Yet the demands on the fitness of the audience kept his readers few and his expensive effort produced a financial failure.[132] Disturbed though he was when cash was not forthcoming, as he phrased his regrets, to "mingle with ... [his] withered laurels,"[133] James trusted in the future and rejoiced that his work was at least enshrined in "new & high honours of type, paper, plates, prefaces."[134] His career had its monument even though the lack of serious critical attention paid to his triumph made James compare his achievement to that of Ozymandias and quote bitterly, " 'look on my *works,* ye mighty, and despair!' "[135]

In spite of all disappointments the appeal to James of fame and fortune is evident to the end. Though renunciation had been a theme more attractive for the artist than those of acquisition and success, for the man the old American implications of triumph were difficult to slough off. He could speak of the happiness of learning to ignore the imperceptive reader as a "peace worth having lived long & wearily to have attained";[136] he could admit to Howells toward the end of his career, "We all fall short of our dreams."[137] But his dreams must not be overlooked. To reduce James to the artist abstracted from human interests is to forget his vast ambition, his puzzled efforts to meet his public, and his hope, intense as that of Ray Limbert in "The Next Time," "of successfully growing in his temperate garden some specimen of the rank exotic whose leaves are rustling cheques."[138] To the last, fame, art, and fortune were the challenge, the lure, and the complication of the writer.

[132] HJ to Edmund Gosse, Aug. 25, 1915, in *LHJ*, II, 497.

[133] HJ to WDH, Aug. 17, 1908, in *ibid.*, II, 99.

[134] HJ to WDH, Nov. 1, 1906 (H).

[135] HJ to Edmund Gosse, Aug. 25, 1915, in *LHJ*, II, 497.

[136] HJ to Grace Norton, Dec. 13, 1903 (H).

[137] March 27, 1912, in *Life in Letters of William Dean Howells*, ed. Mildred Howells (New York, 1928), II, 319.

[138] *Novels*, XX, xvi.

James's Last Portrait of a Lady:
Charlotte Stant in *The Golden Bowl*

Jean Kimball

WELL OVER A DECADE ago Ferner Nuhn speculated at length about the "unexamined and unexploited area"[1] in *The Golden Bowl,* the upside-down story which would surely emerge if the action of the novel were considered from Charlotte Stant's point of view. Matthiessen gently dismissed this view as an "ingenious conjecture," and Mr. Nuhn himself backed away from any claim that the upside-down story was a part of the author's intention. Nevertheless, I should like in this essay to consider the evidence in the novel and in the author's preface that James intended that Charlotte's predicament, the drama of her struggle, be the focus of interest in *The Golden Bowl.*

In contrast to the detailed examination of motive and structure in the prefaces to the other major novels, the preface to *The Golden Bowl* is notably sparse in comment on the subject matter of the novel. Only the first four pages of the preface, which is primarily a discussion of the New York Edition as a whole, concern the novel at all, and these are devoted to James's method of presentation. He tells *how* he has presented his story, but not what it is about. He is particularly impressed, he says, with "the still marked inveteracy of a certain indirect and oblique view of my presented action" [I, v][2] and recognizes in *The Golden Bowl* yet another example of his "preference for dealing with my subject-matter . . . through the opportunity and the sensibility of some more or less detached . . . though thoroughly interested and intelligent, witness or reporter" [I, v]. He reminds the reader that he has "constantly inclined to the idea of the particular attaching case *plus* some near individual view of it" and that he has progressively moved toward the view of his case which "will give me most instead of least to answer for."

---

[1] Ferner Nuhn, *The Wind Blew from the East* (New York, 1940), pp. 133-138.

[2] Text references not otherwise identified are to volume and page in the New York Edition of *The Golden Bowl.* References to other James novels will be identified as follows: PL, *The Portrait of a Lady;* SP, *The Spoils of Poynton;* TM, *The Tragic Muse;* and WD, *The Wings of the Dove,* all in the New York Edition. Henry James, *Notes of a Son and Brother* (New York, 1914). will be identified as NSB.

The entire action in *The Golden Bowl* "remains subject to the register . . . of the consciousness of but two of the characters" [I, v, vi], and these two witnesses are the deeply involved Prince and Princess. Each of them is a "compositional resource" as well as a "value intrinsic" [I, vii] in the novel.

James's insistence on Maggie Verver's functional importance as a reporter of the action does not necessarily disqualify her as the novel's heroine, but it suggests strongly that she may not be, particularly as one remembers *The Wings of the Dove,* which was after all the story of Kate Croy and Merton Densher, even though the author identified Milly Theale as its heroine. He makes no such convenient identification in the preface to *The Golden Bowl,* but I would suggest that the "indirect presentation of his main image" [WD, I, xxii] which James noted in the earlier novel is also the key to this one, that the "particular attaching case" which is the subject of the novel is Charlotte Stant's, and that she is the heroine of *The Golden Bowl.*

Charlotte Stant is descended from a long line of heroines stretching back to the archetype of Henry James's heroic women, Minnie Temple. Like Minnie Temple, who was "a free incalculable product, a vivid exception to rules and precedents" [NSB, 477], Charlotte is an orphan, "a rare, a special product," whose "want of ramifications" gives her, "so detached yet so aware," an "odd precious neutrality" [I, 54]. In her looks there is a family resemblance to Minnie and to Milly Theale. "The face was too narrow and too long, the eyes not large, and the mouth on the other hand by no means small, with substance in its lips and a slight, the very slightest, tendency to protrusion in the solid teeth, otherwise indeed well arrayed and flashingly white" [I, 46]. James remembered in Minnie Temple "the handsome largeish teeth that made her mouth almost the main fact of her face" [NSB, 469], and Milly Theale's face had "rather too much forehead, too much nose and too much mouth" [WD, I, 118]. Charlotte Stant, in Mrs. Assingham's estimation, is "the person in the world . . . whose looks are most subject to appreciation. It's all in the way she affects you" [I, 40]. Mrs. Stringham, too, saw that Milly Theale's beauty, "for stupid people . . . would take a great deal of explaining" [WD, I, 117], and had to content herself with terming Milly's appearance "so 'awfully full of things' " [WD, I, 118]. As for Charlotte Stant, "the intelligence in her face could at any moment make a circumstance of almost anything" [I, 47].

When Charlotte first appears, Amerigo, reacting to her, is aware that in her

the "strong-minded" note was not, as might have been apprehended, the basis. . . . He had besides his own view of this young lady's strength of mind. It was great . . . but it would never interfere with the play of her extremely personal, her always amusing taste [I, 45].

There is an echo here of Isabel Archer, who "had a natural taste" [PL, I, 61], and "whose taste played a considerable part in her emotions" [PL, I, 73], but more specifically this appraisal echoes James's comment on his cousin:

To express her in the mere terms of her restless young mind, one felt from the first, was to place her, by a perversion of the truth, under the shadow of female "earnestness"—for which she was much too unliteral and too ironic, . . . superlatively personal and yet . . . independent [NSB, 78].

Charlotte Stant wears "the air of her adventurous situation, a reference in all her person, in motion and gesture, in free vivid yet altogether happy indications of dress . . . to winds and waves and custom-houses" [I, 45], and Minnie Temple, whose dream of travel was frustrated by ill health, had nevertheless a "greater range of freedom and ease and reach of horizon than any of the others dreamed of" [NSB, 77]. Charlotte is described by Maggie as "brave and bright . . . in the face of things that might well have made it too difficult for many other girls" [I, 180], and James says of Minnie that "no one to come after her could easily seem to show either a quick inward life or a brave, or even a bright, outward" [NSB, 78].

These correspondences are perhaps superficial, though the cumulative effect of them becomes something at least to reckon with. However, there is one scene in *The Golden Bowl* in which Charlotte is seen as a heroine in the same sense as Minnie Temple, "in the technical or logical as distinguished from the pompous or romantic sense of the word; wholly without effort or desire on her part . . . everything that took place around her took place as if primarily in relation to her" [NSB, 461]. This is the scene with Mr. Gutermann-Seuss and his numerous family, the scene which precedes Adam's proposal of marriage. What emerges is "the predominance of Charlotte's very person, in her being there exactly as she was, capable . . . of the right felicity of silence, but with an embracing ease, through it all" [I, 215]. Adam finds himself "quite merged in the elated circle formed by the girl's free response to the collective caress of all the shining eyes" [I, 216].

James has described Minnie's spirit from many different perspectives, but they add up to the conclusion that she was

the very figure and image of a felt interest in life, an interest as magnanimously far-spread, or as familiarly and exquisitely fixed, as her splendid shifting sensibility . . . might at any moment determine [NSB, 77-78].

Charlotte, whose "vision acted for every relation" [I, 105], is gifted with this same "felt interest in life." At Mr. Gutermann-Seuss's

The frank familiar young lady . . . noticed the place, . . . noticed the treasure produced, noticed everything, as from the habit of a person finding her account at any time, according to a wisdom well learned of life, in almost any "funny" impression [I, 213].

And Adam has found another way in which Charlotte can be useful to him, for "it really came home to her friend on the spot that this free range of observation in her . . . would verily henceforth make a different thing for him of such experiences" [I, 213].

The big question posed for James by the character of his cousin is amplified by the drama of Charlotte Stant in *The Golden Bowl*. He felt strongly "the naturalness of our asking ourselves what such spirits would have done with their extension and what would have satisfied them; since dire as their defeat may have been we don't see them, in the ambiguous light of some of their possibilities, at peace with victory" [NSB, 491]. If Minnie Temple had lived, how could "her restlessness of spirit, the finest reckless impatience" have been "assuaged or 'met' by the common lot" [NSB, 462]? Charlotte Stant, with all her "ambiguous possibilities," walks open-eyed into a situation with all the ingredients for unhappiness. Like Minnie Temple, who was "absolutely afraid of nothing she might come to by living with enough sincerity and enough wonder" [NSB, 462],

Charlotte has "the habit, founded on experience, of not being afraid" [I, 45],[3] but she might well be fearful, for when she agrees to marry Verver, she takes her place in a strange, constricted existence, set up by Verver and his daughter, an ironic, inverted Garden of Eden in which the only role for her is that of the serpent.

The echoes of the Garden of Eden myth in *The Golden Bowl* are inescapable, though not, I think, rigidly systematic, and certainly not theological. And all the echoes are off-key. Fawns itself, where "no visibility of transition showed, no violence of accommodation . . . emerged" [I, 135], is an insistent echo. In its "uncorrected antiquity" it is "conscious . . . of no violence from the present and no menace from the future" [II, 309]. The big country place gives its inhabitants "the sense . . . of one's having the world to one's self" [I, 125]; its "noble privacy" is indeed "out of the world" [I, 211]. But Fawns is rented; the innocence which it shields owes everything to "a rare power of purchase" [II, 360], and the irony implicit in the magnificent retreat is heightened by its "shining artificial lake" [I, 125], underlined by a second mention of "its majesty of artificial lake" [I, 135]. Adam Verver, its master, who finds it "complicating to be perpetually treated as an infinite agent," is himself aware that "this attribution of power" is a direct consequence of his fortune, "that as he had money he had force" [I, 131]. "Quantity," as the Prince later recognizes, "was in the air for these good people and Mr. Verver's estimable quality was almost wholly in that pervasion." He is in fact "so nearly like a little boy shyly entertaining in virtue of some imposed rank that he *could* only be one of the powers, the representative of a force—quite as an infant king is the representative of a dynasty" [I, 324]. Adam's power, which is never less than absolute and never other than beneficent in the eyes of his daughter, carries with it to a less prejudiced observer a slightly unpleasant ambiguity.

For Adam Verver is first of all, and perhaps finally, not a creator, but a collector, and he makes no distinction between objects and people. He collects the Prince for his daughter, even as, in reverse order, God created Eve for Adam. It is "the instinct, the particular

---

[3] Contrast Maggie Verver, who lives "in terror" [I, 181], for whom knowledge is not only a "fascination," but "a fear" [II, 140], and increasing knowledge "an aggravation of fear" [II, 163]. In the climactic scene with Charlotte on the terrace it is "fear all the while that moved her" [II, 247].

sharpened appetite of the collector [which] had fairly served as a
basis for his acceptance of the Prince's suit" [I, 140]. "Nothing,"
the author remarks in an aside, "might affect us as queerer, had we
time to look into it, than this application of the same measure of
value to such different pieces of property as old Persian carpets, say,
and new human acquisitions" [I, 196].[4] Mr. Verver, of course, has
the vast wealth necessary to indulge his "passion for perfection at
any price" [I, 146]; otherwise he might well appear another Gilbert
Osmond, "the incarnation of taste," who "judges and measures,
approves and condemns, altogether by that" [PL, II, 71]. For Mr.
Verver, "as a taster of life," puts "into his one little glass everything
he raised to his lips." This "tool of his trade" has "served him to
satisfy himself" both about his son-in-law and about a Bernardino
Luini he had heard about at the same time, both about Charlotte
and about "an extraordinary set of oriental tiles of which he had
lately got wind" [I, 196]. Nor does the resemblance between
Verver and Osmond end with their mutual interest in rare pieces.
Each of them has a devoted little daughter for whom he provides
an extraordinary young stepmother, and in this life situation the
resemblances multiply.

In the very early notes about *The Golden Bowl* James recognized that "a necessary basis for all this must have been an intense
and exceptional degree of attachment between the father and
daughter—he peculiarly paternal, she passionately filial."[5] He could
scarcely have failed to realize as he turned the theme over during
the next twelve years that he had already presented just such a pair
in *The Portrait of a Lady,* Gilbert Osmond, for whom "paternity
was an exquisite pleasure" [PL, II, 162], and little Pansy Osmond,
who told Isabel Archer, "If he were not my papa I should like
to marry him; I would rather be his daughter than the wife of—
of some strange person" [PL, II, 28].

Pansy, Isabel told Lord Warburton, had "an immense wish
to please her father" which would "probably take her very far"
[PL, II, 219]. At a crucial juncture in *The Golden Bowl* Charlotte

---

[4] Note also Mrs. Gereth in *The Spoils of Poynton,* who is so dominated by "the passion
. . . of the collector" [SP, 13] that her "ruling passion had in a manner despoiled her
of humanity" [SP, 37].

[5] *The Notebooks of Henry James,* ed. F. O. Matthiessen and Kenneth Murdock (New
York, 1947), p. 131.

suggests that Maggie's equally strong desire to please her father may have taken her farther than she really wants to go. As Charlotte assesses the import of Maggie's telegram to Adam about his proposed marriage, she questions the Prince's reaction, considers the possibility that "he mayn't be able to join in the rosy view of our case that you impute to Maggie," and Adam replies that "he'll just have to accept from us whatever his wife accepts; and accept it . . . just because she does. That . . . will have to do for him" [I, 232].[6] Charlotte then points out to him that the quality of Maggie's acceptance makes all the difference, that "the reality of his belief will depend . . . on the reality of hers," and that Amerigo may see only that "Maggie may mainly desire to abound in your sense, whatever it is you do," remembering "that he has never seen her do anything else" [I, 233-234]. When Adam inquires, "To what catastrophe will he have observed such a disposition in her to lead?" Charlotte replies, "Just to *this* one!" for, she continues, "I can't quite help noticing . . . Maggie wires her joy only to you. She makes no sign of its overflow to me" [I, 234-235].

"Castastrophe" is a strong word, but the action which follows Charlotte's marriage to Adam justifies it. When she tells Maggie, in their final painful interview at Fawns, that her "difficulty" has been the close relationship between father and daughter, this is not an excuse she is presenting on the spur of the moment; it is a reiteration of her initial premonition. "The struggle with it," she tells Maggie, "hasn't been for me, as you may imagine, in itself charming; I've felt in it at times . . . too great and too strange an ugliness" [II, 316]. Many critics, Matthiessen among them, have felt in *The Golden Bowl* "too great and too strange an ugliness," and it is the author's intent that they should. Maggie's unwillingness to comprehend either for her father or for herself any relationship which supersedes the "decent little old-time union" [I, 135] of father and daughter is basic to the tangle and the tragedy of *The Golden Bowl*.

She has herself married "without breaking . . . with her past," without giving up her father "by the least little inch" [II, 5]. Her

---

[6] Note that though Amerigo acquiesces in this view of his obligation "to lead the life, to breathe the air, very nearly to think the thoughts, that best suited his wife and her father" [I, 268-269], he feels strongly Adam's usurpation of his own role as father: "How can I not feel more than anything else how they adore together my boy?" [I, 307].

marriage "had never . . . suggested to either of them that they must . . . reckon with another presence." It is her father's marriage that makes the difference, that destroys "their old freedom, their never having had to think . . . of any one, of anything but each other" [II, 80]. Until the final book of the novel Maggie does not accept Charlotte as her father's choice for a wife, never swerves from her conviction that Adam married "all and only for me" [II, 170].

As a matter of fact, however, Adam marries Charlotte, not only to put Maggie "at peace," but also for "his own actual sense of felicity" [I, 208]. This is a repetition of the marriage in *The Portrait,* for Osmond married Isabel, not only for Pansy's security, but also for the convenience of his own vanity, because he saw in the girl "a high spirit attuned to softness, . . . the softness . . . all for one's self, and the strenuousness for society, which admired the air of superiority" [PL, II, 79]. Adam Verver acquires his young wife "to do the 'worldly' for them" [I, 318], and at the same time enjoys feeling "eased and . . . 'done' for" by Charlotte, who "by becoming for him a domestic resource had become for him practically a new person" [I, 201]. She provides for him "a surface delightfully soft to the pressure of his interest" [I, 202]. Charlotte, in fact, as she practices the "regulated, the developed art of placing him high in the scale of importance" [I, 205], is in effect repeating Isabel's unintentional deception of Gilbert Osmond. For Isabel "had effaced herself when he first knew her; she had made herself small, pretending there was less of her than there really was" [PL, II, 191].

Isabel Archer was not eager to marry—"there are other things a woman can do" [PL, I, 212], and Charlotte expresses the same opinion to the Prince, reminding him that "existence . . . doesn't depend on . . . having caught a husband" [I, 57]. It "may contain after all, in one way and another, so much" [I, 58]. Isabel, however, married Osmond because, in large part, the "desire for unlimited expansion" was "succeeded in her soul by the sense that life was vacant without some private duty" [PL, II, 82]. Interested as she was in the general human scene, "she would be willing . . . to renounce all her curiosities and sympathies for the sake of a personal life" [PL, II, 197-198]. Charlotte tells Verver when he proposes, "I should like to have an existence. I should like to have a motive for one thing more than another—a motive outside of myself" [I, 219].

For Isabel "Pansy . . . represented part of the service she could render, part of the responsibility she could face" [PL, II, 83]; Mrs. Touchett in fact said tartly, "We shall have my niece arriving at the conviction that her mission in life's to prove that a stepmother may sacrifice herself—and that, to prove it, she must first became one" [PL, I, 398]. Interestingly enough, Mrs. Assingham credits Charlotte with a similar motivation.

When Charlotte returns from America, Fanny tells the Colonel that Charlotte "wants to be magnificent," and that she is capable of "carrying out her idea." When the Colonel asks, "And what *is* her idea?" Fanny answers, "To see Maggie through . . . through everything. She *knows* the Prince. And Maggie doesn't" [I, 84]. Charlotte "has had her conception of being able to be heroic, of being able in fact to be sublime . . . to become, for her best friend, an element of *positive* safety" [I, 85]. This theory may be dismissed as a touch of pure irony, but Mrs. Assingham herself does not withdraw it. She assures the Colonel, in their midnight conversation which sums up the first volume, that the situation in which the Prince and Charlotte find themselves is "too extraordinary to be believed," but that they "believe in it themselves. . . . It's their chance for what I told you when Charlotte first turned up. It's their chance for the idea that I was then sure she had" [I, 368]. She speculates that "there's nothing they're not now capable of—in their so intense good faith . . . their false position. It comes to the same thing" [I, 376], and there is an echo of Isabel Archer's "ardent good faith. She was wrong, but she believed; she was deluded, but she was dismally consistent" [PL, II, 74-75].

Charlotte deliberately puts herself into a false position, with rather an excess of good faith, but as she does, she presents her case to Fanny Assingham. It is on the occasion of the Ambassador's reception that Charlotte makes her "point," which is "sharp, bright, true; above all . . . her own" [I, 255]. In this remarkable scene, which is Charlotte's first appearance after her marriage, she specifically outlines her situation to Fanny, a summary which is "in the interest of the highest considerations, . . . good humour, candour, clearness and, obviously, the *real* truth" [I, 256]. It is important that the author deliberately labels Charlotte's statement "true" and "the *real* truth," in contrast, for example, to his ironic interpolation about Maggie—"for she was believing herself in relation to the truth!" [II, 84].

This one big scene between Charlotte and Fanny is a complete and convincing outline of the "unexploited" drama in *The Golden Bowl.* Charlotte has by this time been married long enough to see her unhappy situation in its entirety, to know that if, as the Prince tells her, she is "strange," "how could she be anything else when the situation holding her, and holding *him,* for that matter, just as much, had so the stamp of it" [I, 251]? She places herself publicly with Amerigo so that Fanny may see them together, for she is impatient, almost eager, "to *be* suspected, sounded, veritably arraigned, if only that she might have the bad moment over, if only that she might prove . . . that she could convert it to good" [I, 249-250]. She suspects that the Colonel has already given Fanny, "as a fine little bone to pick, some report of the way one of her young friends was 'going on' with another." The careful reader should note, however, that it is Charlotte's "liberal assumption" that the Colonel "knew perfectly . . . that she wasn't going on with any one" [I, 254].

On her way to her arraignment by Mrs. Assingham, Charlotte is perfectly aware that she is "exposed a little to the public," but exposed also "to much more competent recognitions of her own" [I, 247]. She has arrived at the statement which she makes to Fanny entirely on her own; "no one, not even Amerigo—Amerigo least of all, who would have nothing to do with it—had given her aid" [I, 255]. It is important to remember through all the ambiguities that are to follow this scene, that Charlotte is acting as a completely independent agent, according to her own lights, which will never be entirely revealed to anyone. Maggie is aware of this independent quality in both her crucial scenes with Charlotte at Fawns. On the terrace, she has a "glimpse of [Charlotte's] conceivable idea, which would be founded on reasons all her own, reasons of experience and assurance impenetrable to others but intimately familiar to herself" [II, 240]. Three weeks later, in the garden, she is again aware, as Charlotte is "finding . . . her way," that "there was something she was *saving,* some quantity of which she herself was judge; and it was . . . like watching her from the

solid shore plunge into uncertain, into possibly treacherous depths"
[II, 314].

Charlotte's plunge into possibly treacherous depths recalls a
figure which the Prince uses in describing their situation to Fanny,
a figure placing these two in a category which James has elsewhere
termed "regenerate." The Prince tells Fanny that he and Charlotte
are "in the same boat," which is "Mr. Verver's boat" [I, 267], which
"is a good deal tied up at the dock, or anchored . . . out in the
stream." Both he and Charlotte "have to jump out from time to
time to stretch [their] legs," and sometimes "one has to take a
header and splash about in the water." He advises Mrs. Assingham
to "call our having remained here together to-night . . . one of the
harmless little plunges, off the deck, inevitable for each of us" [I,
270]. Gabriel Nash, in *The Tragic Muse,* defines for Nick Dormer
the distinction between the "regenerate" and the "unregenerate" in
an almost identical figure:

What we like, when we're unregenerate, is that a new-comer should . . .
come over to our side, . . . get into our little boat . . . whatever it is, and
help us to row it. . . . A passenger jumps over from time to time, not
so much from fear of sinking as from a want of interest in the course or
the company. He . . . splashes about, on his own account. . . . The regenerate, as I call them, are the passengers who jump over in search of
better fun [TM, I, 168-169].

James spoke of Milly Theale as his "regenerate young New Yorker"
[WD, I, xi], and it should be clear that any of his heroines qualifies
for Gabriel Nash's regenerate category. Charlotte Stant, who
"visibly knows how to swim" [I, 270], is true to her heritage.

Maggie Verver, on the other hand, is much happier in the
boat. At the beginning of her awakening in the second volume she
tries to pretend that "nothing had happened to her. She hadn't,
so to speak, fallen in; she had . . . not got wet," though she begins
to wonder "if she mightn't, with or without exposure, have taken
cold" [II, 7]. And later, when she has her farewell scene with her
father:

It was wonderfully like their having got together into some boat and
paddled off from the shore where husbands and wives, luxuriant complications, made the air too tropical. In the boat they were father and

daughter. . . . Why . . . couldn't they always live, so far as they lived together, in a boat [II, 255]?

Even as she prepares to part from Adam, "she might have been wishing . . . to keep him with her for remounting the stream of time and dipping again, for the softness of the water, into the con- tracted basin of the past" [II, 258].

It is just Maggie's desire to dip again into the "contracted basin of the past" which Charlotte describes to Fanny as the source of the failure of her own marriage. She tells Fanny that she has "simply to see . . . that Maggie thinks more on the whole of fathers than of husbands," and when Fanny objects that Maggie "adores" her hus- band, Charlotte agrees, but adds that she simply "doesn't think of him" [I, 257]. On the other hand a "large allowance" of her father's company is "of the first necessity to her" [I, 258]. Char- lotte concludes her exposition with the reminder, "The only thing is that I have to act as it demands of me," and in answer to Mrs. Assingham's frightened echo, she says, "Isn't it acting, my dear, to accept it? I do accept it" [I, 261]. The unhappily married Isabel came to the same conclusion, that "when a woman had made such a mistake, there was only one way to repair it—just immensely (oh, with the highest grandeur!) to accept it" [PL, II, 161]. When Charlotte points out to Fanny that "your husband doesn't treat you as of less importance to him than some other woman" [I, 261-262], she has reached the deep water into which Fanny cannot follow her, for she has named Maggie as the "other woman," the threat to her marriage, long before Maggie begins to consider her in the same light. What Mrs. Assingham breathlessly calls "Mr. Verver's per- fectly natural interest in his daughter" she asserts is "the greatest affection of which he's capable . . . in spite of my having done all I could think of to make him capable of a greater" [I, 262].

To dismiss Charlotte's analysis as a glib and involved excuse for misconduct with the Prince is not only to ignore the weight of other evidence in the novel which supports it, but also to distort the whole tone of the scene, a tone which comes to a sort of crescendo as Charlotte leaves Fanny:

She spoke . . . with the noblest moderation of tone, and the image of high pale lighted disappointment she meanwhile presented, as of a creature patient and lonely in her splendour, was an impression so firmly imposed that she could . . . enjoy the last word . . . with a perfection void of any vulgarity of triumph. She merely completed, for truth's sake, her demonstration [I, 263-264].

Charlotte has "made her point . . . once for all, so that no more making was required" [I, 264]; it is in essence that the relationship between the father and daughter is so strong, so primary, that Charlotte is deposed from her rightful position as Adam Verver's wife and must accept a subordinate role as adjunct and convenience to the primary relationship. As the Prince comments to Mrs. Assingham, "For Mrs. Verver to be known to people so intensely and exclusively as her husband's wife . . . he should manage to be known . . . a little more as his wife's husband" [I, 272].

This is an impossible position; Charlotte is undoubtedly rashly mistaken to try to make the best of it, to accept the "forms" which, according to Fanny, Maggie and Verver *"impose* on Charlotte and the Prince" [I, 391]. But she does. She tells Mrs. Assingham, "I've hoped against hope, for I recognise that . . . I was duly warned. . . . He did tell me he wanted me just *because* I could be useful about her. . . . So you see I *am"* [I, 262]. Her conception of being useful about Maggie is to accept what the Prince later thinks of as the "grotesque theory" that she and Amerigo should "go about" together "in a state of childlike innocence, the state of our primitive parents before the Fall" [I, 335]. Both she and Amerigo are aware of the hazards of the arrangement; Mrs. Assingham says that they are afraid "of their own danger, . . . that danger being their position," which "contains, luckily . . . everything *but* blindness: I mean on their part" [I, 369]. But Charlotte says to the Prince, "What in the world else can we do?" [I, 297]. To accept such an arrangement and yet keep straight "represents for us a conscious care of every hour" [I, 312], but they pledge themselves to take that care.

The whole scene between Charlotte and the Prince, which ends with the kiss with which they seal their pledge,[7] is charged with ambiguity, but their good faith should be seriously considered.

---

[7] This kiss has been called "adulterous" by Jacques Barzun, but it should be remembered that renunciation is for James one of the fundamental passions. Note that the renunciation scene between Maggie and her father also ends in a strong embrace [II, 275], and also Isabel's renunciation of an **easy** happiness follows Caspar Goodwood's "white lightning" kiss [PL, II, 436].

Through all the conversation Charlotte speaks "with a nobleness not the less effective for coming in so oddly; with a sincerity visible even through the complicated twist by which any effort to protect the father and the daughter seemed necessarily conditioned for them" [I, 309-310]. And to the Prince her "luminous idea" of "the privilege, the duty, the opportunity, had been the substance of his own vision; they formed the note he had been keeping back to show her that he wasn't, in their so special situation, without a responsible view" [I, 310]. The whole thing is described as "taking place at a very high level of debate—in the cool upper air of the finer discrimination, the deeper sincerity, the larger philosophy" [I, 300-301].

Irony? Perhaps. But there is a deeper irony if Charlotte and the Prince are sincere. They will never be believed; society has a name for a close relationship between them, as it has not (or at least had not when this novel was written) for the strange infidelity of their respective *"sposi."* One could hardly fling the accusation of incest at these charmingly naïve people; as Charlotte says, "It's not a question of anything vulgar or horrid" [I, 305]. Still, whatever the relationship may be called, its closeness and its exclusiveness leave the other two "immensely alone" [I, 308], and it is not unreasonable that they should pool their loneliness, given, that is, their acceptance of the strange predicament.

The Prince is an honorable man; aware of "dangers from within," he is "intelligent enough to feel quite humble" [I, 16]. He says quite seriously that he is "not a hyprocrite . . . I don't lie nor dissemble nor deceive" [I, 15], and Mrs. Assingham tells the Colonel that, "to do him justice, I believe he absolutely doesn't [lie]" [I, 72]. His answer to Maggie's accusation about the original Golden Bowl expedition with Charlotte is: "You've never been more sacred to me than you were at that hour—unless perhaps you've become so at this one" [II, 199], but when Maggie refuses to acknowledge his assurance, he retreats into an "extreme reserve" [II, 220] and does not again specifically defend himself. But his final ambiguous word on Maggie's "knowledge" is, "If ever a man since the beginning of time acted in good faith—!" [II, 350].

Charlotte, standing before Maggie "beautiful and free, her whole aspect and action attuned to the firmness of her speech" [II, 247], assures her, "I'm aware of no point whatever at which I may have failed you . . . nor of any at which I may have failed any one in whom I can suppose you sufficiently interested to care" [II, 248]. This is a comprehensive assurance, and since it comes so straight from a character who is through the novel credited with "nobleness," "sincerity," "a generous rigour of conscience," "explicit honesty," "true directness," and similar qualities, it should not be so readily dismissed as an outright lie. Maggie does not even consider that it may be true; this is a possibility which would complicate her "simple certainty" [II, 182], and Maggie is, as Charlotte remarks to the Prince, "very, very simple" [I, 311]. She admits at the same time that she does not understand Maggie. "I can't put myself into Maggie's skin. . . . It's not my fit—I shouldn't be able, as I see it, to breathe in it. But I can feel that I'd do anything to shield it from a bruise" [I, 311].

Charlotte's resolve to shield Maggie may be a noble one, but dangerous. She seems not to realize that simplicity may be brutal as well as sweet, that the cruelty of childhood is one of the less lovely aspects of the innocent time, and the more striking as it appears hand in hand with the sweetness. Maggie is very much a child; Mrs. Assingham perceives this with some concern when she realizes that Maggie holds her responsible for the situation because of her "original affectionate interest":

On this affectionate interest the good lady's young friend now built before her eyes—very much as a wise or even as a mischievous child, playing on the floor, might pile up blocks, skilfully and dizzily, with an eye on the face of a covertly-watching elder [II, 102].

The blocks Maggie piles up, however, are human feelings, and this fact has frightening implications, because Maggie does not have the understanding to play without hurting. Her lack of understanding is underscored by a repeated image in the second volume, the image of the card game. It is introduced early in the volume:

She thought of herself, instinctively, beautifully, as having dealt, all her life, at her father's side and by his example, only in reasonable reasons. . . . She felt herself—as at the small square green table between the tall old silver candlesticks and the neatly arranged counters—her father's playmate and partner [II, 34].

When Maggie watches the real card game at Fawns, as Charlotte, Adam, Amerigo, and Fanny play "round the green cloth and the silver flambeaux" [II, 232], it is pointed out that "cards were as nought to her and she could follow no move, so that she was always on such occasions out of the party" [II, 233]. The card game is such a straightforward symbol that Maggie's inability to "follow the moves" cannot reasonably be restricted to its literal sense. If Maggie has an imperfect understanding of the game of life, then she has serious weaknesses as a witness of the action in which she participates. And she is the star witness of the second volume; she doubles as a "compositional resource" in this volume.

Her limitations as a witness are pointed up in Mrs. Assingham's interpolated analysis, directed to the Colonel, of Maggie's state of mind and her view of the action [II, 121-136]. The whole conversation is ironic and really very funny, but it is not simply an exercise in comic relief. Mrs. Assingham, deliberately seeing the situation through Maggie's eyes, reminds herself and her husband that "we're not talking of course about impartial looks. We're talking of good innocent people deeply worked upon by a horrid discovery and going much further in their view of the lurid, as such people almost always do, than those who have been wider awake all round from the first" [II, 127]. Her observation that "no imagination's so lively, once it's started, as that of really agitated lambs" [II, 128] could well serve as a motto for the Princess's volume of *The Golden Bowl*.

Although "there had been, through life, as we know, few quarters in which the Princess's fancy could let itself loose," she has a field day with the relationship between the Prince and Charlotte. Her imagination

shook off restraint when it plunged into the figured void of the detail of that relation. This was a realm it could people with images; . . . they swarmed there like the strange combinations that lurked in the woods at twilight; they loomed into the definite and faded into the vague, their main present sign for her being . . . that they were always, that they were duskily, agitated [II, 280].

Even before the final visit to Fawns, Maggie has looked into the "recesses of her imagination . . . almost without penetration" [II, 219], and by the time of her final interview with Charlotte she is a thoroughly agitated lamb indeed.

There were always too many [possibilities], and all of them things of evil when one's nerves had at last done for one all that nerves could do;

had left one in a darkness of prowling dangers that was like the predicament of the night-watcher in a beast-haunted land who has no more
means for a fire. She might, with such nerves, have supposed almost
anything of any one [II, 299-300].

Agitated as she undoubtedly is, she is sustained in her course of
action by her very simplicity, "her small still passion for order and
symmetry, for objects with their backs to the walls" [II, 152]. She
is determined to keep "in tune with the right" [II, 250], but her
conception of the right is dominated by her "sense of possession . . .
almost too violent either to recognise or to hide" [II, 207]. She owns
the Prince, just as her father owns Charlotte, and the one thing she
is certain of is that they must never lose a valuable piece. When
it seems probable to her that the Prince and Charlotte, if they are
to remain in the Ververs' inventory, will have to be separated, the
corollary, that she and her father will have to separate as well, makes
her "quail." Their separation is "thinkable, but only on the basis
of the sharpest of reasons" [II, 74]. The goal she sets herself is to
keep both her father and their possessions, but in this she fails, for
when the golden bowl is broken, she finds that she can "carry but
two of the fragments at once" [II, 182]. She separates from her
father, but she keeps Amerigo.

It should always be remembered that Maggie Verver is every
inch her father's daughter in her acquisitive instinct; she tells the
Prince in the very beginnng, with no trace of embarrassment, that
he is a *"morceau de musée"* [I, 12], and that it is his history that
"made me originally think of you. It wasn't—as I should suppose
you must have seen—what you call your . . . particular self" [I, 9].
She and her father, she tells her husband-to-be, have been "like a
pair of pirates," and their "treasure is buried . . . pretty well everywhere—except what we like to see," like the Prince, for instance,
who is in the class of "things we take out and arrange as we can,
to make the hotels we stay at and the houses we hire a little less
ugly. Of course," she admits, "it's a danger, and we have to keep
watch. But father loves a fine piece . . . and it's for the company
of some of his things that he's willing to run his risks" [I, 13-14].
They have had, she assures the Prince, "extraordinary luck. . . .
We've never lost anything yet" [I, 14].

Small wonder that Amerigo, even though used to "assenting,

from principle and habit, to more than he understood" [I, 138], is conscious after this of "an appeal to do something or other, before it was too late, for himself" [I, 20]. When he turns to Fanny Assingham for guidance, however, she reminds him that he hardly needs a guide since he is "practically *in* port. The port . . . of the Golden Isles" [I, 27]. When Adam Verver is introduced in Book Second, there is a flash back to the moment when he realized that "to rifle the Golden Isles" was to be "the business of his future" [I, 141]. The Prince represents for him a piece of loot from the Golden Isles of European culture. The irony of the symbol is that it applies at the same time to what the Prince sees in Adam, for Adam is the proprietor of the Golden Isles—the security provided by American wealth. The irony and the ambiguity extend to the central symbol of the novel, the Golden Bowl.

From the point of view of the Ververs, the Prince is the Golden Bowl; Verver tells him so. The applications of the symbol to the Prince's character and his European heritage have been thoroughly explored in other criticisms. But there is a broader meaning emanating from the Bowl, related to the golden age of innocence which it suggests in the biblical source of the symbol:

. . . the days of thy youth, while the evil days come not, nor the years draw nigh, when thou shalt say, I have no pleasure in them. . . .
Or ever the silver cord be loosed, or the golden bowl be broken.[8]

The Golden Bowl, in this sense, is the receptacle which encloses them all in the false security of their "see-no-evil" world, their ironic Eden. This bowl, too, is not really gold, but gilded by money, and it is threatened by "realities looming through the golden mist that had already begun to be scattered" [II, 31].

The Golden Bowl of Mr. Verver's wealth becomes for Charlotte a prison. The sight of her suggests to Maggie "gilt wires and bruised wings." In her "spacious but suspended cage, the home of eternal unrest," she is "a prisoner looking through bars, . . . bars richly gilt but firmly though discreetly planted" [II, 229-230]. Charlotte knows when she sees the Bowl that something is the matter with it, for "if it's so precious how comes it to be cheap?" [I, 114]. But she is charmed with the cup, cracked or not. She says to the Prince, "Don't you think too much of 'cracks' and aren't you too

[8] Eccles. 12: 1, 6.

afraid of them? I risk the cracks" [I, 359]. Her attitude is a marked contrast to the Prince's, who answers, "Risk them as much as you like for yourself, but don't risk them for me" [I, 360], and also to Maggie's infantile demand for "a happiness without a hole in it big enough for you to poke in your finger . . . the golden bowl —as it *was* to have been . . . , the bowl with all our happiness in it. The bowl without the crack" [II, 216-217].

Charlotte's attitude toward the cracks is thoroughly Jamesian. Throughout his fiction James is concerned with the "insuperable difficulties which present themselves in people's lives and from which the only issue is by forfeiture."[9] Isabel Archer recognized that "I can't escape unhappiness" [PL, I, 186]. "I can never be happy . . . by separating myself . . . from life. From the usual chances and dangers, from what most people know and suffer" [PL, I, 187].

When Charlotte makes her appearance in the beginning of *The Golden Bowl,* the conversation between the Prince and Fanny builds up to her entrance with all the intent of any first-act introduction of the star of a play, even to the cue line, "She's back" [I, 43], which ends the chapter. They make it perfectly clear that she is that vital element in any drama, the complication, for "a handsome clever odd girl staying with one is always a complication" [I, 43]. The Ververs add this complication to their simple existence "to give us a life" [II, 95], and the way in which she was done this is summed up by Maggie in the final book of the novel. This last book is the dénouement of the drama, and the subject is still Charlotte Stant. To the Prince Maggie says:

She's wonderful and beautiful, and I feel somehow as if she were dying. Not really, not physically. . . she's naturally so far, splendid as she is, from having done with life. But dying for us—for you and me; and making us feel it by the very fact of there being so much of her left [II, 346].

"It's as if," Maggie concludes, "her unhappiness had been necessary to us—as if we had needed her, at her own cost, to build us up and start us" [II, 346]. Such is Maggie's justification of Charlotte Stant, which echoes Kate Croy's justification of Milly Theale: "She died for you then that you might understand her. From that hour you *did.* . . . And I do now. She did it *for* us" [WD, II, 403].

[9] Quoted in Matthiessen, *The James Family* (New York, 1948), p. 501.

Maggie and her father part "absolutely on Charlotte's *value.* ...,
her gifts, her variety, her power" [II, 365], but for Charlotte her
only consolation is that, whatever her suffering and defeat, she *is*
valuable. She has this recognition in common with Isabel Archer,
who nevertheless asked herself, "When had it ever been a guarantee
to be valuable? Wasn't all history full of the destruction of precious
things? Wasn't it much more probable that if one were fine one
would suffer?" [PL, II, 392-393]. James's affirmative answer to this
last question comes as consistently through *The Golden Bowl* as
through any of his other novels, for to the end "it is the tragedies
in life that arrest my attention more than the other things and say
more to my imagination."[10]

[10] *Ibid.*

James's "Moral Policeman":
William Dean Howells

Oscar Cargill

I

Opening the Door

THE LONGEST IMPORTANT ASSOCIATION in American letters was that of William Dean Howells and Henry James.[1] In the beginning it was the friendship between a young writer of fiction, eager for a regular outlet, and the newly appointed assistant editor of the magazine which each was most willing should prosper. Howells, as Fields's junior on the *Atlantic Monthly,* had the realization of James's hopes in his hands, and to judge from the letter which James wrote to be read at the party in New York City honoring Howells on his seventy-fifth birthday, on March 2, 1912, James felt he could not have had a more sympathetic friend in power:

My debt to you began well nigh half a century ago in the most personal way possible, and then kept growing and growing with your own admirable growth—but always rooted in the early intimate benefit. This benefit was that you held out your open editorial hand to me at the time I began to write—and I allude especially to the summer of 1866—with a frankness and sweetness of hospitality that was really the making of me, the making of the confidence that required help and sympathy and that I should otherwise, I think, have strayed and stumbled about a long time without acquiring. You showed me the way and opened me the door;

[1] For the relations of Howells and James at the beginning of each's career as a writer of fiction, see Cornelia Kelley, *The Early Development of Henry James* (Urbana, 1930), pp. 73-80; Van Wyck Brooks, *New England: Indian Summer* (New York, 1940), pp. 224-249; Clara Marburg Kirk and Rudolph Kirk, *William Dean Howells,* AWS (New York, 1950), pp. lvii-lxix, lxxvii, and clxvi-clxvii; and Leon Edel, *Henry James: The Untried Years* (Philadelphia, 1950), pp. 268-276. More general: F. O. Matthiessen, *The James Family* (New York, 1947), pp. 498-518. Edward Wagenknecht, "Of Henry James and Howells, 1925," *Virginia Quarterly Review,* I, 453-460 (Oct., 1925), contains nothing pertinent, but is a review of Oscar Firkins, *William Dean Howells, A Study* (Cambridge, Mass., 1925) and Van Wyck Brooks, *The Pilgrimage of Henry James* (New York, 1925), both in themselves disappointing on the relationships of the two men.

you wrote me and confessed yourself struck with me—I have never forgotten the beautiful thrill of *that*. You published me at once. . . .²

This assumption of cordiality is borne out by Howells's earlier
reminiscence. James "had already printed a tale—'The Story of a
Year'—in the *Atlantic Monthly*," Howells recalled not quite ac-
curately,³ "when I was asked to be Mr. Fields's assistant in the
management, and it was my fortune to read Mr. James's second
contribution in manuscript. 'Would you take it?' asked my chief.
'Yes, and all the stories you can get from the writer.' One is much
securer in one's judgment at twenty-nine than, say, at forty-five; but
if this was a mistake of mine I am not yet old enough to regret it.
The story was called 'Poor Richard.' "⁴ But the most substantial
proof that Howells "opened me the door" is, of course, the publishing record. As assistant editor of the *Atlantic* (March 1, 1866⁵-
1871) and as editor-in-chief (July 1, 1871-Feb. 2, 1881⁶), Howells
accepted from Henry James and published five novels, six *novelle*,
seven short stories, a farce, eight art articles, eight travel sketches,
and six reviews and notices.⁷ One of these novels, *The American*,
Howells induced Francis P. Church, editor of the *Galaxy*, to turn
over to him after learning from James himself that he would have

² "A Letter to Mr. Howells," *North American Review*, CXCV, 558-562 (April, 1912).
"Your letter will help me to take away some of the moments of self-blame, and I can think,
'Well, there must have been something in it; James would not abuse my dotage with
flattery; I probably was not always such a worm of the earth as I feel myself at present' "
(W. D. H. to H. J., March 17, 1912, *Life in Letters of William Dean Howells*, ed. Mildred
Howells, 2 vols., Garden City, 1928, II, 316).
³ James had contributed "The Story of a Year" and "A Landscape Painter" and had
submitted a critical article on George Eliot which had been accepted before Howells joined
the staff in the spring of 1866 (Kelley, p. 73). It would appear that while Fields had
assented to taking James's *fourth* contribution, Howells actually passed on it: "Mr. James
has given me the ms. of a story about which he has already spoken to you, and I find it
entirely acceptable.
"If you haven't made up the March number entirely yet, wouldn't it be well to get
this story into it? . . . The title of course to be changed" (W. D. H. to James T.
Fields, Jan. 4, 1886 [1867], James C. Austin, *Fields of "The Atlantic Monthly,"* San
Marino, Calif., 1953, p. 148 and n. 17). "In regard to the March number we have now
115 pp. inclusive of James's story" (W. D. H. to J. T. F., Jan. 21, 1867, transcript,
Arms, Gibson, and Marston). "My Friend Bingham" appeared in March, 1867; *Poor
Richard* in June, July, and August. James's recollection makes his debt to Howells in regard to *Poor Richard* even larger; see *Notes of a Son and Brother* (New York, 1914), p. 437.
⁴ *Century*, XXV, 25-29 (Nov., 1882); and Kirk and Kirk, *William Dean Howells*,
p. 346.
⁵ Austin, p. 145.
⁶ *Life in Letters*, I, 162, 294.
⁷ See Le Roy Phillips, *A Bibliography of the Writings of Henry James* (New York,
1930), pp. 137-190.

preferred to send it to the *Atlantic,* being dissatisfied with the owners of the *Galaxy.* James had sent the story to the New York magazine because he had felt the timing inopportune for the *Atlantic.*[8] *The Europeans* was in the hands of the *Galaxy* for serial publication at the time of its merger with the *Atlantic* and was also turned over to the surviving magazine.[9] Despite this fortuitous arrival of one of James's serials Howells was, on this showing, the friendliest of James's editors.

Howells's receptivity to James's work was fostered in a period of close communication with the younger man, which began probably in the fall of 1866 when the Jameses returned from Swampscott.[10] "I cannot recall my first meeting with Henry James, or for that matter, the second or third or specifically any after meeting," Howells wrote in 1920. "All I can say is that we seemed presently to be always meeting, at his father's house and at mine, but in the kind Cambridge streets rather than those kind Cambridge houses which it seems to me I frequented more than he. We seem to have been presently always together, and always talking methods of fiction, whether we walked the streets by day or night, or we sat together reading our stuff to each other; his stuff which we both hoped might make itself into matter for the *Atlantic Monthly,* then mostly left to my editing by the senior editor Mr. Fields."[11] In regard to the substance of those frequent and protracted dialogues[12] on "the methods of fiction" Howells gives us only one further hint, which, however, may be of the utmost importance:

We [Howells and his wife] were of like Latin sympathies, he [James] was inveterately and intensely French, and with the Italian use of our three or four years' life in Italy we could make him feel that we met on a common ground. James could not always keep his French background back, and sometimes he wrote English that the editor easily convicted of

---

[8] H. J. to W. D. H., Feb. 3, 1876 (*Selected Letters,* ed. Leon Edel, New York, 1955, pp. 65-66); Howells to Church, Feb. 29, 1876; "If you have found, with Madcap Violet on your hands, that you can't use Mr. James's new serial conveniently, won't you turn it over to me?" Howells to Church, March 5, 1876: "I should be glad to know within a week what your decision is in regard to Mr. James's story" (Church's note on verso of second letter, "MSS sent per Exch. Mch 11/76," transcripts, Arms, Gibson, and Marston).

[9] Frank Luther Mott, *A History of American Magazines* (3 vols., Cambridge, Mass., 1938), III, 369.

[10] Kelley, p. 73. For confirmation see *Life in Letters,* II, 399, and *Notes of a Son and Brother,* p. 437.

[11] *Life in Letters,* II, 397.

[12] *Ibid.,* I, 116, 137; II, 388.

Gallicism; but this was the helplessness of early use and habit from his life and school in France throughout boyhood.

. . . I had learned to like his fiction from such American subjects as *Poor Richard,* but now it was such a French theme as *Gabrielle de Bergerac* which had employed his art. . . . We were sufficiently critical no doubt as an editorial family should be, but we richly felt the alien quality and circumstance of the tales and novels which I eagerly accepted from him. . . .[13]

It would appear from this that some of the discussions between James and his editor may have revolved on the question of how far it was appropriate to write and to print in America any fiction which was "French" in its character. Howells was not the only one at this time to object to the Gallicisms in James's prose; his brother William protested against them[14] and so did J. C. Heywood in the New York *Sun;*[15] but the French "background" which James could not always keep "back" was more than scattered Gallicisms in his style—it was "the alien quality and circumstances" of the tales as well. Fields had apparently warned Howells against the young contributor's penchant for pessimism and Howells, amused, had repeated the proprietor's words to James.[16] The latter had begun his career with a sensational story of a French mistress who, in plotting the death of her husband, achieved the death of her lover.[17] *Gabrielle de Bergerac,* which Howells cites as having disturbed him and his wife, tells the story of a girl who elopes with her tutor because the tutor has been wrongly accused by her brother of making her his mistress and subsequently has been dismissed. Yet it should be noted that Howells published this novella despite Fields's caution and despite its theme.

That Howells should have had qualms about issuing a tale of wrongfully accused innocence is not surprising to those who have

[13] *Ibid.,* II, 398. In "Novel-writing and Novel-reading," a lecture which Howells prepared for Major Pond in 1899, discovered recently by W. M. Gibson and to be published shortly in the *Bulletin of the New York Public Library,* our knowledge of these talks will be slightly extended.

[14] Ralph B. Perry, *The Thought and Character of William James* (2 vols., Boston, 1935), I, 298.

[15] E. P. Mitchell, *Memoirs of an Editor* (New York, 1924), p. 205.

[16] Henry James, "Mr. and Mrs. James T. Fields," *Atlantic,* CXVI, 27 (July, 1915); H. J., *The American Essays,* ed. Leon Edel (New York, 1956), p. 273.

[17] "A Tragedy of Error," *Continental Monthly,* V, 204-216 (Feb., 1864); reprinted by its discoverer, Leon Edel, with a prefatory note, in the *New England Quarterly,* XXIX, 291-317 (Sept., 1956).

been made acquainted with his neurotic prudery.[18] Yet Howells was very conscious of his limitation and at times struggled against it. Prior to going to Venice as consul in the Civil War, Howells had contributed Heinesque poems and, in defiance of "the Misses Nancy of criticism," an essay of qualified approval of Whitman to the *Saturday Press*—that notorious outlet for the New York bohemians.[19] He may have even hoped that Henry Clapp and his cohorts might adopt him, for he went to New York to meet them but was completely discouraged, according to Professor Cady, by his reception. Italy and marriage to Elinor Mead, relative of John Humphrey Noyes and sister to a sculptor, should not have put great obstacles in the way of his self-improvement. At any rate, when Howells returned to America and established himself in New York as a free lance, he again made overtures to the *Saturday Press* through the device of praise for it in his "Letter from New York" in the Cincinnati *Daily Gazette*.[20] It was during this tentative period in New York that Howells made his only lasting enemy by attacking that syrupy mound of respectability, Dr. Josiah Gilbert Holland.[21] It was to this incipient, but hesitant, mild iconoclast, with his common "Latin sympathies," that the young James appealed—and appealed persuasively enough to get *Gabrielle de Bergerac* published.

Ironically, Howells was treated to his most drastic lesson in public taste during this very period of his presentation of his more

[18] Edwin Harrison Cady, "The Neuroticism of William Dean Howells," *PMLA*, LXI, 229-238 (March, 1946). Cady supplies an abundance of evidence (hypochondria, homesickness, horror at sex and brutality, etc.), but there is much more. Note Howells's reaction to Stevenson and Gorki (*Life in Letters*, I, 232; II, 220). Professor William Gibson calls my attention especially to Howells's attitude as a boy toward a "fallen" seamstress, taken in by his father. "Heaven knows how I came by such a devilish idea of propriety . . . ," Howells confesses (*Years of My Youth*, New York, 1916, p. 42).

[19] Edwin H. Cady, *The Road to Realism: The Early Years, 1837-1885, of William Dean Howells* (Syracuse, 1956), pp. 85-87.

[20] Compare the condescension in the memorial to George Arnold when Howells was hoping for permanent exclusive employment with the *Nation* ("*The Press* holds a place of its own, and there is the old personal flavor in the liking and dislike for it; but the principal literary interest of New York centers around *The Nation* and *The Round Table*," to which H. was a contributor—Nov. 20, 1865) with the frank praise Howells expressed when he had made an arrangement with the *Nation* which was not exclusive and he knew that he might possibly supplement his income by contributing to the *Press:* "I hope that you see Mr. Clapp's *Saturday Press*. It is not the old *Saturday Press*, certainly, but it is wonderfully good, and grows better from week to week" (Jan. 9, 1866). For dates, see *Life in Letters*, I, 102, 104.

[21] Cady, *The Road to Realism*, pp. 122-125.

venturesome young protégé in the pages of his magazine, when at the urgency of Dr. Holmes, but with the disapprobation of James Russell Lowell, he published, while Fields was in Europe, "The True Story of Lady Byron's Life" by Harriet Beecher Stowe in the *Atlantic* in September, 1869. Howells may have been afraid to reject it for fear of losing so important a contributor,[22] he may have yielded too readily to Holmes (another important contributor), but on the whole, his reasons for publishing the story are almost as strange as Mrs. Stowe's in writing it. Perhaps in part it was a boldness inspired by association with a more emancipated, younger man. "Howells seemed to approve," says James C. Austin. "The public reaction to the article was far beyond anything the *Atlantic* had ever gone through."[23] The magazine and the author were abused and subscriptions were canceled wholesale. The effect of this, if not to shock Howells back into prudery, was to teach him an extraordinary editorial caution. No more daring adventures for the *Atlantic* in the field of morals.

On the score of what the public would accept, Henry James would have had every inclination to defer to his editor. "James was younger, his experience of the world of men and the practical world in which one sold and published writing much less than Howells'."[24] That Howells, despite his generous reception of James's work, increasingly annoyed James by persistent criticism of the "immoral" implications of his tales, especially after the Lady Byron episode, and by his pressure on the author to respect the tabus of his age is not beyond demonstration. Howells actually refused only one story from James in fifteen years[25] but that possibly for the

[22] Austin, pp. 290-295.

[23] *Ibid.*, pp. 294-295. "The September is equally good, though Mrs. Stowe's sensation of course benumbs the public to everything else in it. So far her story has been received with howls of rejection from almost every side where a critical dog is kept. The *Tribune* and one or two Western papers alone accept it as truth; but I think the tide will turn, especially if its publication in England elicits anything like confirmation there" (W. D. H. to Fields, Aug. 24, 1869, *Life in Letters*, I, 147). Cady (*The Road to Realism*, pp. 136-137) tries to play down Howells's part in this notorious episode, in keeping with his theory of Howells's utter rejection of bohemianism after his trip to New England in 1865. This is not the way I read the evidence. The foregoing letter supports Austin's view as more acceptable.

[24] Cady, *The Road to Realism*, p. 152.

[25] "I looked at his stuff for the *Atlantic* except one 'humorous' story"; "We . . . felt the alien quality and circumstance of the tales and novels which I eagerly accepted from him, even one of a supposed humorous cast which we both grieved to find inacceptable" (*Life in Letters*, II, 388, 398).

wrong reasons. If the story was "The Light Man,"[26] with its patently assumed sophistication and cynicism, Howells could have rejected it for its clumsy narrative method—that of longish diary entries—but he probably objected to its tone. A more irritating episode, possibly, occurred in connection with the publication of "The Madonna of the Future." James, who was traveling, evidently entrusted proofreading on this contribution to his father. Howells objected to the length of the tale, and "besides he had a decided shrinking from one episode—that in which Theobald tells his love for, and his visit from the Titian-ic beauty, and his subsequent disgust with her worthlessness, as being risky for the magazine; and . . . he objected to the interview at the end between the writer and the old English neighbor, as rubbing into the reader what was sufficiently evident without it." James's father conceded that Howells was "too timid" in both cases, yet he consented to the deletion of two episodes on the provision that the editor run the remainder in a single issue. Howells revised the tale to cover the deletions and this was the way in which it appeared. James naturally resented this tampering with his work, but he had to assent to it:

> With such a standard of propriety, it makes a bad look-out ahead for imaginative writing. For what class of minds is it that such very timorous scruples are thought necessary? . . . Evidently Howells has a better notion of the allowances of the common public than I have, and I am much obliged to him for performing the excision personally, for of course he will have done it neatly.[27]

Howells added fuel to James's resentment by telling him, after the tale had been published, that, much as he liked the piece, he found "the insistence on the cats and monkeys philosophy" a blemish,[28] and later, when he reviewed the volume in which it was collected,

---

[26] It appeared in the *Galaxy* for July, 1869, pp. 49-68. I do not connect its rejection with the Lady Byron episode because of the dates, but James may have been annoyed at the acceptance of one and the rejection of the other, which could not have occurred too far apart.

[27] H. J., Sr., to H. J., Cambridge, Jan. 14, 1873; H. J. to H. J., Sr., Rome, Feb. 1, 1873 (Matthiessen, pp. 121-123).

[28] W. D. H. to H. J., Cambridge, March 10, 1873 (*Life in Letters*, I, 175-176). The reference is to the molder of satirical figurines, who got his human types from studying cats and monkeys: "Cats and monkeys, monkeys and cats; all human life is there!" (*A Passionate Pilgrim*, Boston, 1875, pp. 313-314, 325). This seems a trivial thing for Howells to have objected to.

laid precisely the same stricture on the story.[29] James may well have concluded that Howells's caution ran beyond the reticence of his readers. Yet, when Howells objected to the ending of *The American* (which, however, he allowed James to keep), James, while defending the verisimilitude of his conclusion, conceded, "But whether the Atlantic ought to print unlimited tragedy is another question—which you are doubtless quite right in regarding as you do. Of course, you couldn't have for the present another evaporated marriage from me! I suspect it is the tragedies in life that arrest my attention more than the other things and say more to my imagination."[30]

But if James conceded to Howells that his editor knew more about public taste than he did, he thought highly neither of that taste nor of its zealous guardian, though he concealed his feelings from the latter. In writing to Grace Norton on November 27, 1870, he allowed his estimate of Howells's timidity to color his evaluation of him as a writer.

> Poor Howells is certainly difficult to defend, if one takes a standpoint the least bit exalted; make any serious demands and it's all up with him. He presents, I confess, to my mind, a somewhat melancholy spectacle— in that his charming style and refined intentions are so poorly and meagrely served by our American atmosphere. There is no more inspiration in an American journey than that! Thro' thick and thin I continue however to enjoy him—or rather thro' thin and thinner. There is a little divine spark of fancy which never quite gives out. . . .[31]

To Charles Eliot Norton, an especial friend of Howells then in Europe, James wrote in January, 1871, to praise Howells's *Suburban Sketches* as belonging, "by the wondrous cunning of their manner, to very good literature" and to admit that American civilization

[29] "Recent Literature," *Atlantic*, XXXV, 490-495 (April, 1875). James had not added in *The Passionate Pilgrim* the episodes which Howells had deleted; hence reiteration of the private criticism in the review must have seemed especially gratuitous.

[30] H. J. to W. D. H., March 30, 1877 (Matthiessen, pp. 500-501). There is no absolute proof that James did not change the ending at Howells's insistence; it may have been like that of the dramatization, which assigns concealment of disloyalty to Mme de Belle-garde as a motive in the death of her husband.

[31] Edel, p. 23. Edel says the letter refers to *Suburban Sketches;* William M. Gibson and George Arms give the publication date of this volume as Dec. 9, 1870 (*A Bibliography of William Dean Howells,* New York, 1948, p. 22). James may have seen the proof sheets, but *No Love Lost* (1869) seems an equally good choice; its subtitle is "A romance of travel." "A Day's Pleasure," serialized in the *Atlantic* (July-September, 1870), seems, however, on the score of triviality to be the best choice of all.

might provide, up "to a certain point a very sufficient literary field."
He added, however, that "it will yield its secrets only to a really
grasping imagination. This I think Howells lacks."[32] After Howells
became editor-in-chief of the *Atlantic,* James wrote the same correspondent:

> Howells is now monarch absolute of the *Atlantic* to the increase of
> his profit and comfort. His talent grows constantly in fineness but hardly,
> I think, in range of application. I remember your saying some time ago
> that in a couple of years when he had read Sainte-Beuve &c. he would
> come to his best. But the trouble is he will never read Sainte-Beuve, nor
> care to. He has little intellectual curiosity, so here he stands with his
> admirable organ of style, like a poor man holding a diamond and won-
> dering how he can wear it. It's rather sad I think. . . .[33]

The unfairness of this comment[34] reveals that James's annoyance
was deep; later in the seventies, as Leon Edel has amusingly shown,
James deliberately started teasing Howells indirectly about his narrowness. On February 3, 1876, he told Howells that Edmond de
Goncourt contemplated writing a novel on "a whore-house *de
province.*" To which, Howells responded that he thanked God
that he wasn't a Frenchman. In his next letter, on May 28, 1876,
James told how he had been visiting in Paris the supposedly ille-
gitimate daughter of an English peer, a certain Baroness:

> She lives in a queer old mouldy, musty *rez-de-chaussée* in the depths
> of the Faubourg St. Germain, is the greasiest and most audacious lion
> huntress in all creation, and has two most extraordinary little French
> emancipated daughters. One of these, wearing a Spanish mantilla and
> got up apparently to dance the cachacha, presently asked me what I

---

[32] H. J. to C. E. N., Cambridge, Jan. 16, 1871 (*Letters*, I, 30). Norton had provided
the cash for Howells to buy his first home in Cambridge (*Life in Letters*, I, 106).

[33] H. J. to C. E. N., Cambridge, Aug. 9, 1871 (Edel, p. 276). Why the Nortons turned
their early letters from James over to Howells in 1903 is a mystery; perhaps Howells asked
for them in connection with an article he contemplated writing. See below. Howells
wrote Norton, April 26, 1903: "In a way I think their criticism very just; I have often
thought my intellectual raiment was more than my intellectual body, and that I might
finally be convicted, not of having nothing *on,* but of that worse nakedness of having
nothing *in.* He speaks of me with my style, and such mean application as I was making
of it, as seeming to him like a poor man with a diamond which he does not know what
to do with; and mostly I suppose I *have* cut rather inferior window glass with it. But
I am not sorry for having wrought in common, crude material so much; that is the right
American stuff . . ." (*Life in Letters*, II, 172-173).

[34] It is an amusing byplay that Howells later compares James to Sainte-Beuve as a critic
("Recent Literature," *Atlantic*, XLII, 118, July, 1878). Had Norton reported the stricture?
Howells could not then have seen the letter.

thought of *incest* as a subject for a novel—adding that it had against it that it was getting, in families, so terribly common.

"We do not know," Edel remarks, "whether Howells made any rejoinder on this occasion."[35] Edel misses the deadly thrust in this, however—the reminder to Howells that he had printed the most notorious allegation of incest of the century in the Byron case. Edel does report, on the other hand, how James "with unconcealed delight" had told that "a mother, after reading a novel by Howells, took elaborate precautions that it should not be read by her daughter. It seemed to James a pleasant irony that a novel by a writer scrupulously careful to keep his work 'wholesome,' who pleaded for happy endings and simple romantic tales from him, should be forbidden a *jeune fille*."

Coupled with Howells's efforts to persuade James to be less venturesome in challenging the limitations of magazine fiction was pressure on the younger man to adopt Hawthorne as a model. Miss Kelley, who first noted the existence of this pressure, observes that, although Howells shared with James an interest in George Eliot, Howells confessed that he found a "more potent charm" in Hawthorne's "more artistic handling" of the problem of evil than he found in George Eliot's treatment.[36] If the issue of Hawthorne's adumbration of evil were ever a contention between the two men—and one cannot help feeling that it was—then James's extended preferential comparison of J. G. Lockhart's *Adam Blair* with *The Scarlet Letter* in his critical study of Hawthorne was intended more for the eye of Howells than for that of any other reader:

> *Adam Blair* is the history of the passion, and *The Scarlet Letter* the history of its sequel. . . . I confess that a large portion of the interest of *Adam Blair,* to my mind . . . , lay in noting its difference of tone. It threw into relief the passionless quality of Hawthorne's novel, its element of cold and ingenious fantasy, its elaborate imaginative delicacy. These things do not constitute a weakness in *The Scarlet Letter;* indeed in a

[35] Edel, p. 274.

[36] Kelley, pp. 77-80. Miss Kelley concludes that Howells's preference for Hawthorne led James into experimenting to achieve a "more artistic handling" of his materials—even a romantic treatment of them. She maintains that James's contributions to the *Atlantic* in 1868-1869 were more romantic than those he made to the *Galaxy* and she points out that, after the "last and best" of the *Atlantic* contributions, Howells wrote James, ". . . when you've a fame as great as Hawthorne's, you won't forget who was the first, warmest and truest of your admirers, will you?" Miss Kelley may be generally right, but this "last and best" tale was *Gabrielle de Bergerac,* about which, as we have seen, Howells had qualms.

certain way they constitute a great strength; but absence of something warm and straightforward, a trifle more grossly human and vulgarly natural, which one finds in *Adam Blair,* will always make Hawthorne's tale less touching to a large number of even very intelligent readers, than a love-story told with the robust, synthetic pathos which served Lockhart so well.[37]

But one should note also James's insistence that "Lockhart's story is *as decent, as severely draped,* as *The Scarlet Letter.* . . ."[38] The stories and novels of James certainly deal with passion in a warmer, more natural and direct way, while still keeping it decently draped, than do those of Hawthorne. If this were a result of the long discussions with Howells, then Howells contributed to James's development by providing him with a foil before he demonstrated his skill to the public.

One contribution of Howells to the younger man, however, is so patent as to need no demonstration—he improved James's style. The Gallicisms that we have noted gradually disappeared; James's prose became more simple and supple—the result was that in the 1880's these two American novelists were writing the best narrative prose in English.[39]

II

"Finer . . . than . . . Dickens and Thackeray"

Of the practicing critics who treated his work over the years, Henry James owed most, probably, to William Dean Howells. It was Howells who regularly dropped into his writing encomiums for James's fictions, who kept interest in him perpetually alive. James "is . . . extremely gifted—gifted enough to do better than anyone has yet done toward making us a real American novel," Howells wrote Stedman at the end of 1866.[40] "Each one of Mr. Henry James's books is as broad as any one of Balzac's; and we believe his *Princess Casamassima* is of a scope and variety quite unknown to them," he observed in a general essay in 1887.[41] Yet it was Howells who, with the best intentions in the world as critic,

[37] *Hawthorne,* E. M. L. (London, 1879), p. 115.
[38] *Ibid.,* p. 116. Italics mine.
[39] James greatly admired Howells's style. "This charm of style Mr. Howells' two books on Italy possess to perfection" (H. J., *North American Review,* CVI, 336, Jan., 1868). See also letter to C. E. Norton, Nov. 27, 1870 (above).
[40] *Life in Letters,* I, 116.
[41] "Breadth in Literature," *Harper's,* LXXV, 639 (Sept., 1887).

created the greatest difficulty for James as an artist dependent on his pen. Moreover, though Howells was generally laudatory, the reservations that he voiced were peculiarly irritating to James and outweighed the praise when relations between the two men were strained. Thus the comment in Howells's review of *A Passionate Pilgrim and Other Tales* that "it would be better if the assumed narrator were able to keep himself from seeming to patronize the simpler-hearted heroes, and from openly rising above them in a worldly way" probably stuck longer in James's memory than Howells's praise of the whole collection: "[these stories] remain to us a marvel of workmanship. In richness of expression and splendor of literary performance, we may compare him with the greatest, and find none greater than he. . . ."[42] Or such a moralistic quibble as that over Monsieur de Mauves's advice to his wife to take a lover: "a difficulty with so French a situation is that only a French writer can carry due conviction of it to the reader. . . ."[43]

Impressed as Howells was with James's fiction, he thought very little of him as a critic, writing of *French Poets and Novelists:*

> His reviews of other writers are not precisely criticism, but they possess a pleasant flavor of criticism, agreeably diffused through a mass of sympathetic and often keenly analytical impressions. It is saying a great deal when we admit that he reminds us more of Sainte-Beuve than any other English writer; but he is more of a *causeur* than the author of the famous *Causeries,* and less of a critic in a systematic sense.[44]

Though he called James's *Hawthorne* "a delightful and excellent essay, refined and delicate in perception, generous in feeling, and a worthy study of the unique romancer," Howells really emphasized in his feature review the common American reaction and may have been thought to have stimulated it:

> Forty-six, fifty, sixty-four, are not dates so remote, nor are Salem and Concord societies so extinct, that the people of those places cannot [*sic*] be safely described as provincial, not once, but a dozen times; and we foresee, without any very powerful prophetic lens, that Mr. James will be in some quarters promptly attainted of high treason. . . . We think the epithet is sometimes mistaken. . . . If Hawthorne was "exquisitely provincial," one had better take one's chance of universality with him

[42] "Recent Literature," *Atlantic*, XXXV, 490, 494 (April, 1875).
[43] *Ibid.*, p. 492.
[44] "Recent Literature," *Atlantic*, XLII, 118 (July, 1878).

than with almost any Londoner or Parisian of his time. . . . It is not enough to say of a book so wholly unexampled and unrivaled as *The Scarlet Letter* that it was "the finest piece of imaginative writing put forth in America"; as if it had its parallel in any literature. . . .[45]

Close publication of *Daisy Miller* and of Howells's *The Lady of the Aroostook,* with their somewhat similar "international" heroines, Daisy and Lydia Blood, in situations alike challenging to their reputations,[46] led readers, especially British readers, to link the two American authors together. Howells's treatment of the English uncle, Henshaw Erwin, in his novel, and James's *An International Episode* tied them further in the satirical handling of English folk, aroused resentment,[47] and led to their being labeled the "new [American] School" as early as 1880.[48]

At this inopportune time Howells, who suffered a real Anglophobia,[49] was invited to write a long appreciative article on "Henry James Junior"[50] in which he compared the American author with the best established English novelists, all to the advantage of the former.

It seems to me that an enlightened criticism will recognize in Mr. James's fiction a metaphysical genius working to aesthetic results. . . . No other novelist, except George Eliot, has dealt so largely in an analysis of motive, has so fully explained and commented upon the springs of action in the persons of the drama, both before and after the facts. These novelists are more alike than any others in their processes, but with George Eliot an ethical purpose is dominant, and with Mr. James an artistic purpose. . . . Isabel has her great weaknesses, as Dorothea had, but these seem to me, on the whole, the most nobly imagined and the most nobly intentioned women in modern fiction; and I think Isabel is the more subtly divined of the two. . . .

It is a little odd . . . [that James's] power of engaging your preference for certain of his people has been so little commented on. Perhaps it is

[45] "James's Hawthorne," *Atlantic*, XLV, 284, 282, 283 (Feb., 1880). Howells does not refer to the Lockhart-Hawthorne comparison, and James's acknowledgment of the review is urbane but reiterative of his point of view (H. J. to W. D. H., Jan. 31, 1880, *Letters*, I, 71-72).

[46] See James Woodress, *Howells and Italy* (Durham, N. C., 1954), pp. 165-168.

[47] James wrote his mother on Jan. 18, 1879, in regard to his novelette, that the English "take it ill of me as against my British entertainers. It seems to me I have been very delicate, but I shall keep off dangerous ground in the future" (*Letters*, I, 67).

[48] *Graphic*, XX, 595 (Dec. 11, 1880).

[49] See Howells's letter to J. R. Lowell, June 22, 1879 (*Life in Letters*, I, 271).

[50] *Century*, XXV, 25-29 (Nov., 1882).

because he makes no obvious appeal for them. . . . [It] comes about
through their own qualities, and is not affected by insinuation or by
downright petting, such as we find in Dickens nearly always and in
Thackeray too often.

The art of fiction has, in fact, become a finer art in our day than it
was with Dickens and Thackeray. We would not suffer the confidential
attitude of the latter now, nor the mannerism of the former, any more
than we could endure the prolixity of Richardson or the coarseness of
Fielding. These great men are of the past—they and their methods and
interests; even Trollope and Reade are not of the present. The new school
derives from Hawthorne and George Eliot rather than any others. . . .
This school . . . finds its chief exemplar in Mr. James. . . .[51]

"I suppose you have seen that I have stirred up the English
papers pretty generally by what I wrote of Dickens and Thackeray
in my paper on James," Howells wrote Roswell Smith, on November 19, 1882, from Switzerland. "I don't remember what I said,
but so far as they have quoted me, I stand by myself, and should
only wish to amplify and intensify the opinions that they object to.
I knew what I was talking about, and they don't know at all what
they are talking about."[52]

Howells had indeed stirred up indignation in England.[53] Leading off with a review of Howells's *A Modern Instance* in 1882, the
Graphic stigmatized the book as "a typical novel of the newest
fashion," written "in the celebrated manner of Henry James, Junior,
which consists of saying nothing in a great many words."[54] John
Nichol, concluding his *American Literature, An Historical Sketch,
1620-1880*, felt impelled to warn James and Howells jointly against
their method: "Together they stand in peril of betraying their
mission by overworking their mines."[55] The *Quarterly Review* was

[51] Kirk and Kirk, *William Dean Howells*, pp. 349-350, 352-353. I cite this text, rather
than that of *Century*, because of its availability.
[52] *Life in Letters*, I, 329.
[53] Donald McLeish Murray, "The Critical Reception of Henry James in English Periodi-
cals, 1875-1916," Ph.D. diss., N.Y.U., 1950; Donald M. Murray, "Henry James and the
English Reviewers, 1882-1890," *American Literature*, XXIV, 1-20 (March, 1952). Clarence
Gohdes was the first apparently to notice the effect in England of Howells's essay on
James (*American Literature in Nineteenth Century England*, New York, 1944, p. 130).
Recently Edwin H. Cady (*The Road to Realism*, pp. 218-220) has reviewed the attacks on
Howells solely; he makes the interesting suggestion that Andrew Lang was one of the
anonymous attackers.
[54] XXXVI, 583 (Nov. 25, 1882). (Murray, *The Critical Reception of Henry James in
English Periodicals;* also my source in the next nine notes.)
[55] (Edinburgh, 1882), pp. 389-397.

caustic. Contrasting the "charm and beauty" of Frances Hodgson Burnett's *Louisiana* with the "artificial mannerisms" and "tawdry smartness" of *Daisy Miller,* it raised the question of whether James was even qualified to report on "American" character types, since, as Howells had indicated in the biographical notes in his article, James was of Irish and Scots descent and did not even live in America. It castigated the lack of story in his "studies" and found only "philosophical instruction and dawdling sentimentality." The *Portrait of a Lady,* for example, was simply "dull, unspeakably dull." As for the slur on Dickens and Thackeray, one could remember their characters, but who could recall one of the *personae* of Howells?[56] Arthur Tilley, in "The New School of Fiction" in the *National Review,* echoed the *Quarterly's* strictures on lack of plot and of vital motive and on labored analysis but was more moderate in tone.[57] The *Spectator* mocked James with an idea and phrase it picked up from James's review of *The Correspondence of Carlyle and Emerson* in the *Century*:[58] "In Mr. Henry James's view of life . . . we have the lowest form of the rapidly dwindling Puritanic faith, a thin sort of pessimism. . . ."[59] Karl Hillebrand in the *Contemporary Review,* citing Howells's opinion of Dickens and Thackeray, lumped Howells and James as "North Americans in whom this ignoring of the past and forgetting of all proportion show themselves most crudely."[60] Simultaneously *Temple Bar* published an essay, "The New School of Fiction," which found these writers possessed of "futility" and "tenuity" and lacking "red blood."[61] James's *Portraits of Places,* appearing in 1884, was patronizingly reviewed[62] and his *Tales of Three Cities* drew from the *Pall Mall Budget* the opinion that by adding two tales and one city, James had made no improvement on Dickens: his form was "infinitely conceited" and his subjects "infinitely trivial."[63]

James had returned to America, after an absence of six years, late in 1881; he was called to Boston from Washington by the illness of his mother and, following her death, made that city his headquarters until May when he returned to England. On March 18, 1882, Howells wrote John Hay on the cordial renewal of his friendship:

[56] CLV, 212-217 (Jan., 1893).
[57] I, 257-268 (April, 1883).
[58] XXVI, 265-272 (June, 1883).
[59] LVI, 702-703 (June 2, 1883).
[60] "Old and New Novels," *Contemporary Review,* XLV, 390 (March, 1884).
[61] LXX, 383-388 (March, 1884).
[62] *Spectator,* LVII, 160 (Feb. 2, 1884).
[63] XXXII, 28 (Dec. 19, 1884).

Henry James is spending the winter only a few doors from us. (We left our country house after my sickness, and came into town.) I see him constantly, and we talk literature perpetually, as we used to do in our walks ten years ago. He is not sensibly changed, and, reflected in him, I find that I am not.[64]

James returned to London in May and in July secured lodgings in South Kensington for the Howellses, who were to have a holiday in England and Europe.[65] In mid-September, Howells, reporting his felicity, attributed it largely to the younger novelist: "H. J., Jr., has been an adoptive father in housing and starting this orphan family in London. Just now he has gone to France."[66] The Howellses themselves left immediately after for Switzerland to spend two months on Lake Geneva, and it would appear that the essay "Henry James Junior" was written at Villeneuve. James could have had no time to examine it or realize its effect on his return to London in December, for he was called back to the United States "almost at once" by a message announcing the serious illness of his father.[67] He could not have fully comprehended the storm Howells had raised in England until his return there in August, 1883. Before this, Howells had written to Thomas S. Perry, from Florence, regretting his paper *so far as it had involved James in controversy,* with the hope, perhaps, that Perry would convey this thought to James. There is no evidence that he did:

The British lion . . . seems to have been born . . . without a cuticle. It is only necessary to insinuate that all English novels are not perfection. One of my London friends actually asked me if I didn't hate Thackeray and Dickens because they were English! . . . I have been scarcely if at all troubled by the row about me, and *have been chiefly vexed because it includes James.*[68]

James showed no immediate inclination to disavow the connection

[64] *Life in Letters,* I, 311. Howells was then living at 16 Louisburg Square.

[65] "We are here in a very charming lodging [18 Pelham Crescent], which James had taken for us and in which we sat down to a dinner that was cooking for us on our way up from Liverpool. . . . James has been with me today and has been very kind" (W. D. H. to J. R. Osgood, Aug. 1, 1882, *Life in Letters,* I, 315-316).

[66] W. D. H. to C. E. Norton, Sept. 14, 1882 (*Life in Letters,* I, 321). The "two months" became three. There is a curious reference (*Life in Letters,* I, 333) to a "skull cracking" of abuse and criticism for the article on James. But the letter containing these references has apparently been deleted.

[67] *Letters,* I, 83.

[68] W. D. H. to T. S. Perry, Florence, March 13, 1883 (*Life in Letters,* I, 332). Italics ours.

Howells had forced on him. A summary article on "Anthony Trollope" in the *Century Magazine* for July, 1883, connected that novelist, who had just died, with Dickens and Thackeray (though ranking him beneath them) but marked his demise as "the complete extinction of his school." James castigated Trollope for writing too much—his "fertility was gross, importunate," and for an utter lack of a sense of form—"it is probably safe to affirm that he had no 'views' whatever on the subject of novel-writing."[69] Here was much to cause English readers to align him with Howells. A month later, differing with Warner on the primary purpose of the novel, which Warner had maintained to be entertainment, James had insisted that it is to "represent life" and had said that *some* got this illusion from the novels of Miss Austen, others from those of Dumas, and still others "in the pages of Mr. Howells."[70]

A published lecture[71] by Walter Besant on *The Art of Fiction* was brought to James's attention especially by an article in the *Pall Mall Gazette* attacking his *An International Episode* for its psychological treatment as "fiction without adventure" and leaning upon Besant for support.[72] This drew from James his famous essay "The Art of Fiction" in which he briefly makes his contemner ridiculous, calls the conception of the novel held by Dickens and Thackeray *naïf,* attacks Besant at certain points (especially on the score of "conscious moral purpose"), and then brilliantly expounds the theory he had advanced in "Alphonse Daudet"—that the purpose of the novel is to represent life.[73] Robert Louis Stevenson, whom James had brought into the discussion,[74] urbanely took up the gage in "A Humble Remonstrance"[75] but in an addendum leveled the sharpest attack on Howells to which he was subjected in the controversy:

. . . none ever couched a lance with narrower convictions. His own work and those of his pupils and masters singly occupy his mind; he is

[69] *Partial Portraits* (London, 1888), pp. 97-133.
[70] "Alphonse Daudet," *Century* (Aug., 1883); *Partial Portraits*, pp. 227-228. "I haven't yet read all of James's paper, but what he said of Warner's theory of fiction was all gospel" (W. D. H. to John Hay, Boston, July 30, 1883, *Life in Letters,* I, 351).
[71] Given at the Royal Institution in April, 1883.
[72] See *Partial Portraits,* pp. 400-404.
[73] *Longman's Magazine,* IV, 502-521 (Sept., 1884); also *Partial Portraits,* pp. 375-408.
[74] See *Partial Portraits,* pp. 402-403.
[75] *Longman's,* V, 139-147 (Dec., 1884). *The Works of Robert Louis Stevenson,* Thistle Edition XIII: *Memories and Portraits,* pp. 344-358.

the bondslave, the zealot of his school; he dreams of an advance in art like what there is in science; he thinks of past things as radically dead; he thinks a form can be outlived: a strange immersion in his own history; a stranger forgetfulness of the history of the race! Meanwhile by a glance at his own works . . . much of this illusion would be dispelled. For while he holds all the poor little orthodoxies of the day . . . the living quality of much that he has done is of a contrary . . . complexion. . . . A poet, a finished artist, . . . he has other passions than those he loves to draw. The obvious is not of necessity the normal; . . . and the danger is lest, in seeking to draw the normal, a man should draw the null. . . .

Though in part the Stevenson attack was retaliation for a deliberate snub by Howells,[76] it was the first time a critic had separated Howells from James in the controversy, and James, concerned about the effect of that controversy on his own work in England, decided after reflection to take advantage of it. He had not at the moment any hope of diverting Howells from his battle with the English. Hence, he resolved to write an article on Howells which would plainly set forth such differences that two would no longer be considered one by the critics. He did this in a critical study in *Harper's Weekly* entitled "William Dean Howells," which ironically emphasized the narrow artistic convictions and all the poor little orthodoxies of the day to which Howells subscribed. He traced Howells's Anglophobia to his isolation in Venice during the Civil War when he had to put up with the London *Times* for news and with the talk of British tourists for conversation. He praised Mr. Howells's "unerring sentiment of the American character" while lamenting the impression a prospective visitor might get of American society from "the terrible practices at the country hotel in *Dr. Breen* and at the Boston boarding house in *A Woman's Reason.*" He felt that Howells was "animated by a love of the common, the immediate, the familiar and vulgar elements of life."

He thinks scarcely anything too paltry to be interesting, that the small and vulgar have been terribly neglected, and would rather see an exact

[76] In 1882, mutual friends, including Henry James, had suggested a meeting with Stevenson; this had been arranged, but Stevenson having read Howells's *A Modern Instance,* "which he took for a general condemnation of divorce," felt it his duty to inform Howells, "My wife did me the honour to divorce her husband." "Howells made no reply to this letter," says his daughter; neither did he go to see the Stevensons. This may account for Stevenson's label "fantastic." Stevenson wrote in 1893 "to apologize for all the offenses I have ever been guilty of" and Howells graciously offered him his hand (*Life in Letters,* I, 332-333; II, 37-38).

account of a sentiment or character he stumbles against every day than a brilliant evocation of a passion or a type he has never seen and does not even particularly believe in.

James scoffed at novels in which "the only immoralities are aberrations of thought, like that of Silas Lapham, or excesses of beer, like that of Bartley Hubbard." He found Lapham's wife and Lemuel Barker's mate "exhaustive renderings of the type of virtue that worries." And he suggested, in conclusion, that style counted for less and less with Howells and that he appeared increasingly "to hold composition too cheap."[77]

The attack must appear brutal even to the admirers of James, but it is not without parallel in other artistic careers and it was not wholly undeserved. Howells's reiterated proprietorship in James[78] created an uncomfortable attachment and adversely affected James's fortunes. Further, it made James responsible for ideas he did not hold. Howells should have been forewarned by the differences with him that James freely expressed[79] and by James's growing impatience with the tabus in English and American writing.[80] On James's part a final motive might be found in a small desire to teach Howells that his criticism was not wholly "impressionistic!"

III

"Grow Old Along with Me"

It is hard to believe that James did not think Howells might resent the devastating article in *Harper's Weekly* despite its thin sprinkling of praise. Howells had been dealt a heavy blow immediately after the Stevenson attack. So far as is known, however, he gave no visible sign of having felt either. There is no published letter between June 18, 1886, when the article appeared, and December 25, 1886, when Howells wrote James in part as follows:

[77] XXX, 394-395 (June 19, 1886).

[78] Two varieties: ". . . I shall seem to be making an unwarrantable claim when I express my belief that the popularity of his stories was largely confined to Mr. Fields's assistant" ("Henry James, Jr.," Kirk and Kirk, *William Dean Howells*, p. 347); " 'But I'm bound to say that I don't find our countrymen so aggressive, so loud, as our international novelists would make out. I haven't met any of their peculiar heroines as yet, sir' " (*Indian Summer*, Boston, 1885, p. 37).

[79] See notes 35 and 45 above.

[80] "For Trollope the emotions of a nursery-governess in Australia would take precedence of the adventures of a depraved *femme du monde* in Paris or London"; "I should . . . say not that the English novel has a purpose, but that it has a diffidence" (*Partial Portraits*, pp. 123, 406).

Your most kind letter from Milan caused great excitement and re-
joicing in this family. What could I ask more even if I had the cheek
to ask half so much? One doesn't thank you for such a thing, I suppose,
but I may tell you at least of my pride and pleasure in it. I'm disposed
to make the most of the abundance of your kindness, for in many quarters here the book meets with little but misconceptions. If we regard it
as nothing but an example of work in the new way—the performance of
a man who won't and can't keep on doing what's been done already—
its reception here by most of the reviews is extremely discouraging. . . .
I find myself not really caring a great deal for the printed animosity,
except as it means ignorance. I suspect it's an effect of the frankness
about our civilization which you sometimes wondered I could practice
with impunity. The impunity's gone now, I assure you.[81]

Obviously James had written Howells in appreciation of one of the
latter's novels; Mildred Howells, who equally obviously was not in
possession of the conciliatory letter, surmises that the book was
either *The Rise of Silas Lapham* or *The Minister's Charge.*[82] It was
the latter, and James's letter must have been in part a retraction, for
he had censured each in *Harper's Weekly*. Howells's feeling that
he had no right to ask what James had freely offered is based on
his contrition for having involved James in controversy by his
comparison of James's abilities with those of the great English
novelists.[83] Howells responded publicly to James's private overture
with a wholly laudatory review of *The Princess Casamassima*—the
most generous he had written up to that time—in the "Editor's
Study" in *Harper's* in April, 1887: "We find *no* fault with Mr.
Henry James's *Princess Casamassima:* it is a great novel; it is his
greatest, and it is incomparably the greatest novel of the year in our
language."[84] Correspondence between the two novelists was resumed (though there are gaps in what has been published); but
Howells, despite the experience that had jeopardized their friend-

---

[81] *Life in Letters*, I, 387.

[82] *Life in Letters*, I, 386. It was definitely *The Minister's Charge* (H. J. to W. D. H.
from Hotel de la Ville, Milan, May 17, 1890, *Letters*, I, 163-164). *The Minister's Charge*
(which had run in the *Century* from Feb. to Dec., 1886) was published in book form on
Dec. 11, 1886, in America (Gibson and Arms, *A Bibliography of W. D. H.*, pp. 109-110).
James was in Milan as early as Dec. 16, 1866 (*Letters*, I, 122). He went again in 1888
(Richardson, p. cxvi).

[83] See letter to T. S. Perry, March 13, 1883, quoted above.

[84] LXXIV, 829. "Howells told me the other night that he had written a rousing eulogy
of your *Princess* for the next *Harper* and he hadn't a fault to find with it" (William
James to H. J., March 10, 1887, Matthiessen, *The James Family*, p. 330).

ship, continued to belabor the British in his columns and reviews. James was moved to mild protest at the beginning of 1888.

> If we could have that rich conversation I should speak to you too of your monthly polemics in *Harper* and tell you . . . of certain parts of the business in which I am less with you than in others. It seems to me . . . you . . . sometimes make mistakes of proportion, and in general incline to insist more upon restrictions and limitations, the *a priori* formulas and interdictions, of our common art, than upon that priceless freedom which is to me the thing that makes it worth practising. . . . I am surprised sometimes, at the things you notice and seem to care about. One should move in a diviner air. . . .[85]

How much Howells dwelt on "the *a priori* formulas and interdictions" may be judged from his *Criticism and Fiction,* gathered from the "Editor's Study" in 1891. But this book also goes beyond the article on James in its defamation of English writers,[86] while lavish in its praise of James:

> . . . I value more such a novel as Mr. James's *Tragic Muse* than all the romantic attempts since Hawthorne. . . . To spin a yarn for the yarn's sake, that is an ideal worthy of a nineteenth-century Englishman . . . ; but wholly impossible to an American of Mr. Henry James's modernity. . . . To such a mind as his the story could never have value except as a means; it could not exist for him as an end; . . . it could be the frame, not possibly the picture.[87]

But James did not take umbrage at this,[88] for the better English reviewers and critics no longer lumped his work with that of Howells. In marking Howells off as fanatical, Stevenson had begun a process which was to culminate in the opinion of the *National Observer* in 1896 that "Mr. Howells' combativeness" had drawn on James quarrels he might otherwise have avoided.[89] Along

[85] *Letters,* I, 135-136.
[86] For example: "The misfortune rather than the fault of our individual critic is that he is the heir of the false theory and bad manners of the English school"; "The art of fiction, as Jane Austen knew it, declined from her through Scott, and Bulwer, and Dickens, and Charlotte Brontë, and Thackeray, and even George Eliot, because of the mania of romanticism . . ."; "An English novel, full of titles and rank, is apparently essential to the happiness of such people; their weak and childish imagination is at home in its familiar environment. . ." (*Criticism and Fiction,* New York, 1891, pp. 32, 74, 79-80).
[87] *Criticism and Fiction,* 118-119.
[88] James's tenderness for Howells had been increased by the death of Winifred Howells on March 3, 1889 (*Life in Letters,* I, 422-426).
[89] XVI, 681-682 (Oct. 24, 1896) (Murray).

the way James's temperate and highly reflective "The Art of Fiction" had further helped in the separation, as had such a highly
particularized attack as that in the *Speaker* in 1890 upon Howells,
whom it characterized as "the great man who was to slay Dickens
and Thackeray and to lead the children of Washington out of the
Egyptian darkness of Romanticism."[90]   Attacks on James continued,
to be sure; in fact, he was to complain bitterly of the reviewers,
but there was less coupling of the names of Howells and James, and
the latter's work was now more commonly censured in England
for what were regarded as intrinsic faults.

Although the fine tribute to *The Princess* and the praise of *The
Tragic Muse* may be taken as gestures of friendship and indications
that all was forgiven, there is some evidence that James's treatment
of him in *Harper's Weekly* still rankled slightly with Howells.   In
the series of articles in the *Ladies' Home Journal* which became *My
Literary Passions* (1896), Howells, according James scant treatment,
ambiguously observed, "I have my reserves in regard to certain
things of his; if hard pressed I might undertake to better him here
and there, but after I had done that I doubt, if I should like him
so well."[91]   In Howells's *Literary Friends and Acquaintance* (1900)
there is a pleasant recollection of Henry James, Sr., but no mention
of his namesake.[92]   In his two-volume treatment of the *Heroines
of Fiction,* where the reader might readily have expected some
presentation of the great gallery of feminine types that James had
created, Howells accords only a brief treatment to Daisy Miller.[93]
Further, Howells neglected to send James copies of his books, and
James complained of the neglect.   The fact that James purchased,

[90] *Speaker*, II, 721 (Dec. 27, 1890) (Murray).   Alice James felt the attack exaggerated
Howells's importance (*Alice James, Her Brothers, Her Journal,* ed. Anna Robeson Burr,
New York, 1934, p. 219).

[91] Only one paragraph.   XII, 13 (Jan., 1895).   But Howells also said, "In literary
handling no one who has written fiction in our language can approach him . . ." (*My
Literary Passions,* New York, 1895, pp. 224-225).

[92] (New York, 1900), pp. 265-269; also p. 151.   James himself may have been responsible for the omission: "You asked me . . . if I should object to being made a feature of
your composed reminiscences. . . .   I won't pretend I like being written about—the sight
of my own name on a printed page makes me as ill . . . as that of one of my creations
makes me well.   I have a morbid passion for personal privacy. . . .   I wince even at
eulogy. . . .   But on the other hand, I like, I love to be remembered by you and I surrender
myself to your discretion" (H. J. to W. D. H., Jan. 29, 1893, *Letters,* I, 198).   Did
Howells, remembering the *Century* article, think James was afraid to have Howells write
about him?

[93] (2 vols., New York, 1901), II, 164-176.

from scant earnings, *Ragged Lady* (1898), "The Pursuit of the Piano," and "two or three other things" in order to read him "again as continuously as possible" may have somewhat mollified Howells's feelings.[94]   Howells sent him his next book of fiction, a collection of short stories, *A Pair of Patient Lovers* (1901).[95]   Thereafter the exchange of letters and of books was the regular practice of the two men.[96]

But one great difference continued to exist between Howells and James, and the latter had pointed this up not only in his emphasis upon the "priceless freedom" of the novelist in his letter of remonstrance to Howells, but also in the *Harper's Weekly* attack.   It is apparent that, to James, Howells was too reticent on the score of morals to be the emancipator of fiction he should have been.   This much can be inferred from his remark on the wives of Lapham and Barker and from his observation that Howells preferred sentiment to passion.   On May 17, 1890, James wrote Howells about *A Hazard of New Fortunes,* which he had just read, and stressed the limitation of this reticence:

The *Hazard* is simply prodigious. . . .   You are less *big* than Zola, but you are ever so much less clumsy and more really various, and moreover you and he don't see the same things. . . . there's a whole quarter of the heaven upon which . . . you seem consciously—is it consciously?—to have turned your back. . . .[97]

When Howells was abroad again in 1897 James may have pointed up his thoughts on freedom in fiction to his friend, though much of their talk centered on practical ideas which Howells had for the marketing of James's work.[98]   It seems likely that James placed

[94] H. J. to W. D. H., June 29, 1900 (*Letters*, I, 350). "The Pursuit of the Piano" was in *Harper's Monthly*, C (April, 1900), 725-746.

[95] H. J. to W. D. H., Aug. 10, 1901 (*Letters*, I, 375).

[96] James pressed the continuance of this practice; see H. J. to W. D. H., Dec. 11, 1902 (*Letters*, I, 409-410).

[97] *Letters*, I, 164-165.

[98] "I had a very great pleasure the other day in a visit, far too short—only six hours—from dear old Howells, who did me a lot of good in an illuminating professional (i.e. commercial) way, and came, in fact, at quite a psychological moment" (H. J. to Mrs. William James, Dec. 1, 1897, *Letters*, I, 267; also I, 277). "I had two days in London, and saw James continuously and exclusively. I never saw him more divinely interesting, and he told me I had been useful to him, and giving him a new business perspective. He seemed to have got needlessly but deeply discouraged, and I was able to reassure him of his public here" (W. D. H. to C. E. Norton, Dec. 27, 1897). Howells got back to America on Nov. 6; hence the meetings were in October (*Life in Letters*, II, 83).

things in the *Cosmopolitan,* the *Chap Book, Collier's Weekly,* and the American edition of *Literature* at Howells's suggestion.[99]

But the greatest service that Howells was to render James, beyond restoring his confidence, was to help him place *The Ambassadors* in the *North American Review.*

My feelings don't permit me to wait to tell you that the communication I have just had from you surpasses for pure unadulterated charm any communication I have *ever* received. I am really quite overcome and weakened by your recital of the generous way in which you threw yourself into the scale of the arrangement, touching my so long unserialized serial, which is manifestly so excellent a thing for me. I had begun to despair of anything, when, abruptly, this brightens the view. For I *like,* extremely, the place the *N.A.R.* makes for my novel. . . . Charming to me also is the idea of your own beneficent paper in the same quarter— the complete detachment of which, however, from the current fiction itself I equally appreciate and applaud. . . .[100]

Howells's "own beneficent paper," to which James alludes, was "Mr. Henry James's Later Work" printed in the *North American Review*[101] in January, 1903, immediately before the first instalment of *The Ambassadors.* In some ways this is the most remarkable document in the whole relationship between the two men. Howells had made in his *Criticism and Fiction* perhaps the most notorious justification for reticence in regard to illicit love in American fiction in the entire critical annals of the nineteenth century, arguing that authors and editors were compelled to reticence because a preponderance of the readers were young girls. He contended, further, that the manners of the novel had been steadily improving, and that the role of the novelist had become "something like that of a physician or priest . . . bound by laws as sacred as those of such professions." He felt that the critics who demanded "passion" had only the "passion of guilty love" in mind; he contended that it took more skill to develop other passions in the novel: grief, avarice, pity, ambition, hate, envy, devotion, and friendship.[102] In his essay "Mr. Henry James's Later Work" he seems utterly and astonishingly to

[99] He was very much excited also by the prospect of being included in Howells's "Great Authors and Newspapers enterprise" (*Life in Letters,* II, 132).

[100] H. J. to W. D. H., Lamb House, Rye, Jan. 8, 1903 (*Letters,* I, 414).

[101] CLXXVI, 125-137; also in *The Question of Henry James,* ed. F. W. Dupee (New York, 1945), pp. 6-19. It would not appear that James had seen this paper when he wrote.

[102] *Criticism and Fiction,* pp. 147-157.

reverse himself. The bulk of the essay is a dialogue between Howells and an interlocutress to whom he assigns the today inadmissible point of view *which he himself had upheld* in *Criticism and Fiction:*

[She:] ". . . But do you think he ought to picture such life because it exists?"

"Do you find yourself much the worse for the *Wings of the Dove?*" I asked. "Or for *The Sacred Fount?* or for *The Awkward Age?* Or even for *What Maisie Knew?* They all picture much the same sort of life."

"Why, of course not. But it isn't so much what he says—he never says anything—but what he insinuates. I don't believe that is good for young girls."

"But if they don't know what it means? I'll allow that it isn't quite *jeune fille* in its implications, all of them; but maturity has its modest claims. Even in the interest of a knowledge of our mother-civilization, which is what Mr. James's insinuations impart, as I understand them."

"Well, young people cannot read him aloud together. You can't deny that."

"No, but elderly people can, and they are not to be ignored by the novelist always. I fancy the reader who brings some knowledge of good and evil, without being worse for it, to his work is the sort of reader Mr. James writes for. I can imagine him addressing himself to a circle of such readers as this *Review's* with a satisfaction, and a sense of liberation, which he might not feel in the following of the family magazines, and still not incriminate himself. I have heard a good deal said in reproach of the sort of life he portrays, in his later books; but I have not found his people of darker deeds or murkier motives than the average in fiction. I don't say, life."

"No certainly, so far as he tells you. It is what he *doesn't* tell that is so frightful. He leaves you to such awful conjectures. For instance, when Kate Croy ———"

"When Kate Croy ———?"

"No, I *won't* discuss it. But you know what I mean; and I don't believe there was ever such a girl."

"And you believe there was ever such a girl as Milly Theale?"

"Hundreds! She is true to the life. So perfectly American. . . ."[103]

---

[103] *North American Review*, CLXXVI, 130-131 (Jan., 1903). There is a special irony in Howells's exertions in this instance, for in some degree Strether in *The Ambassadors* had been suggested to James by Howells (*The Notebooks of Henry James*, ed. F. O. Matthiessen and K. B. Murdock, New York, 1947, pp. 226, 370, 373-374; see also H. J. to W. D. H., Rye, Aug. 10, 1901, *Letters*, I, 376).

Has Howells *completely* shifted his ground, as has just been assumed? No, the implication here seems to be that subject matter, like James's, is still unfit for the young girl, but she doesn't read the *North American Review* anyway; mature people do, and James is entitled to address them here on subjects excluded from "family" magazines, especially since he is treating English society. That is, we might be justified in assuming that Howells's attitude is permissive—he is solely bent on justifying the serialization of *The Ambassadors* in this particular review with its limited circulation. The fact that he finds James's people compelled by no "murkier motives" and committing no "darker deeds" than "the average in fiction" suggests that he was defending James in part from the strictures that had been laid on his morality the previous June by Frank Moore Colby[104] and from the "reproaches" Howells had heard readers make. This raises the question: Is the whole dialogue a piece of self-defense, a justification of himself for having persuaded the *Review* to print *The Ambassadors,* in case the editors were attacked for it? Is the qualified retraction of his former well-known position, on the other hand, a possible limited surrender to James's argument for freedom for the novelist? Is it meant, in a word, as much for James as for the reader of the *Review* or for the general public? There is no clear answer to any of these questions because Howells's own position with regard to the proprieties is in no way clear. He wrote five novels after this, *The Son of Royal Langbrith* (1904), *Miss Bellard's Inspiration* (1905), *Fennel and Rue* (1908), *The Leatherwood God* (1916), and *The Vacation of the Kelwyns* (1920), which show no departure from his previous standards of reticence. Further, the "Gorki case" in 1905, in which Howells withdrew from the planned dinner to the Russian novelist because he was accompanied by his common law wife, displays a prudery as bad as anything recorded in Howells's youth.[105] On the other hand, Howells accorded two sympathetic reviews and contributed an introduction to Stephen Crane's *Maggie*[106] and was the first American editor to include a story by Theodore Dreiser in an anthology.[107] The best that can

[104] "The Queerness of Henry James," *Bookman,* XV, 396-397 (June, 1902).
[105] *Life in Letters,* II, 219-220.
[106] "Life and Letters," *Harper's Weekly,* XXXIX, 556-557 (June 15, 1895); "New York Low Life in Fiction," New York *World,* II, 18 (July 26, 1896); "An Appreciation," *Maggie, A Child of the Streets* (London, 1896), pp. v-vii.
[107] *The Great Modern American Stories* (New York, 1920).

be said would appear to be that Henry James's long protestation against his friend's narrowness succeeded in modifying Howells's attitude slightly towards the daring work of others but liberalized Howells's own compositions not a whit.[108]

Although the influence of Henry James was negligible in diverting Howells from his "Victorian . . . preference of decency," Howells's attention to his friend and his solicitude for him increased as both their lives narrowed to a close. The record is one of continuous service: he acted as James's agent and he helped to prepare the way for James's visit to America in 1904.[109] James visited Howells at his summer place in Kittery, Maine, and in Cambridge his feet had fallen into the old path of "shared literary secrets . . . , the dreams of youth, the titles of tales, the communities of friendship, the sympathies and patiences . . . of dear W. D. H.," hoping it would lead to its old terminus, Fresh Pond—only to find that extension of the "Park System" had practically swallowed the pond.[110] There were other visits between the two men, but of their last meeting, there is no published record; Howells was in England in 1913 and in all likelihood saw his old friend then.[111] In that year, he joined with T. S. Perry in discouraging some well-meaning fund raisers who meant to present James a gift for the purchase of furniture for Lamb House, since they knew how little James would care for such a gift.[112] In 1910 he had contributed a letter, "One of the Public to the Author" to *The Henry James Year Book,* which pleased James much more. Howells said in part:

> After so many years ago your eager editor, and ever since your applausive critic, I ought not to feel bound to insist now upon my delight in the charms of your manner, the depth of your thought, the beauty of your art, which the grouping of these passages freshly witnesses even to such a veteran lover of your work as I; and in fact I do not feel so bound. I do not so much fulfill a duty as indulge a pleasure in owning my surprise at the constant succession of your felicities here.[113]

[108] ". . . our novelists . . . write many things they ought to be ashamed to read to women. . . . But perhaps they *are* ashamed and only hold out writing so for art's sake; I cannot very well speak for them; but I am still very Victorian in my preference of decency" (W. D. H., *Years of My Youth,* New York, 1916, pp. 145-146).

[109] *Letters,* I, 358, 360; II, 8; *Life in Letters,* II, 132.

[110] *Letters,* II, 102; H. J., *The American Scene* (New York, 1907), pp. 68-69.

[111] *Life in Letters,* II, 254, 257, 287, 297, 305, 328.

[112] *Ibid.,* II, 327.

[113] *The Henry James Year Book,* ed. Evelyn Garnaut Smalley (London, n. d.), p. 2.

In 1911 Howells led the effort in the United States and wrote the President of the Academy to attempt to secure the Nobel Prize for literature for Henry James; in 1915, though he expressed grief for "losing" James, he defended to Brander Matthews James's right to become a British citizen—and whimsically remarked that he himself was thinking of becoming a citizen of Maine.[114] A month after James's death in 1916 he laid aside with relief an article on James when the contractor for it failed him, remanding his memories "to the past where I should have suffered so much in calling them up."[115] Yet the last effort of his own life, undertaken before his fatal illness four years later but worked on after he was bedfast, was a review of *The Letters of Henry James* and the beginning of an article which was to be entitled "The American James."[116] In their long lives, Howells and James had inflicted hurts on each other, but not more so than is common with persons closely associated, a fact which each seemed to appreciate, and their double striving, with Howells perhaps making the greater concessions,[117] made it a path of amity at the end, as it was in the beginning.

[114] *Life in Letters*, II, 294-295, 352.

[115] *Ibid.*, II, 356.

[116] *Ibid.*, II, 394-399.

[117] Note especially the way in which Howells reacted to the James letters, n. 33 above. It perhaps was helpful to the renewed friendship that Howells did not review James after 1903.

I am indebted to Professor William Gibson, who, though not thoroughly in accord with everything it contains, has helped me immeasurably with this article.

The sentences from the unpublished letters of William Dean Howells contained in footnotes 3 and 8 are reproduced by permission of W. W. Howells and may not be quoted again without his permission. The first is from a MS letter in the Henry E. Huntington Library at San Marino; the latter two, in the New York Public Library; both libraries have granted permission to reproduce.

Past Perfect Retrospection in the Style of James
Hisayoshi Watanabe

> "What was to be in the retrospect more distinct to him. . . ."
> —*The Wings of the Dove,* Book Sixth, I.

T HE AIM OF THIS ESSAY is to show the unusual importance of the past perfect tense and retrospection in the late novels of Henry James—especially to describe the effect of his use of this tense and to consider its relation to his art. In his late works, James tends to enlarge the sphere of the past perfect tense and in complementary fashion to reduce that of the normal narrative tense, the past. The effect is of reduced action and event; those movements which remain are more indirect, less palpable, less objective. The inaction is the corollary of a greater subjectivity in a world of remembrance, reflection, impression, and interpretation. Such a style is important to the unity of the last novels in its relation to the sustaining of the consciousness of the central character. Related as these many matters are, the use of the past perfect tense is at once a symptom and an important factor; analysis of it may better our understanding of the other elements of James's art.

Appropriately enough, since the novel most pleased James himself, *The Ambassadors* uses the past perfect tense for retrospection most effectively. There are of course moments in every novel when the past perfect tense is natural and necessary, because the author relates actions prior to those which are happening at the time. Such moments may be brief glimpses into the past or long flashbacks, but in the traditional novel they are rare—simply because to proceed through reminiscence is to risk slowing the novel and reducing its vividness. The point to be made about James's use of the past perfect tense is, therefore, dual: he uses it more often than other writers and he uses it precisely in order to explore the reminiscences of his characters.

The first book and the first chapter of the second book in *The Ambassadors* move slowly toward the inner world of retrospection. The next chapter takes place on "his second morning in Paris," when Strether goes to "the bankers of the Rue Scribe" to pick up the letters sent him by his patroness, Mrs. Newsome. Having moved, though slowly, through a chronological succession, we await Strether's next step. Instead James suddenly turns to reminiscence of the previous day's events:

> They [Strether and Waymarsh] *had hastened* to the Rue Scribe on the morrow of their arrival, but Strether *had* not then *found* the letters the hope of which promoted this errand. He *had* as yet *had* none at all; *hadn't expected* them in London, but *had counted* on several in Paris, and, disconcerted now, *had* presently *strolled* back to the boulevard with a sense of injury that he felt himself taking for as good a start as any other. It would serve, this spur to his spirit, he reflected, as, pausing at the top of the street, he looked up and down the great foreign avenue, it would serve to begin business with.[1]

The page-long, detailed account is in such fashion presented naturally in the past perfect tense. The tense is natural with reminiscence: the question is rather why James did not begin the chapter with the first day—and the past tense—rather than skipping a period only to return to it.

When Strether at last gets the letters, he wanders through the Paris streets, choosing a park as a suitable place to read them. As he begins to read them on his bench, he lapses into deep thought, analyzing the state of his own mind at first, and then, with James's mature skill in such matters, is led into the recollection of his past life. We are given, though very sparingly, what has been concealed from us: what had been going on in America before he left on his mission, what is behind the mission, what relation he holds to the Newsomes. The retrospection ranges from his youth to his recent days in Europe.

Although the retrospection here is unusually lengthy, similar things take place throughout the earlier half of the novel. The technique is characteristic of all his later novels and is peculiarly Jamesian. It is as if everything had been established before the

---

[1] *The Ambassadors* ("The Novels and Stories of Henry James," London: Macmillan, 1923), I, 67. The italics in this and other quotations are mine. Subsequent references to James's works are to this edition.

story opens, as if in reading we are made acquainted piece by piece with established facts. As Joseph Warren Beach says, in reading James's novels we have "a sense of being present at the gradual unveiling of a picture."[2] In such unveiling, revelation comes not through normal narration in the past tense but through dialogue and the retrospection of the central character. The past perfect tense is necessary for retrospection, dealing as it does with anterior events in the consciousness of the central character. The method is especially successful in the case of *The Ambassadors* because Strether is of a meditative nature, and his concern with his past and the significance of the present events leads to rumination rather than action.

The past perfect tense is necessary in the passages from earlier sections of the novel, because they deal with time periods prior to those into which they are introduced. That is, the pluperfect is necessary because James uses retrospection so often and for such purposes. Few novelists before or since have a character put his hand to a doorknob at the beginning of a chapter, ponder throughout the chapter, and turn the knob to enter the room at the end of the chapter, as James has Adam Verver do in *The Golden Bowl*. The significant thing, therefore, is not that the past perfect tense is necessary in such situations, but that James should so consistently use situations that require it. Even more remarkable, however, he sometimes uses the tense when there is no recollection of anterior time. In Book Four of *The Ambassadors* occurs a passage which comes in the normal sequence of narration and yet begins with the past perfect:

Chad *had* one day *offered* tea at the Boulevard Malesherbes to a chosen few, a group again including the unobscured Miss Barrace; and Strether *had* on coming out *walked* away with the acquaintance whom in his letters to Mrs. Newsome he always spoke of as the other party, so oddly, to the only close personal alliance observation *had* as yet *detected* in Chad's existence. Little Bilham's way this afternoon was not Strether's, but he *had* none the less kindly *come* with him, and it was somehow a part of his kindness that as it *had* sadly *begun* to rain they suddenly found themselves seated for conversation at a café in which they *had taken* refuge. He *had passed* no more crowded hour in Chad's society than the one just ended. . . .

² *The Method of Henry James* (New Haven, 1918), p. 39.

"What game under the sun is he playing?" He signified the next moment that his allusion was not to the fat gentleman immersed in dominoes on whom his eyes *had begun* by resting, but to their host of the previous hour, as to whom, there on the velvet bench, with a final collapse of all consistency, he treated himself to the comfort of indiscretion. "Where do you see him come out?"[3]

The effect of the use of the past perfect tense here is to render action not as action but as existing facts, depriving portions of the passage of immediate vividness but giving others a greater concentration—a Jamesian intensification. What had happened before the two friends came to the cafe is less important: it is, as it were, pushed away, weakened by the use of the past perfect tense, just as the part described in the past tense obtains a corresponding, contrasting stress: the two friends sitting "on the velvet bench" of the cafe are presented vividly before our eyes.

A page or two later James employs the past perfect tense somewhat differently. The talk coming to an end, Strether and little Bilham are about to leave the cafe:

As the half hour meanwhile had ebbed Strether paid his score and the waiter was presently in the act of counting out change. Our friend pushed back to him a fraction of it, with which, after an emphatic recognition, the personage in question retreated.

"You give too much," little Bilham permitted himself benevolently to observe.

"Oh I always give too much!" Strether helplessly sighed. "But you don't," he went on as to get quickly away from the contemplation of that doom, "answer my question. Why isn't he free?"

Little Bilham *had got up* as if the transaction with the waiter had been a signal, and *had* already *edged out* between the table and the divan. The effect of this was that a minute later they *had quitted* the place, the gratified waiter alert again at the open door. Strether *had found* himself deferring to his companion's abruptness as to a hint that he should be answered as soon as they were more isolated. This happened when after a few steps in the outer air they *had turned* the next corner. There our friend *had kept* it up. "Why isn't he free if he's good?"

Little Bilham looked him full in the face. "Because it's a virtuous attachment."[4]

Those usages of the tense which are italicized obviously do not

[3] *The Ambassadors*, I, 154-155.
[4] *Ibid.*, I, 158.

have their being because they deal with anterior time or because an effect of concentration is sought. The movements described in the past perfect tense ought normally to have been reported in the past tense, since they take place during the conversation now going on before us. The passage obliges us to recognize a new possibility of the past perfect tense. Something other than the movements occupies Strether's mind. He is expecting an answer from Bilham, but, the answer being suspended, he is left in wonderment while the actions here described proceed. Strether's intent consciousness pervades the whole paragraph, looming far larger than the surface actions. We do not see directly how little Bilham "got up" from the seat, how he "edged out between the table and the divan," for what is written in the past perfect tense ("had got up," "had edged out") is not present in our attention. It is through Strether's consciousness that we can see the external actions (including his own). It is, as it were, the reflection of the actions cast on Strether's consciousness that we see. What, then, concerned James here was not the objective description of the actions but the impression made on Strether's otherwise preoccupied mind by the external occurrences. Such a method may be said to produce a double image of what is going on outside Strether's mind and what is going on inside it.

The Ambassadors derives its unity from Strether's sustained consciousness, but it is when his consciousness becomes more sustained than usual that James employs the unusual technique. Early in the novel Strether, who has not yet discerned Chad's situation, one day goes to a theater with Maria Gostrey and Waymarsh. Chad enters their box unexpectedly, surprising Strether by his change from his older American coarseness. Strether perceives this at a glance and lapses into deep thought. Civility requires him to introduce Chad to the inestimable Maria Gostrey; such a moment would seem to deserve treatment as a great event, but Strether is shown introducing him in the past perfect tense:

> He *had introduced* Chad, in the first minutes, under his breath, and there was never the primness in her of the person unacquainted; but she *had* none the less *betrayed* at first no vision but of the stage, where she occasionally found a pretext for an appreciative moment that she invited Waymarsh to share . . . .[5]

[5] *Ibid.*, I, 121.

This passage is inserted among pages of Strether's profound contemplation, and the act of introduction (his own act!) is described
as if it were registered in his memory only faintly. Strether's consciousness here is so expanded and so strained that there is no room
for any objective description of the external events to enter. If the
introduction were presented in the past tense, Strether's consciousness would suddenly be broken by the intrusion of objective narrative in a way for James's style at once awkward and false.

Such technique makes Strether's mind seem constantly teeming
with something, preoccupied with something, and he is therefore
likely to fail to observe vividly the trifling events going on around
him. Such an impression of ours is confirmed when James says
of him during a conversation with Chad, "he heard his interlocutor
ask him if he mightn't take him over about five";[6] or again when
he remarks to Maria Gostrey: "I'm always considering something
else; something else, I mean, than the thing of the moment. The
obsession of the other thing is the terror. I'm considering at present
for instance something else than *you*."[7]

The impression left by *The Ambassadors* is that of the hero's
intense consciousness pervading the whole. No small part of the
focus on Strether's consciousness derives technically from the use
of the past perfect tense so consistently that by the close of the
novel we are scarcely aware whether a single passage in the pluperfect is anterior action or present action barely perceived by Strether.
His consciousness grows more and more intense, dominating our
awareness of the experience of the novel. Such an effect is characteristic of James's purpose through most of his career. As he says
in the Preface to *The Spoils of Poynton,* he reviewed the novel

once more, too, with the re-entertained perception that a subject so lighted,
a subject residing in somebody's excited and concentrated feeling about
something—both the something and the somebody being of course as
important as possible—has more beauty to give out than under any
other style of pressure. One is confronted obviously thus with the
question of the importances; with that in particular, no doubt, of the
weight of the whole, or of something ominously like it, that one may
decently permit a represented figure to appear to throw.[8]

[6] *Ibid.*, I, 208.
[7] *Ibid.*, I, 17.
[8] P. xv.

In *The Golden Bowl,* such a purpose, and with it the use of the past perfect tense, seems to me to be developed to extreme lengths. At once upon opening the book the reader finds himself in the world of the past perfect tense and retrospection. Prince Amerigo is walking along the London streets remembering how he came to be engaged to Maggie Verver, the rich American girl. His retentive memory recalls even his conversations with her at the time of their engagement:

"Why, his 'form'," he *had returned,* "might have made one doubt."
"Father's form?" she *hadn't seen* it. "It strikes me he hasn't got any."
"He hasn't got mine—he hasn't even got yours."
"Thank you for 'even'!" the girl *had laughed* at him.
"Oh, yours, my dear, is tremendous. But your father has his own. I've made that out. So don't doubt it. It's where it has brought him out—that's the point."
"It's his goodness that has brought him out," our young woman *had,* at this, *objected.*
"Ah, darling, goodness, I think, never brought any one out. Goodness, when it's real, precisely, rather keeps people in." He *had been interested* in his discrimination, which amused him. "No, it's his *way.* It belongs to him."
But she *had wondered* still. . . .⁹

This goes on for pages, and the reader cannot help wondering. Conversation directly presented with the conventional narrative formula—"he said"—normally seems the most vivid to a reader, who supposes the conversation to be going on before him as he proceeds into the novel. Here, however, the usual response to dialogue is denied us by James's casting the non-dialogue, narrative portions into the past perfect tense. We feel somewhat bewildered, uncertain about our temporal response to the experience presented. We obtain our bearings only from an occasional narrative insertion such as, "The young man remembered now . . ." or "He recalled what, to this, he had gravely returned."

The world of consciousness rendered in *The Golden Bowl* is so expanded and so intensified that it takes on a portentous, obsessive quality. The most ordinary matters, turned up at random in the novel, reveal how effectively and persistently the internal world is rendered by the past perfect tense:

⁹ *The Golden Bowl,* I, 6-7.

What *had happened,* in short, was that Charlotte and he *had,* by a single turn of the wrist of fate—"led up" to indeed, no doubt, by steps and stages that conscious compunction *had missed*—*been placed* face to face in a freedom that partook, extraordinarily, of ideal perfection, since the magic web *had spun* itself without their toil, almost without their touch.[10]

Of the novel's two parts, the former is narrated from the point of view of the Prince, the latter of Maggie Verver. In the passage just quoted, the Prince is shown remembering and interpreting "what had happened" but a moment before. Anything that happens in the external world has no value or meaning in itself; it comes to have value and meaning only after it has been absorbed by the memory and presented through the consciousness of the observer. The effect is heightened to an unusual degree by the way in which the opening passage of the novel (quoted above) plunges us at once into a double time scheme in which the novel's present is at the outset departed from to convey its past. Such complexity at times takes on a remoteness which may haunt us with uncertainty or uneasiness. Since in *The Golden Bowl* there is perhaps more of the past perfect than of the past tense and nearly as much of the subjunctive as of the indicative mood, the actual, the palpable, seems to elude our grasp.

Originally intended for a short story, the plot of *The Golden Bowl* is very simple. We might therefore assume that James would stress as much as possible what little action the plot possesses, but in fact the action is suppressed as much as possible. Even those actions essential to the plot are not reported directly. To take a crucial event, Maggie buys the golden bowl unaware of its flaw. Afterwards, the shopman, showing compunction, visits Maggie and asks her to let him have it back. Noticing by chance two photographs representing the Prince and Charlotte, he remarks that he knows these persons; that they had come to his shop long before; that the lady had insisted on buying this very bowl and presenting it to the gentleman; and that the gentleman had said with a laugh that he would not accept such an ominous present. All this is disclosed to the reader *after* the bowl has been broken, not through the narrative of the author, of course, but through Maggie remembering her frankness about the matter with her husband. Such compli-

[10] *Ibid.,* I, 266.

cated presentation of important action cannot but be given in the past perfect tense.

It would have been impossible, however, even for James to write novels without making anything happen in the presence of the reader, as we can see from one of the most impressive scenes in *The Golden Bowl*—that of the destruction of the bowl:

> "Well then, if it's because of this—!" And Fanny Assingham, who *had been casting* about her and whose inspiration decidedly *had come,* raised the cup in her two hands, raised it positively above her head, and from under it, solemnly, smiled at the Princess as a signal of intention. So for an instant, full of her thought and her act, she held the precious vessel, and then, with due note taken of the margin of the polished floor, bare, fine and hard in the embrasure of her window, she dashed it boldly to the ground, where she had the thrill of seeing it, with the violence of the crash, lie shattered. She *had flushed* with the force of her effort, as Maggie *had flushed* with wonder at the sight, and this high reflection in their faces was all that passed between them for a minute more. After which, "Whatever you meant by it—and I don't want to know now—has ceased to exist," Mrs. Assingham said.
>
> "And what in the world, my dear, did you mean by it?"—that sound, as at the touch of a spring, rang out as the first effect of Fanny's speech. It broke upon the two women's absorption with a sharpness almost equal to the smash of the crystal, for the door of the room *had been opened* by the Prince without their taking heed.[11]

The dramatic effect of this smashing of the bowl derives from its presentation in the immediacy of the past tense. In a novel like this the past tense produces a striking effect in itself when the verbs express physical action. But even here the movement is exclusively the raising, holding, and dashing of the bowl, for the attendant occurrences that precede and follow it are presented in the past perfect tense. After the event the Prince enters, as if by the breaking of a spell in a fairy story, as Matthiessen puts it, but the event is reported in the past perfect tense.[12] The scene is, strangely, static. It is as if everything else happened at the same time with the destruction of the bowl, and as if everything were standing still for a moment around the shattered bowl. The result is one of those pictorial scenes of which James was proud—or per-

---

[11] *Ibid.,* II, 157-158.
[12] See F. O. Matthiessen, *Henry James: The Major Phase* (New York, 1944), p. 85.

haps rather of a photograph stopping and holding a moment of sudden action.

The technique employed in the scene of the breaking of the golden bowl can be best understood by contrast with other techniques in James's own earlier fiction. Fortunately, there is a very similar episode in *Roderick Hudson*:

"I want to begin," he cried, "and I can't make a better beginning than this! Good-bye, Mr. Barnaby Striker!" He strode across the room, seized a hammer that lay at hand, and before Rowland could interfere, in the interest of art if not of morals, dealt a merciless blow upon Mr. Striker's skull. The bust cracked into a dozen pieces, which toppled with a great crash upon the floor. Rowland relished neither the destruction of the image nor his companion's expression in working it, but as he was about to express his displeasure the door opened and gave passage to a fresh-looking girl. She came in with a rapid step and startled face, as if she had been alarmed by the noise. Meeting the heap of the shattered clay and the hammer in Roderick's hand, she gave a cry of horror. Her voice died away as she saw Rowland was a stranger, but she had sounded her reproach. "Why, Roderick, what on earth have you done?"[13]

The two episodes are nearly identical in construction—a sudden resolution impels one character to destroy a work of art in the presence of another, and a third character is introduced, surprised, to the scene.

The great difference between the two passages is expressed by the verbal tenses used. In *Roderick Hudson,* with one exception ("she had sounded"), all the verbs are in the past tense, and the passage is naturally more active than the parallel one in *The Golden Bowl.* The fact argues, not that the earlier novel is superior to the later, but that James was following different purposes. *Roderick Hudson* is a novel in which the past tense dominates. As James says in the Preface to this novel years later, "I was dealing, after all, essentially with an Action."[14] In a succession of actions, each must claim its share of attention unless special stress is given by other means. But in *Roderick Hudson,* the same stress is laid on all the verbs. We can only wonder which fact is more important, that the bust was broken or that a girl "came in with a rapid step and startled face" and "gave a cry of horror." In the case of *The*

[13] *Roderick Hudson,* pp. 33-34.
[14] P. xxii.

Golden Bowl, on the other hand, the stress is laid on the act of dashing the bowl, making it possess a symbolic meaning.

The scene in the later novel gives the effect of double image mentioned earlier. With the past perfect and the past functioning together, one image overlaps another. In the temporal foreground the two women stand with the broken cup between them and in the background the Prince at the door. There is a psychological truth in the technique—it reproduces the way we perceive things at a "great" moment when our attention is concentrated, with images coming to us overlapped. As it is actually perceived, time does not appear homogeneous; it is felt at some times thick, and at other times thin. The author of *Roderick Hudson* was incapable of this discrimination, and his time scheme elapses at the same monotonous pace.

The most famous episode of *The Golden Bowl* is that of the first real confrontation of Maggie and Charlotte. As the opening of the chapter shows (the episode belongs to the latter half of the novel), James uses Maggie's consciousness for his narrative point of view:

They *had been* alone that evening—alone as a party of six, and four of them, after dinner, under suggestion not to be resisted, sat down to "bridge" in the smoking-room. They *had passed* together to that apartment, on rising from table, Charlotte and Mrs. Assingham alike indulgent, always, to tobacco, and in fact practising an emulation which, as Fanny said, would, for herself, had the Colonel not issued an interdict based on the fear of her stealing his cigars, have stopped only at the short pipe. Here cards *had* with inevitable promptness *asserted* their rule, the game forming itself, as had often happened before [here a normal past perfect], of Mr. Verver with Mrs. Assingham for partner and of the Prince with Mrs. Verver. The Colonel, who *had* then *asked* of Maggie license to relieve his mind of a couple of letters for the earliest post out on the morrow, was addressing himself to this task at the other end of the room, and the Princess herself *had welcomed* the comparatively hushed hour—for the bridge-players were serious and silent— much in the mood of a tired actress who has the good fortune to be "off," while her mates are on, almost long enough for a nap on the property sofa in the wing.[15]

The past perfect tenses suggest the troubled state of Maggie's mind —an important change takes place a few pages later. Maggie is

[15] *The Golden Bowl,* II, 204.

hovering in the dark upon the terrace adjoining the room where cards are being played.

Several of the long windows of the occupied rooms stood open to it, and the light came out in vague shafts and fell upon the old smooth stones. The hour was moonless and starless and the air heavy and still—which was why, in her evening dress, she need fear no chill and could get away, in the outer darkness. . . . She walked to the end and far out of the light; she returned and saw the others still where she had left them; she passed round the house and looked into the drawing-room, lighted also, but empty now, and seeming to speak the more, in its own voice, of all the possibilities she controlled.[16]

The shortness and simplicity of the sentences and the use of verbs in the past tense brings a remarkable contrast—as if the musical key had suddenly been changed. When such an objective description of the setting and her brisk movements is introduced suddenly amid the expanded inner world of her consciousness, the atmosphere changes at once. Our expectation of something new and important is soon fulfilled by the most dramatic scene of the novel —the confronting of Maggie and Charlotte. The action proper is followed by objective comment:

The two women, at all events, only hovered there, for these first minutes, face to face over their interval and exchanging no sign; the intensity of their mutual look might have pierced the night. . . .[17]

"The two women" are here observed equally, but thereafter we shift once again to the inner world of Maggie. The shift into the objectivity of the past tense and out again heightens the drama, so that the duel-like event may seem to come upon Maggie as if from without. James then shifts to the inner world of the characters gradually, reporting the effect of their impact upon each other in terms of Maggie's consciousness and again with the past perfect tense and a mood of passiveness:

By the time she was at her companion's side, for that matter, by the time Charlotte *had,* without a motion, without a word, simply *let* her approach and stand there, her head was already on the block, so that the consciousness that everything *had gone* now blurred all perception of whether or no the axe *had fallen.* Oh, the "advantage," it was perfectly

[16] *Ibid.,* II, 208.
[17] *Ibid.,* II, 213.

enough, in truth, with Mrs. Verver; for what was Maggie's own sense but that of *having been thrown* over on her back, with her neck, from the first, half broken and her helpless face staring up? That position only could account for the positive grimace of weakness and pain produced there by Charlotte's dignity.

"I've come to join you—I thought you would be here."

"Oh yes, I'm here," Maggie heard herself return a little flatly.

"It's too close in-doors."

"Very—but close even here." Charlotte was still and grave—she *had* even *uttered* her remark about the temperature with an expressive weight that verged upon solemnity; so that Maggie, reduced to looking vaguely about at the sky, could only feel her not fail of her purpose. "The air's heavy as if with thunder—I think there'll be a storm." She made the suggestion to carry off an awkwardness—which was a part, always, of her companion's gain; but the awkwardness didn't diminish in the silence that followed. Charlotte *had said* nothing in reply; her brow was dark as with a fixed expression, and her high elegance, her handsome head and long, straight neck testified, through the dusk, to their inveterate completeness and noble erectness. It was as if what she *had come* out to do *had* already *begun,* and when, as a consequence, Maggie *had said* helplessly, "Don't you want something? Won't you have my shawl?" everything might have crumbled away in the comparative poverty of the tribute.[18]

Drama takes place in James's novels when the equilibrium of the internal world is broken by an action from outside—when the sensitive mind undergoes a new experience. The past perfect tenses here suggest the intensity of Maggie's self-consciousness, an effect heightened to symbolism by the images of the heavy air and the threat of storm.

James's use of the past perfect tense is the opposite of the so-called historical present, which brings forth, for the sake of vivification, what belongs to the world of the past tense to that of the present tense. His mind is of contrary make to those of the authors, like Dickens, who seek the immediacy of the historical present. Dickens seems to wish to bring his readers into the closest possible contact with the happenings in his stories, while James's tendency is obviously to separate his readers from the happenings themselves by interposing between them the consciousness, the intelligence, the retrospection of his characters.

[18] *Ibid.,* II, 214-215.

The complicated indirection of James's later novels is not a method discovered by a man young and inexperienced in the art of the novel. We would not expect to find it in his first novel, *Roderick Hudson*—indeed, it would be possible to follow its development through successive novels. So minute an inspection is out of the question here, but James's technique in his first novel and his mature reactions to that technique will serve to show the distance he traveled as an artist and his own awareness of his development.

In certain respects *Roderick Hudson* is the root of his later growth. In its American-European setting, its presentation of disintegrating personality, and in the likeness of Rowland Mallet to Strether, we may even find resemblances to *The Ambassadors*. Yet the style, and especially the time scheme, are worlds apart. In his Preface to *Roderick Hudson*, written during the period of his later novels, he tells his reaction upon rereading his first novel:

It stared me in the face that the time-scheme of this story is quite inadequate, and positively in that degree that the fault but just fails to wreck it. The thing escapes, I conceive, with its life . . . . Everything occurs, none the less, too punctually and moves too fast: Roderick's disintegration, a gradual process, and of which the exhibitional interest is exactly that it is gradual and occasional, and thereby traceable and watchable, swallows two years in a mouthful, proceeds quite not by years, but by weeks and months, and thus renders the whole view the disservice of appearing to present him as a morbidly special case.[19]

Was there ever another novelist who complained of his own work that it is "too punctual" and "too fast" in its movement? The "time-scheme" is truly, as James says, one of the weak points of the novel. He seems unable to arouse our interests with a rapid this-and-then-this sequence—not that he would have succeeded in a novel "dealing, after all, essentially with an Action" if he had slowed the speed with more digressions or more "ciceroning." Two quotations show his problem and an early solution of it. At times he is capable only of a fairy-tale sequence of no depth:

The young men walked away at a steady pace, over hill and dale, through woods and fields, and at last found themselves on a grassy elevation studded with mossy rocks and red cedars. Just beneath them, in a great shining curve, flowed the generous Connecticut. They flung

[19] Pp. xviii-xix.

themselves on the grass and tossed stones into the river; they talked, they fell into intimacy, like old friends. Rowland lit a cigar and Roderick refused one with a grimace of extravagant disgust.[20]

The feebleness and unreality of this passage are perhaps due as much to the misuse of the author's talents as to his inexperience. The purely objective narration is devoid of psychological elements. Here is an omniscient author, but strange enough, the omniscient author knows little in his aloofness from human behavior. Significantly, even in his first novel, when James psychologizes, his prose strangely gains power. In the following passage Rowland is thinking of Mary Garland, the cousin of Roderick, whom he loves secretly:

He felt himself, in a word, a man cruelly defrauded and naturally bent on revenge. Life owed him, he thought, a compensation and he should be restless and resentful till he should find it. He knew—or seemed to know—where he should find it; but he hardly told himself, thinking of it under mental protest, as a man in want of money may think of funds that he holds in trust. In his melancholy meditation the idea of something better than all this, something that might softly, richly interpose, that might reconcile him to the future, that might freshen up a vision of life tainted with staleness—the idea, in short, of compensation in concrete form found itself remarkably resembling a certain young woman in America, shaped itself sooner or later into the image of Mary Garland.[21]

Here, James's prose strikes us as being properly applied. In the delicacy of represented psychology, in the happiness of simile, and also in the complexity of syntax, it suggests the style of his last years. By entering the consciousness of a character, James found for a moment his proper interest, if not yet his matured technique. Toward the end of *Roderick Hudson,* however, there is a passage in which the late style is realized. (I am unable to ascertain whether it is the result of later revision, but the point remains the same.) Significantly, it is a passage of retrospection in which Rowland recalls a Swiss mountain inn that he had once visited:

He had a very friendly memory of a little mountain inn, accessible with moderate trouble from Lucerne, where he *had* once *spent* ten idle unadventurous days. He *had* at that time *been trudging,* knapsack on back, over half Switzerland, and, *having had* a sturdy conscience about

[20] *Roderick Hudson,* pp. 27-28.
[21] *Ibid.,* p. 274.

covering ground, it was no shame to him to confess that he was mortally tired. The inn of which I speak appeared to have but recently exchanged the care of the stalled ox for that of the hungry tourists; but Rowland at least *had felt* himself only a feebler ruminant. It stood in a high shallow valley, with flower-strewn Alpine meadows sloping down to it from the base of certain rugged rocks whose outlines were grim against the sky. Our friend had seen grander places that pleased him less, and whenever afterwards he wished to think of Alpine opportunities at their best he recalled this grassy concave among the steeper ridges and the August days passed in resting at his length in the lee of a sun-warmed boulder, with the light cool air astir about his temples, the wafted odours of the pines in his nostrils, the tinkle of the cattle-bells in his ears, the vast procession of the mountain-hours before his eyes and a volume of Wordsworth in his pocket. His face, on the Swiss hillsides, *had been scorched* to a brilliant hue, and his bed was a pallet in a loft, which he shared with a German botanist of colossal stature—every inch of whom quaked at an open window. These *had been* drawbacks to selfish ease, but Rowland hardly cared whether or how he was lodged, for his place of preference and of main abode was under the sky, on the crest of a slope that looked at the Jungfrau. He remembered all this on leaving Florence with his friends . . . .[22]

The retrospection is somewhat obtrusively presented—"afterwards . . . he recalled," and "He remembered all this. . . ." But the verbs in the past perfect tense give the passage a certain assurance and, strangely, it is quite realistic in spite of the fact that the description is lifeless and shallow in itself. In one's memory what one has done and seen long before comes back in much the same way as this—only in fragments and much diluted. The weak side of James's early prose style is fortunately concealed under the cloak of memory.

In order to be convincing, James needed to develop the point of view of one of his characters. In the Preface to *Roderick Hudson* he suggests that he became aware of the need while writing the novel and so adopted half-way Rowland's point of view:

I might produce illusion if I should be able to achieve intensity. It was for that I must have tried, I now see, with such art as I could command; but I make out in another quarter above all what really saved me. My subject, all blissfully, in face of difficulties, had defined itself— and this in spite of the title of the book—as not directly, in the least, my

[22] *Ibid.,* pp. 406-407.

young sculptor's adventure. This it had been but indirectly, being all the while in essence and in final effect another man's, his friend's and patron's, view and experience of him. One's luck was to have felt one's subject right—whether instinct or calculation, in those dim days, most served; and the circumstance even amounts perhaps to a little lesson that when this has happily occurred faults may show, faults may disfigure, and yet not upset the work. It remains in equilibrium by having found its centre, the point of command of all the rest.[23]

The realization served him in his next novel—as an examination of his use of the past perfect tense in the opening chapter of *The American* would show. He had not developed the full, rich, and intricate sense of retrospective consciousness in this novel written a year later; but the move toward what may be called a somewhat objective representation of the consciousness of the past led gradually toward the late style. Physical action is progressively replaced by thought, the event by retrospective consciousness of it, and his use of the past perfect tense gradually acquires complexity until it achieves the double-image sequence combining two time processes or the dramatic contrasts of shifts from past perfect to past tenses and back again. Strether's observation of the maturing of Chad while in Europe seems equally appropriate for the artistic maturation of James himself:

He *had* formerly, with a great deal of action, *expressed* very little; and he now expressed whatever was necessary with almost none at all.[24]

[23] Pp. xxii-xxiii.
[24] *The Ambassadors*, I, 134.

James and the Morality of Fiction
Robert J. Reilly

I

IF THE NOTION OF HEIGHT is a natural metaphor, always implying superiority of some kind, then it is a metaphor singularly appropriate to the true Jamesian—or Jacobite, in Geismar's acid phrase. For the Jamesian, the work of James is really above and beyond most other fiction; it is a high palace of art which he enters with genuine reverence, by virtue of those qualities which James himself required of the ideal critic—perception at the pitch of passion, insight that is only once removed from the original creative act. In James's work the Jamesian perceives the quintessence of conscious art; he learns to delight in the process of total artistic consciousness presenting, or projecting, vessels of consciousness nearly as full as its own. And after Bach, who can descend to Strauss, or even Wagner? For the Jamesian, only James is really satisfactory—other fiction seems fumbling and accidental, or easy and obvious, or simply gross. The Jamesian nearly always speaks from heights; it is impossible for him not to judge by Jamesian standards, because in order to become a Jamesian he has had to ascend to these standards.

Below, they argue still, long after Frank Moore Colby said it all so well, that James's people have no bodies, that they are unattached consciousness casting no shadows. But that complaint has no more force for a Jamesian than for a Platonist. The Jamesian has long since discovered that the only means he has of defending Hemingway or Lawrence is to hope that they have dimly tried to construct James's dramas of consciousness but have only rarely been equal to it, have darkly scuffled about in the vestibule of physical reality until by accident or luck they have strayed inside and seen for a moment the altar of human consciousness. The Jamesian does not care that James's people have no bodies, or at most bodies like gold to airy thinness beat, for he long ago learned from James that to deal with the body is to retreat from truth, or from the only reality that matters. The singularity of man, for the Jamesian, is man's consciousness, not his body. If dogs and sheep wrote novels, they would deal with physical reality. But if anything is recorded in the book of human life it is the actions of human consciousness, the sunlight of the human mind, not the refractions and shadows that the mind casts through the body— these James and the Jamesians leave for history and the lower forms of imitative literature.

Nor is the Jamesian ruffled by the other ancient rebukes: that James's people are hypersensitive, almost extrasensitive, alert to mental tones and pitches beyond normal human perception, like dogs hearing an apparently silent whistle; that they speak an impossible language never heard on land or sea; that their passions consists in their intricate analyses of each other, and their detumescences in psychological discovery. Against all these, and more, the Jamesian has sealed his mind; for him these are phantom issues; the only real issue is the premise from which they proceed. That premise is simply that the norm for judging fiction is established by combining many of the characteristic aims and techniques of the great body of twentieth-century realistic fiction: the newspaper realism of Dreiser's details, the panoramic social view of Dos Passos's trilogy, the celebration of physical sex in Lawrence, the calculated formlessness in the stream of consciousness of Joyce and Faulkner, the mindless violence in Hemingway. If one adds to these the general twentieth-century preoccupation with mental freaks, neurotics, and endless surrogates of formal religion, one has what might be called the normative twentieth-century novel. Set next to it, James's work seems of another world, for James has not Dreiser's realism, nor Dos Passos's social conscience, nor Lawrence's overt sexuality, nor Joyce's and Faulkner's free flow of the unconscious, nor Hemingway's violence. But for the Jamesian the norm is James. It is not James who fails to do what these others do, but they who fail to do what James does. James is orthodox; they are heretical. And if James is the norm, then Dreiser's realism is dreary and insignificant, and Dos Passos has strayed into social history, and Lawrence has elevated a body function into a religion, and Joyce and Faulkner have let the formlessness of their material

dictate their aesthetic order, and Hemingway has written boys'
books. For the Jamesian they all fall short: some are windy and
intrusive pessimists, some are word-drunk, some are lost in the
secondary and easily pictured reality of the body, and none has
sufficiently felt "the torment of form."

But there is at least one ghost that the Jamesian adept has not
laid, one question that hauntingly recurs like Peter Quint's white
face outside the windows at Bly. That is the question of the moral
character, or direction, of James's work; whether or not the work
can be said to subscribe to a moral viewpoint, even in the most
general way; and, if so, whether this moral viewpoint is traditional or wholly personal to James. The question is a peculiarly
tormenting one for the Jamesian; however he answers it, he seems
for the first time vulnerable to the assaults of the crowd.

The first inclination of the avowed Jamesian when faced with
the moral question of James's fiction is to stand aloof, to treat the
whole issue ironically, as James himself did in "The Art of Fiction"—to reduce the question to absurdity by means of analogy:
"Will you not define your terms and explain how (a novel being
a picture) a picture can be either moral or immoral?"[1] But to
answer thus is to leave James open to the accusation of *fin de siècle*
aestheticism, to seem to lodge him uncomfortably with Whistler
and Wilde, a grouping that the anti-Jamesians would cherish only
a little less than an admission of James's homosexuality. Worse,
the Jamesian knows how wrong such a grouping is. Though in
his passion for technique James often spoke as if that were his
whole concern, the Jamesian knows that this was not James's moral
indifference but his singlemindedness. His prefaces and notebooks
are as full of technical data as a painter's notebook or a cabinet-
maker's—comments on the looseness of the first-person point of
view, the importance of foreshortening, the desirability of an intense perceiver as protagonist. They are largely the records of a
craftsman's successes and failures, and if they do not often deal
with the large questions of life, neither do Da Vinci's sketchbooks.
On the other hand, if the Jamesian asserts what is for him very
apparent, that there is a positive moral quality in James's work but
that it is not easily described, not fixed to any traditional dogmatic

[1] *The Future of the Novel*, ed. Leon Edel (New York, 1956), p. 24.

religion, then James seems liable to another indictment: that he was cynically using morality because, consummate artist that he was, he found moral decisions dramatic and difficult to "do." From this point of view his morality is unspecifiable because it is relatively unimportant; any vague kind of religion would do, as for a writer who is concerned to dramatize a soldier's cowardice under fire any kind of war will do. According to this indictment, all the famous Jamesian "renunciations"—Isabel Archer's, Fleda Vetch's, Lambert Strether's—occur because they are interesting psychological or spiritual processes, not because what produced them is important. The moral motivation behind them is in fact irrelevant, or at best nominal; if one could conceive of any other cause bringing them about, then that would have done as well. The branches are dramatic; the roots are not. But the Jamesian knows truth from opinion, and he knows that James was anything but a cynical manipulator of religion, that James's attitude toward traditional religion is at least partly revealed in that magnificent scene in *The Ambassadors* in which Strether watches Mme. de Vionnet praying in Notre Dame and comes very close to envying her faith, before he steps back into his role of the Jamesian gentleman visiting a monument.

Perhaps it would give aid and comfort to the Jamesians to remind them that this problem is not peculiar to James, that the question of an author's moral attitudes seems naturally to arise in every case where the author's reputation is almost wholly "aesthetic" or "artistic," when an author invariably appears in every book of literary history but only rarely in a book dealing with intellectual history or philosophic attitudes, for the very good reason that there is not in his work any identifiable moral code or set of attitudes that can be extracted, abstracted, and discussed. No one is puzzled by the moral qualities of Hemingway's fiction, for example, because the Hemingway "code" or "world view" is relatively easy to abstract; one can discuss it as he can that of Milton or Camus or Zola, because in all these cases the moral or religious pattern seems not so much an organic part of the work as a paradigm which the work fills out and gives body to. But with Shakespeare, Conrad, and James the moral patterns, the figures in the carpets, are much harder to trace and are only partly detachable; and this is certainly in part because the textures of the carpets are so rich, the writers are so manifestly great artists in command of their mediums. Thus it happens with writers like Shakespeare and James that the question sooner or later arises: what are their moral views? what is the moral direction of their work? And because they are clearly the master workers, it is natural that the questions ultimately shift from the moral direction of their specific work to the moral possibilities of the mediums themselves, and the questions become general and speculative: is drama moral? is fiction moral? It is one of the marks of the great artist that he forces attention to the form in which he works as if, like Homer, he had invented his medium and had left his shaping impression everywhere through it.

It is these related problems of the morality of James's fiction in particular and the morality of fiction in general that I wish to deal with here, though warily and tentatively, as befits one scaling lofty peaks in rarefied air. But as a prologue to the problems, it may be wise to point out, if not clear away, some of the thickets of difficulty which surround them.

First, there is the obvious fact that in dealing with an artist's moral views one has two bodies of evidence. He has what the artist has himself said about morality, outside the art works— unless, like Shakespeare, he has said nothing at all that we know of. And he has the moral view, or attitudes, to be found in the art work itself. It is not self-evident that these views will coincide, though we usually assume they do. But as you cannot argue with any assurance from the moral views in *Lear* to the personal moral views of Shakespeare himself, so you cannot argue the reverse of the process—that what James said discursively about morality is automatically reproduced in aesthetic form in his fiction. And clearly, the more dramatic and objective the art work is—Shakespeare's plays, James's late novels—the more difficult it is to assign to its author any moral view or views advocated by a character in the work. It was this impenetrable dramatic quality of Shakespeare's work that so distressed Johnson: Shakespeare had so faithfully held the mirror up to life that though he reflected all the elements of a moral system, he nowhere ordered them into a system. But in some of the commentaries on James's morality this distinction between primary and secondary evidence is ignored, and it is assumed that what James said in his letters, for example, is clear and ample evidence of a certain moral view to be found in his work. It is true that the letters contain many moral formulations and also many unforgettable comments on the human condition. That they throw light on James's fiction is indisputable; but they are not a substitute for the fiction; more important, they are not redactions of the fiction. Even supposing that James was perfectly accurate in his self-analysis, that he did have "the imagination of disaster" and did see life as "ferocious and sinister,"[2] the question remains still: do the phrases describe James's imagination or James's work? Further, as an unreconstructed New Critic might have it, are the letters (and the prefaces and the notebooks) necessary for us to appreciate the qualities of the fiction? What is objectively "there" in the fiction if we do not properly see it until the letters point it out? Did we see the depicted life in *The Golden Bowl* as ferocious and sinister before we read James's fine phrase? Do the letters (and prefaces and notebooks) sharpen our perceptions or introduce us to qualities we have not seen before? If, as James insisted, a novel consists of what is dramatized, what is represented, what is pictured—then what is outside the picture is irrelevant, does not formally exist. The old joke about *The Waste Land* was that the structure is in the footnotes, and the implied principle is relevant to James's work; for if we judge it by his own standards—holding that fiction is representational, not discursive—then what is not dramatized has no bearing. The meaning of the picture is in the picture or nowhere.[3]

Another way of suggesting secondary evidence in such a way as to make it seem primary evidence from the fiction itself is to dwell on the temperaments of James's father and brother William and to imply that James shared these temperaments. Thus Graham Greene makes much of the father's and brother's encounters with evil—the "vastations" which both seem to have undergone—and

---

[2] *Letters to A. C. Benson and Auguste Monod*, ed. E. F. Benson (London, 1930), p. 35.

[3] Of the form of *The Awkward Age*, James wrote that it was a "form all dramatic and scenic—of presented episodes, architecturally combined and each making a piece of the building; with no going behind, no *telling about* the figures save by their own appearance and action and with explanations reduced to the explanation of everything by all the other things *in* the picture" (*The Letters of Henry James*, ed. Percy Lubbock, New York, 1920, I, 333).

then notes too that Henry's sister Alice had strong suicidal tendencies. The inference that Greene draws from these facts is that James,
too, had this sixth sense for evil, that his imagination was "clouded
by the Pit."[4] He goes on to argue that James's awareness of evil
was so intense and so Puritanical that one thinks he might be talking about Jonathan Edwards. But if we may use secondary evidence
to comment on secondary evidence, one would suppose that if James
had this almost Calvinistic sense of evil, his brother William would
have noticed it. But the letters show that William had no more
sympathy with Henry's work—and no more understanding of it—
than Wells had. The recent emphasis on James's awareness of
evil in the world is perhaps an attempt to make him seem contemporary, as we have made Melville, Hawthorne, and Emily
Dickinson seem to be contemporary with Camus and Wallace
Stevens. We currently value the literature of negation and try
to extend our present norms backward in time whenever we can.
This is an understandable procedure; any intellectual view "recti-
fies" the whole of literature, so long as the view is accepted—as
Eliot pointed out years ago. But earlier readers of James were not
necessarily blind to the existence of evil in his work, as some contemporary critics seem to assume. It is rather that the earlier judgments of his work were more purely literary than our own. As
Colby noted, James could deal with any kind of horrors that he
chose to and his books could still be left open in the nursery, because his style was "his sufficient fig leaf."[5] But recent critics, with
intense dedication, have brushed form aside to get at meanings
that for earlier readers existed only in a dim way behind what they
saw as an indeterminate veil of words.

One of the more interesting oddities of James criticism is the
way James himself has so often pointed the way for his interpreters,
somewhat in the manner by which a fox will lead hounds over
ground he knows. If one reads James's preface to one of his novels
and then turns to the critical commentary on the novel, he has
a distinct sense that the commentary exists within a framework
that has been "given"—like the innumerable medieval commentaries on the "given" *Sentences* of Peter Lombard. This practice

---

[4] "Henry James: The Private Universe," *The Lost Childhood* (New York, 1952), p. 26.
[5] "In Darkest James," *Imaginary Obligations* (New York, 1905), p. 321.

goes back at least as far as Percy Lubbock's *The Craft of Fiction*, which analyzes fictional techniques in wholly Jamesian terms, and continues to its absolute *reductio* in a recent book on James in which the writer makes an incredible attempt to imitate the Jamesian style, like a demented sparrow trying to hover on imaginary eagle wings.[6] Even the omissions in James criticism are interesting in this respect. One must search hard to find any serious comment on *Washington Square*, which James did not include in the New York Edition and so did not comment on formally. Yet, if one can avoid James's judgment by exclusion and look at the book on its merits, one finds that it is clearly not inferior to *The Spoils of Poynton*, for example, and is in addition one of the wittiest of James's stories. And in the matter of the novelist's moral views, or the moral qualities of his fiction, most of the critics approach the problem in ways that James himself sketched out, and they state in James's terms moral issues in the fiction which James himself introduced in his backward-looking prefaces. Fleda Vetch is a case in point. To one who had not read James's preface her moral behavior would surely seem bizarre, would seem in fact almost a classic of moral hyperscrupulousness. As a moral agent, if she does not belong with the neurotics in Faulkner or Tennessee Williams or with Strindberg's Miss Julie, she surely belongs with the ritualistic moralists of love in the court of Marie de Champagne. But James indicated in his preface that she had "character" and that he took her conscience seriously, and thus this view echoes through the commentaries.

The next difficulty is one which James's fiction shares with other psychological fiction and perhaps with all fiction that assumes a certain degree of free will in its characters, all fiction that is not professedly "naturalistic" or deterministic. Any discussion of the moral elements of James's work has to touch on what we call the "moral acts" or "moral choices" of his characters: Isabel Archer's decision to return to her husband, Strether's decision to return to

[6] Robert Marks, *James's Later Novels* (New York, 1960). Thus: "The ambition of this book is the imputation to him, with an equanimity of confidence, of some ideas—both of life and form—cherished as convictions, those of which his novels and stories are dramatizations and embodiments, supreme ideas and recurrent techniques of his thought that constitute an underlying point of view sharp and bright by which his work all hangs together, which impart to it a unity, a character, a tone, and from which it derives its final value" (pp. 10-11).

America, Newman's decision to renounce vengeance on the Bellegarde family. James himself, characteristically, has led the discussion of many of these moral choices and has evaluated them
from what might be called the orthodox or conventional point of
view—as if Isabel Archer's choice, for example, is a perfectly "free"
choice for which she is to be commended or censured. But if you
examine her decision—or Strether's or Newman's—you find that
in every case the moral choice is in accordance with, and really
seems to proceed from, the temperament or "humor" of the character. In other words, the more closely you examine the decision,
the less it seems to be a perfectly free moral choice and the more
it seems to be an automatic or determined one. And the more you
know about a given character—the more fully and delicately he
is analyzed by the author—the less likely it becomes that you can
ever accept his decisions as free in any real sense. It may be put
as an inverse ratio: the greater the psychological knowledge we
have of a character, the less the illusion of free choice, and total
knowledge absolutely precludes this illusion. If this is so, then the
process of psychological analysis in fiction is self-destructive—so long,
that is, as the writer wishes to maintain the illusion of his people's
free will; the ultimate aim, the presentation of character "in the
round" or "in depth," if it is ever wholly successful, presents not a
living being but an automaton. Perhaps, then, the only kind of fiction that can give us totally believable moral agents is non-analytical
fiction in which the characters are depicted entirely from the outside, where we have no knowledge of the working of the character's
consciousness, fiction that approximates the wholly dramatic quality
of the stage play.

And in this respect literature, as Johnson said, may appeal to
life for justification. The difficulty in ascribing praise or blame in
life varies according to how well we know the person whose acts
we are judging. The perfect stranger is the easiest to judge, and
is proved most easily a villain; but even a little knowledge leads
to leniency. And we hardly ever pass a strictly moral judgment on
one of our own acts because we know so well the complexities of
the situation—our own strains and stresses, the shaping influence
of time and place, and so on. Of people we know, we say that they
acted "characteristically," implying that their acts were predictable,

as proceeding from their temperaments. But for "predictable" we almost have to read "unfree," for if the decision accords with the temperament, then it seems nearly automatic, unless we assume that all of us are choosing all the time, deciding every minute to be what we are. That is a *reductio* of a well-known existential tenet, and it is simply impossible that it should be true in practice. What all this means is that the closer James, or any other psychological novelist, comes to imitating life, or existential human reality, the more nearly impossible it becomes for him to depict a real moral choice; for, assuming the possibility of moral choice, it is apparently either incredibly more complex or incredibly more simple than we generally assume it to be. And in either case one can no more isolate it in fiction than he can in real life. If this is so, most of the elements in the fiction that we use as evidence of James's moral opinions are irrelevant. In the same way, let us hope, most of the elements in life on which we base our moral judgments, and on which others base their moral judgments of us, are also irrelevant. Judge not, say the Scriptures, that ye be not judged, meaning presumably that we are all hopelessly wicked or that all judgments are partial and thus wrong.

It is hypothetically possible that the difficulty I have been describing here is one of which James himself was unaware; in that case we should have in the fiction the portrayal of acts which James himself saw as free but which we (on reflection) cannot recognize as such, and if this were true then the fiction would still hold up as evidence of James's moral views. But I believe it is a mistake to underestimate the sophistication of James's mind, or to assume there were many problems related to his art of which he was ignorant. If we consider his passion for process as such, for causality as such, for action and reaction in the realm of human behavior, we should be very surprised if we found that at a certain point in his study of this process he had simply abandoned it, as if he had gone carefully up a tortuous staircase only to leap out a fifth-story window. The possibility surely occurred to him that in dealing with process he might well be dealing *only* with process, with endless or circular causality. We make much of some of James's remarks about his characters, about his ability to see them as "real," but this capacity does not cancel out the possibility that in some

way or other, or at least intermittently, he also saw them as determined. "What will she *do*?" he asked concerning Isabel Archer
as he went about setting up her character, and we are inclined to
see this curiosity as charmingly ingenuous. But of course the answer
is that she will do what James will make her do once he has
decided for himself what kind of person she is; his curiosity cannot be from total but only partial ignorance. His curiosity, in the
beginning stages of his composition of the novel, can only apply
to the specific circumstances under which this "set" character
will "issue into action" (in A. C. Bradley's fine phrase). Or if her
character is not wholly settled on an a priori basis, if James himself kept discovering (or making up) new aspects of her character
as he went along, the fact still remains that she acts characteristically; that is, it does not matter whether James created her instan-
taneously (as it were) or by a kind of creative evolution: she is
still what she is. "What will she do?" She will do what a train
will do once it has been set on rails that have already been built.
In a word, she will become—at least for James, and for the reader
too, if James's analysis is successful—predictable. All experience
is against free will, as Johnson once commented, and all belief is
for it. To give James his intellectual due and in order not to sell
him short, I think we must assume that at best he wrote "as if"
free will were present in human affairs but without much positive
reason for thinking so; and while such an attitude perhaps does
not weaken his art, it surely makes the art unreliable evidence in
a discussion of James's moral views. If James did not take this
view, or something like it, if he did not suspect at least occasionally
that analysis of human behavior seems to lead always to the whirli-
gig of determinism, then that famous passage in *The Ambassadors*
seems wholly cryptic—that remarkable scene that James himself
called the core of the book, in which Strether advises Little Bilham: " 'Live all you can; it's a mistake not to.' " Then, having
urged Little Bilham toward a choice, Strether adds:

"What one loses one loses; make no mistake about that. The affair—
I mean the affair of life—couldn't, no doubt, have been different for
me; for it's at the best a tin mould, either fluted and embossed, with
ornamental excrescences, or else smooth and dreadfully plain, into which,
a helpless jelly, one's consciousness is poured—so that one 'takes' the

form, as the great cook says, and is more or less compactly held by it; one lives, in fine, as one can. Still, one has the illusion of freedom; therefore don't be, like me, without the memory of that illusion."[7]

I do not argue that Strether's view is necessarily James's, only that Strether could not have said it if James had not first thought it. Scott Fitzgerald once remarked that "the test of a first-rate intelligence is the ability to hold two opposed ideas in the mind at the same time, and still retain the ability to function."[8] He might well have been describing the accumulated wisdom of the race on the subject of responsibility in human behavior, the double view of human existence that sees human acts in life, and human acts in art, as only provisionally understandable and as ultimately ambiguous. I do not think we can fairly deny James this perception.

Finally, in respect to this matter, it has been noted by critics that James typically relieves his characters of financial needs—Isabel Archer is the most obvious case—and the assumption is that he does this in order to set them free from the partly determining force of poverty and the limited horizons of the very poor. But this assumption also underestimates James if it implies that James thought he was thus setting his people "free." He may have been freeing them of a particular factor in mental life because, for any of a number of reasons, he did not want to deal with it except in rare cases such as those of Hyacinth Robinson and Kate Croy. But it is absurd to believe that because James's people are "comfortably fixed" they live in a moral vacuum; if one siphons away one potentially determining factor in life, another rushes in to take its place; life, in fact, abhors a moral vacuum. To remove potentially determining factors is to remove the atmosphere from the earth; man acts amid existential stresses—interior and exterior forces so strong and so apparent that the Naturalist believes them overwhelming—and these stresses comprise the elements of human choice, in fact the very conditions of choice. An absolutely unconditioned human act is inconceivable, like a poem without the conditioning factor of language. James may have wanted to exchange one set of conditions for another because he found one more interesting or more complex than the other; but, with his passion for

[7] *The Ambassadors*, New York Edition, I, 217-218.
[8] *The Crack-Up*, ed. Edmund Wilson (New York, 1956), p. 69.

analysis, he surely was not trying to uproot his people from existential reality, for if he did he would have nothing to analyze. We sometimes speak of James's characters as if they were solipsists, or as if James thought they were; but even the subtlest of their mental processes has "reality" as its object; it is the action-reaction of a sensitive being who has been "put in relation" with something outside himself. James, for all his distrust of the pessimistic pattern that the Naturalists "projected" onto human life, was always aware of the vital tension between human consciousness and the outer world. So little did he want to isolate his people from the world that, like a transcendentalist, he more than once remarked on the fact of consciousness as a web, as a homogeneous tissue in which inner and outer reality shaded into each other in blendings so subtle that one could hardly specify boundaries.

II

There have been notable attempts both to state and to resolve the specific problem of the morality of James's fiction, attempts sufficient in quality and number to emphasize its importance and persistency as a critical issue for some half a century. Joseph Warren Beach was among the first to note one of the phenomena already mentioned, that James's characters are rarely affected by ethical or religious orthodoxies. Beach argued that the characters' moral sense was not separable from their aesthetic sense and that this integrity of consciousness placed James in the transcendental moral tradition of Emerson, Thoreau, and Hawthorne.[9] David Daiches held that there is a progression in James's work, that early work such as *Roderick Hudson* contains "specific"[10] and "overt"[11] morality but that in the late novels the morality does not exist "apart from their totality of meaning, apart from the 'felt life' the author presents through the novel."[12] Yvor Winters credited James with a belief in a peculiarly American moral sense, a moral outlook that was a product of the centuries-long discipline of the Roman, Anglo-Catholic, and Calvinist churches, a moral sense finally destroyed

[9] *The Method of Henry James* (New Haven, 1918), pp. 141-144.
[10] "Sensibility and Technique (Preface to a Critique)," *Kenyon Review*, V, 577 (1943).
[11] *Ibid.*, p. 576.
[12] *Ibid.*, pp. 576-577.

by Emerson's "anti-moral"[13] philosophy and by the immoralities
of "the new financial aristocracy which had arisen after the Civil
War. . . ."[14] C. B. Cox found elements of Stoicism in James's religious views.[15] F. O. Matthiessen argued for a "religion of consciousness"[16] in James's work and held that James placed his characters on a scale of good and evil that is based on their "awareness,"[17] the stage of sensitivity to which their consciousness has
advanced. John H. Raleigh also posited a religion of consciousness
in James's characters but on grounds that James's philosophical
assumptions were derived from the British empirical tradition of
Locke. "The consciousness most sensitive to impressions is liable
to be the most moral. So in James there is an equation between
the esthetic and the moral sense, and the individual who most
appreciates the beauty of a Renaissance painting is also the most
moral."[18] Quentin Anderson traced the moral structure of James's
later work to James's use of his father's Swedenborgian religious
views and argued that the work of the "major phase" is in fact
a single "divine novel"[19] based on the father's religious convictions.
Dorothea Krook held that James's world view is not to be attributed
to any single source but was formed by "the ambient air of nineteenth-century speculation, whose main current was the preoccupation with the phenomenon of self-consciousness."[20]

Considering these critical commentaries I believe two things
are evident: (*a*) all are interesting in themselves, and (*b*) none of
them wholly explains the moral phenomenon of James's work. If
it is possible to have such a thing as an unhelpful truth, what might
be called a non-operative truth, then Beach's view is such a truth,
and so is that of Daiches. To the reader who finds himself afoot
"in darkest James" (Colby's phrase) it is not very useful to be told
that James's people act as they do because, in effect, they have a
"unified sensibility," whether that unity be described as transcendental or not. Nor is it very useful even to the advanced reader of

---

[13] *In Defense of Reason* (New York, 1947), p. 306.
[14] *Ibid.*
[15] "Henry James and Stoicism," *Essays and Studies*, N.S. (London, 1955), VIII, 76-88.
[16] *Henry James: The Major Phase* (New York, 1944), p. 131.
[17] *Ibid.*, p. 146.
[18] "Henry James: The Poetics of Empiricism," *PMLA*, LXVI, 111 (March, 1951).
[19] *The American Henry James* (New Brunswick, N. J., 1957), p. 349.
[20] *The Ordeal of Consciousness in Henry James* (Cambridge, England, 1962), p. 411.

James to be told that the moral quality of James's fiction is not separable from the "totality of meaning" of the work. Though we may agree with Aristotle that we know things in their causes, we must also say that there are different spheres of causality and that a metaphysical cause throws little light on a question of psychology or morality. Beach and Daiches explain without satisfying. Strether's rejection of the good life remains just as cryptic, or maddening, as if Beach and Daiches had not spoken. The crudest kind of dismissal of Strether as a bloodless neurotic is really more satisfactory, in the sense that it at least is on the same level of causality as the act itself. It may be wrong, but it is relevant.

As to Winters's assertion of an American moral sense, it serves well enough as a kind of working description of only part of James's work, and it is logically indefensible if taken as explanation. It is true that some of James's Americans act as if their moral nature were different from that of some of James's Europeans— Christopher Newman, Daisy Miller, Strether, Isabel Archer, for example. But that is really a matter of contrast for dramatic purposes. Set next to the general moral corruption of the Bellegarde family, Newman's morality seems bright and refreshing and wholly different from theirs. But the two members of the Bellegarde family with whom Newman has the closet relations—Claire (who rejects his love in order to become a nun) and her brother Valentin (who, while on his death bed, apologizes for his family's corruption)— act according to moral beliefs quite as distinct of those of Newman. In fact, what the contrast really shows, and what many of the Jamesian American-European contrasts show, is the relatively ingenuous American moral view versus the relatively complex European moral view. But that is no argument for the moral sense being peculiarly American but rather for the moral sense being universal. In fact, when we look over the great range of James's people, we find that if it is the moral sense that makes people moral, then all James's people have it but not under the same conditions of life. And Winters's whole thesis about the moral sense— whatever its limited usefulness as description—can hardly be more than a mental construct parading as a historical phenomenon. If the moral sense is viewed as a product of ages of Roman Catholic and Anglo-Catholic thought, then how can it be peculiar to America, where this thought came only so recently? If an infusion of American Puritanism modified it, then that seems only another way of saying that the original sense remained unmodified—but of course remained. But even if Winters's ingenious intellectual history were truer than it is, it would still have little to say about the basic problem of the morality of James's fiction. Because Winters was working on an irrelevant level of causality, like Beach and Daiches he seems to be saying that James's people act as they do because they are what they are.

Cox has surely hit on one of the most important aspects of James's protagonists—what he calls their "rigid self-control and consistent moral behaviour"[21]—for nothing can be more clear than that they act according to a code which, if not personal, is at least never revealed. But rigid self-control and consistent moral behavior are not peculiar to Stoicism and are in fact distinguishing characteristics of any religion that holds to an ethical system. If James, as Cox believes, rejected the Stoic notion of *apatheia*, or the determination not to feel, then it seems clear that James rejected Stoicism itself, since it is *apatheia* that is the core of Stoicism. And since it is evident that James's people do feel, and feel profoundly, about a great many things, then if there are self-control and consistent moral behavior in the fiction they come from a different source.

The notion of a "religion of consciousness," as advocated by Matthiessen and Raleigh, perhaps comes closest to saving the Jamesian appearances. It accords with what most readers feel in the fiction, and it has the added advantage of according with James's comments outside the fiction. There can be no doubt that James in some way graded his characters according to their degrees of consciousness. I say "in some way" because it is not immediately evident that the gradation is as simple as Raleigh's comments would suggest—that the person of the most advanced consciousness, most likely to appreciate a Renaissance painting, is likely to be the most moral. One thinks of Gilbert Osmond, Madame Merle, John Marsh, Charlotte Stant—all belong to the class that James called his "super-subtle fry," yet all are presumably evil in one way or another. Matthiessen makes the matter less simple, and thus probably closer

[21] Cox, p. 77.

to truth: the character having the refined Jamesian consciousness sees the greatest number of moral possibilities. And yet, if one turns from speculation and examines the work itself, the one thing that strikes the reader is the essential similarity of mind among all the important Jamesian characters, the fact that James hardly ever dealt with characters who had not advanced to this refinement of consciousness. In the Jamesian world there are people we see as good and those we see as evil, but a little reflection suggests that the difference between them is not to be found in levels of consciousness but where the difference is always said by moralists to reside—in the will. Where all people are nearly equally advanced in self-consciousness the moral differences among them cannot derive from this self-consciousness. Matthiessen's argument would be much stronger if he could point to cases of obvious evil in James and say, in effect, "This man is evil because he is lumpish and unrefined, because he has not advanced to Strether's level of self-consciousness." But this is impossible to do. If Newman is the moral hero of *The American* it is not because his consciousness is more refined than that of the Bellegarde family; it is obviously *less* refined, less analytical, less articulate. Christina Light is as conscious an agent as any of James's protagonists, yet she is clearly in the ranks of those ranged against the Jamesian heroes. And what is true of her is also true of Madame Merle, the greedy publisher in *The Aspern Papers*, Mrs. Gereth in *The Spoils of Poynton*, the aesthetic novelist in "The Author of 'Beltraffio,'" and many others. It is not really that James's villains are relatively unconscious but rather that James deals primarily with characters whom we assume to be "good." Most of the intricate Jamesian analysis is devoted to his protagonists, whom we identify with, and whom we assume to be heroes. This is so generally the case that when we are treated to the examination of a consciousness set against the protagonist we are likely to mistake it for something else—who has not been in sympathy with Merton Densher of *The Wings of the Dove* or with the prince in *The Golden Bowl*? Most of James's evil characters are not necessarily unconscious, only unanalyzed. Moreover, it is not always indisputably true that the refined consciousnesses that James presents us with are necessarily to be taken as heroes; they may in some cases be merely interesting protagonists. James himself may have thought of his protagonists as heroes, and thus have led the way in our critical estimates of them, but there really is no reason to assume that we have to admire Maggie Verver or Fleda Vetch, or even Strether or Isabel Archer, any more than we feel forced to admire the intricately analyzed people in Durrell's quartet or in Faulkner. If we allow ourselves this freedom with James, if we pay him the deserved compliment of accepting his people as dramatic presentations, as we do for contemporary novelists in general, then we are relieved of the necessity (surely a burdensome one) of thinking of Fleda Vetch as a moral heroine or of Charlotte Stant as a moral monster. We are free to be impatient with Strether, sympathetic to Mme. de Vionnet, suspicious of Maggie Verver, infinitely bored with Milly Theale; we are free, in short, to form opinions of these people as if they were real, as if life itself rather than James had thrust them at us. It is the compliment we pay to Shakespeare, almost the highest one we can pay to an imitative writer, and James himself could have asked for no more. But if we pay this compliment we abandon the conventional distinctions between heroes and villains, and with them the real basis for Matthiessen's argument for a religion of consciousness.

Quentin Anderson's provocative thesis, that James's later work is a subtle allegorizing of his father's Swedenborgian religious views, has not been generally accepted, though one critic has called it "an exciting work of interpretive criticism and scholarship."[22] Anderson argued that much of the later Jamesian imagery is really to be read as a use of Swedenborgian "emblems"—the House of Life, the Tree of Life, the Portrait, the bowl or the "great containing vessel"[23]—and that these emblems are "rigidly determined by an intention which must be called allegorical."[24] The most basic objection to this glossing of James's images is that what Anderson sees as emblems are really only the "literary currency of the day,"[25] or, as Leon Edel has called them, no more than a "verbal inheritance"[26] from the elder James. And it is Edel who

[22] Unsigned review of Anderson's book in *Modern Fiction Studies*, III, 181 (Summer, 1957).
[23] Anderson, p. 347.
[24] *Ibid.*, p. 350.
[25] *Modern Fiction Studies*, p. 182.
[26] Review of Anderson's book, *American Literature*, XXIX, 494 (Jan., 1958).

has said what seems to be the last word on the subject, not by leveling a specific objection but by asserting a general and far-reaching truth about James's work as a whole. Any allegorical reading of James's work that places him alongside Dante (as Anderson's reading does) ignores the profound truth that James was above all things a novelist, that he proudly represented himself as such, and that his work "is rooted not in the *Divine Comedy* of Dante but in the *Human Comedy* of Balzac."[27]

Now these critical commentaries we have been examining range from the assignment of causes at one end of the scale, through what may be called working descriptions, to allegorical interpretation, and finally to very broad general statement, as in Dorothea Krook's comment that James was preoccupied with the phenomenon of self-consciousness. Matthiessen's argument, whether wholly right or not, is probably most successful in the sense that it makes the reader feel more "at home" with James, though the argument suffers, as most of the others do, from the attempt to present a single moral pattern and then fit all of James's people into it. But what the reader—and perhaps even the Jamesian—needs in order to be comfortable with James is to feel that the moral world that James presents is not unique. It is even possible that one of the great laws of art is that analogy is more helpful than exegesis; analysis of a new and novel work of art is not as useful as comparison, for it is only by comparison, or analogy, that the seeming uniqueness of the art work is accommodated. A reader innocent of most contemporary fiction might be bowled over by *The Catcher in the Rye*, and might then discover by exegesis something of the cause of his reaction. But the more general meaning of the book, the significance of its form, everything that makes Holden Caulfield so pitifully symbolic of the current phase of the human condition—all this the reader comprehends from analogy, from reading books comparable to Salinger's, from seeing into the minds of other adolescent searchers such as Holiday Golightly and Ike McCaslin and Frankie (F. Jasmine) Addams. And so it is with the phenomenon of James's morality; the reader can be made comfortable with it, not so much by having it explained, as by seeing it reproduced elsewhere. It is the odd blandness, the opacity, of James's moral

[27] *Ibid.*, p. 495.

dramas that puzzle the reader, that he can in fact hardly describe. It is James's seeming acceptance of the moral postures of his protagonists without comment (as Beach noted) as if all of them were of equal value—Strether's, and Fleda Vetch's, and Maggie Verver's; it is this apparent equalitarianism of moral views that puts the reader off, that raises the question whether James was not, like Jefferson, tolerant to the point of indifference, treating all moral views impartially because he saw them as all equally wrong. It is this apparently all-accepting quality of James's moral outlook that remains enigmatic unless there is an analogue for it.

That analogue, I believe, is to be found precisely in the concluding chapter of his brother William's *Varieties of Religious Experience*. I do not argue that Henry was a pragmatist; his famous remark that he was amazed to discover to what extent he had been a pragmatist all his life may or may not have been ironic and in any case is only secondary evidence. Nor do I argue that William's work is a source in any direct way. I argue simply that to know William's religious cast of mind—as he reveals it at the end of his survey of the variety and quality of religious feelings and experiences—is the best practical way of coming to some kind of accommodation with the moral qualities of Henry's fiction.

William's "conclusion" is a marvel of deism in the original sense of that term, as we apply it, for example, to the work of Lord Herbert of Cherbury. Like Herbert's work, William's is a wholly sympathetic attempt to find the least common denominator of all religions—not, as with Paine and Voltaire and later agnostics like Ingersoll, in order to ridicule all religions on the grounds of their essential similarity but in order to save them on that same basis. Nothing could be more amiable, more understanding, more tolerant than William's discussion of "the religious life."[28] Such life, William holds, is based on the belief that the visible world is made significant by the more spiritual world of which it is a part, that man's proper end is "union or harmonious relation" (p. 485) with that spiritual world, that communion with that world produces psychological and material effects in the visible world—"work is really done" (p. 485). Psychologically, religion gives man "zest," which "adds

[28] *The Varieties of Religious Experience* (New York, 1923), p. 485. The following several page references to this book are indicated in parentheses in the text.

itself like a gift to life" and which "takes the form either of lyrical enchantment or of appeal to earnestness and heroism" (p. 485); religion gives "an assurance of safety and a temper of peace" and, toward others, "a preponderance of loving affections" (p. 486).

Within this framework of common beliefs marked by common characteristics there is room for endless variety of individual religious acceptance. Not all men will have "identical religious elements" (p. 487); in fact, "no two of us have identical difficulties, nor should we be expected to work out identical solutions" (p. 487). Each of us has his "peculiar angle of observation" from which he perceives "a certain sphere of fact and trouble, which each must deal with in a unique manner" (p. 487). And this pluralism, or multiplicity of religious acceptances, is as it should be, because it brings about human awareness of the multiplicity of the qualities of "the divine" (p. 487). "The divine can mean no single quality, it must mean a group of qualities, by being champions of which in alternation, different men may all find worthy missions. Each attitude being a syllable in human nature's total message, it takes the whole of us to spell the meaning out completely" (p. 487). Thus, "for each man to stay in his own experience . . . and for others to tolerate him there, is surely best" (p. 488).

For William, the most important thing about these individual and perhaps unique experiences is that they are real; they are facts of consciousness. And facts of consciousness have more verifiable reality than objects as such, than things "outside" human consciousness. Such outer objects are "ideal pictures of something whose existence we do not wholly possess" (p. 499)—they share their reality with our experience of them. Thus "things in themselves" constitute no more than "a mere abstract element of experience" (p. 499); they are not "full facts" (p. 499) until they are registered on a human consciousness which has "an attitude towards the object *plus* the sense of a self to whom the attitude belongs" (p. 499). Not things, but things as felt, are what constitute reality. It is as if when an "abstract element" became registered on a human consciousness it was raised, not exactly from potency to act, but from a lower act to a higher; and this higher act, or existence, is what William calls reality. In other words, what is "subjective"—not the phenomenon but the *felt* phenomenon—is what is real. This subjective reality is, of course, susceptible of gradation, but for William the gradations do not seem important, as (let us say) the gradations of bliss in heaven do not seem important when that bliss is set against "non-bliss" or earthly life.

Now it is in human consciousness, in this reality-maker, that the religious experiences exist; it is in the human consciousness that religious experiences, like all other phenomena, are made real. It follows that all subjective religious experiences have value in the sense that they are real, for "as soon as we deal with private and personal phenomena as such, we deal with realities in the completest sense of the term" (p. 498). Thus we may say that, for William, whatever registers on human consciousness is wholly real, and what is wholly real is "good," in the sense of having significance, in the sense of *being* and having connections with other realities— for "a full fact . . . is of the *kind* to which all realities whatsoever must belong; the motor currents of the world run through the like of it; it is on the line connecting real events with real events" (p. 499).

Religious feelings, then, are real and do real work. And it is religious feelings and the conduct they lead to which form, for William, the indispensable element of the religious life. These feelings and conduct are common to all religions—"the feelings . . . and the conduct . . . are almost always the same, for Stoic, Christian, and Buddhist saints are practically indistinguishable in their lives" (p. 504). It is in the theories, the intellectual superstructures that men erect on these common feelings, that men differ. These theories William calls "additional beliefs" or "over-beliefs" (p. 504) or even "individualistic excrescences" (p. 503), and they are secondary to the essence of religious life. Dogmas, creeds, ideas, symbols "are not to be regarded as organs with an indispensable function, necessary at all times for religious life to go on" (p. 504). The "faith-state" brought about by the religious feelings "may hold a very minimum of intellectual content. . . . It may be a mere vague enthusiasm, half spiritual, half vital, a courage, and a feeling that great and wondrous things are in the air" (p. 505). When the faith-state is associated with a creed (even a creed of minimal intellectual content), then there occurs the phenomenon we call "religion," which profoundly affects the "action and endurance" (p. 506) of men. William quotes Professor Leuba:

"The truth of the matter can be put in this way: *God is not known, he is not understood; he is used*—sometimes as meat-purveyor, sometimes as moral support, sometimes as friend, sometimes as an object of love. If he proves himself useful, the religious consciousness asks no more than that. Does God really exist? How does he exist? What is he? are so many irrelevant questions. Not God, but life, more life, a larger, richer, more satisfying life is . . . the end of religion. The love of life, at any and every level of development, is the religious impulse." (pp. 506-507)

Such is William's view of what we might call operative religion, and it is at once evident that it is open to many of the same objections that Henry's work has had to bear. The "religious life," for example, is wholly subjective; we all have our own peculiar "angles of vision"; we all "use" God in our own way, according to our needs and our capacities. But most important, behind William's commentary lies a belief almost too obvious to be seen: the religious life is a way to the source of psychic power, a means of producing "work," a cause of energy which literally moves its recipients to action. As a force, and of itself, it is unknowable except in its effects; but those effects are enormously signficant in the sense that they are real phenomena—and for "real" we must read "valid." A "faith-state" is a valid phenomenon, a part of the interconnected world of other real phenomena. And if it is real, and thus valid, it requires no justification or defense; it simply is, and the only thing that one can put against it for comparison is not other real phenomena but only the nothingness of non-being. William's view is not one of cynical tolerance of all religious points of view but rather an almost exuberant glee in their infinite variety, a profoundly religious conviction that "the divine" is not exhausted in any one view, nor even perverted in any one view. What can be seen in an infinite number of ways is infinite; the sun that is capable of infinite refractions is an infinite sun. William is not a philosopher of the Negative Way but of the Positive: all views of God are true views, all angles of vision are accurate. Or more precisely, all views of God are true so far as they remain primary and largely a matter of feeling; perversion begins when one begins to add "over-beliefs" or "additional beliefs" or "individual excre-scences" to the elemental faith-state—when (by analogy) the church fathers began to erect a church on the "primitive Christianity" of the apostles. If we were trying to put a name to William's religious views, I believe we should be driven to the term I have already mentioned in connection with him—deism, but (again) deism in its original sense before it became associated with political radi-calism. Tolerant though he is of all religious "over-beliefs," Wil-liam's sympathy is clearly with "natural religion," not the religion of visible forms but the religious affections of the inner life. The very effort itself to discover the least common denominator of all formal religions must indicate a dissatisfaction with those religions. Dogma, Chesterton once remarked, is merely articulate religion. True religion, William might have replied, is really inarticulate dogma.

A moral universe in which all individual religious feelings are equally valid; a sense of the divine mind revealing itself endlessly in these peculiar religious feelings; a distrust in the hardening forms that conventional religions assume; a delight in the infinite variety of religious affections in their inchoate state—it really seems we might as easily be talking of Henry as of William. If there is one thing that is clear about Henry's protagonists it is that their moral attitudes are personal, deeply felt, and "real" in the sense of pro-ducing real work done. And Henry's interest in—even sympathy with—these peculiar attitudes is legendary. The kind of moral world that William arrived at inductively, Henry created out of his "moral consciousness"[29]—a world in which no moral act is uninteresting, or untypical, or unimportant. Henry's fiction, in fact, might well serve as a series of *exempla* for the last chapter of William's book: Henry's people all perceive "a certain sphere of fact and trouble, which each must deal with in a unique manner," and each of Henry's people stays "in his own experience." The religious cast of mind that William and Henry share simply re-jects the notion of typicality, of fidelity to a norm. A moral agent, for both brothers, is always *sui generis*, as the theologians tell us that every angel is a species. Both brothers show this profound

[29] *The Letters of Henry James*, ed. Lubbock, I, 115.

respect for singularity, for the always fascinating individual case. They have the psychologist's love of endless particularity. If the case seems aberrant, seems to deviate from the norm—as with Fleda Vetch, perhaps—that is only because all norms are provisional. In the long run it will be seen that what human nature is capable of is the only true definition of human nature—existence precedes essence, as Sartre might say; every moral attitude is "a syllable in human nature's total message." Strether's rejection is perhaps one such syllable, uttered from the depths of his being, beneath the predictable over-beliefs of churches like Mme. de Vionnet's, uttered from down deep (as Emily Dickinson said) where the meanings are.

What we miss in Henry's fiction is not morality but the "over-beliefs" that we generally associate with morality. Henry's religion, as Eliot said, is marked by an "indifference to religious dogma" but an "exceptional awareness of spiritual reality."[30] Henry's tolerance of formal religious structure is just as real as his brother's, but his true sympathies are just as obviously with the "free" religious elements that make up the individual human mind. If we see Henry's famous "rejections" in his brother's terms, then perhaps what are often thought of as their weaknesses become virtues. Fleda Vetch's hyperconscientiousness, Strether's amiable withdrawal, Catherine Sloper's prescinding from all vital life are valid precisely because they do not proceed from a fixed moral code but from unique moral beings. By contrast, those Jamesian people who remain even loosely within an orthodox moral framework seem shallow and predictable—Mme. de Vionnet, who maintains her nominal Catholic marriage; or the prince in *The Golden Bowl*; or Christina Light. The typical Jamesian protagonist is an Emersonian individual who exists in an unintellectualized faith-state that will lead him to unique moral action. He is not in touch with law but with the divine.

Creeds and schools in abeyance,
Retiring back awhile sufficed at what they are, but never forgotten,
I harbor for good or bad, I permit to speak at every hazard,
Nature without check with original energy.

[30] Matthiessen, p. 145.

Whitman's lines are an apt description of Henry's protagonists: as William described them and Henry dramatized them, they are moral originals.

III

There remains, finally, the large question of which the specific morality of James's fiction is a part. It is the ancient question of the moral possibilities of fiction itself, or of imitative art in general, the question that James posed so ironically: How can a novel, since it is a picture, be either moral or immoral? It is almost the oldest question in art, and no critic has been able to evade it successfully. Against the maligners of fiction, or drama, or epic poetry—no matter what the era—the defender of these forms has had to argue for their moral goodness, if only because the accusers have always fixed on the obvious moral harm that "stories" can do. The accusers—Plato, Gosson, the compilers of the Index Librorum Prohibitorum, any local master of revels—have always had a clear-cut case drawn from the common sense of the world. Certain depictions of life inflame the passions, present vice and depravity as attractive, and in general allow the reader to see the conventional social and moral laws as antiquated or impractical or even absurd. It follows from this (the accusers always assume) that the reader is either forced into, or strongly tempted toward, immoral or anti-social behavior, or at the least that he has endangered the foundation of his moral life. This consequence is not strictly demonstrable, of course, but it is rarely challenged. Instead, the defenders of art—Aristotle, Sidney, Coleridge—have generally asserted that art (or "great art" at least) is somehow edifying, is somehow a force for moral good. They have had to assert this because the alternative is unthinkable. For if great art is not *utile* as well as *dulce*, if it does not sweetly teach in some way or other, then great art is in the long run only a game, only a kind of superior pastime, only accidentally different from tennis or bridge. But of course it is just as difficult to show how great art enhances practical morality as it is to show that some art causes practical immorality. Neither side can really make the deductive leap from the general assumption to the particular case; the nature of the problem will allow no such happy precision.

The defenders of drama and fiction and epic poetry have always advanced the thesis that these forms "imitate" or "represent" life and that this imitation or representation needs little or no justification. The history of literary theory shows the greatest possible variety of opinion about what this imitation consists of. Aristotle is perhaps at one end of the spectrum, arguing for a kind of ritualized and stylized reproduction of life; at the other end are the advocates of absolutely literal "realism" whose stock in trade is the strongest possible illusion of reality—Farrell, O'Hara, the makers of contemporary movies; and between these extremes are innumerable positions—the varying kinds of representation to be found in Shakespeare, O'Neill, Proust, Joyce, and Albee. It is this variety of opinion that cripples the defenders of imitative art in any kind of polemical situation. They are forced to fight with blunted weapons, for they have no univocal terms. There is not one of the words or phrases ordinarily used in a discussion of the problem that is not ambiguous. Imitation, representation, mimesis, reproduction, holding the mirror up to life, illusion of reality, objective and subjective reality—even the term life—none of these lends itself to sharp practical discussion, and no one (as Chesterton said) ever went into battle shouting a distinction in terms.

But perhaps it would not darken counsel to suggest that not all the moral implications of mimesis have been sufficiently drawn out. Any argument for imitative art assumes that the imitation—whether "literal" or "ritualistic" or "symbolic"—imitates the "essence" of life, if not all the accidents, that art re-creates the qualities of life that make life what it is. It follows that if "essential life" contains any moral elements, serious imitative art will reproduce these elements. That is, if life is essentially homiletic, imitative art will also be homiletic. If life is morally bland, has no reference to morality, then imitative art will be bland and will have no reference to morality. But surely it is the essence of life that it is a texture of "real" occurrences which we all accept no matter what our philosophical or religious affiliations. A man may be a Platonist or Buddhist and not "believe" in the reality presented to his consciousness through his senses, but that does not prevent him from dying, nor does it prevent his mourning the deaths of his loved ones and friends. A man may not believe in linear or sequential time, but that does not prevent his growing old. A man may be a solipsist, but that does not prevent his being run over by a bus. A man accepts this reality existentially, as his lungs accept air, though his philosophy may explain it away. This reality of sequential time, of change and growth, of bodies occupying space, may or may not be the ultimate reality; it may even be a universal delusion; but however we think of it, even if only as a kind of tentative reality, it is the reality which is relevant to man's moral life. A man deals morally with these realities or he does not deal morally at all. He loves or lusts or hates always with time's winged chariot at his back, knowing that the object of his passion will change and eventually disappear from human perception, as his passion and even he himself will change and disappear. If he inflicts mental pain on another, or betrays another, or wishes another well, he does these things not as one disembodied consciousness to another, but as a consciousness associated with a body in a time and place to another consciousness similarly defined. It is in the context of time and place and body that we are good or evil—

> Love's mysteries in souls do grow,
> But yet the body is his book.[31]

As soon as we think of our existential self in any way abstracted from this world of common experience—as in death, or in mystical experience, or in severe psychosis, or even in dreams—we assume automatically that the self no longer exists in the moral sphere. Our union with common human experience is the "subtle knot"[32] that makes us moral man.

We may say, then, that life has relevance to morality in the profoundly significant sense that it provides the context in which we perform our moral acts; it provides the real "things as such" among which we must trace our moral paths. And it follows that if imitative art reproduces the essential quality of life, then it too provides these real things—the sense of time passing, the immanence of death, the transience of human relationships, the certainty of anguish to come. If it is true that a man must be conscious of his acts before they can be said to be either moral or immoral—if,

[31] Donne, "The Ecstacy."
[32] *Ibid.*

in Matthiessen's phrase about James's protagonists, we must be aware of moral possibilities—then we may say that imitative art performs the same function that life itself does. They both provide, not morality, but the conditions of morality; they provide the realities of which we must be aware if we are to act as moral agents. Moreover, if imitative art is a kind of "second life," or reminder of life, it may act as a corrective of, or substitute for, life so far as morality is concerned. It is often possible to ignore life, at least for a while—to act as if time does not pass and as if death were not immanent; in fact it is this state of contrived ignorance that most of us struggle to maintain. It is, of course, only a temporary state, because life, through a death or a failure, sooner or later shocks us back to the reality of things. But in the meantime, to the extent that we live a kind of vegetable existence, we can hardly be said to be moral agents at all. We live in a kind of non-moral fog; the sharp outlines of the great realities of life lose their distinction, as skyscrapers lose their form and magnitude in mist. It is at times like these, when life itself is in abeyance, that imitative art can restore true vision, can bring back the awareness of things as they are that is the condition of the moral life. With a precision that life itself has only intermittently, a scene from a novel can raise us from moral potency to moral act, can nourish our moral life with the sunlight and rain of reality, so that we become again "intense perceivers" of life, have again the heightened awareness of things as such that makes us capable of meaningful choice. If we have allowed ourselves to forget the prison that sheer physical lust places us in, and if life leaves us for a while to our fancy of lust in prospect, a scene from James brings us back. Merton Densher, after seducing Kate Croy, finds himself on the dreadful treadmill of mental repetition of the act:

The door had but to open for him to be with it again and for it to be all there; so intensely there that . . . no other act was possible to him than the renewed act, almost the hallucination, of intimacy. Wherever he looked or sat or stood, to whatever aspect he gave for the instant the advantage, it was in view as nothing of the moment, nothing begotten of time or of chance could be, or ever would; it was in view as, when the curtain has risen, the play on the stage is in view, night after night, for the fiddlers.[33]

Seeing Densher's portion of reality, we are brought back to our own; and surely this notion of imitative art as memento of reality is somehow at the bottom of every argument, classical or modern, for the edifying influence of mimesis. And perhaps James was aware of this when he made the famous comment that the "moral" sense of the work of art is wholly dependent "on the amount of felt life concerned in producing it." Fiction is no more moral than life, but no less either. The substantial connection between life and imitative art is that neither is the cause of either goodness or wickedness but that both present to man the essential condition of morality. It is a relationship ironic enough to have met with James's approval.

[33] *The Wings of the Dove*, New York Edition, II, 236-237.

A "Shade of a Special Sense":
James and the Art of Naming

Joyce Tayloe Horrell

I

IN RECENT YEARS students of Henry James's fiction have noticed many examples of suggestive naming. Scholarly comments run all the way from Dorothy Hoare's brief generalization, "James' names are always odd,"[1] to Quentin Anderson's lengthy theory that Milly Theale is an anagram of a Greek word.[2] The attention given to names arises naturally as careful readers become increasingly aware that practically everything in James is deliberate and serves some artistic purpose. What needs examining now is the length to which he carried symbolic naming and how such an unrealistic— in some writers even allegorical—device functions in his work.

James's most explicit statement on appropriate naming appears in *Partial Portraits*, where he deplores Trollope's tendency to go too far and strain credulity. "A Mr. Quiverful with fourteen children (which is the number attained in *Barchester Towers*) is too difficult to believe in. We can believe in the name and we can believe in the children; but we cannot manage the combination." However, James added that when Trollope was "content not to be too comical, his appellations were fortunate enough," and names such as Mrs. Proudie and Gatherum Castle he felt were "rather able to minister to illusion than destroy it." In the same essay James says that "Thackeray's names were perfect; they always had a meaning, and (except in his absolutely jocose productions, where they were still admirable) we can imagine, even when most figurative, that they should have been borne by real people."[3] For James, then, credibility demanded exercising some slight restraint so as to avoid complete burlesque but did not exclude even the most blatant of connota-

[1] Dorothy M. Hoare, *Some Studies in the Modern Novel* (Philadelphia, 1953), p. 30.
[2] Quentin Anderson, *The American Henry James* (New Brunswick, N.J., 1961), pp. 241ff.
[3] Henry James, *Partial Portraits* (London, 1905), pp. 117–118.

tive possibilities where the tone of the story sustained the relationship of character to name.

James's preoccupation with names appears in his *Notebooks*, where for years he hoarded any he thought likely to be useful in future fiction. But these lists are more than a reservoir; as the editors of the *Notebooks* point out, they are a clue to the associative power words had for their collector.[4] For example, Barran followed by Count (p. 127), or Server, Lender, Taker, Pounder (p. 245), or Taunt-Tant (p. 119), show how one name often suggests another because of a related meaning or, as with Millington-Mallington-Malville-Mulville, a similar sound (p. 132). Sometimes the names are really quite ordinary words which become proper names only when capitalized: Undertone, Fiddler, Chancellor, and Medley. It is also interesting that James sometimes achieved visual disguise through spelling modifications without changing the sound of the word or its evocative power, as shown in the following: Monier or Monyer (p. 119), Allaway or Alloway (p. 127), Mariner or Marriner (p. 127), Gainer or Gaynor (p. 178), Bender or Benda (p. 194).

In the stories themselves, however, because there is seldom a clear statement of the original word to which a name is related, various pronunciations and some imagination must be employed before an association emerges. Often James encourages speculation by deliberately calling attention to certain names. His signals vary and may be anything from a casual but significant mispronunciation of a name by one of the other characters to a whole set of complications that arise because a character does or does not have the right kind of name. In *Daisy Miller* the middle-class commercial background of the name Miller is emphasized in a seemingly absentminded remark by the social-conscious Mrs. Costello, who refers to Daisy's friendship with the Italian gigolo as "that young lady's—Miss Baker's, Miss Chandler's—what's her name?—Miss Miller's intrigue" (XVIII, 76).[5] In *The Reverberator*, James used suggestive mispronunciation when Miss Francie is called "Miss—what's her name?—Miss Fancy." The mistake emphasizes the contrast between

[4] F. O. Matthiessen and Kenneth Murdock, eds., *The Notebooks of Henry James* (New York, 1947), p. 7.

[5] Unless otherwise stated, all volume and page references cited in the body of the paper are to *The Novels and Tales of Henry James*, New York Edition (New York, 1907–1917).

the two Dosson sisters; Fidelia and Francie are fidelity and fancy in
the sense of caprice (XIII, 79). Mrs. Bread, in *The American*, already has a name that fits her wholesome character, but Newman,
whom she has befriended, adds, "Mrs. Cake she ought to be called.
She's very sweet" (II, 257). At other times James does no more than
assert the essential rightness of a name as in "A Landscape Painter,"
when the narrator comments, "Miss Miriam—her name is Miriam
—and it exactly fits her,"[6] or in "Mora Montravers," when the
heroine's uncle, pondering what Mora is really like, says, "She is,
one does feel, her name."[7] Even where the comments are most
ambiguous, they direct attention to the relationship between character and name.

Further evidence that James matched names to characters—and
even a glimpse of the process—appears in the preliminary notes to
The Ivory Tower. Although he does not reach a final decision about
all the people he has in mind, he does reveal why certain names
and characters are satisfying combinations. He chose Augusta
Bradham, "Gussie" Bradham, "for the big social woman." For the
hero, he considered Graham Rising with Gray Rising as a nickname, but decided "to keep [it] for another occasion," finally
landing on the more down-to-earth Gray Fielder as suitable for a
"very special young man with no tiresome 'artistic' associations."
For the friend of the hero, the name Horton "Haughty" Crimper
won out over Wenty Hench "for the small amusement of the
Haughty." Abel Gaw, the shrewd billionaire, is characterized as a
bird of prey—perched like a "ruffled hawk" with "his beak, which
had pecked so many hearts out, visibly sharper than ever" and "his
talons nervous" (XXV, 6). The harsh sound of the name fits the
imagery. Gaw's former business partner, a more estimable person,
is named Betterman. In looking for a name to use for the second
girl in the novel, who is an opportunist and a fortune hunter (very
similar to Kate Croy in *The Wings of the Dove*), James considered
Moyra Grabham an "excellent thing [that] was in *The Times* two
or three days ago; its only fault [was] a little too much meaning,"
and he wanted to keep "everything of the shade of the real."[8] He

[6] *The Complete Tales of Henry James*, ed. Leon Edel (Philadelphia and New York,
1962), I, 124.
[7] Henry James, "Mora Montravers," in *The Finer Grain* (New York, 1923), p. 64.
[8] In his *Notebooks* James occasionally refers to the *Times*. See p. 63 for a letter
indicating his practice of storing up names he finds in the newspapers.

did not use Grabham, however, as it seemed to clash with Bradham, which he wanted to keep because it had "no shade of a special sense."[9]

From these notes several concepts emerge, useful in analyzing the meaning of the names in James's fiction, the most important being that James chose names in some cases because they were amusing—Haughty; in some cases because they had meaning in terms of character—Gray Fielder, Moyra Grabham; in some cases because they had none—Bradham; and in other cases because he felt attracted to the name for no discernible reason. Consequently not all the names in his stories will have meanings and certainly some will have such private associations they will remain secret although open of course to interpretation.

One other relevant bit of information about naming is an anecdote, told by Edith Wharton, of how James's sense of humor and love of word play found expression in the creation of names. She reports how, on motor trips made over the countryside near Rye, James, bursting with good humor, made a practice of inventing stories as they drove along, sometimes suiting them to the landscape or villages passed through.

James was delighted by . . . the magic of ancient names, quaint or impressive, crabbed or melodious. These he would murmur over and over to himself in a low chant finally creating characters to fit them, and sometimes whole families, with their domestic complications and matrimonial alliances, such as the Dymmes of Dymchurch, one of whom married a Sparkle, and was the mother of Scintilla Dymme-Sparkle, subject of much mirth and many anecdotes.[10]

This is James parodying his own method, humorously matching a character to a name rather than the other way around, but clearly showing at once his love of word play and his concern that a name suggest the personality and attributes of the character.

II

From the *Notebooks*, then, and scattered remarks elsewhere, it is plain that James considered naming an important part of his writing and was aware that, in theory at least, the suggestive name could contribute meaning without destroying realism. The way he

[9] James liked the "ham" ending and used it at least sixteen times.
[10] *A Backward Glance* (New York, 1934), p. 249.

solved the problem of keeping "everything of the shade of the real" emerges more clearly from an examination of where the names come from and how they function. Though most of the names for which any significance can be found are taken from ordinary words chosen for their suggestive powers, some can be grouped together because they have a common source of meaning. For example, many names come from nature—mostly flowers and animals; others come from history and myth. By far the largest group, however, is made up of names that do not lend themselves to neat categories but run the whole gamut of James's image-making powers. Of this latter group, some, like the dependable Goodwood or the social climbing Misses Climbers in *The Portrait of a Lady*, are easy to detect; others are more subtle and can be convincingly discussed only in terms of their use within a particular story.

In drawing names from the world of nature James could expect the associations raised in the minds of the readers to be fairly uniform. For a nice, fresh, innocent but rather common variety of American girl, he chose Daisy. Like the field flower, she has grown up uncultivated but quite lovely and natural. Another young girl, Gilbert Osmond's convent-bred daughter in *The Portrait of a Lady*, is called Pansy, which carries a similar image of open-faced innocence, but also suggests a carefully nurtured plant. The distinction James makes between the two kinds of innocence—one natural and retained in spite of exposure to the evils of the world and the other a cultivated innocence produced by isolation from the world—is inherent in the names. Pansy is a hothouse plant; Daisy is a wild flower. Pansy is paired with Rosier, a nice horticultural arrangement. Daisy dies, partly at least, as all field flowers do, from exposure to the cold—but it is not just the chill air of the Colosseum that kills her; the emotional climate created by the frigid Winterbourne, whom she loves, is also to blame. Another child of nature is Mary Garland in *Roderick Hudson*, whose name links her to the foliage of the New England woods which produced her and also suggests victorious associations which James wanted for this character. Twice James used Vetch for characters who flourished, as does the little covering plant by the same name, in the most unpromising environment and circumstances.[11] In *The Princess*

[11] Oscar Cargill, *The Novels of Henry James* (New York, 1961), p. 241. Mr. Cargill points out not only the connection of name and plant but also the ugliness of the

Casamassima, Anastasius Vetch is a man who has "the nerves and sensibilities of a gentleman, yet whose fate had condemned him to play the fiddle at a second rate establishment" (V, 24). Fleda Vetch, the heroine of *The Spoils of Poynton,* is a young girl whose "sensibility was almost as great as her opportunities for comparison had been small" (X, 23).

Somewhat unflattering images are suggested by the characteristics of various animals. Mr. Feeder and Mrs. Chew in *Lady Barbarina* satirize charity and social grace, respectively. The names Mangler and Maresfield in *The Chaperon* suggest the cruelty and stupidity of some members of English society, and a woman "who had so big a house that she couldn't fill it unless she opened her doors, or her mouth, very wide," is Mrs. Bray (X, 468). A simple sound shift—*f* to *v*—reveals the meaning of the name Mrs. Fermin, a particularly "odious" guest in *The Spoils of Poynton* (X, 8). From domestic fowls, there are the flashy, strutting Pococks in *The Ambassadors* and Mrs. Gosling, a rather stupid, goose of a woman in "Longstaff's Marriage." The names of two men, Jay in *The Chaperon* and Wendhover in *A London Life,* suggest birds, and they are in love with sensitive young women who rise above conventional society, Laura Wing and Rose Tramore.

A second source of suggestive naming is history and myth. The names of several characters have already received attention from James scholars, especially names derived from discoverers. Roderick Hudson, Christopher Newman, and Prince Amerigo suggest the spirit of adventure and exploration of preceding centuries.[12] The inspiration for heroines comes from myth rather than history, and any number of eager young American girls owe their origins to James's fascination with the Artemis legend. Several of this type are linked to Diana, the chaste goddess of the hunt, by their names as well as their looks and personality. In a very early story, "Adina," the title, which is the heroine's name, is an anagram of Diana, but

sound, p. 229. For James's views on ugly sounds, see *The Question of Our Speech* (Boston, 1905).

[12] For further discussions of Roderick Hudson, see Cargill, *Novels,* p. 26; for Christopher Newman, see F. W. Dupee, *Henry James* (New York, 1956), p. 84. Prince Amerigo's name seems to have been chosen for somewhat different motives. He is an adventurer who has risked little. In marrying the American heiress, Maggie Verver, he parallels the achievement of his ancestor, that other "pushing man who followed, across the sea, in the wake of Columbus" and succeeded in giving his name to the continent (XXIII, 78).

this seems to have gone undiscovered in spite of the pointed remark, "Her pretty name of Adina seemed to me to have somehow a mystic fitness to her personality," and of the many obvious similarities between this story and the Diana-Endymion myth.[13] In another story, "Longstaff's Marriage," James used a combination of the goddess and her habitat to create the name—Diana Belfield—and related this heroine to the myth with a heavier hand than usual for him. She had "the beauty foreshadowed by her name." She had a "tall, light figure, nobly poised head, weighted with a coronal of auburn braids," and walked with a "gliding step." With her she had a big dog but, as a special concession to realism, no bow and arrow—just a closed umbrella over the shoulder. "Thus equipped, she looked wonderfully like that charming antique Goddess of the chase which we encounter in various replicas in half the museums of the world." She also has the same views as the goddess on love. She is "passionately single, fiercely virginal" and "found the idea of marriage insupportable: a fact which completes her analogy with the mystic divinity."[14] James's best-known Artemis figure is Isabel Archer in *The Portrait of a Lady* and here he tried a kind of runic sentence. His heroine is a beautiful archer, and though she is in every way a more subtle and complicated figure than the earlier ones, she has much in common with them.[15] Slim, beautiful, and chaste, her coldness to men is the despair of Goodwood and Warburton: "Something pure and proud . . . there was in her—something cold and dry an unappreciated suitor . . . might have called it." And it is not coincidence that her first appearance in the book is accompanied by the friendly bark of the Touchett dogs (III, 71).

Other mythological names are of little assistance in unlocking meaning, the parallels being very general at best. At least three times James used Aurora, once in contrast to Christina Light. He used Urania for a lady with "heavy tread," and the sweetly troublesome Pandora Day seems self-explanatory. The myth of the friendship between Hyacinth and Apollo may account for so unusual a

[13] Henry James, "Adina," in *Travelling Companions* (New York, 1919), p. 273. Quentin Anderson, in *The American Henry James*, has noted that Scrope, another character in the story, is an anagram of corpse.

[14] Henry James, "Longstaff's Marriage," in *Master Eustace* (New York, 1920), pp. 57–59.

[15] A discussion of mythical, literary, and biographical sources for Isabel Archer and of her similarities to Diana Belfield may be found in Cargill, *Novels*, pp. 83–86. See also Leon Edel, *Henry James: The Untried Years* (New York, 1953), pp. 331–332.

name as Hyacinth for the hero in *The Princess Casamassima.* The legend of St. George, the dragon slayer, embellished with Jamesian irony, gives some significance to the meaning in *The Lesson of the Master*, where a successful author, St. George, turns into something of a dragon and saves a struggling writer by marrying the girl the novice loves, thus rescuing him from the danger of matrimonial joy that would destroy his talent.

The third group of purposeful names is made up mainly of connotative words. Although the meanings of many of these I see as highly conjectural, others are so obvious that the master might well have found them objectionable in Trollope. For example: Rumble, Monarch, Deedy, Betterman, Goodenough, Bloodgood, Miss Sturdy, Chad (just one letter away from the cad he is), Lord Desmesne (whose ancestral estate capitulates to the frontal assault of Mrs. Headway), Miranda Hope, Violet Ray, Sir Digby Dence (a bureaucrat), Mrs. Bread, Miss Vane, Mrs. Brash, and the Wentworths, from whom as Richard Poirier points out all the "worth . . . has went."[16] Names of places are sometimes equally blatant: Properley, Blackport-on-Dwindle (dreary town), Dedborough, Medley, Hovel, Prestidge, Bigwood, Undertone (the quiet estate of Lord and Lady Wispers), Matcham (James used this twice and both times with mating associations), Carrara Lodge (a sculptor's house), Catchmore, and—for a tough town to get elected to Parliament from—Harsh.

Other names, though less glaringly suggestive than those listed above, can still be seen to function purposefully. James employs names in a variety of ways to add to the humor or mildly satirical tone of certain stories. Often they are a means by which he sharpens his reader's awareness of social class, profession, or nationality. The relationship between a name and social success is the basis of one entire story. In "Fordham Castle" Mrs. Abel F. Taker (Lily from Peoria) finds her inelegant name a barrier to social advancement. Miss Mattie Magaw ("so dreadful even singly, a combination not to be borne") is in a similar predicament (XVI, 411). Mrs. Taker abandons her husband and assumes a new and more pretentious name, Mrs. Sherrington Reeve, and Miss Magaw hides her mother away and begins calling herself Miss Vanderplank. This nominal transformation is sufficient to gain admission to the society of Ford-

---

[16] *The Comic Sense of Henry James* (London, 1960), p. 105.

ham Castle, Wilts, for both ladies. At the other end of the spectrum
James finds the British affectation of hyphenated names a means
ready at hand for ridiculing social pretension as shown by Mrs.
Vaughn-Vesey, Mrs. Stock-Stock, and Silberstradt-Schreckenstein,
the last of which James must have liked since it occurs in two
stories.[17] The British use of initials after their name to designate
official honors is mocked by exaggeration in A. B. C. Beadle-Moffet,
K.C.B., M.P. James also pokes fun at British pride of ancestry by
using a name such as Lord Theign of Dedborough for a man whose
chief characteristic is his stiff-necked concern with preserving tradition and maintaining the dignity of his place in British life. Similarly, Sir Arthur Desmesne of Longlands is a name that, when attached to a mama's boy who cannot defend himself in "The Siege
of London," parodies the chivalric tradition his name embodies.
And the Marquise de Bellegarde in *The American* has committed
murder to protect her married name, but she is equally proud of
her maiden one, Emmeline Atheling, which surely carries her
Anglo-Saxon origins back to the ridiculous.

James's sense of humor expresses itself at times in the naming of
certain professional people. One nurse is Mrs. Catching; the three
who bustle about the sickrooms of *The Ivory Tower* are Misses
Goodenough, Mumby, and Ruddle. The physicians in attendance
are Dr. Hatch and Dr. Root. Had James not shied away from the
example of Trollope, the former might have turned up as an obste-
trician and the latter a dentist. With an irony that borders on bad
taste, James used the name Sir Matthew Hope for the physician
in charge at the fatal illnesses of Ralph Touchett in *The Portrait of
a Lady* and Charles Carteret in *The Tragic Muse*. An active feminist
and physician in *The Bostonians* is called Mary Prance. Lawyers
also seem appropriately named: Mr. Hardman, Mr. Crick, "that
dryest of men" (XXV, 239), Barnaby Striker (half of the New
England law firm of Spooner and Striker), and the solid sounding
Stoddard and Hale.

James seems to have endowed one profession with distinction,
however, by the very unsuitability of the names. Governesses, even
those who are minor characters, are rarely left in the anonymity
their role seems to merit but are given unusual names as this list
indicates: Miss Bold or Bald (she is so insignificant no one remem-

---

[17] *Notebooks*, p. 73.

bers which it is), Mlle Bouquet, Miss Hack, Miss Merriman, Miss Steet, Miss Teagle, Miss Bogle, Moddle, Mrs. Wix, Miss Overmore, and Miss Turnover. In *A Bundle of Letters,* Lady Battledown has conquered the vagaries with which life names governesses by calling them all Johnson as soon as they enter her service. But James never resorted to so simple a solution, and he is able to add even more mystery to his most important governess of all, the haunted heroine of *The Turn of the Screw,* by giving her no name.

III

In varying degrees, a great many English novelists have shown a moral and even allegorical impulse in the choice of names, and what seems to emerge from the discussion thus far is that James is following in a tradition in prose fiction that starts with Lyly and has never completely ended. James differs only in the degree of sophistication with which he names, paying more attention to disguise than most and minimizing the moral judgments usually involved in the whole process of labeling characters. That James is no innovator is hardly surprising since it has long been recognized that his plots are mainly reworkings of such never-fail formulas as seduction with sentiment, and his characters have their origins in the villains, heroes, and poor little rich girls common to novelists of all ages. His special genius is to take materials of the ordinary novel and transform them by his advanced technique. So it is with the names; his modifications—one calling for more subtle method and the other permitting greater freedom—give a new dimension to the whole tradition of suggestive names in literature. What he is able to do is go beyond the usual typing of a character or a group and relate the names to the total meaning of his story. Out of context, many of these names seem entirely realistic, while in the total framework of the story they become part of a single impulse that binds together theme, characters, and imagery. To use James's figure, some of the stories are like an intricately woven carpet in which the names are threads necessary to complete the design beautifully, and so well blended as almost to defy separation. Insofar as such names can be explained, it is in terms of their relationship to theme or central idea, and imagery is often the best indication of their meaning.

For example in "The Death of a Lion," James condemns the

public acclaim a writer receives from those who, with no understanding of his work, use him for their own interests—the magazine editor to increase circulation and the society matrons to enhance their own culturally barren images. So it is that Neil Paraday is pushed into prominence by a series of articles on his personal life and, as a result, becomes the chief exhibit in the "Universal Menagerie" of a rich brewer's wife (XV, 123). That such prominence is essentially phony—a show—is borne out by the imagery of the circus which suggests one meaning of the lion in the title, but reduces its jungle grandeur to captive entertainment. Other imagery plays upon the royal associations of the lion and mocks the idea of a literary king. Paraday is a "prime attraction," a "king of the beasts" in a millennium-like menagerie where "the animals rub shoulders freely with the spectators and the lions sit down for whole evenings with the lambs" (XV, 122, 123). He was made "royal" when the *Empire* "fired, as if on the birth of a prince, a salute of a whole column." He is proclaimed, and anointed, and crowned, "and while the guns of publicity boom, he is raised to the throne" (XV, 110). The passage parodies the ceremony, and what the imagery suggests—the sham, the noise, the brevity and capriciousness of such honors—the names reinforce. In this phony world, nothing is what it seems. A big baldheaded writer with red mustaches calls himself Dora Forbes, so his novel *The Other Way Round* (a title which reflects his own switched sex) will titillate the public more since they will think a woman wrote the naughty passages. A young woman writer, Miss Collop, calls herself Guy Walsingham and advocates what is euphemistically called "the larger latitude" in her novel *Obsessions*. Their literary fraud is indicated by their false names.[18] A portrait painter is Mr. Rumble who in "one roaring year" not only painted the novelists above but also Mrs. Bounder, who figured in a juicy divorce case, and Miss Braby, an actress who had an "incident" in America (XV, 135). The fame of these people is created by enterprising editors such as Mr. Pinhorn, whose name combines the smallness of his mind with the loudness of his editorial mouth. The intimate, personal articles are written by Mr. Morrow, named for his concern for the next deadline. The love of novelty, which motivates the society lady who takes

[18] This seems to hold true for all of James's novelists. The good ones write under their own names.

up celebrities, is suggested by her name, Mrs. Weeks Wimbush—each artist is a week's whim. The houses of the promoters are named, with typical nouveau riche swagger, Bigwood and Prestidge.[19] Neil Paraday becomes a paragon for a day to whom these people kneel in a ceremony that parodies genuine acclaim. But the name Neil takes on a meaning beyond the mockery of ceremony through a set of religious images deriving from the genuine worship of the narrator for his literary idol. An adoration inspired by Paraday's genius is indicated by references to "sacrifice and communion," "altar and temple," "acts of homage," and "feats of submission" (XV, 134, 131). These glorify the writer of the "mystic scroll" and make the kneeling a real ceremony—an act of devotion to a great writer, not a curiosity (XV, 149). Ironically, the most harmless person in the story has the most "ominous name"; she is a fellow worshiper, Miss Fanny Hurter (XV, 133). This ability in James to strain language and image to their limit and thereby create meaning and enlarge symbols is typical of his genius. F. W. Dupee points out that James is

a kind of visionary of the small fact, [who] compels a maximum of meaning from a minimum of evidence. In a James novel, the style, the dialogue, the imagery, the symbolism, the various narrative devices, all constitute the high pressure under which . . . the minutiae of life and sensibility are transformed into great witnesses.[20]

James wastes nothing, as the names testify.

The same unity is to be found with more playful effect in many of the social comedies, such as "Lady Barbarina," where horses and ancestry seem to be the touchstone. Indeed the two are most amusingly mingled, it being impossible, occasionally, to decide whether a statement such as "There is a thorough-bred" refers to horse or human (XIV, 6). The story exaggerates the notion that the superiority of the English gentry is the result of the same kind of careful breeding practices that produced their fine horses. James makes the names part of the exaggeration. The father of the heroine is Lord Canterville; the family estate is Pasterns. Lady Barb—as

[19] R. P. Blackmur writes of this name, "Paraday is seduced into going to a house party at Mrs. Wimbush's country place which is called Prestidge—a surface quality obtained, if you remember your etymology, by sleight of hand" ("The Country of the Blue," in *The Question of Henry James*, ed. F. W. Dupee, New York, 1945, p. 206).

[20] *The Question of Henry James*, p. x.

Barbarina is usually called—has a name that lends itself to multiple interpretation. Obviously it is a rather un-English appellation, and no reason for its being so is given. Since a "barb" is a "horse native to the stock of Barbary," her name supports the parallel with horses that James is intent upon. To her American suitor, Dr. Jackson Lemon, purity of breeding is what makes her so desirable. She has genetic possibilities for improving the stock of his ordinary family. In addition, there is a fleeting suggestion of barb as a kind of thorn in this otherwise beautiful flower. Her second name, Clement, suggests the apparent mildness of the creature as long as she is given free rein, but her suitor scarcely noticed "there was a certain superior dumbness in her eyes" (XIV, 74). Both the animal and the floral interpretations are supported by the imagery Dr. Lemon uses when he discovers too late that "if she should plant herself, no power on earth would move her; and her blooming, antique beauty, and the general loftiness of her breeding came fast to seem to him but the magnificent expression of a dense, patient, ponderous power to resist" (XIV, 137). What he had thought was nobility, deeply ingrained in this thoroughbred, turned out to be stubbornness. He might as well have mated with a Missouri mule. There is also the possibility that James, because he is comparing "civilized" Britons with "barbarian" Americans, felt the sense generated by the name in this direction also, and one reference to American barbarism supports the supposition that this meaning was not lost on him. Worth noting is the fact that the name is a near-anagram of Arabian. There is even a possibility that James's change in the spelling (from Barberina to Barbarina) for the New York Edition was the result of a belated discovery of the anagram possibility.[21]

Other names in the story are Dr. Feeder, "whose name expressed not inaptly his numerous acts of charity," and Mrs. Chew. Both names smack of the animal imagery that dominates the story. Two other names, both suggestive of the characters so labeled, are Herman Longstraw—a long-legged cowboy—and Jackson Lemon, the American whose experience in British breeding circles leaves him somewhat soured and also financially well squeezed.

[21] Another noticeable change in the revisions James made for the New York Edition was to substitute the nickname "Barb" for the full name in his earlier version, emphasizing thereby her irritating qualities. See Herbert Ruhm, *Lady Barberina and Other Tales with Variants* (New York, 1961).

IV

It may be something of a shock to admirers of James's artistry to see characters reduced to whatever meaning can be found in a word or two. Anagrams, runic sentences, and misspelled words seem superficial for James and inconsistent with the high literary purpose he espoused. By using flowers, myths, history, and connotative words, James reversed the process described by Ernst Pulgram by which "proper names become nouns" through their "connotative potential."[22] In James the word (not always a noun) was incorporated into a name so that a rich man became Cashmore, a gentleman who longed for the past became Longdon, or a lady who retreats from reality, substituting something "nice"—romanticism—for something "bad"—a philandering husband—is Euphemia. The man who comes to rescue her is Bernard, and if he wore a keg of brandy around his neck, he couldn't be more obvious! However, in spite of the rather appalling facetiousness of an occasional name, James did not just create a character to fit a label. He found or invented a name to fit a character being created in his imagination, and although the names may suggest a stereotyped figure, certainly James did not stop when he had fulfilled the intention expressed in a name. Instead of limiting the character, the name often suggests possibilities for extension of meaning. Whether or not the technique stimulated a proper response to the universal often indicated by the name can only be answered for one story at a time, but James justified his method when he wrote, "I saw clumsy Life again at her stupid work." He was thinking of a real life anecdote that could have significance but needed Art to shape it (X, vii). Life might be so prodigal as to name a beautiful and innocent young girl searching for life's experiences Jane Jones, but the artist should not. All of these qualities and more could be suggested by naming such a girl out of a myth. For the sensitive reader, the name would not limit but expand meaning; for the casual reader James had no great concern.

V

It is also possible to see changes in James's own interests and style reflected in the names. In the early social criticisms of Americans and Europeans, there was little need to be concerned about

[22] *Theory of Names* (Berkeley, Calif., 1954), p. 20.

obviousness. The people are very nearly caricatures and are made so by highlighting their external characteristics, for which no better tool exists than the image-making name. The openly aggressive Mrs. Headway belonged to a concept of the world that was enlivened by external and overt peculiarities which James emphasized and exaggerated for "the amusement of the thing." The transition from satire to idealization is not difficult to make stylistically if one remembers that both depend upon emphasis. Daisy and Isabel and Christopher were idealizations of a type, at least partly recognizable, and therefore characterizable, by external means.

But gradually, after 1885, changes in attitudes and values, in degree if not in kind, took shape. The simple dichotomy of innocence versus worldliness, based on national origins, gave way to a highly complicated view of the social scene, and the moral problems of the protagonists are apt to be far less idealistic and much more sordid than before. The waters in which the heroines of this period sail are often muddied by poverty and divided loyalties to loved ones whose conflicting demands do not allow of any easy solution. Even the young women themselves are different. More often English than American and perceptive beyond their years, they see moral gradations that could never have occurred to the simple heroines of earlier novels. Instead of being ignorant of what the world is like, they are aware of all the subtle forces at work to influence their decisions, and the price of retaining personal integrity is often alienation and renunciation. Such a heroine is Fleda Vetch in *The Spoils of Poynton*. F. W. Dupee points out that she "embodies . . . 'the moral sense' and the fate of the moral sense in a corrupt or obtuse world [which] is the common subject" of several novels where the heroines are "rendered angular, charmless and unbeautiful . . . by being made unwanted children or solitary governesses or impoverished dependents. Even their names—Vetch or Wix— are apt to be grotesquely homely."[23] Oscar Cargill employs the ugliness of Fleda Vetch's name to support his contention that she "was not meant to represent perfection in taste." No character whose aesthetic principles were of any significance could be so unattractively named.[24]

It is equally possible that her name is, like Isabel Archer's, a

[23] *Henry James* (2nd ed.; New York, 1956), p. 162.
[24] *Novels*, p. 229.

kind of runic sentence. Especially when considered in conjunction with the images of flight and escape which occur in the novel, it could mean she fled the tentacles of material temptation and moral corruption which, like the vine her last name is, would have entangled her.[25] However, unlike Isabel Archer, this name does not conjure up a picture—no portrait of a virgin goddess here—but rather suggests the character's moral dilemma. James does not let us see what Fleda Vetch looks like, but we grasp something of her feeling of being trapped by the ugliness of life and her own situation. It is a name which reflects the greater ambiguity, both in meaning and style, so typical of James in this period and shows his increasing interest in exploring the inner life.[26]

Although James always wrote glowingly of point of view, the *Notebooks* and prefaces record an almost ecstatic joy during the 1890's in challenging his own powers by deliberately choosing a limited center of consciousness. In abdicating the role of omniscient author, James ran the risk, albeit willingly, of ambiguity, even obscurity. In some cases, the names may be a clue to his intention if not his result. *What Maisie Knew* is a novel in which the boundaries imposed by the point of view were particularly narrow. Without too noticeably violating the child's consciousness on which the events are registered, James tried to show the effect of adults, most of whom are more or less depraved, on Maisie's gradually developing moral attitudes. However, one of the real questions the book leaves unanswered is what did Maisie know. Mrs. Wix, who has seen all that Maisie has seen, is afraid to think about it, and Maisie herself cannot, at her age, put it into words. Actually, James probably left the reader hanging as to the exact state of Maisie's moral sense on purpose, but the names in the novel do indicate what he intended each character to contribute to its development.

The family name of Farange suggests the extent, literal and figurative, to which both parents go to avoid responsibility. They

[25] In the preface to this novel, James explains his interest in what might seem an insignificant girl by saying that, for him, a kind of "treasure is stored safe from the moment . . . so fine an interpretation and criticism as that of Fleda Vetch . . . is applied . . . to the surrounding tangle" (X, xiv). For a discussion of the flight imagery, see Alan H. Roper, "The Moral and Metaphysical Meaning of *The Spoils of Poynton*," *American Literature*, XXXII (May, 1960), 182–196.

[26] Names of secondary characters do not necessarily show any change in function. For example, the uncomplicated female who pursues the hero with single-minded persistence is called—unambiguously enough—Mona.

range from Africa to America before the novel ends and have
already left their morality by the wayside before the story opens.[27]
The immoral governess who marries Maisie's father and later becomes the mistress of her stepfather is Miss Overmore, both halves
of her name suggesting her excesses in love. Maisie's recognition that
Miss Overmore is too much comes out late in the novel when Mrs.
Wix, who has always disliked the other governess, appears to have a
change of heart and speaks favorably of her. Maisie assumes, with
her child's logic, that Miss Overmore has been making love to Mrs.
Wix. After all, this was how Miss Overmore won over Maisie's
father and stepfather.

For Mrs. Wix, who tries so desperately to instill a sense of
morality into her little charge, James probably had in mind wicks,
the alteration in spelling providing a visual disguise without changing pronunciaton. Wix, with its suggestion of the homey kerosene
lamp, is perfect for this lady. She sees life through her "straight-
eners," as she calls her glasses, and provides whatever moral illumination she can. Although at their first meeting Maisie notices the
drabness of the lady, there "were things that in a few days' talk
with Mrs. Wix quite lighted up" (XI, 23). Sir Claude clouds the
whole moral horizon by being, in spite of his wandering eye and
inability to hold out against Miss Overmore, genuinely fond of the
little girl. Besides, he is irresistible to women. Even Mrs. Wix
comes close to surrendering to his masculine charm and attentive-
ness, and when Maisie is with him, she goes about "as sightlessly as
if he had been leading her blindfold" (XI, 342). Only at the very
end of the book does Maisie, after an unsuccessful attempt to save
him from his own frailty, appear to have removed the blindfold.

To the child who wends her small way through a labyrinth of
complicated and bewildering adult relationships, James gave a name
that suggests by its sound some of the wonder and amazement the
child feels. At the same time, it is, metaphorically, her situation.
She is in a maze. That she emerges from its bewildering passages is
due largely to the illumination of Mrs. Wix, who never quite goes
out, morally speaking. It would seem James does not entirely en-
dorse any of these characters and calls attention to their faults

---

[27] Oscar Cargill points out that they are nearly always coming and going in fast-
moving vehicles, symbolic of their effort to get away (*Novels*, p. 258). Originally, James
considered Hurter for the family name, but rejected it later, perhaps because it was too
obvious (*Notebooks*, p. 134).

through their names. The Faranges are escapists, Miss Overmore is immoderate, and Sir Claude, lovable as he is, is morally hazy. Only Mrs. Wix has a name that suggests the power to shed light, and even that is rather narrowly defined. Had James thought her capable of real brilliance, he would have named her Mrs. Chandelier.[28]

The question why Henry James used symbolic and suggestive names so extensively does not lend itself to an easy answer, partly because their function does not always seem to be the same. Frequently they are no more than an expression of humorous word play and are bestowed on such minor characters as to seem hardly worth the effort. At other times, however, the names are so closely related to theme and imagery that all three seem to rise from the same impulse. Whatever the reasons, it is clear that such names occur in nearly all of his novels and stories, and they undergo modifications to suit his own changing interests and attitudes. The names are one of the ways James used Art to improve "clumsy Life."

[28] Mrs. Wix's dead daughter, whose grave she and Maisie visit, was named Clara.

Marriage and the New Woman in *The Portrait of a Lady*

Annette Niemtzow

T HE QUESTIONS OF MARRIAGE, his father's questions, were urgent within the domestic circle in which the novelist Henry James was raised. If *The Portrait of a Lady* mocks the transcendental innocence in which his father revelled,[1] still, the overall pattern of the book, in which Isabel Archer chooses to return to her dismal marriage, reflects ideas about the relationship between husband and wife, akin to those which Henry James, Sr. espoused. The most concise presentation of the father's views appeared first in a series of debates, which began in 1852 in the New York *Tribune,* between himself, Horace Greeley, and the inveterate reformer, Stephen Pearl Andrews; and then appeared again in a series of papers on marriage which were published in the *Atlantic Monthly* in 1870.[2]

In the second *Atlantic* article, entitled "Is Marriage Holy?" the elder James posits a hypothetical situation (the reverse occurs in *The Portrait*) in which a wife has offended her marriage vows. What is the husband to do? His answer comes fast: "Pray tell me then, my reader, what business it is of yours and mine, that any man's wife in the community, or any woman's husband, has either veritably or conjecturally committed adultery, and should be legally convicted or legally absolved of that unrighteousness. What social right has any man or woman to thrust the evidence of a transaction so essentially private, personal, and irremediable up to the light of day?"[3] Or, as he states the case more dramatically: "Thus, to keep to the case supposed, when the civil magistrate says to me, 'Your wife has violated the conjugal bond, and so exposed herself to

---

[1] See, for example, Donald Stone, *Novelists in a Changing World* (Cambridge, Mass., 1972), pp. 219–220.

[2] The works referred to are Stephen Pearl Andrews, Horace Greeley, and Henry James, Sr., *Love, Marriage, and Divorce, and the Sovereignty of the Individual* (Boston, 1883) and Henry James, Sr., "The Woman Thou Gavest With Me," *Atlantic Monthly,* XXV (Jan., 1870), 66–72; "Is Marriage Holy?" *Atlantic Monthly,* XXV (March, 1870); and "The Logic of Marriage and Murder," *Atlantic Monthly,* XXV (June, 1870).

[3] Henry James, Sr., "Is Marriage Holy?" p. 366.

condign punishment at my hands,' I shut my ears to his invitation. I dare not listen to its solicitations. The awful voice of God within me forbids me to do so, compels me rather to say to him, 'Get thee behind me, Satan!' "[4] We, as readers, stand puzzled. Was this famous iconoclast inveighing vigorously against divorce?

Not that Henry James, Sr. was opposed to divorce as theory. In his well-known exchange with Greeley and Andrews, he had pleaded effectively to the contrary: "I have invariably aimed to advance the honor of marriage by seeking to free it from certain purely arbitrary and conventional obstructions in reference to divorce. For example, I have always argued against Mr. Greeley that it was not essential to the honor of marriage that two persons should be compelled to live together, when they held the reciprocal relation of dog and cat, and that in the state of things divorce might profitably intervene, provided the parties guaranteed the State against the charge of their offspring."[5] And yet, Andrews himself offered the most precise, if harsh, judgment when he declared James was "of the class of purely ideal reformers,"[6] one of a "good many persons transcendentally inclined, . . . whose views of prospective human improvement take no broader and more practical shape than that of *spiritualizing* whatsoever things, however stupid, which happen now to exist among us."[7]

James favored divorce, in the end, for the same reasons he favored the elimination of all legalism. The abolishment of contracts was supposed to effect a recognition of the original spiritual state inherent in marriage, but too often obscured by its laws. Marriage laws were, for him, like many social laws, concrete articulations of human instincts. To change them would bring about only spiritual improvement, not practical change (James, of course, would never have acknowledged the distinction). Convinced as he was that "constancy would speedily avouch itself as the *law* of the conjugal relations, in absence of all legislation to enforce it,"[8] he never

---

[4] Ibid., p. 362.

[5] Henry James, Sr.'s letter "To the Editor of the New York *Observer*, printed in the New York *Tribune* on November 13, 1852, included in the Andrews, Greeley, and James volume, *Love, Marriage, and Divorce, and the Sovereignty of the Individual*, p. 24.

[6] Ibid., p. 10.

[7] Ibid., p. 74.

[8] Ibid.

suspected that a man or woman might choose divorce, given it as an option.

And so, when faced with a specific case of domestic discord or adultery, as in his imagined case or in the Beecher-Tilton scandal,[9] James responded with a brisk "Get thee behind me, Satan!" Divorce remained, to his thinking, only a private, ethical dilemma. As he stated the question for his couple in "Is Marriage Holy?": "my sole debate with myself is, whether I shall make my private grief a matter of public concern, and so condemn my wife to open and notorious shame."[10] His solution was clear. He dreaded that divorce too be reduced to sets of laws, rather than be treated as an individual moral problem: "I cannot imagine, for example, that any man or woman whose own bosom is the abode of chaste love could ever be tempted by any selfish reward to fasten a stigma of unchastity upon anybody else."[11]

His then was a complex position on divorce, surrounded more by metaphysics than by mores, for always, the elder James proved more a Swedenborgian than a Fourierist, more a spiritual theologian than a social reformer. For him, marriage remained part of a universal allegory, as he demanded ample spirituality of even its conventional form: "For I cannot help regarding the marriage of man and woman as a crude earthly type or symbol of a profounder marriage which, in invisible depths of being, is taking place between the public and private life of man, or the sphere of his natural instinct and that of his spiritual culture. . . ."[12] Within such an infinitely entangled view of marriage and personal morality, it is no wonder that the senior James decreed marriage, once undertaken, a private, not public, concern. Although he had theorized that divorce might be an attractive means to end marital laws in his early discussions,

[9] James alluded directly to the scandal between the famous minister Henry Ward Beecher and Elizabeth Richards Tilton in the December, 1872, letter which he wrote to one "H.Y.R." "H.Y.R." obliged by writing to Andrews and sending James's letter; Andrews printed both letters in *Woodhull & Claflin's Weekly*, the same publication which had announced Beecher's sexual promiscuity with his parishioner. These later papers are included in the 1883 edition of *Love, Marriage, and Divorce, and the Sovereignty of the Individual*. While the *Atlantic* papers appear a bit too early to connect themselves directly to the published scandal, the Beecher-Tilton affair was hearsay in New York prior to Mrs. Tilton's disclosure (July, 1870) to her husband of her adultery. It may be that "Is Marriage Holy?" anticipates the public notice of the affair.

[10] Henry James, Sr., "Is Marriage Holy?" p. 362.

[11] Ibid., p. 366.

[12] Henry James, Sr., "The Woman Thou Gavest with Me," p. 71.

he recognized that divorce created another nexus of legal complications. As such, it appeared to him as a reckless surrender of personal
commitments. This he reluctantly suggested when dealing with a
particular case in his later *Atlantic Monthly* essay.

Although it was written ten years after the father's work, the
younger James's novel remains curiously sensitive to the position his
father expounded on the question of the ethical status of divorce.
In a letter to William James, March 8, 1870, James himself had
commented favorably on the elder James's testament to the horror
of legalistic divorce and the inviolability of the institution of marriage. "Among the things I have recently read is Father's Marriage
paper in the Atlantic—with great enjoyment of its manner and
approval of its matter."[13] It is this same approval that seems to guide
the last hundred pages of his novel, in which the narrator's approval
of Isabel's decisions echoes the father's position.

As we recall, after her fatal glimpse of Madame Merle and
Osmond together, Isabel's moral earnestness forces her still to re-
consider her visits to Ralph Touchett, her beloved cousin, because
of her husband's opposition:

I have already had reason to say that Isabel knew her husband to be dis-
pleased by the continuance of Ralph's visit to Rome. That knowledge
was very present to her as she went to her cousin's hotel the day after she
had invited Lord Warburton to give a tangible proof of his sincerity;
and at this moment, as at others, she had a sufficient perception of the
sources of Osmond's opposition. He wished her to have no freedom of
mind, and he knew perfectly well that Ralph was an apostle of freedom.
It was just because he was this, that it was a refreshment to go and see
him. It will be perceived that she partook of this refreshment in spite of
her husband's aversion to it, that is, partook of it, as she flattered herself,
discreetly. She had not as yet undertaken to act in direct opposition to
his wishes; he was her appointed and inscribed master; she gazed at
moments with a sort of incredulous blankness at this fact. It weighed upon
her imagination, however; constantly present to her mind were all the
traditional decencies and sanctities of marriage. The idea of violating them
filled her with shame as well as with dread, for on giving herself away
she had lost sight of this contingency in the perfect belief that her husband's intentions were as generous as her own. She seemed to see, nonetheless, the rapid approach of the day when she would have to take back

[13] Percy Lubbock, ed., *Henry James, Letters* (New York, 1955), I, 27.

something she had solemnly bestown. Such a ceremony would be odious and monstrous; she tried to shut her eyes to it meanwhile. Osmond would do nothing to help it by beginning first; he would put that burden on her to the end.[14]

Isabel is thinking of disobedience or divorce—we cannot be sure which, though either would be morally culpable—and before her rise "the decencies and sanctities of marriage." "Shame" and "dread" overwhelm her; and while she wants to shut her eyes, she is forced to face the ethical questions of marriage. The woman who once flaunted, "I don't want to begin life by marrying. There are other things a woman can do," is transformed into the custodian of domestic organization. Despite her unconventional visits to Ralph, her path to renunciation is straight.

While Isabel never forsakes her belief in freedom, she surrenders it to an ethic understandable only to a world that appreciated and bowed to the elder James's work:

"Yes, I'm wretched," she said very mildly. She hated to hear herself say it, she tried to say it as judicially as possible.

"What does he do to you?" Henrietta asked, frowning as if she were inquiring into the operations of a quack doctor.

"He does nothing. But he doesn't like me."

"He's very hard to please!" cried Miss Stackpole. "Why don't you leave him?"

"I can't change that way," Isabel said. (p. 449)

Although Henrietta Stackpole, James's spectre of the new woman, sees divorce as a possibility, Isabel differs from her friend, who is public, while she, Isabel remains essentially private:

"I don't know whether I'm too proud. But I can't publish my mistake. I don't think that's decent. I'd much rather die."

"You won't think so always," said Henrietta.

"I don't know what great unhappiness might bring me to; but it seems to me I shall always be ashamed. One must accept one's deeds. I married him before all the world; I was perfectly free; it was impossible to do anything more deliberate. One can't change that way," Isabel repeated.

"You have changed, in spite of the impossibility. I hope you don't mean to say you like him."

[14] Henry James, *The Portrait of a Lady*, ed. R. P. Blackmur (New York, 1961), p. 256. Hereafter all references to *The Portrait* will cite this edition and will appear in the text.

Isabel debated. "No, I don't like him. I can tell you, because I'm weary of my secret. But that's enough; I can't announce it to the rooftops." (p. 449)

It is her sense of privacy that forces her to reject divorce as a possibility. Because she passionately believes in her freedom to choose, she also believes, as the elder James did, that she alone is accountable for her choices. Her final acceptance of her oppressive condition is predicated on her sense that a woman accepts public responsibilities to the marriage institution itself when she becomes a wife. As she says to Henrietta and again to Ralph, her creed is simple: "If I were afraid of my husband that would be simply my duty. That's what women are expected to be" (p. 463). If the tone James gives her is understandably bitter, ironic about the female condition, he unceasingly pushes her into an eternal pit in the name of salvation and blesses her with the title lady, in reward for her moral sacrifice. In a way acceptable to his father and coincidentally to American society at large, James creates a character too moral to flee what is abhorrent and smothering.

In American society of the 1870's, no woman could blithely walk out the door of her marriage, despite Henrietta's invitation to do so. As Matthiessen reminded us, "Our age no longer feels as he—and she—did about the strictness of the marriage vow."[15] But they did, and *The Portrait of a Lady* is a book largely about the seriousness of this vow. Isabel makes this clear time and time again: "What he thought of her she knew, what he was capable of saying to her she had felt; that they were married, for all that, and marriage meant that a woman should cleave to the man with whom, uttering tremendous vows, she had stood at the altar. She sank down on her sofa at last and buried her head in a pile of pillows" (p. 496).

As Isabel buries her head, James plays a wonderful literary trick on her. He places before her—magically—the Countess Gemini, whose name suggests her false position. The Countess's person is transformed into an apparition of Isabel's own fears about what she herself may become. What James has done is to unite objective physical reality with Isabel's psychological state, as Isabel becomes aware of her sister-in-law's presence: "When she raised her head again the Countess Gemini hovered before her" (p. 496). The

[15] F. O. Matthiessen, *Henry James: The Major Phase* (New York, 1947), p. 182.

word "hovered," added by James in his focused revision, captures the dream level on which the Countess's appearance affects Isabel. She arrives as a physical being, but presides as a spirit conjured up by Isabel's mind: a concrete representation of Isabel's fear of being an adultress. Like her predecessor, Hester Prynne, Isabel, burdened with strong moral sensibilities, is capable of placing the visibilia of adultery on her own chest, if society is too corrupt or derelict to punish her. She is, as the Countess retorts, "a woman with such a beastly pure mind" (p. 497); this fact not only blinds her to the affair which had existed between Osmond and Madame Merle, but also cuts her off from fleeing the cloistered fortress in which Osmond holds her.

To take this argument one step further is to realize that the charge often levelled at James's heroine, that she suffers from a near psychotic fear of sexuality, is hopelessly misplaced. One critic, William Bysshe Stein, for instance, denounces Isabel as a "fleshless robot, a contemptuous prig who flaunts her impotent femininity in the guise of innocence." He finds her "oblivious to the force of nature, the vis inertiae with which the female had long controlled the world. Instead, like the men, she was obsessed with the abstractions of independence and freedom."[16] To him, Isabel's repression is proof of her sickness. But Stein is suffering from historical parochialism as well as from an odd, if not untypical, fantasy about women's sexuality. To Henry James (who was not, after all, Henry Adams), Isabel was a delightful, albeit difficult, rebel. *The Portrait of a Lady* is not "James's treatment of the stagnant emotions of the Victorian female";[17] rather, it is a study of how a woman is to behave if she is to be a "lady." While the novel begins as a study of a single woman, searching for options other than marriage, who must control her sexuality because it could shatter her and society's notion of what is "decent," it ends as a study of the same woman, now married, who continues to control her sexuality because it threatens her respectability, morality, and marriage. When Isabel asserts, "I don't want to begin life by marrying," she is adventurous, not frigid.

For instance, what of Isabel and Caspar Goodwood? Isabel, as we

[16] William Bysshe Stein, *"The Portrait of a Lady:* Vis Inertiae," *Western Humanities Review,* XIII (Spring, 1959), 177.

[17] Ibid., p. 181.

see her, is both fearful of and attracted to him. Her encounters with him are always anxious because she is aware of his insistent physical presence. To Isabel, "He was the finest young man she had ever seen, was indeed quite a splendid young man; he had inspired her with a sentiment of high, of rare respect. She had never felt equally moved to it by any other person" (p. 41). But more, for her: "He was tall, strong and somewhat stiff; he was also lean and brown. He was not romantically; he was much rather obscurely, handsome; but his physiognomy had an air of requesting your attention, which was rewarded according to the charm you found in blue eyes of remarkable fixedness, the eyes of a complexion other than his own, and a jaw of somewhat angular mould which is supposed to bespeak resolution" (p. 41). Isabel even defends Caspar's physical appearance against the attack of his ally, Henrietta Stackpole:

"He's dying for a little encouragement. I see his face now, and his earnest absorbed look while I talked. I never saw an ugly man look so handsome."

"He's very simple-minded," said Isabel, "and he's not so ugly."
(pp. 97–98)

The only complaint Isabel offers against Caspar's appearance is that his chin, suggestive of his sexuality, protrudes *too* aggressively, but she is clearly not unaware of his appeal: "She wished him no ounce less of his manhood, but she sometimes thought he would be rather nicer if he looked, for instance, a little differently. His jaw was too strong and set and his figure too straight and stiff" (p. 114). From the opening of *The Portrait,* Isabel complains that the main trouble with Goodwood's attractiveness is that the option it offers, marriage, would end all her hopes for experiment. Again and again, she asserts what she wants; we have no reason to doubt her. Of marriage she says, "There are other things a woman can do" (p. 144); and she offers praise to Henrietta for carving a trail for her weaker sisters: "Henrietta, for Isabel, was chiefly a proof that a woman might suffice for herself and be happy" (p. 56). Yet Isabel is not Henrietta, who functions efficiently, undauntedly as a woman of a new type. (When Ralph Touchett tries to push Isabel into that mould, she answers him curtly, "Women are not like men," p. 144.) And yet she is not the traditional woman either. Isabel Archer

seeks a life of her own; ultimately she finds that her own requisite is
that it not be shocking.

It is in her interview with Goodwood in her hotel room that
Isabel's image of herself as a woman open to all possibilities starts
to waver because of the challenge he presents. For him, Isabel has
only one definition; she is to be his wife. Threatened, she feels
compelled to assert her right to independence in a confrontation
with a man who appears to her "naturally plated and steeled, armed
essentially for aggression" (p. 148). Still, he presses her, until
despite herself, she must admit that she was thinking of him when
she refused Warburton:

> "You do me very little justice—after my telling you what I told you
> just now. I'm sorry I told you—since it matters so little to you."
> "Ah," cried the young man, "if you were thinking of me when you
> did it." And then he paused with the fear that she might contradict so
> happy a thought. (p. 152)

Not only does Isabel not contradict him; she admits that he is right,
"I was thinking of you a little." She refuses him, of course, but
her explanation is crucial: "I don't wish to be a mere sheep in
the flock; I wish to choose my own fate and know something of
human affairs beyond what other people think it compatible with
propriety to tell me" (p. 154). Isabel explains that she seeks possibilities in life that Goodwood would end; and yet, she leaves the
door open to the future, because she is attracted to him: "They
stood so for a moment, looking at each other, united by a hand-clasp
which was not merely passive on her side" (p. 155; italics mine).

Is there any wonder that Isabel breaks down, trembling, at the
end of the interview? Determined to be independent, yet aware
of her own sexuality, Isabel gets a frightening vision—an unveiling
of herself as a "loose woman":

> She had laid her hand on the knob of the door that led into her room,
> and she waited a moment to see whether her visitor would not take his
> departure. But he appeared unable to move; there was an immense un-
> willingness in his attitude and a sore remonstrance in his eyes. "I must
> leave you now," said Isabel and she opened the door and passed into the
> other room.
> This apartment was dark, but the darkness was tempered by a vague
> radiance sent up through the window from the court of the hotel, and

Isabel could make out the masses of the furniture, the dim shining of the mirror and the looming of the big four posted bed. (p. 155)

The darkness here is suggestive of the darkness that Goodwood threatens her with again, in their final meeting; and like the Countess Gemini, who will "hover" before Isabel later as a menacing reminder of adultery, the bed "looms" at her with frightening force. Questions of morality and sexuality are so intertwined in Isabel's mind that her response is never mild. Because she feels her sexuality so strongly, she feels in danger of falling.

Isabel's imagination can, in fact, turn beds into menacing creatures and sisters-in-law into warnings. She possesses an almost obscene— certainly no frigid—imagination, filled with disturbing sexual fantasies. She recalls a day-dream about "drifting": " 'A swift carriage, on a dark night, rattling with four horses over roads that one can't see—that's my idea of happiness' " (p. 158). This "idea of happiness" has its source in French pornographic novels, as Henrietta is only too quick to grasp: " 'Mr. Goodwood certainly didn't teach you to say such things as that—like the heroine of an immoral novel' " (p. 158). And Isabel manages to flee the possibility that she will become such a heroine, as James avoids making his novel "immoral" —in the end.

Isabel Archer marries Osmond because she finds no options other than marriage. With him, she is not made to feel so passionately those emotions which cripple her, which force her to remember her anatomy more than her mind. Unlike Henrietta, soon to be queen of American journalism, Isabel was drifting aimlessly, without a vocation. Osmond and his daughter Pansy give her one, "There was exploration enough in the fact that he was her lover, her own, and that she should be able to be of use to him" (p. 326). Or, "She would launch his boat for him; she would be his providence; it would be his providence. . . . As she looked back at the passion of those full weeks she perceived in it a kind of maternal strain—the happiness of a woman who felt that she was a contributor, that she came with charged hands" (p. 393).

The Portrait of a Lady, then, is a record of the thwarted search a woman makes for a vocation; and of her surrender to marriage for fear that she may rip asunder the mores which are her own. Isabel is a boxed woman, one of a new breed, but one who does not realize—or believe—that sexual freedom is a prerequisite for other kinds. In her painful marriage, it is of sex, of an affair, that she thinks, to her own shock: "She was not a daughter of the Puritans, but for all that she believed in such a thing as chastity and even as decency. It would appear that Osmond was far from doing anything of the sort; some of his traditions made her push back her skirts. Did all women have lovers? Did they all lie and even the best have their price?" (p. 398). But she cannot—will not—"push back her skirts"; she instead pushes them down.[18] For, to her, the moral laws are set; she must resist her sexuality or run the risk of living in "concubinage." Of this, the younger as well as the elder James approved.

The metaphors of the book (other than the eye imaginary, which has been rightly identified as Emersonian) may also be attributed to suggestions of the elder James, who drew a crucial contrast between private and public worlds. As Richard Chase has reminded us, "The idea of leaving and entering a house, the contrast of different kinds of houses, the question of whether a house is a prison or the scene of liberation and fulfillment—these are the substance of the metaphors in *The Portrait of a Lady*."[19] Ralph and Osmond define that metaphor as each one dwells in privacy and admits guests first to the anteroom prior to admission to the inner apartment. When Caspar Goodwood gives Isabel that famous kiss, they are, of course, out of doors, outside the houses which define the private world in which married life thrives; and the kiss not only challenges her sexuality but her privacy. Isabel opts to respect the notion of a private world, to reenter the door to the house. James captures the tension as she tremulously forms her decision:

So had she heard of those wrecked and underwater following a train of images before they sink. But when darkness returned she was free, she was free. She never looked about her, she only darted from the spot. There were lights in the windows of the house; they shone far across the lawn. In an extraordinarily short time—for the distance was considerable—she had moved through the darkness (for she saw nothing) and reached the door. Here only she paused. She looked all about her; she listened a little;

---

[18] It may be that "pushing back her skirts" means "pushing them down." At any rate, Isabel's intentions are the same. She chooses chastity. I am grateful to Professor Edwin Cady of the journal *American Literature* for this second reading.

[19] Richard Chase, *The American Novel and Its Tradition* (Garden City, N.Y., 1957), p. 121.

then she put her hand on the latch. She had not known where to turn, but she knew now. There was a very straight path. (pp. 542–543)

The setting itself again becomes psychological and reveals the terms of Isabel's struggle—all had been "dark"; Isabel was not "free" as she "put her hand on the latch." For James, these two remarks are not contradictory, for, like Hawthorne, he seems to define freedom as a willful entrance into the flow of conventions which themselves might be incarcerating. Involved in such a landscape, with a morality fixed so that the world outside domestic forms is dark while the forms alone are light, Isabel understandably races to the door for safety. And it is Gardencourt, rather than Osmond's house, to which she returns—for James is drawing analogues between hostile and hospitable houses in the bourgeois environment; he is arguing for a rule of conduct that is unwavering, despite even the most terrible circumstances—as Isabel's are. James forces Isabel, in short, to satisfy the moral code that the elder James prophesied would come if legal marriage contracts were dissolved and she does so "freely" and "consciously," as she must, to be moral.

But the idea that James may be said to dramatize a point of view which regards the social responsibilities of marriage vows as crucial—a point of view which he shared with, indeed, may have derived from, his father—should not alter the readily accessible fact that James was equally a critic of bourgeois marital life. Indeed, the bourgeois and marital life seem linked. In critiques as corrosive and therapeutic as the angriest social indignation spewed out by thinkers of temperaments different from his, such as Chopin and Shaw, James inevitably singled out the acquisitive spirit of the bourgeoisie. But is it accidental that his father too had singled out the evil inherent in this spirit? It is from this domestic source that James derives his criticisms.

James's short stories abound with such criticism; "Rose-Agathe," a story published in 1878, is the most pointed of these tales dealing with marriage. It is a parody of the acquisitive nature of marriage and love; and it offers as the love-sick hero a collector who invites the narrator to catch a glimpse at the darling with whom he is in love:

In spite of our approach she stood motionless, until my friend went up to her and with a gallant, affectionate movement placed his arm around her waist. Hereupon she gazed at me with a brilliant face and large quiet eyes.

"It is a pity she creaks," said my companion as I was making my bow. And then, as I made it, I perceived with amazement—and amusement— the cause of her creaking. She existed only from the waist upward.[20]

"Rose-Agathe" is a black comedy, drawn with perverse humor to describe a society in which marriage is merchandising and women are mannequins.

Even the good-hearted Christopher Newman of *The American,* who aimed at nothing but to make money until his thirty-fifth year, does not escape James's charge that he assesses a would-be wife as if he were buying a "fine piece":

"Well," he said, at last, "I want a great woman. I stick to that. That's one thing I can treat myself to, and if it is to be had I mean to have it. What else have I toiled and struggled for, all these years? I have succeeded, and now what am I to do with my success? To make it perfect, as I see it, there must be a beautiful woman perched on the pile, like a statue on a monument. She must be as good as she is beautiful, and as clever as she is good. I can give my wife *a good deal,* so I am not afraid to ask a good deal myself. She shall have everything a woman can desire; I shall not even object to her being too good for me; she may be cleverer and wiser than I can understand, and I shall only be the better pleased. I want to possess, in a word, *the best article in the market."* (Italics mine)[21]

The late novels, often cited as evidence of James's withdrawal into aesthetic isolation, offer such analyses too. In the opening scene of *The Golden Bowl,* Maggie Verver and the Prince explain that the appropriating spirit controls Adam Verver, the American industrialist:

"You're at any rate a part of his collection," she had explained— "one of those things that can only be got over here. You're a rarity, an object of beauty, an object of price. You're not perhaps absolutely unique, but you're so curious and eminent that there are very few others like you—you belong to a class about which everything's known. You're what they call a *morceau de musee."*

[20] Henry James, "Rose-Agathe," *The Complete Tales of Henry James* (London, 1962), p. 140.
[21] Henry James, *The American,* ed. R. P. Blackmur (New York, 1960), p. 51. Italics mine.

"I see. I have the great sign of it," she had risked, "that I cost a lot of money"[22]

The two are right; James is depicting a world of collectors. When Maggie and the Prince have a child themselves, the boy, the Principino too, is treated not as a person but as an object in the family. Like the pathetic child of *What Maisie Knew* (which too indicts a bourgeois mother and father who view their offspring as a possession to be volleyed between them), the Principino serves as a "new link between wife and husband" and even more as a "link between mama and grandpa."[23] *The Golden Bowl* stands connected closely to James's earlier works which offer critiques of "innocent" men, like Adam Verver, who share in Osmond's penchant for treating people, especially women, as if they were objects.

Gilbert Osmond personifies the collector. To him, Isabel is not only a source of fortune, but a precious object in herself—suitable for a place in his collection. His words to Madame Merle on Isabel (similar to those of Newman) are those of a connoisseur in quest of a precious object:

"Is she beautiful, clever, rich, splendid, universally intelligent and unprecedentedly virtuous? It's only on those conditions that I care to make her acquaintance. You know I asked you some time ago never to speak to me of a creature who shouldn't correspond to that description. I know plenty of dingy people; I don't want to know any more."

"Miss Archer isn't dingy; she's as bright as the morning. She corresponds to your description; it's for that I wish you to know her. She fills all your requirements." (p. 225)

The overabundant adjectives that Osmond unwinds suggest there is an element of caricature in James's attitude toward Osmond's "requirements" for a woman, just as there is in his attitude toward Isabel's dream of a "prince"; but while Isabel's visions are naive, Osmond's are mercantile. He views his daughter too as a precious possession; and James shows us that, as her father-owner, Osmond is intent not to sell her for less than a great fortune. The marriages in *The Portrait of a Lady* are centered in money and are the means by which people seek to advance themselves in society. Osmond himself exemplifies the worst bourgeois spirit—which substitutes

[22] Henry James, *The Golden Bowl* (New York, 1963), p. 23.
[23] Ibid., p. 115.

bibelots for people; he, in fact, is even willing to accept the overall social view his collector's mentality drives him towards. He says of Lord Warburton:

"He owns about half England; that's his character," Henrietta remarked. "That's what they call a free country!"

"Ah, he a great proprietor? Happy man!" said Gilbert Osmond.

"Do you call that happiness—the ownership of wretched human beings?" cried Miss Stackpole. "He owns his tenants and has thousands of them. It's pleasant to own something, but inanimate objects are enough for me. I don't insist on flesh and blood and minds and consciences." (p. 279)

Osmond, however, cannot make such a fine discrimination; and James unhesitatingly castigates him for his values. For James is not what John Leonard has dubbed "an English department avatar because he incarnated a dream of the Genteel Artist, the Writer preserved in formaldehyde."[24] Instead, despite his self-proclaimed conservatism, James was in part a Hyacinth Robinson, trapped between a world of art and a world of politics; and while he tried to exorcise that part of his consciousness, moving more and more into art, more and more into allegory, James never fully lost the moral indignation he had been raised with. He continued to probe and realize facts about the real world.

James, for instance, makes it clear throughout *The Portrait* that Osmond, although an extreme, is no aberrant fortune hunter in a society of pure people. Just as the women in the novel seem to be transformations of each other (Isabel=Mrs. Touchett=Henrietta= Osmond's mother=Pansy), the men too mirror each other, and each reflects a bit of Gilbert Osmond. Osmond, as I have suggested, is pure villain, thriving on a poisonous state of mind which would incapacitate such comparative innocents as Ralph Touchett or Ned Rosier. Yet Ralph allies himself with Gilbert Osmond by his desire to tamper with Isabel and by his faith in money as a means for control. To him—a collector of boxes—Isabel becomes at one moment "a yard of calico" (p. 49); and James explicitly compares him to Osmond, saying that Osmond "consulted his taste in everything— his taste alone perhaps, as a sick man consciously incurable consults

---

[24] John Leonard, "Review of Leon Edel's *Henry James: The Master,*" *New York Times* (Feb. 14, 1972), p. 27.

at last only his lawyer; but that was what made him so different from every one else. Ralph had something of this same quality, this appearance of thinking that life was a matter of connoisseurship; but in Ralph it was an anomaly, a kind of humorous excrescence, whereas in Mr. Osmond it was the keynote, and everything was in harmony with it" (pp. 244–245). Rosier too is solidly cast in the collector's mold; even his love for Pansy, tender though it seems, is saturated with the acquisitive spirit. He looks to Osmond as a hero: "the fact that Gilbert Osmond had landed his highest prizes during his impecunious season confirmed his most cherished doctrine—the doctrine that a collector may be poor if he only be patient" (p. 338). These men mirror each other, because James is trying to offer a portrait of a society of collectors, like Osmond, and spectators, like Isabel, who between them divide the world into objects and specimens. In such a world—in which the bourgeois household filled with precious objects (including the wedded couple themselves) is the center—there is hardly room for human sympathy.

And yet, how could James, knowing all this, still create a marital prison for Isabel Archer? Committed as he was to a stable world of manners, James could not afford to allow the experimental female to walk away from domesticity. Isabel, as I have suggested, is allowed to "choose" her fate, just as Hester Prynne is allowed to "choose" hers, but she has no options except marriage. *The Portrait of a Lady* opens with the question of whether or not a woman must marry, but moves quickly, conservatively, to the question of whom she will marry. Isabel's alternatives become limited to one of four men. Further, James passionately believed this stable world of manners was essential to the writer of fiction. As we can remind ourselves, he had written of Hawthorne's case: "This moral is that the flower of art blooms only where the soil is deep, that it takes a complex social machinery to set a writer in motion."[25] Conventions which perhaps lacked spirituality were ironically the soil necessary for art.

Still, there is another tendency in *The Portrait;* and this was part of the initial plan for the book: "After Isabel's marriage there are five more installments."[26] From the conception of *The Portrait,*

---

[25] Henry James, *Hawthorne* (Ithaca, N.Y. 1956), p. 2.
[26] Henry James, *The Notebooks of Henry James,* ed. F. O. Matthiessen and Kenneth Murdock (New York, 1947), p. 15. Entry of March 18, 1879.

James was insisting on requirements for an open-ended, rather than maritally complete, novel. The ending of *The Portrait* is crucial if we are to understand the complex interaction that James's art has with the social order of his time. If, as I have argued, James's writing was not biographically or personally removed from questions urgent to him, yet critics such as Poirier and Stone are at least partially correct when they assert that James had "confidence in the power of language to make us citizens of the world we crave rather than in the world where we actually live"[27] or that "James, by shifting his values from the world to his own inner world and their own artistic standards, successfully salvaged the writing of fiction—and the need for fiction—for the modern world."[28] By his discovery of equivocal endings, James found a literary solution which created possibilities of freedom for himself as an artist, as well as the possibilities of freedom for the women he admired, even if their actions might be dangerous to his world. In *The Portrait of a Lady,* for example (as in *The Bostonians* or in *The Golden Bowl*) the final scene refuses to be final; it reserves for James as for us the possibility, on one hand, of believing that the heroine has no future (that she is trapped by social history, i.e., marriage) and, on the other, of believing that she has a future (that she may flee society, i.e., marriage). It was James's discovery of the open-ended novel that shocked his contemporaries reviewing *The Portrait* who saw in it a prediction of adultery between Isabel and Caspar; they were not far wrong. For James had through art moved us from the marriage novel to the verge of the divorce novel. His scorn for the happy ending, the marital ending, was an aesthetic commitment, to be sure, but was an aesthetic commitment in consonance with newly visible nineteenth-century social reality and with James's quiet, albeit anti-social and critical, sympathies.

James's fights over the "marriage ending" were not unique to *The Portrait*. Before and after writing the novel, James squabbled over his refusal to capitulate to coventional finales. When he serialized *The American* in the *Atlantic Monthly,* William Dean Howells argued that Newman should marry his aristocratic lady, and James retorted, "They would have been an impossible couple. . . . I should have felt as if I were throwing a rather vulgar

---

[27] Richard Poirier, *A World Elsewhere* (New York, 1968), p. 210.
[28] Donald Stone, p. 337.

sop to readers who don't really know the world."[29] The debate on
Guy Domville's ending was more lengthy, with backers who felt
that they could not buy a play without a happy ending. James was
adamant, saying that returning his priest hero to the monastery was
"the only ending I have ever dreamed of giving the play."[30]

Withdrawing his heroes (heroines too) from marriage may have
been James's aesthetic retreat from society: "The obvious criticism
of course will be that it is not finished—that I have not seen the
heroine to the end of her situation, but I have left her *en l'air*. This
is both true and false. The whole of anything is never told; you
can only take what groups together. What I have done has that
unity—it groups together. It is complete in itself—and the rest may
be taken up or not, later."[31] But it involved a social position as well.
What James is challenging is his contemporaries' belief in marriage
as an apocalypse; he assaults the conventional temporal paradigms
to which these beliefs had forced the novel to give consent. Following the Austen tradition, marriage ended time, and the novel had
committed itself to reducing reality to a paced and defined human
plot. To use Kermode's terminology, the plot of life was seen as
"tock-tock";[32] and in most novels, birth was "tick," marriage, the
inevitable and final "tock." In such an ordered world (and in
such ordered novels), the interval in between was precisely that—
an interval, a period charged with anticipation and existing only
for the sake of the ending. The marital apocalypse, like any
apocalypse, was expected to reorder time, structure its random flow
and provide it with meaning. But this is, as we moderns know, a
lie—a dream of social order and rigidity, of easy answers. James,
however,—and this perhaps is a too long neglected fact of what
constitutes his major vision—exploded that lie and the novel with
it. *The Portrait* makes clear what other writers ignored, that often
marriage created rather than solved problems; as we learn daily,
even if the princess marries the prince, the grimmest possibilities
remain. What *The Portrait* offers, then, is an adjustment that is
contradictorily and simultaneously a move to realism and, in Poirier's

---

[29] Quoted in Leon Edel, *Henry James: The Treacherous Years* (Philadelphia, 1969), p. 23.
[30] Ibid.
[31] *The Notebooks of Henry James*, p. 18.
[32] See discussion in Frank Kermode, *The Sense of an Ending* (New York, 1968), pp. 43–46.

phrase, a move to the world elsewhere. While James's book, written, on one hand, by a member of the James family, tames the experimental woman[33] and restricts her physical options for her psychic salvation; on the other, it is James himself who proves bolder than he permits his heroine to be. Isabel thinks of herself as an adventurer, asserting her belief in free will, in the Emersonian system, but she emerges before us as a voice shouting "I want to live," rather than "I am living"; to her, the present seems merely a promise of the future, and despite her assertion that she does not want to begin life by marrying—by her sense of time—she is tacitly consenting to the premise of the marital ending. James, on the other hand—through the implication of his endings—was insisting on the pregnant interval between "tick" and "tock." What he wrote was, to adapt the Kermode language, "tick-tock."

The Portrait of a Lady exploded the domestic novel, converted it into the more fluid form open to the modern novel, made way, in effect, for Joyce and Stein. If James was no modern in being unable to conceive that there might be other options open to Isabel (Quentin Anderson has suggested, for instance, that she might have become an artist), *The Portrait of a Lady* still offered something new to the novel. Indeed, its strength, rather than its failing (as Anderson—and we too—would have it) may curiously reside in James's narrow, conventional vision of women. For his limited vision was not simple; if he wanted to trap Isabel, he wanted as well to free her. It is the tension in the novel, which comes from the struggle between his (and her) desire for confinement and his (her) move to freedom that creates the explosive architecture of *The Portrait*. It might be said too, that the new woman led James on a new path to modernism, as he unsystematically made the marriage novel— like the marrying world about him—burst its mold to tell her tale.

---

[33] For Henry James, Sr.'s hostile attack on feminist women, see "Woman and the Women's Movement," *Putnam's Monthly Magazine*, I (1853), 279–288.

Feminist Sources in *The Bostonians*

Sara deSaussure Davis

ALTHOUGH HENRY JAMES'S KNOWLEDGE of his subject matter in *The Bostonians* has been impugned or ignored since 1885, specific historical events, issues, and personalities of the feminist movement from the Civil War to the early 1880's indicate that James developed the novel from the actualities of that period of the women's movement.[1] To add historical sources to the material from which James created the plot and characters of *The Bostonians* is not to forget that he had literary sources as well. The numerous studies of those literary sources, however, are disproportionate to the paucity of scholarship on real-life sources.[2] Curiously, the novel most similar to *The Bos-*

Author's Note: I would like to thank the University of Alabama Research Grants Committee for their generous summer funding.

[1] James began the doubts himself when he wrote to William James about the novel in 1885, that he had "the sense of knowing terribly little about the kind of life I had attempted to describe" (*The Letters of Henry James*, ed. Percy Lubbock, I, New York, 1920, 115–116). In 1933, without giving any evidence, Granville Hicks asserted that James knew nothing at all of the fight for women's rights (*The Great Tradition*, New York, 1933, p. 113). More recently, in a collection of essays entitled *"The Air of Reality"* David Howard comments on "how much of the extraordinary world of reform in this period is not [in the novel]" and contends that James neglects "the particular reform questions, especially the woman question" (*"The Air of Reality,"* ed. John Goode, London, 1972, pp. 65, 66).

[2] Studies of literary sources include the following: Marius Bewley, *The Complex Fate* (London, 1952), pp. 11–31 ff.; Oscar Cargill, *The Novels of Henry James* (New York, 1961), pp. 123–145; Robert L. Selig, "The Red-Haired Lady Orator: Parallel Passages in *The Bostonians* and *Adam Bede*," *Nineteenth-Century Fiction*, XVI (Sept., 1961), 164–169; Robert E. Long, "The Society and the Masks: *The Blithedale Romance* and *The Bostonians*," *Nineteenth-Century Fiction*, XIX (Sept., 1964), 105–122; David B. Green, "Witch and Bewitchment in *The Bostonians*," *Papers on Language and Literature*, III (Summer, 1967), 267–269. More recently, Robert McLean has examined James's debt to the pastoral tradition, "*The Bostonians*: New England Pastoral," *Papers on Language and Literature*, VII (Fall, 1971), 374–381; and Lyall H. Powers traces the influence on *The Bostonians* of stories by Daudet, Turgenev, Howells, and James himself in *Henry James and the Naturalist Movement* (East Lansing, Mich., 1971), pp. 42–87. Maria Jacobson makes an excellent case for James's use of both the Civil War romance and the feminist novel in "Popular Fiction and Henry James's Unpopular *Bostonians*," *Modern Philology*, LXXIII (Feb., 1976), 264–275.

Three exceptions to our ignorance of historical sources for the novel have been provided by William James, who attacked his brother's use of Sara Peabody in the creation of Miss Birdseye (See *Letters*, ed. Lubbock, pp. 115–116); Robert Emmet Long, "A Source for Dr. Mary Prance," *Nineteenth-Century Fiction*, XIX (June, 1964), 87–88; and Howard Kerr, *"Mediums, and Spirit-Rappers, and Roaring Radicals": Spiritualism in American Literature, 1850–1900* (Urbana, Ill., 1972), pp. 190–222. The latter is an excellent study of Cora Hatch and spiritualism as an influence on the characterization of Verena Tarrant. Kerr's

tonians, The Princess Casamassima, has received serious attention as
a portrayal of the anarchists and revolutionaries of the 1880's,[3] but the
fact that *The Bostonians* succeeds better as a novel appears to have
rendered corroboration of historical validity unnecessary or un-
desirable.

Unlike the subrosa anarchist activities that informed *The Princess,*
feminist activities were more highly visible; the women's movement
was anxous to communicate its plans and ideas to the public. James,
therefore, shared the increasing awareness on the part of Americans
and English alike concerning the movement. More particularly, he
drew his knowledge from the circumstances of his travels and friendships, using not only the general subject matter of the debate over
feminism but specific figures and events associated with it. From 1865
to 1885, his trips back and forth among the three major cities of
feminist activity—London, Boston, and New York—increased his
sense that feminism was a powerful, important aspect of social
change. Additionally, James was personally acquainted with various
people associated with the movement, including Louisa May Alcott
and Julia Ward Howe. Most influential on the novel as contemporary, real-life sources were Anna Dickinson and her relationship to
three of her supporters: Wendell Phillips, Susan B. Anthony, and
Whitelaw Reid. James knew the two men well; and if he did not
know Anna Dickinson personally, he knew of her, as his early writing reveals. She was a major personality in a particularly fascinating
story of feminist activities, and James used her as a model for Verena
Tarrant.

In the spring of 1863, while Henry James was at Harvard, sensitive
to the fact that all around him others, including his two younger
brothers, were participants in the war, Anna Dickinson publicly supported the war in both Cambridge and Boston during her many

analysis does not, of course, preclude Anna Dickinson as an additional source in the creation
of Verena.
[3] Historical studies of *The Princess* include: Louise Bogan, "James on a Revolutionary
Theme," *Nation,* CXLVI (April 23, 1938), 471–472, 474; Clinton Oliver, "Henry James as
Social Critic," *Antioch Review,* VII (Summer, 1947), 243–258; George Woodcock, "Henry
James and the Conspirators," *Sewanee Review,* LX (Spring, 1952), 219–229; Oscar Cargill,
"*The Princess Casamassima:* A Critical Reappraisal," *PMLA,* LXXI (March, 1956), 97–117;
Robert W. Kretsch, "Political Passion in Balzac and Henry James," *Nineteenth-Century
Fiction,* XIV (Dec., 1959), 265–270; W. H. Tilley, *The Background of The Princess
Casamassima,* University of Florida Monographs, Humanities No. 5 (Gainesville, Fla., 1960);
Mildred E. Hartsock, "*The Princess Casamassima:* The Politics of Power," *Studies in the
Novel,* I (Fall, 1969), 297–309; and Taylor Stoehr, "Words and Deeds in *The Princess
Casamassima,*" *ELH,* XXXVII (March, 1970), 95–135.

engagements in the Northeast. Although James evidently did not see her speak then, he mentions Dickinson in a review in 1868 as "the famous lecturer—whom we have not heard. . . ."[4] Indeed, if he had not seen her in person in 1863, he would have to have heard of her; everyone did. She had risen to fame from anonymity, an obscure Quaker girl from Philadelphia, in a matter of months in 1863, one of the bleakest periods of the war. She attracted large audiences with her fervor and magnetism; the words consistently used by contemporary newspapers to describe her effect are "magic," "charm," "mesmerism."[5] But the "magic" was not without substance. Although she is not credited with having original ideas, she did give persuasiveness to those of others, and her speeches "showed her to be highly informative, if strongly opinionated" on political and social questions of the day.[6] She was in such demand as a lyceum and political speaker that she received as much as $20,000 a year in fees. The public was fascinated with her and followed the detailed news and gossip of her in the papers. When she began to speak for woman suffrage, after 1866, she was described by *The American Gentlemen's Newspaper* as "the only pretty, well-shaped, and womanly-looking advocate that progressive ideas ever had for an oratorical champion in this country."[7]

During the Civil War Susan B. Anthony and Wendell Phillips competed for the speaking talents of young Dickinson. Anthony and Phillips are still well known, but their relationship with Dickinson seems almost to have vanished from public memory. In 1863, the Republicans hired Anna Dickinson to help their presidential campaign, and she succeeded in turning the states of New Hampshire and Connecticut to the war cause and the Republican party.[8] During one of her speeches Dickinson attracted the attention of Anthony, who was "taken captive. Susan was seized by a vision of what Anna Dickinson might become in the future."[9] Anthony was determined that Dickinson should be the evangel of the woman's cause, as soon as the war was over, and sought constantly to get her to speak for woman

[4] "Dallas Gailbraith," *Nation*, VII (Oct. 22, 1868), 330.
[5] Giraud Chester, *Embattled Maiden: The Life of Anna Dickinson* (New York, 1951), p. 65 and *passim*.
[6] Chester, p. 89.
[7] As quoted in Chester, p. 95.
[8] Susan Katherine Anthony, *Susan B. Anthony: Her Personal History and Her Era* (Garden City, N.Y., 1954), pp. 178–179.
[9] Anthony, p. 178.

suffrage. Personal attraction between the two women added intensity to their relationship; her biographer says, "Susan's attachment to Anna Dickinson became the most passionate affection of her life."[10] Anthony's letters record her intense, fervid love for Dickinson. Anthony addressed the younger girl as "Dicky darling Anna" and "Dear Chick a dee dee."[11] In one letter Anthony wanted to give her "one awful long squeeze," and she tried to make her promise "not to *marry a man.*"[12] She also wrote to Dickinson, "I have *plain* quarters—at 44 Bond Street—*double bed*—and big enough and good enough to take you *in*—So come and see me."[13]

In the struggle to ensure the young orator's talents for the Women's Rights Convention to be held in the fall of 1866, Anthony apparently met resistance from Wendell Phillips, Dickinson's Boston friend and sponsor since 1861. Anthony made "this cryptic reference to a counter-influence: 'I know the pressure to keep you [Anna] from doing in the one direction.'. . . The influence to which she referred could only have been that of Anna's great friend, Wendell Phillips."[14] Anthony's biographer adds, "They [Susan Anthony and Phillips] were competing for the possession of her soul."[15] During the summer before the 1866 women's convention, both Dickinson and Henry James were at the small Massachusetts resort of Swampscott, where it seems possible—given the similar setting and events used in the novel—that he might have met her or at least have heard gossip about her while the tug-of-war raged between Anthony and Phillips.[16] At any rate, their political and personal rivalry prefigures a later one that occurred between Anthony and Whitelaw Reid for Dickinson, a triangle that provided both plot and characters in *The Bostonians.*

When James began writing fiction in the late 1860's, suffrage in particular and women's rights in general acquired a special intensity

[10] Anthony, p. 176.

[11] Andrew Sinclair, *The Better Half: The Emancipation of the American Woman* (New York, 1965), pp. 75–76.

[12] As quoted in Sinclair, p. 76.

[13] As quoted in Sinclair, p. 76 (emphasis Anthony's). Carroll Smith-Rosenberg's fine article, "The Female World of Love and Ritual: Relations between Women in Nineteenth-Century America," *Signs,* I (Autumn, 1975), 1–29, helps me to place in a cultural context this relationship so that it seems neither explicitly lesbian nor anomalous. But Anthony's request that Dickinson not marry is contrary to the tradition Smith-Rosenberg describes.

[14] Anthony, p. 199.

[15] Anthony, p. 199.

[16] Leon Edel notes that James was in Swampscott then, in *Henry James* (Philadelphia, 1953), I, 241–242. Dickinson's stay there is mentioned in Anthony, p. 197.

because the campaign for Negro enfranchisement threatened specifically to exclude women from citizenship and voting rights. The *Revolution,* edited by Anthony and Elizabeth Cady Stanton, began publication January 8, 1868; activities and membership in women's groups increased; the Working Women's Association and the New England Women's Club were founded. In 1868, 172 women voted for the first time, in a small town in New Jersey, in the presidential election. But in that same year the Fourteenth Amendment was ratified. It used the word "male" before "citizen" for the first time and thus raised the question of whether women were actually citizens. The new amendment also meant that another amendment to the Constitution would be necessary for women to vote in federal elections. Faced with the prospect of this new task, suffrage workers disagreed on the methods of winning the right to vote and separated into two camps, the National Women's Suffrage Association led by Anthony and Stanton, and the American Women's Suffrage Association, headed by Julia Howe.

In May, 1870, James returned from Europe to America and to Cambridge, where he lived with his parents until May, 1872. During these two years James apparently haunted the streets of Cambridge, seeking diversion and fictional subject matter: Edel records that James attended demonstrations, meetings, seances, and speeches by reformers.[17] These two years were among the most active and sensational before suffrage was won. When James arrived in 1870, the organizational meeting for the Massachusetts Woman Suffrage Association had just been held in Boston, and the *Woman's Journal* had begun publication there with Julia Howe as one of the editors. Utah and Wyoming enacted woman suffrage, and for the first time women went to the polls in Massachusetts: forty-two women voted in Hyde Park, then a suburb of Boston, led through a snow storm by the aging Grimké sisters. Their example inspired some 150 women in ten states and Washington, D.C., to try to vote in 1871 and 1872. These unsuccessful attempts were followed by court actions that also failed.[18]

Another highly publicized event of the 1870's involving feminists and influencing James's vision of the movement was the Beecher-

[17] Edel, *Henry James* (Philadelphia, 1962), II, 22–26.
[18] Eleanor Flexner, *Century of Struggle: The Woman's Rights Movement in the United States* (Cambridge, Mass., 1959), p. 165.

Tilton scandal. News of the adultery between the pious, liberal minister Henry Ward Beecher and Elizabeth Tilton, wife of Theodore Tilton, was published in November, 1871, in *Woodhull and Caflin's Weekly* by Victoria Woodhull. More than the adulterers were exposed; another aspect—pointedly sexual—of the movement was revealed. Mrs. Woodhull, a self-styled suffragist who was also a supporter of "free love, spiritualism, and quack-healing,"[19] did not aid the women's rights cause with her bruiting of the scandal. And although Beecher had been the former president of AWSA (Julia Howe's group), that organization did not suffer as much as the NWSA, because Anthony and Stanton actively supported Mrs. Tilton in the case, believing that of the three people involved, she was the main victim since she was not even allowed to testify in court in her own behalf.[20]

James was in New York City when Theodore Tilton sued Beecher for misconduct, four years after the scandal was first revealed. The trial received sensational coverage in the newspapers. Even *The Nation,* for which James was writing while living in New York, followed the trial week by week, deploring the partisan coverage given by other papers. In 1875 the press discovered that Susan Anthony personally knew Mrs. Tilton's intimate story. As a houseguest of Mrs. Tilton one night in 1870, Anthony had spent the night as an unwilling confessor to Mrs. Tilton's penitent. Anthony was appealed to publicly to reveal what she knew. Her reputation as a truth-sayer was eulogized. Reporters followed her everywhere, pressuring her to make a statement; her responsibility was great, and she carefully refused to say a word. Perhaps because of her reputation neither lawyer called her to the stand.[21] This was one of two widely publicized accounts James could have read about Anthony's moral integrity. The Beecher-Tilton trial of 1875 thus contrasted two opposing faces of the women's movement: Victoria Woodhull and Susan Anthony, with the adulterous and helpless wife, Mrs. Tilton, somewhere in between.

During this two-year visit in America, James also witnessed the presidential campaigning for 1872, when Horace Greeley and Ulysses Grant (along with Victorian Woodhull) were in the running. During

19 Flexner, p. 153.
20 Flexner, p. 154.
21 Anthony, pp. 316–317.

the campaign a struggle similar to that between Susan Anthony and Wendell Phillips in 1866 was again taking place for the speaking talents and affection of Anna Dickinson. This second triangle provided the plot and the three major characters of *The Bostonians;* and James's use of the story, moreover, suggests that his observation of and personal acquaintance with feminists contributed to his fiction, particularly that of the 1880's. The second triangle involved Whitelaw Reid, a young New York *Tribune* correspondent, who together with Phillips vied openly for Dickinson. The newspapers in Boston and New York speculated frequently on the supposed romance between Reid and Dickinson,[22] while those in the confidence of Boston society and politics watched the rivalry with interest. Phillips and Reid supported Greeley for President, while Anthony was campaigning for Grant. According to Anthony's biographer, Reid swayed Dickinson to Greeley, so that "one of the casualties of the campaign was Susan's friendship with Anna"; the two women quarrelled not because of whom each supported but because of Reid.[23] Dickinson's support of Greeley represented an ostensible betrayal of the feminist cause, since in the *Tribune* Greeley and Reid had taken stands against woman suffrage. The role of the handsome thirty-five-year-old bachelor Reid in the affair seemed apparent to those speculating on marriage between him and the unmarried Dickinson.

James returned to Cambridge from Europe for a visit in August, 1874, the year Anthony was conducting a lecture tour to pay for debts from her feminist paper, *The Revolution,* and for the debts she had incurred during her trial for having voted "illegally." She had lectured in New York state all summer, then went West during the fall where Bronson Alcott heard her.[24] Ironically at the time Dickinson was pressing Anthony for payment of a $1,000 note, Dickinson's speaking career was just about at an end; she had changed from abolitionist and feminist topics to "social evil" and had lost her audiences. Anthony, on the other hand, despite her age, was being praised as follows: "No longer in the bloom of youth—if she ever had any bloom—hard-featured, guileless, cold as an icicle, fluent and philosophical, she wields today tenfold more influence than all the

[22] Anthony, p. 276.
[23] Anthony, p. 276.
[24] Anthony, p. 309.

beautiful and brilliant female lecturers. . . ."[25] In spite of her superficial unattractiveness and her apparent coldness Anthony finally
faced the public herself. By 1876, when she had earned enough
money to clear her debts, the news was carried nationally with congratulations. One paper said that she paid her debts like a man:
"Like a man? Not so. Not one man in a thousand but would have
. . . settled at ten or twenty cents on the dollar."[26] Anthony's was the
kind of honor that would have appealed to James; and it was associated in this instance as in the Tilton-Beecher trial specifically with
female morality. James was in Paris in 1876, but it seems likely he
would have sought the sequel to Anthony's story, which had been so
current when he was in New York in 1875.

James visited the United States twice more before 1890; both visits
preceded his writing of *The Bostonians* and were instrumental in
shaping that novel. He arrived in Boston from England in late 1881,
the year the NWSA was holding a series of conventions in New
England. In December he went to New York twice, the first time
staying with Edwin Godkin, the former editor of the *Nation,* and
"getting impressions" of the city.[27] After Christmas he attended a
banquet given him in New York by Whitelaw Reid. Although Reid
had earlier been the public rival of Anthony for Anna Dickinson, she
had since refused Reid's marriage proposals and had begun a second
career in 1876, as author and actress. Reid and his *Tribune* were
infamous for attacking her and for leading the New York dramatic
critics in a vicious public battle against her.[28] At the December
banquet, whether or not Reid was willing to discuss her, no doubt
she was mentioned among the guests. During the same month,
Dickinson's successful play, *An American Girl,* closed in New Orleans; the play had run in New York the previous fall, starring
Fanny Davenport, and had been on tour since then. Dickinson's
obvious talents and their unpredictable reception must have been
especially interesting to James, who that same week had speculated
in his journal about the meaning and value of success.[29]

In January, 1882, James went to Washington, D.C., where he

[25] As quoted in Anthony, p. 310, from a St. Louis newspaper.
[26] As quoted in Anthony, p. 311.
[27] Edel, *Henry James* (Philadelphia, 1962), III, 25.
[28] Chester, pp. 168–234.
[29] Edel, III, 25.

visited with the Henry Adamses. Leon Edel believes that James's thoughts on arriving in the capital for the first time were those he later gave a character in *The Bostonians*.[30] Other elements associated with this visit to America which found their way into the novel included James's renewed acquaintance with Reid, his response to political activities in Washington, and his stay at Beacon Hill from January to May. Debate had begun in Congress, just weeks before James arrived in the capital, over whether to appoint a select committee on woman suffrage;[31] and the suffragists were evidently lobbying successfully because the committees they requested were appointed that year by both houses.

During 1882 the death of James's parents, who died within eleven months of each other, led directly and indirectly to psychological insights that he would incorporate into *The Bostonians*. He was summoned unexpectedly from Washington to Cambridge at the death of his mother, whom Edel says James believed had been at times sacrificed to family oppression.[32] His observation may have contributed to his preparation for a novel about women's rights. James returned to Europe in May, 1882, only to be recalled to Cambridge in December to his father's death-bed. Subsequently, James kept house with Alice James and discovered that her friend and nurse Katherine Loring "had quite taken over the foreground of Alice's life. . . ."[33] The first notes for *The Bostonians* were recorded April 8, 1883, in Boston. James had an opportunity that spring and in late 1884 to observe the intense, symbiotic emotional relationship between Alice and Kate Loring. He was thus provided with the psychology for his already extant plot and characters.

Included in his April, 1883, notes on the novel is his belief that it should be "an American story . . . very national, very typical."[34] When he left Cambridge and the United States for the last time before writing *The Bostonians,* his sense of America, according to Edel, was of the " 'numerosity' of the womenfolk. . . . Henry felt he was in a city of women, a country of women. . . ."[35] He might

[30] Edel, III, 26.
[31] *Nation,* XXXIII (Dec. 22, 1881), 484.
[32] Edel, III, 36–37.
[33] Edel, III, 67.
[34] *The Notebooks of Henry James,* ed. F. O. Matthiessen and Kenneth B. Murdock (New York, 1961), p. 47.
[35] Edel, III, 67.

well have thought so. One of the most discussed subjects in the
Nation for that year was female education: thirteen articles (both
news and editorial) appeared there from January to June, 1883.
Harvard Annex (the forerunner of Radcliffe College) was conducting a campaign from Cambridge to raise $100,000 to put the college
on a permanent basis, while in New York Columbia University was
debating whether to accept women. The *Nation* followed this latter
story closely and held "that anything done in New York in the way
of recognition of women's claim to and fitness for a collegiate education is really a great thing. . . ."[36] Women's rights had by 1883 been
an issue long enough that the *Nation* noted ironically such supposed
effects of "equality" as women strikers who used clubs to keep scabs
and sheriffs at bay and a woman who shot her husband to death.[37]

Though the *Nation* feared in the spring of 1883 that interest in
suffrage was dying out everywhere except in Massachusetts and was
struggling even there against "the supineness of the 'better element,' "[38] James found renewed suffrage activity when he returned to
London in August. Joseph Chamberlain had broken with the
women's movement in the early 1880's, spawning a wave of retalia-
tory demonstrations for suffrage all over England from 1880 to 1884.
In addition to these impressive demonstrations, the movement had
achieved several specific victories. The University of London granted
full membership to women in 1880, as did all the new provincial universities thereafter. In 1882 the married woman's property act became
law in England. In 1883 Mrs. Josephine Butler held a "great meeting
of prayer," a kind of sit-in dramatically held in the Westminster
Palace Hotel to pressure the Parliament then meeting for repeal of
the Contagious Diseases Acts, a celebrated feminist issue. The acts
were not repealed until 1886, but the vote in 1883, which was favorable, abolished the detested compulsory examination.

Just after his return to England James wrote T. S. Perry that
"Nothing *lives* in England today but politics."[39] So when James
began writing *The Bostonians* in London during the summer of
1884, he would have been justified in feeling that women's rights was

---

[36] *Nation*, XXXVI (May 17, 1883), 413.
[37] *Nation*, XXXVI (May 31, 1883), 455; *Nation*, XXXIX (Dec. 4, 1884), 473,
respectively.
[38] *Nation*, XXXVI (March 8, 1883), 204–205.
[39] As quoted in Edel, III, 84.

a topical subject with a future. He had a powerful sense of the vitality of the movement and its potential influence on society and the individual. From observation of the movement in America he drew the principal characters of his novel: Susan Anthony, Whitelaw Reid, and Anna Dickinson are transmogrified into Olive Chancellor, Basil Ransom, and Verena Tarrant. In *The Bostonians* twenty years of feminist activities are distilled and scrutinized there by the artist's vision.

The striking similarity between the triangle of Anthony-Dickinson-Reid and of Olive-Verena-Basil is easily recognizable, once the historical facts are known. James altered several important aspects of the historical triangle, however. In probing the relationship of Olive and Verena and the possibilities of a lesbian attachment, James goes beyond what was known or publicly realized about Anthony and Dickinson. As Edel has pointed out, James in all likelihood drew additionally from his observations of the friendship between Kate Loring and Alice James.[40] Yet James's speculation about the potentially lesbian nature of the Dickinson-Anthony relationship was not unreasonable, as Anthony's biographer hints.[41] James also changed the outcome of Reid's proposal to Dickinson. By having Basil carry off Verena in the end (as Reid fails to win Dickinson) James possibly sought to avoid too close a parallel between his real-life sources and his fictional characters. Another reason for the change is that in being false to the actual facts of Dickinson's relation to Reid, James was true to his overall sense of the feminist movement; Ransom's "winning" Verena is symbolically and historically appropriate to the history of the movement at that time.

The story of Verena seems almost an allegory of postwar feminism, and James's vision of the women's rights movement is provocative and historically valid because the most powerful enemy of the movement in the 1870's (and for some time thereafter) was, in fact, postwar reactionary thought and the fear of black votes, best symbolized by the Southerner. Antisuffrage forces were strengthened by the apathy of many women and by the bad publicity resulting from various scandals (such as the Tilton-Beecher affair) and idiosyncratic cults associated with suffrage. The objections of "gentlemen" who

[40] Edel, III, 67.
[41] Anthony, p. 176.

believed privilege preferable to rights also added their dead weight; but, as James indicates, those objectors were their own best proof of the reverse of the argument. In Basil's wresting Verena away from the podium, James shows those "gentlemen" willing to use physical force unscrupulously in their attempts to thwart the aims and implied threats of feminism. Verena has the rhetorical ability to persuade but lacks personal conviction and experience. She succumbs to Basil because she is too naive to resist. Her naiveté parallels that of the early feminist movement. Ironically her marriage to Basil will educate her to the experience necessary for integrity as a feminist: "It is to be feared that with the union, so far from brilliant, into which she was about to enter, these [tears] were not the last she was destined to shed" (p. 464).[42] Her period of "education" signals the beginning of the quiescent years of American and English feminism, from the 1880's until 1890, when feminist activity was renewed on a much stronger basis.

James used more than the outline of Dickinson's story, however. He assimilated numerous details from her life, the lives of those associated with her, and details from the feminist movement. Like Anna Dickinson, Verena has had meteoric, overnight success. Basil Ransom says, "I am told you made an immense sensation . . . that you leaped into fame" (p. 241). The words used to describe Dickinson's effect on her audiences—magic, charm, mesmerism—are synonyms for those James applies to Verena: "enchanting," "fascinating," "charming," "engaging" (pp. 61, 144, 240). The physical beauty of Anna Dickinson recorded by the *American Gentlemen's Newspaper* is, of course, a fundamental part of Verena's charm. James comments, "There had never been a more attractive female speaker before the American public" (p. 144). In fact, Selah Tarrant's prominence in the papers suffers because of the attention given to his "daughter's *physique*" (p. 104, emphasis James's). Anna Dickinson was originally from Philadelphia, the daughter of a man who died while speaking publicly for abolition. James radically altered Selah into a caricature of a public speaker, but Selah still comes from "down in Pennsylvania" (p. 104).

Dickinson is not the only person whose activities have been trans-

---

[42] *The Bostonians*, ed. Irving Howe (1886; rpt. New York, 1956), Mod. Lib. Ed. All further references to the novel are taken from this edition.

lated into *The Bostonians*. In addition to her role in courting Dickinson for the movement and for herself, the beginning of Susan B. Anthony's own speaking career suggests the real-life source for Olive Chancellor's terrible confrontation of the Music Hall audience at the end of the novel. Olive, like Anthony in 1874, risked the hostility and rejection of a public accustomed to the pretty but deceptively pleasant face of a young, beautiful girl. An awareness of Anthony's contemporary reputation—two-sided as it was—adds weight to a more sympathetic view of Olive.

The third member of the real-life triangle that informed the major characters of *The Bostonians,* Whitelaw Reid, bequeathed to Basil Ransom his Southernness. In James's first notes for the novel Ransom was destined to be from the West; but Ransom becomes a Mississippian for the novel. Reid, originally a Westerner from Ohio, spent some time after the Civil War plantation-farming in Alabama and Mississippi. His efforts were evidently not successful; he returned to Xenia, Ohio, and then joined Horace Greeley on the New York *Tribune*.[43] The pattern suggests the post-Civil War actions of Ransom, who like Reid gives up Mississippi plantation life for journalism in New York. Charles Samuels has argued that James changed Ransom's origins from West to South to accord with the hot-blooded virility appropriate to the stereotyped Southerner.[44] But a Westerner would seem equally capable of symbolizing the uncouth "masculinity" of Ransom. Realizing Reid's biographical influence in the evolution of Ransom, one wonders if James was not swayed by a desire to disguise his debts to Reid's life. Too, James wished to draw upon contemporary popular notion about the South and Southern hostility to feminism. In the 1870's, the time of *The Bostonians,* the Southern gentleman epitomized, as a Westerner could not, reactionary objection to feminist goals. After all, Utah and Wyoming were the first states to enact woman suffrage.

Reid's career as a journalist and his use of the *Tribune* to seek personal revenge against Anna Dickinson are reduced to minor themes

---

[43] Chester, p. 114.
[44] Samuels, *The Ambiguity of Henry James* (Urbana, 1971), p. 98. Charles Anderson argues that James drew (somewhat faultily) on the myth of the Southern cavalier, who is devoted to chivalry and conservatism, in "James's Portrait of a Southerner," *American Literature*, XXVII (Nov., 1955), 310–331. Jacobson traces Ransom to James's use of the Civil War romance, pp. 269 ff.

in the novel. James seems to have combined these two elements with characteristics from the life of the great Boston liberal Wendell Phillips, Dickinson's first important sponsor; the result is Mathias Pardon, the pandering, fey journalist who professes, "I want to work for their [women's] emancipation. I regard it as the great modern question" (p. 146). Like Phillips and Reid, who arranged the political stumping of Dickinson, Pardon "knew Parties who, if they had been present, would want to engage Miss Verena at a high figure for the winter campaign" (p. 64). Like Phillips and Reid, Pardon also sues for the talents of the young orator: "Would Miss Chancellor be willing to divide a—the—well, he might call it the responsibilities? Couldn't they run Miss Verena together?" (p. 145). When Olive refuses his offer, Pardon threatens her with the powers of the "vigilant daily press" (p. 147), which would demand an account from her. Pardon, however, is a pathetic figure lacking any real power or force. The dramatic intensity of Reid's and Phillips's war against Anthony is distilled, of course, into the more personal vendetta of Basil Ransom. James culled too from the newspaper gossip about Reid and Dickinson the popular belief that the only way to silence Dickinson/Verena is "to stop your mouth by kissing you.!"[45]

James also assimilated contemporary feminist ideas into the novel. But since he was a novelist, he expresses these themes by scenes of dramatic conflict among the characters rather than political speeches. In Verena's arguments with Basil, James couches the fundamental feminist beliefs of the 1870's: that universities should be open to women (p. 233); that female political power and suffrage would "usher in the reign of peace" (p. 248); that assuming the responsibilities for husband and children no longer comprises a career as a matter of course (p. 344); and that women should have "equal rights, equal opportunities, equal privileges" (p. 233).

James tries to approximate the ideological differences between the two major American feminist groups by opposing the aims of Olive with those of Mrs. Farrinder (p. 166); though his distinction between the two groups is not particularly accurate in detail, it suggests adequately enough the nature of the split between AWSA and NWSA along conservative and radical lines. More precise is James's observation that feminist activities were entering a new sphere dur-

[45] Chester, p. 125.

ing the 1870's because of the fight against the Fourteenth Amendment. Mrs. Burrage remarks that the movement "has entered into a new phase . . . the domain of practical politics" (p. 317). James carefully avoids dealing specifically with the Negro suffrage amendment, which denied women the vote; however, by pitting Olive and Ransom as antagonists, James suggests the role Southerners played in handicapping women because of their fear of black women voters. Mrs. Burrage and her son are not the only ones who recognize the new domain of politics, of course. Miss Birdseye proclaims that the law book is the feminists' Bible.

Finally, Olive's despair at the end of the novel, her realization that she is giving up her life "to save a sex which, after all, didn't wish to be saved, and which rejected the truth . . ." (p. 422), evinces the hopelessness appropriate to the mid-1880's, when feminist activities slowed considerably and when James actually began writing *The Bostonians*. Although he did not seem to realize the slow-down when he began the novel, his materials took him to that discovery—historically correct—by the end of the book.

The distinction to be made in analyzing James's use of Anthony and Dickinson is that he was not trying to portray them as people in an historically authentic or complete manner; he was drawing from a brief period of their lives certain facts and characteristics to add to the amalgam of Olive or of Verena as feminists of the American 1870's. Furthermore, his attitude in the novel toward these two characters and his attitude towards the feminist movement are separable. His attitude towards Olive and Verena (Basil, too, for that matter) changes in the novel, depending on whether the character is acting as a type—Olive, for example, as the rich New England spinster, cultivating romantic illusions about poor shop girls is satirized—or as an individual—Olive wrestling with her desires and tormented by her conscience in making the decision to "free" Verena is portrayed tragically. James said in his notebook that he wanted in *The Bostonians* to write about certain American types,[46] which he does to satirical perfection; but when his characters begin to define their individuality against their "type," James invests them with his own greater interest and illumines them by their own larger humanity.

[46] *Notebooks*, pp. 46–47.

When Olive decides she does not have the right to possess Verena, Olive earns the traditional Jamesian approval.

James's attitude toward the movement is complex and ambivalent; the attitude is revealed only by a thorough analysis of the themes and characterization and is complicated by the slippery irony of the narrative voice.[47] His method, by and large, was reportage, as Oscar Cargill has termed it,[48] and he strives for objectivity by being as satirical of the opponents of the women's movement as of the women's movement itself. The target of James's mordant satire on both sides of the issue is fixed beliefs, codified responses to life—Basil's chivalric code and Olive's political beliefs—as well as the hypocrisy and moral blindness that result from such codes. Very much like *Huckleberry Finn,* a selection of which was published concurrently with *The Bostonians* in the *Century* (February, 1885), James's satire reveals that these fixed beliefs give rise to frauds who prey upon the weaknesses, false sentiments, and unexamined beliefs of well-intentioned people. Twain's comment notwithstanding—he said he'd rather be condemned to John Bunyan's heaven than have to read *The Bostonians*—the similarities are strong between Selah Tarrant and the Duke and the King. Furthermore, James, like Twain, is consistently suspicious of the group in whatever form. James cannot portray the group behavior of the women's movement without comedy or satire, but as his next two novels, *The Princess Casamassima* and *The Tragic Muse,* reveal, he supports the goals of feminism when they are individually pursued and achieved.[49]

When *The Bostonians* was published in 1884, Boston readers, beginning with William James, reacted quickly against Henry's initially satirical portrait of Miss Birdseye; the prominence of that family name assured Miss Peabody the concern of her fellow Bostonians. No one, including reviewers, however, remarked on the similarity of Verena Tarrant to Anna Dickinson, who had been closely associated

---

[47] For an analysis of these themes and problems, see my article, "*The Bostonians:* A Revaluation," *Tulane Studies in English,* Special Issue Honoring Richard P. Adams (Fall, 1978).

[48] Cargill, p. 131.

[49] Twain too gets caught in something of James's dilemma; in *Huck Finn* in the Boggs-Sherburn incident, Sherburn is clearly wrong in having killed Boggs, yet when the group of men come to his house to protest, Twain's sympathy cannot remain with the group and swings to the power of Sherburn.

with prominent Boston liberals and reformers in the 1860's. Nothing was said of this correlation when the novel came out for several reasons. By 1885 Wendell Phillips had been dead almost a year and Dickinson had dropped from public notice. And, too, the wit present in the characterization of the youthful and resilient Verena probably seemed less offensive than the satire of an old woman whose important activities were behind her. Furthermore, Dickinson was a Philadelphian from an unknown family whose name would not have qualified her for public defense in Boston. Finally, the feminists who might have raised objections to the novel were busy writing their own history and were uninterested in the unflattering picture of women's rights in *The Bostonians.* A lengthy review of the novel in the *Woman's Journal* termed the satire "caricature" and condemned James as untrue to both human nature and to art.[50] The reviewer therefore had a vested interest in not seeing any link between the major figures of the novel and feminists of the 1870's.

A final reason that these parallels attracted little attention is that the novel appeared just after the movement in the United States and England had momentarily peaked. The inactivity lasted from 1884 to 1897; as Ray Strachey states, "the press and public were tired of hearing of it [woman suffrage] . . . a regular Press boycott set in, and the dead period of the movement came on."[51] The public surfeit of women's rights issues which is evident from 1884 to 1890 contributed in a large measure to the poor reception of *The Bostonians.* The average novel reader was uninterested, and the "better sort" were apathetic or antagonistic; the suffragists were writing their own history.

But James had seen and absorbed into *The Bostonians* the public and political as well as psychological aspects of feminism. The two major women figures in the novel are his first political characters: Verena sacrifices her public career for a private life; Olive sacrifices her private life for a public one. James's exploration of women who step beyond the concern of family life and who seek liberation in the "world outside" became one of the principal themes of his fiction of the 1880's.

Women in political affairs during the nineteenth century repre-

---

[50] Lucia T. Ames, *"The Bostonians," Woman's Journal,* XVII (March 18, 1886), 82–83.
[51] *"The Cause": A Short History of the Woman's Movement in Great Britain* (London, 1928), p. 284.

sented the ultimate conflict between radically opposing values—personal and sexual versus social and political—and focused ideas of crucial artistic interest to James. It is not too much to say that his study of feminism led James to the social issues that provide the themes of his next two major novels: anarchist activities in *The Princess Casamassima* (1885–1886) and the conflict between art and politics in *The Tragic Muse* (1890). James's attention to contemporary affairs perhaps comes as a surprise to those readers whose idea of him is shaped by the late novels; however, in addition to the evidence of the three "social" novels themselves, we have James's own statement to Robert Louis Stevenson in 1888, that he wanted "to leave a multitude of pictures of my time, projecting my small circular frame upon as many different spots as possible."[52] In *The Bostonians* he left more of a picture "of [his] time" than Jamesian criticism has hitherto realized.

[52] As quoted in *The Complete Tales of Henry James*, ed. Leon Edel (Philadelphia, 1961), I, 7.

Criticism and Autobiography in James's Prefaces

William R. Goetz

T HE PREFACES that Henry James wrote for the New York Edition
of his works, and to which he devoted much of his time between
1906 and 1908, are surely one of the major achievements of the
author's late period. Yet the Prefaces have only rarely been viewed
by James's critics as a literary work in their own right.[1] Instead,
critics have tended to use the Prefaces for ulterior purposes, in one
of two ways: either they have taken up the individual essays as
commentaries or critical aids to the novels and stories they discuss,
or they have taken the entire series of essays as constituting James's
major statement on the "theory of the novel." Neither of these
methods of application, however, has enjoyed total success. On the
one hand, the use of the Prefaces as practical criticism of James's
novels has usually proved fruitless, because the Prefaces have a remarkable way of failing to address the thematic content of the
works at hand. Since most of the criticism devoted to James has
been thematic, critics have not always known what to do with the
purely technical discussions on the craft of fiction which the Prefaces offer as a substitute for any direct interpretation of the novels'
content. Even on the rare occasions when James does comment on
the explicit themes of a work, his most immediate reference is usually
to the *source* of the story (for instance, to the literary notebooks in
which it took shape), which is usually quite different from the published work. The critics who rely on these remarks thus end up
often by commenting unwittingly on the Preface, or on the notebooks, rather than on the fictional work itself.

On the other hand, the claim that the Prefaces contain a general
theory of the novel has had a substantial *prima facie* success, from
the time of Percy Lubbock to that of Wayne Booth. Any number
of James's pronouncements concerning "point of view," the "organic"

---

[1] The most important exception to this tradition has been Laurence B. Holland, who
devotes a section of his book on James to the Prefaces. See Holland, *The Expense of Vision:
Essays on the Craft of Henry James* (Princeton, N.J., 1964), pp. 155–182.

form of fiction, the need for a "center of consciousness" and many other topics have been lifted out of the Prefaces and have passed into general currency. But this process of abstraction has not gone unaccompanied by certain presuppositions, the most important of which is that the Prefaces are cast in a purely expository mode and hence constitute a "meta-linguistic" discourse which is firmly set off against the primary instance of language which it is describing, that is, the literary language of the novels and tales. According to this assumption, the Prefaces themselves have a stock of themes which can, without distortion, be lifted from their rhetorical context—a context which would be completely neutral. One problem with this view, however, is that it ignores the attitude the Prefaces themselves adopt toward thematics. It appears perverse to consider solely from a thematic point of view a discourse which, itself, often goes to unusual lengths to avoid thematic issues. Even more important is the fact that, when James does discuss thematics in the Prefaces, it is often in order to put that method into question as a tool of criticism. He wages a continuing polemic against what he calls "the platitude of statement,"[2] which means any statement vouched for immediately by an authorial voice. Or, to use the pair of critical terms inspired by James (though not regularly employed by him), he argues that artistic representation consists always in "showing," never in "telling." He often makes the same point in his essays by insisting on the inseparability of "manner" and "matter." The strictures James applies to the criticism of fictional narrative can be applied equally to the criticism of the Prefaces. The essays' own "matter," their explicit themes, cannot alone furnish a sufficient clue to their real mode of operation.

There is good reason, in fact, to interpret the Prefaces not simply as a critical commentary on James's novels and tales but also as a continuation or repetition of those earlier works. The Prefaces explicitly assume the character of a narrative work, even in their opening paragraph, where James calls them a "thrilling tale" (4), or (later) when he refers to them as "the story of one's story" (313). Moreover, the Prefaces use certain common novelistic devices: a

[2] Henry James, *The Art of the Novel*, ed. R. P. Blackmur (New York, 1934; rpt. 1962), p. 37. All subsequent page numbers in my text will refer to this volume.

first-person narrator and an abundance of invented dialog.[3] Finally, they contain a richness of imagistic and figurative language that is comparable, in scope and function, to that found in James's late novels.

But the temptation to treat the Prefaces as only a new literary fiction runs up against an obvious objection, which arises from the ambivalent nature of the essays' enterprise. Even while the language of the Prefaces seems to fall back into the condition of a fictional and literary language, James is asserting that his language is *not* fictional but has an authentic referential function. The narrative the Prefaces embody is intended to be the story of the author, Henry James, as he exists outside of his literary productions. The story of the novels' composition amounts to nothing less than "the history of the growth of one's imagination" (47). The Prefaces turn out to be as much autobiography as they are textual criticism, and the James who writes the essays would rebel absolutely against the notion that his narrative is nothing but a new fiction.

Thus the Prefaces' refusal of thematism, their adherence to strictly technical questions of novelistic composition, is only half of the story. As long as only this half is recognized, the full, ambivalent purpose of the Prefaces cannot be accounted for. A recent critic, Leo Bersani, reflects a common opinion when he makes the following assessment of the Prefaces' method: "James should continually be proposed as a model for structural criticism. For the Prefaces are the best example I know of a criticism that constantly draws our attention away from the referential aspect of a work of art—its prolongations into reality—and toward its structural cohesion, which is taken as its principal source of inspiration."[4] If "structuralist" criticism, in this sense, were James's only purpose in the Prefaces, then his language would indeed have no referential claims. But although this structural (or at least, formal) commentary is one avowed purpose of the Prefaces, it is by no means the only one. James's other chief purpose is stated fully and clearly in his very first paragraph:

This revival of an all but extinct relation with an early work may often produce for an artist, I think, more kinds of interest and emotion than

---

[3] Invented dialog can be found on pp. 43–44, 64, 106, 112, 116, 168, 173–174, 182, 222–225, 269.

[4] Bersani, "Le Monsonge Jamesien," in *Poétique* No. 17 (1974), p. 51. My translation.

he shall find it easy to express. . . . This accordingly is what I mean by the contributive value—or put it simply as, to one's own sense, the beguiling charm—of the *accessory* facts in a given artistic case. This is why, as one looks back, the private history of any sincere work, however modest its pretensions, looms with its own completeness in the rich, ambiguous aesthetic air, and seems at once to borrow a dignity and to mark, so to speak, a station. . . . Addicted to "stories" and inclined to retrospect, he [the artist] fondly takes, under this backward view, his whole unfolding, his process of production, for a thrilling tale, almost for a wondrous adventure, only asking himself at what stage of remembrance the mark of the relevant will begin to fail. He frankly proposes to take this mark everywhere for granted. (3–4)[5]

The judicial image of *"accessory* facts" signals the rejection of intrinsic, formalist criticism in favor of an autobiographical mode of criticism in which the works' "private history" will be used to corroborate the truth of the author's own creative history. The emphasis on "history," "stories," "process," and "tale" makes it clear that the Prefaces are to assume the form of a new narrative superimposed on the novels' original narrative.

The language of the Prefaces, then, is intended to have the referential status that belongs to any autobiography. But this means that the essays' mode must be seen as a mode of artistic *representation*. The autobiographical subject of the Prefaces (Henry James) must be reconstituted or represented through the language of the essays. The act of representation performed in the Prefaces is thus fundamentally the same as the act of representation previously performed in the novels; the difference in the status of the two discourses (fictional and autobiographical) does not alter the structure of the linguistic sign involved. James himself points up this parallel when he refers to the Prefaces as an act of "re-representation" (335). The result is that artistic representation, or mimesis, is the performative mode of the Prefaces as well as their principal thematic subject-matter. For the technical problems James addresses in his essays are almost all derived from the fundamental topic of mimesis. Notions like "realism" and "representational value" are always the basic themes underlying the particular qualities James attributes to successful fiction: economy of interest, organic form, consistent point of view, and the rest.

---

[5] All italics in the quotations from the Prefaces, here and below, are in the original.

The central position of the theory of mimesis within the Prefaces has often been recognized, of course. But the privileged place that mimesis enjoys in the Prefaces is qualified in two important ways. First, on the explicit thematic level James subjects his own theory to numerous qualifications and even contradictions. In fact the essays exhibit a tension between mimetic and antimimetic hypotheses comparable to the tension I have already mentioned between an objective meta-language and a literary or fictional language. Thus, for instance, James's organicist articles of faith (stating that art imitates life by being formed like an organic object) are constantly put into question by his discussions of artifice and technique, where he writes of various non-organic traits like "foreshortening," "misplaced middles" and "dissimulation." Or again, James's assertion that art springs from the "garden of life" (312) is contradicted elsewhere when he describes art as an "alchemical" transformation that arises only out of the negation of the "form" of life (230).[6]

Thus even on an explicit level James's adherence to mimetic doctrine is in question. But a second way in which that doctrine is qualified is in the clash between the thematic and the performative levels of the essays. As I have said, the Prefaces not only discuss representation as an issue in the novels, they also perform it in their capacity as an autobiographical narrative. The contradiction already present thematically between mimetic and antimimetic statements becomes compounded when the Prefaces' own representational goal is taken into account. That goal appears constantly to be threatened by James's explicit theoretical statements that put into doubt the mimetic continuity between life and art; on the other hand, the claim of the Prefaces to be a referential, autobiographical narrative implicitly carries with it a claim for the effective possibility of the representational function of language.

Interpretation of the Prefaces becomes a problem of adjudicating between the claims made at these two levels, the thematic (or constative, in conformity with the vocabulary of speech-act theory) and the performative. One way to adjudicate is to focus on a certain number of passages that are crucial to the narrative of the Prefaces because they function on both levels at once: not only do they serve as episodes within the Prefaces' own story but they are also meant

---

[6] For similar statements, see pp. 119–120, 161–162, 166–169, and 221–224.

to be descriptions of the earlier act of fictional composition. This double role allows these passages to act as a kind of allegory of narrative, or as an allegory of the process of representation that is implied in any narrative.

The narrative the Prefaces tell is not to be found in the pages of formalist criticism where James studies the laws intrinsic to the novel but in the pages where the novel at hand serves instead as a pretext for the author's autobiographical pursuit. When he studies the novels, James discusses the fictional representation of reality as a special effect to be achieved by special techniques; but in the auto-biographical passages the novels have become documents in an ulterior mimeticist cause: the representation of James that is being performed in these essays. What counts now is not each novel's mimetic relation to the world it mirrors but rather its relation to the artistic biography of its author, the light it can shed on "the history of one's imagination." James uses his memory for the purpose of "glancing at the *other,* the extinct actualities they [the novels] hold up the glimmering taper to. They are still faintly scented, doubtless, with something of that authenticity, and a living work of art, however limited, pretends always, as for part of its grace, to some good faith of community, however indirect, with its period or place" (213). Though the novel indeed fulfills a mimetic function, it is clearly not the one its common reader might expect. The work is a representation not so much of the outside world as of the author's subjectivity; thus James can write that his fiction is "in the highest degree documentary for myself" (196). The work's "authenticity" thus depends on the authority of the writer who created it, and its very survival as a "living" word depends on the link it maintains with the subject whom it represents.[7] The relationship between author and text, however, is not entirely one-sided. The novels themselves stand as the prime evidence bearing testimony to the author's subjective past, so that the reconstitution of his selfhood can be carried out only through the mediation of his works.

Each novel becomes, then, not so much a mimetic copy of an external reality as a palimpsest. The visible surface of the palimpsest is the text as we have it, the text "literally" construed as the story of

---

[7] This organic relationship between author and text, where the author is father of the child/logos, is treated by Jacques Derrida in "La Pharmacie de Platon," in *Disséminations* (Paris, 1972), esp. pp. 89–90.

Isabel Archer, or Lambert Strether; the hidden, partially obliterated layer is the history of the author and his imagination. Thus the text performs two absolutely different semiotic operations, one for the ordinary reader and the other only for James. To the novel's readers, the text produces a signified whole which is the image of a certain (fictional) world. To James, that level of meaning is not the only or even the most important one. The signs of the text also point immediately to a referent that coincides with the real world of the author's past. Moreover, the level of the signified and the level of the personal referent have nothing necessarily in common. That is, James's own memories have nothing to do with the novel's specific images or content; the relation between the two is sheerly contingent and unpredictable. This discordance between the (fictional) signified and the (real-life) referent not only puts into question the unequivocal functioning of the literary work as a semiotic system but it also suggests that there is no common measure, no necessary connection, between the Prefaces' two pursuits: their formalist analysis of the novels and their autobiographical narrative. The two endeavors exist alongside one another in an uneasy relation.

The reason for this breach between the signified and the referent is that the autobiographical narrative is founded on what is essentially a private language, that of the author who alone is able to read the novels as palimpsests. Like any private language, James's will not be subject to verification, so that, in a sense, the categories of truth and fiction are no longer relevant to it. This might of course be said of any autobiography, but it is particularly striking here since James seems to be appealing to the series of his novels as though they offer objective testimony to the history of his consciousness.

The metaphor of the text as a kind of palimpsest is not my invention but James's. In the Preface to *The American,* he describes how a view of the novel's surface (its finished, manifest form) leads on to a view of its "depths": "It is a pleasure to see how again and again the sunken depths of the old work yet permit themselves to be sounded or—even if rather terrible the image—'dragged': the long pole of memory stirs and rummages the bottom, and we fish up such fragments and relics of the submerged life and the extinct consciousness as tempt us to piece them together" (26). This piecing together attempts to fabricate a continuous narrative out of the necessarily fragmentary materials the author's former works yield up. The layers of density of the text correspond to the meaningful depths of the author's mind, of which the text is supposed to be the faithful representation.

In another image, these aqueous depths of the work become a more transparent kind of interior space. The "shrunken concomitants" of one novel, James writes (meaning the scraps of evidence the novel contains from his own past), "lurk between the lines; these serve for them as the barred seraglio-windows behind which, to the outsider in the glare of the Eastern street, forms indistinguishable seem to move and peer; 'association' in fine bears upon them with its infinite magic" (125). In this metaphor the spaced bars of the window stand for the actual appearance of the printed page, with its black lines on a white background. James again upsets our normal notion of the role of the literary sign: he ignores the arbitrary nature of language and instead imagines writing as a sort of pictography, which operates in a spatial, perceptual field rather than a semantic or interpretive one. Once again, James is consciously minimizing the basic relation between the linguistic signifier and its signified in favor of stressing the supposed relation between the text and its referent, a relation which, as I have just argued, is essentially private.

As this passage proceeds the literary work continues to be represented as a kind of palimpsest, so that the author looking into its interior space immediately looks *through* it: "Peering through the lattice from without inward I recapture a cottage on a cliff-side, to which, at the earliest approach of the summertime, redoubtable in London through the luxuriance of still other than 'natural' forces, I had betaken myself to finish a book in quiet and to begin another in fear" (125). The "lattice" and the earlier "seraglio," however different they may be, work together to define the text as an enclosed, protected space. The motif of protection is then doubled at the narrative level by James's account of his retreat from the distractions of London to the calm and isolation of the rural scene to which he retired in order to write the novel. For James, as a retrospective reader of his own works now embarked on an autobiographical venture, one value of the text lies in its power to enclose and preserve the traces of his former self. In another Preface James again describes the role the old novel plays in the "ghostly interest" of summoning up his past: "I find this ghostly interest perhaps even more asserted for me by the questions begotten within the very covers of the book, those that wander and idle there as if in some sweet old overtangled walled garden, a safe paradise of self-criticism" (10). The work appears as a self-contained, organic object, but what James is describing is not an authentic version of intrinsic or formalist criticism, since the novel is not being considered as an entity in its own right but as an aid to "self-criticism." James has elsewhere described the Prefaces as "this infinitely interesting and amusing *act* of re-appropriation" (336), and it is the author's own works that become the *locus amoenus* within which he can withdraw in order to accomplish this self-appropriation. The inside of the literary texts has absorbed and preserved from oblivion the outside, referential reality of the author's past.

What is involved is thus the process of representation itself, the process whereby a literary work can appropriate the presence of an external reality and save it from destruction by giving it a second, interiorized life. The passage in the Preface is thus an allegory of the act of representation, in the sense that it puts into a dramatic, narrative account the structure of the mimetic event involved in the writing of a fictional work. The enterprise of the Prefaces is a repetition, but also a raising to the second power, of the mimetic enterprise of the novels they discuss: hence, as we have seen, James calls these essays a "re-representation." The Prefaces' *"act* of re-appropriation" (the author stresses their performative role) is synonymous with their act of representation. To make the past present once again, through a work of art, is to re-appropriate it, to "make it one's own" (155).

The dualistic imagery of inside and outside, as a metaphor for the process of representation, is crucial to one of the most famous pages in the Prefaces, that which deals with the "house of fiction" (Preface to *The Portrait of a Lady,* p. 46). "The house of fiction has in short not one window, but a million. . . ." It has been pointed out elsewhere that James's stress on the individuality of the author's vision, and on the consequently infinite number of possible literary forms, sets his mimetic theory apart from every positivistic or naturalistic

brand of literary realism.[8] However, as the "house of fiction" metaphor shows, James's tendency toward a subjective relativism does
not at all disturb the basic dualism on which all mimetic theory is
founded. There is an outside (the world, or, as James says, "the
human scene") which antedates the presence of the author; the work
of fiction is then portrayed as an interior space which renders or
represents the outside according to a special subjective bias.

The fate of the "house of fiction" metaphor can be followed
throughout the Prefaces. In fact, the narrative the essays develop is
made up largely of a series of literalized versions of that house. For
instance, as early as the Preface to *The American* (the second essay),
James describes the house in Paris in which he wrote most of that
novel. The Parisian scene is the referent, the earliest writing on the
palimpsest. The deep content of his memory, James writes, "makes
for the faded page to-day a sort of interlineation of sound." This
sound is, quite literally, the sound that rose to the author's windows
from the Parisian street:

> This sound rises to a martial clatter at the moment a troop of cuirassiers
> charges down the narrow street, each morning, to file, directly opposite
> my house, through the plain portal of the barracks occupying part of the
> vast domain attached in a rearward manner to one of the Ministères that
> front on the Place Vendôme; an expanse marked, along a considerable
> stretch of the street, by one of those high painted and administratively-
> placarded garden walls that form deep, vague, recurrent notes in the
> organic vastness of the city. I have but to re-read ten lines to recall my
> daily effort not to waste time in hanging over the window-bar for a
> sight of the cavalry the hard music of whose hoofs so directly and thrill-
> ingly appealed; an effort that inveterately failed. . . . (26–27)

The present-tense verbs of the first sentence reveal how vivid is the
"re-appropriating" and representational power of James's act of
memory. But while the passage accomplishes an act of representation, it also describes one. As with the "house of fiction," the author's
sight is directed outward from within, and this vision stands for the
act of representation itself, the transmission of the force of the active
life outside to the interiority of the work of art. Moreover, the house
in this passage is associated with the *locus amoenus*: it is an enclave

<hr/>

[8] See James E. Miller, Jr., "Henry James in Reality," in *Critical Inquiry*, II (Spring,
1976), pp. 585–604.

situated in the heart of the larger "organic vastness of the city." The "garden walls" are there to indicate the line that separates the protected space of the text from the frenetic life of Paris. The contrast between the protected, passive pursuit of the artist and the vigorous activity of life is underscored by the choice of military manoeuvres to represent the latter. James's remark that this spectacle "thrillingly appealed" is a capsulized formula for the author's fundamental ambivalence toward the outside world, an ambivalence parallel to that of his theoretical statements on the mimetic function of fiction. Though the world is the artist's sole source of material, it poses an unmistakable threat. The suggestion that this threat, embodied here in a military scene, is that of a certain form of death is perhaps counter-balanced by the fact that the military parade is after all only a form of makebelieve or play (like the work of art). Still, the danger hinted at is not to be taken lightly.

The most important immediate result of the present passage, however, is that the effort at an artistic appropriation of external life is essentially a failure. James comments retrospectively that the only result of his endeavors was to "waste time"—and not only because the author may never, as far as the passage tells us, have succeeded in seeing the spectacle anyway. More importantly, it was time wasted because the artist's desire to appropriate life in so immediate a way was misguided in the first place. A key element in James's narrative is the "window-bar" that stands between the writer and the scene outside. In this respect the bar may be said to change the image of the well-known windows or niches of the "house of fiction," which provided transparent points of view for seeing. In semiotic terms, the "window-bar" of the Preface to *The American* can be construed as the "bar" that separates the signifier from the signified, or, *a fortiori,* the bar that separates the total, arbitrary sign from its referent.[9] James's desire for artistic representation (on the performative level, his desire for genuine autobiography) is a desire for the sign and referent to coincide, or at least to stand in some necessary relation to each other. However, the Preface shows that desire being frustrated by the arbitrary nature of the sign. James's repeated failure,

[9] See Ferdinand de Saussure, *Cours de linguistique générale* (Paris, 1972), pp. 97–102, on the arbitrary nature of the sign. The "bar" which is already visible in some of Saussure's diagrams is made explicit by Jacques Lacan in "L'Instance de la lettre dans l'inconscient," in *Ecrits* (Paris, 1966), pp. 493–528.

in the narrative, to overcome the obstacle of the window-bar thus marks an at least temporary abandonment of his mimeticist argument. In fact the defeat within the story of author's mimetic impulse signals the end of the narrative portion of this particular Preface and an abrupt change to a different, more discursive mode. James promptly adopts a didactic tone in order to draw the moral of the story he has just related: "I have ever, in general, found it difficult to write of places under too immediate an impression—the impression that prevents standing off and allows neither space nor time for perspective. The image has had for the most part to be dim if the reflexion was to be, as is proper for a reflexion, both sharp and quiet: one has a horror, I think, artistically, of agitated reflexions" (27). His argument seeks to make a virtue of what his narrative has shown to be a necessity. But his method of compensation argues a certain loss for his art, since he is confessing that his literary text stands in a posterior, secondary relation to the immediacy of life's "image," an image which the mere text cannot hope to render in its orginal vividness. Thus the literary work, which James has optimistically called "the living work of art," finds itself strangely cut off from its life-source. James even writes that his novel had to turn its back on Paris in order "to save as it could its own life" (27). This unsettling conclusion evokes once more the threat that was implicit in the military review of the earlier passage, the threat that real life, far from being the positive source of all art, is potentially the death of the work of fiction.

The antimimetic tendency of this narrative thus leads James to question the very grounds of the artistic work's authenticity (since the work's function has supposedly consisted in its intimate connection to, and representation of, reality), and this is an attitude in which he cannot remain comfortable for long. Therefore the double movement of the Preface to *The American*—the author's simultaneous fear and attraction in front of the spectacle of life, his attempt to appropriate it and the failure of that attempt—is repeated in the very next essay, the Preface to *The Portrait of a Lady*. Here again the author's desire to represent his past self leads to a narrative account of the process of representation itself:

I had rooms on the Riva Schiavoni at the top of a house near the passage leading off to San Zaccaria; the waterside life, the wondrous lagoon spread before me, and the ceaseless human chatter of Venice came in at my windows, to which I seem to myself to have been constantly driven, in the fruitless fidget of composition, as if to see whether, out in the blue channel, the ship of some right suggestion, of some better phrase, of the next happy twist of my subject, the next true touch for my canvas, might not come into sight. (40)

James is describing the mimetic artist in his most mystified state, where he sees no distinction between the materials of life and those of art, and seeks to translate the one immediately into the other (as the passage itself does through a series of metaphors). The repetitive gesture of James's being "driven" to the window symbolizes the persistence of his will to believe in the referential value of his art. Once again, though, the Preface narrates the necessary frustration of this belief, as the novelist is forced to recognize that even "the romantic and historic sites of Italy," precisely because they are rich in expressive value, have nothing to offer the artist. "They are too rich in their own life and too charged with their own meanings merely to help him out with a lame phrase; they draw him away from his own small question to their greater ones" (41). Again the relation of life to art is essentially negative. Life tends not to nourish art but to annihilate it under the force of its own priority, so that at best the writer's work is "lame" or crippled.

In each of these Prefaces, then, James composes a short narrative which puts into a temporal order the different "moments" which, in the more theoretical passages, comprise the author's discussion of mimesis. The narratives are not allowed to stand in their own right but are followed by a summarizing comment which tries to minimize the frustration felt over the defeat of the artist's mimetic impulse. But that frustration is also being counter-acted, in a sense, by the very fact of the narratives' existence. The present discourse that produces the narratives is itself an allegedly successful act of representation in which the present author reaches out beyond the "walled garden" of the past text and re-appropriates into a new work of art (the Prefaces) his former self. This supposed victory of the Prefaces, however, clashes with the story the essays themselves are repeatedly telling. The narratives are not only an allegory of the primary act of fictional representation enacted in the novels, they are also an allegory that turns around to implicate the very discourse that is generating it. The repeated failure, in the narratives, of the artist's effort to appropriate external reality necessarily puts into question the success of the larger narrative, the Prefaces, in their autobiographical quest.

James's idea in this autobiography has been to use his earlier, literary texts as a palimpsest in which he can find the authentic story of his own self as a creative subject. But the stories he constructs consistently point to the difficulty, even impossibility, of such a mimetic, reappropriating act. Thus from a certain point of view these allegorical narratives subvert their own original purpose. For this reason they must constantly be broken off at the point where their failure begins to reveal itself. The result is that the essays, instead of forming the single, continuous story of the author's growth, consist in alternating series of fragmentary, abortive narratives and discursive statements that attempt to redeem the failure of those narratives.

James himself was acutely aware of the dangers inherent in the ambivalent project of the Prefaces, and especially of the dangers inherent in any autobiographical narrative. His awareness manifests itself in one of the most famous critical passages in the Prefaces, the discussion of the first-person narrator in the Preface to *The Ambassadors*. Here James identifies the chief hazard involved in this mode of narration as "the terrible *fluidity* of self-revelation," a quality he also calls a "looseness" in the form of the narrative. This fluidity or looseness results from the first-person narrator's inability to exercise discrimination or control over the narration of his own experience, and becomes a difficulty under which James himself labors in the Prefaces. Instead of practicing the formal restraint that an impersonal narrator can impose, the "I" narrator may wallow in "the large ease of 'autobiography,'" which degenerates all too surely into "the darkest abyss of romance" (320–321). This entire argument is cogent and self-consistent when applied to James's technique in his novels but it offers a peculiar embarrassment to the Prefaces and their own first-person narrator. I have already quoted the statement of intentions with which James opened the Prefaces: his determination to regard the story of his novels as his own "thrilling tale" and to take "the mark of the relevant . . . everywhere for granted" (4). In this optimistic forecast, the author's subjective experience was to be the primary material that would bind the narrative together by assuring the relevance of all its parts. However, as we have seen, this ideal of a single, cohesive narrative gave way in practice to a series of abortive, self-repetitive narratives that frustrate the representational goal of autobiography. Now, near the end of the Prefaces, James as it were gives the theoretical reason for the seeming failure of his project. Far from assuring the unity of his narrative, the first-person narrator is responsible for its "fluidity," its formal incoherence. Relying on "the inserted block of merely referential narrative" (321) to define his past self, the author is actually driven to reconstruct that self in a new work that turns out to be a fictional "romance." James as narrator of his own story suffers the same fate as any of his fictional characters who should try to do the same.

Of course this is not meant to suggest in any way that the Prefaces are a failure. On the contrary, I am suggesting that they may mistakenly be regarded as a failure only if they are taken to be something they are not: for instance, if they are taken to be exclusively a work of "structuralist" criticism (as Bersani would have it) or exclusively an autobiography (as James himself, at least sometimes, seems to wish). What lends these essays a unique interest within the Jamesian canon is the fact that they are clearly trying to be both at once, to pay equal attention to both layers of the text-palimpsest. In other words, the Prefaces tend to put into question a critical assumption for which they themselves, ironically, have proved one of the most historically important models: the assumption that there exists an "intrinsic" criticism of texts which is clearly distinct from the various kinds of "extrinsic" criticism. The Prefaces are so far from acknowledging any such distinction that they do not even try to reconcile intrinsic and extrinsic criticism, since to do so would be at the least to admit that an opposition between the two exists. Instead, the Prefaces mingle the two kinds of criticism without any clearly discernible consciousness that they are doing so. The incommensurability between James's public, formalist study of his novels and his private, "documentary" use of them is never allowed to disturb the apparently smooth, continuous surface of the Prefaces. It is only the contradictions that occur in any attempted reading of the Prefaces—the contradictions between mimetic and antimimetic principles, between narrative and discursive modes—that compel us to feel a discrepancy or incompatibility in the Prefaces' goals.

The task of reading the Prefaces concerns, finally, not only the difficulty of distinguishing intrinsic from extrinsic criticism but also that of distinguishing certain kinds of critical texts from literary ones. Criticism and narrative at the same time, autobiography and "romance," the Prefaces exist on the very margin between James's fictional and nonfictional works, and they go far toward blurring the distinction between the two. They constitute perhaps James's most profound reflection on the self-generating quality of literary language, a reflection which itself remains inscribed within the boundaries of literature.

Strategies for Survival
in James's *The Golden Bowl*

Catherine Cox Wessel

AN image from James's preface to *The Golden Bowl* evokes all that is most alarming in that novel: "I get down into the arena and do my best to live and breathe and rub shoulders and converse with the persons engaged in the struggle that provides for the others in the circling tiers the entertainment of the great game."[1] *The Golden Bowl* is indeed a kind of Coliseum, the product of an advanced civilization whose purpose is to display the beast-like struggle for survival engaged in by James's "deeply involved and immersed and more or less bleeding participants" (Preface, p. 328). The single most important point that can be made about James's book is that such deeply terrifying moral and emotional violence underlies the polished urbanity of its polite social and narrative surface. And, morally speaking, his prefatory arena image excludes no one. James's very readers sit implicated by their presence in the "circling tiers" and their pleasure in the gory "entertainment," while the fraternizing author himself is the imperial sponsor of the "great game."

This imagistic inclusiveness suggests what a close reading of *The Golden Bowl* confirms, that James's is not simply a moral criticism of a particular culture. The novel reveals its author's cynicism about human nature itself and his skepticism about how "civilized" any civilization really is. In this, as in the arena image's conflation of contemporary, "progressive" England with Imperial Rome, James departs from the Victorian effort to believe in patent moral progress and in the power of culture to lead man discernibly toward perfection. His social vision is much more like Freud's than Arnold's. He sees civilization as rechanneling rather than eradicating the instincts that it has learned to deplore. It cannot transform the human nature of which it is a manifestation—it can only refine the forms that

---

[1] *The Art of the Novel*, intro. Richard P. Blackmur (New York: Scribner's, 1934), p. 328. All references to James's prefaces will be to this volume.

American Literature, Volume 55, Number 4, December 1983. Copyright © 1983 by the Duke University Press.

human needs and energies take. Civilization reorganizes but does not abate its members' struggles for power over one another.

The Golden Bowl collapses history within its pages—from, in effect, primeval jungle to ancient Rome to modern London—reflecting James's vision of a species that manifests its deepest, its timeless instincts over and over again in recognizable ways.[2] The human race's primal heritage is depicted literally as lineage, as the blood- and sin-stained family history of Maggie's Roman prince. James's characters even become, imagistically, animals; their competitive relations are figured as violent combat. The most primitive impulses prowl hallucinatorily in a "beast-haunted land" (II, 299). Reduced to their most basic form, the instincts which James thus depicts in his collapsed history—a kind of natural history—are the lust for conquest and the will to possess: power is the instinctual value for which looting and rapine (and this book's gentler forms of material and sexual possession) are forms of currency.

The novel indeed opens on this theme, pronouncing London the contemporary equivalent of Imperial Rome. The very piles of merchandise in shopwindows, as the Prince looks into them on Bond Street, are "as tumbled together as if, in the insolence of the Empire, they had been the loot of far-off victories" (I, 3). For that matter, *The Golden Bowl* projects the imperialistic future, making it plain that the next inheritors of Empire will be the Americans. Adam Verver imagines himself as Keats's Cortez upon his peak in Darien ("a world was his to conquer and . . . he might conquer it if he tried"), though his method of conquest, unusually enough, is to plunder the Old World for the sake of the New, "to rifle the Golden Isles" and transport their most precious contents to American City (I, 141). The American conquistador will be a curious amalgamation of Vandal and Roman.

---

[2] See the comments of two intellectual descendents of Victorian historicism on James's "anti-historical attitude": Raymond Williams, *The English Novel: From Dickens to Lawrence* (London: Chatto and Windus, 1970), p. 133, and Philip Rahv, "Attitudes Toward Henry James," in his *Literature and the Sixth Sense* (Boston: Houghton Mifflin, 1969), p. 102. *The Golden Bowl*'s synchrony extends to its narrative structure, in which there is little suspense and no secrets are left to be unfolded to the reader. At every present moment in the novel, both past and future are taken for granted—as here, where Charlotte and the Prince are shopping for Maggie's wedding gift: "Charlotte, after the incident, was to be full of impressions, of several of which, later on, she gave her companion—always in the interest of their amusement—the benefit." *The Golden Bowl* (New York: Scribner's, 1909), I, 105.

Yet *The Golden Bowl*'s dramatic conflict ensues from Prince Amerigo's deliberate decision to believe that he can actually create a "new history" for himself instead of repeating his Roman ancestors' wicked old ones. "What was this so important step he had just taken [engaging himself to marry Maggie Verver] but the desire for some new history that should, so far as possible, contradict, and even if need be flatly dishonour, the old? If what had come to him wouldn't do he must *make* something different" (I, 16). He is at the story's opening both a medieval Prince embracing Victorian ideals and a Roman embracing American ones: He "wasn't mistaken—his future *might* be scientific. There was nothing in himself at all events to prevent it. He was allying himself to science, for what was science but the absence of prejudice backed by the presence of money? His life would be full of machinery, which was the antidote to superstition, which was in its turn too much the consequence, or at least the exhalation, of archives" (I, 17). Of course, there is plenty in the Prince—in anyone—to prevent a "scientific" rebirth. The "archives" of human history and the "superstition" of Original Sin have more useful human truth in them than this Spencerian or Comtian "science." Indeed, the Prince's own better judgment tells him this, when he thinks of how, in spite of personal virtues, he is "somehow full of his race" (I, 16).

The novel goes on to offer James's most intensive and explicit vision of what that race, the human race, is like. Its settings are figurative jungles or battlefields or arenas because James has moved his narrative locus almost entirely into his characters' minds, because he has captured in dreamlike images the instinctive, emotional, felt quality of their experience. James's last completed novel is the most deeply probing, the most "psychological" of his books: it explores the Darwinistic, behavioral foundations, not the specific outward mechanisms, of human society.[3]

The Golden Bowl's animal images clarify the social vision that had been James's for a long time. For example, he had always made frequent and varied use of images of treasure, money, wealth, and the

---

[3] Not surprisingly, critics who attempt to confine James to a humanistic, meliorist Victorian tradition are unhappy with his later fiction and with *The Golden Bowl* in particular. See, for a recent example, Alwyn Berland in his *Culture and Conduct in the Novels of Henry James* (Cambridge: Cambridge Univ. Press, 1981).

marketplace.[4] But this novel makes it clear, as in those opening descriptions of imperial plunder, that James had a particular understanding of wealth.[5] Just as the tasteful treasures and beautiful objects of art in his stories are often refined representations of sheer economic power, so wealth itself is a human refinement of the physical power and animal cunning of beasts. Economic struggle is a manifestation, not a cause, of human beings' innate lust for power.

The Golden Bowl demonstrates this by allowing its characters to achieve mutual accommodation in the realm of materal wealth. Their arrangement binds the story's principals into a four-way relationship which becomes the ground of their struggles for sexual domination of one another. In the end, the capitalist's wealth reasserts itself as an instrument of aggression—that is, Charlotte's and Amerigo's continuing dependence upon it plays a crucial role in determining the outcome of the sexual battle. But money is not all, even among these fortune hunters and human collectors; and in the course of the novel Maggie clinches her success by adding sexual magnetism to her other powers over the Prince. By structuring his novel so that the struggle for money is mainly a backdrop to its plot's central, sexual struggle, James depicts as specifically as possible in a complex world the power of the more primal sexual drive.[6]

If *The Golden Bowl* demonstrates how desire jeopardizes the individual as a moral, or even a civilized, being, it also acknowledges that (as Freud explained) this drive is the basis of the entire social order. Marriage, the family, and all the institutions that follow are the very forms of sexual desire and sexual dominion, as well as their containment. Even—and this is a critical point—the strength Maggie needs

[4] See especially Laurence Holland, *The Expense of Vision: Essays on the Craft of Henry James* (Princeton: Princeton Univ. Press, 1964), and Bradford A. Booth, "Henry James and the Economic Motif," *Nineteenth-Century Fiction*, 8 (1953), 141–50.

[5] The same is true of other James works from the later period, e.g., *The Wings of the Dove*, *The Ivory Tower*, and "The Jolly Corner." There are discussions of James's animal images in Harry Hayden Clark, "Henry James and Science: *The Wings of the Dove*," *Transactions of the Wisconsin Academy of Sciences, Arts and Letters*, 52 (1963), 1–15, and Daniel J. Schneider, *The Crystal Cage: Adventures of the Imagination in the Fiction of Henry James* (Lawrence: Regents Press of Kansas, 1978).

[6] See Edmond L. Volpe, "James's Theory of Sex in Fiction," *Nineteenth-Century Fiction*, 13 (1958), 36–47. My disagreement with Maxwell Geismar is clear. He contends that "all the primary drives of these later James figures have been compressed into an overwhelming 'curiosity' . . . replacing, in a curious contravention of the late nineteenth century Darwinian-Freudian world, the usual biological motives of food, fear, flight and sex." *Henry James and the Jacobites* (Boston: Houghton Mifflin, 1963), p. 232.

to restore marital order derives from her kindled sexual energy. Maggie can fruitfully break away from the pattern of the nobly renouncing Jamesian heroine precisely because she discovers within herself the vital, competitive animal power that other heroines either would not (Isabel Archer) or could not (Milly Theale) muster. She works to restore civilization's basic unit, the family; but she knows she works toward this civilized end with a motivating energy which is at bottom neither civilized nor moral. "When . . . you love in the most abysmal and unutterable way of all," she tells her father, "— why then you're beyond everything" (II, 262).

The Golden Bowl discreetly seethes with as much sexual energy as any best-selling novel of James's day—or our own—could hope to make genuine. The Prince's exquisitely lingering reappraisal of Charlotte upon her return to England is familiarly sexual, personally possessive. She is a cabinet of treasures to him, an "expanded flower," a well-filled silk purse that chinks as he weighs it in his palm (I, 46–47). The passion with which they are finally again lovers spills out upon the page in a torrent ("as at the issue of a narrow strait into the sea beyond, everything broke up, broke down, gave way, melted and mingled" [I, 312]). Maggie's love for her husband is, if anything, more passionate still, though less sheerly lustful. Her full cup spills over. "So here I am with it, spilling it over you—and just for the reason that's the reason of my life," she silently tells him (II, 18); she is "floated and carried on some warm high tide" (II, 25); and, heart thumping, vision "fevered," restraining herself from "her disposition personally to seize him," in the book's penultimate scene, Maggie, wanting to "wait," finds the physical intensity of her husband's closeness almost too much to bear (II, 341–42). Part of this intensity can be explained by the peculiar and perverse capacity which jealousy has for arousing passion; earlier in the book, Maggie and Amerigo have couched their acknowledgment of this in the safe but accurate form of a domestic joke: she "never admired him so much, or so found him heart-breakingly handsome, clever, irresistible, in the very degree in which he had originally and fatally dawned upon her, as when she saw other women reduced to the same passive pulp that had then begun, once for all, to constitute *her* substance" (I, 165). Sexual desire, even when it happens to be legitimized by law, is not a law-abiding passion.

Still, James does *not* simply reduce his characters' passions or their loving to animal lust. He does not employ the novel's striking animal imagery to describe human sexuality per se. Rather, in truer Darwinian fashion, his characters become animals as they struggle in the difficult, competitive situations to which their passions have consigned them. The two women in particular exchange the roles of predator and prey; both men, more detached (even the appreciative Prince by temperament and by breeding regards the relations between the sexes as somethings of a game), tend to figure as objects for the women's consumption.

The Golden Bowl's early animal images are comical-ironical ones, the pictorial offerings of the characters themselves. The threat behind the human-beast comparison still seems far off. Amerigo describes himself in chapter 1 as a *"crême de volaille,* with half the parts left out." Maggie's father, by contrast, he calls "the natural fowl running about the *bassecour,"* and he and Maggie joke about the Prince's "eating [him] alive—which is the only way to taste him" (I, 8). A little later Fanny pictures Amerigo as "a domesticated lamb tied up with pink ribbon. . . . [not] an animal to be controlled— [but] an animal to be, at the most, educated" (I, 161).

The book's imagistic atmosphere gradually darkens. Maggie tells her father that she is "a small creeping thing," one which "tremble[s] for [its] life" (I, 181); as we enter her consciousness with the crisis of Book Two impending, however, she is crouched, awaiting her husband's return from Matcham, like "a timid tigress" (II, 10). The Prince and the Principino, on the most light-hearted of family outings, are nevertheless "introducing Grandaddy, Grandaddy nervous and rather funking it, to lions and tigers more or less at large" (II, 59). Adam is the lamb now, bleating at Maggie to "Sacrifice me, my own love; do sacrifice me, do sacrifice me!" (II, 83). And at the very heart of *The Golden Bowl,* it is primarily Charlotte whom we see, through Maggie's eyes, as a magnificent beast roaming Fawns's terrace: "The splendid shining supple creature was out of the cage, was at large" (II, 239).

Later, however, the splendid creature will be recaptured. The Princess will see her stepmother as if in "the hard glare of nature . . . virtually at bay, and yet denied"—that peculiarly Jamesian, *human* torment—"the last grace of any protecting truth" (II, 303). With his daughter's aid, Adam Verver has got Charlotte completely under his control: the "likeness of their connexion wouldn't have been wrongly figured if he had been thought of as holding in one of his pocketed hands the end of a long silken halter looped round her beautiful neck" (II, 287). Man is the most dangerous creature in this "beast-haunted land," after all; the most powerful—in spite of his physical unimpressiveness—is Adam.

Many of the novel's exclusively human images also convey violence worthy of the world of animal aggression: war, torture, hand-to-hand combat. The Prince's French sets the tone for this group of images: "*A la guerre comme à la guerre*" (I, 290). Maggie imagines Charlotte as "always," rather tiresomely, "on the rampart" (II, 143); she thinks of herself at one point as "not unarmed for battle" (II, 106), at another, as throwing up her hands like a Wild West character to show that she's not carrying a revolver (II, 310–11). There is a violence to Amerigo in Fanny's smashing of the golden bowl, "a violence calling up the hot blood as a blow across the mouth might have called it" (II, 182). In the scene on the terrace at Fawns, Charlotte has effectively thrown Maggie "over on her back with her neck from the first half-broken and her helpless face staring up" (II, 242). But Charlotte, once again, suffers the most keenly in image as well as in fact: the separation from Amerigo is "like a knife in her heart." Maggie catches a glimpse of "her uncontrollable, her blinded physical quest of a peace not to be grasped," hears in the quaver of Charlotte's voice "the shriek of a soul in pain" (II, 311–12, 292).

Maggie chooses her battleground and her weapons with care. She cannot win the peace and love she longs for by crying out, in an unjust universe, for justice, nor can she compete with Charlotte physically on Charlotte's frankly sexual or grandly theatrical terms. But Maggie does not, like so many of James's protagonists before her, eschew the power struggle altogether; nor, since she wants her husband's heart as well as his presence, does she rely on her money to keep him. Rather, she achieves a real victory by fighting Charlotte with the human strengths of intelligence and canny self-restraint. The prowling beast that Charlotte, leaving the bridge game at Fawns, allows herself to become can be bested by a human being who uses her wits.

That card game is the novel's image for the game of wits and patience Maggie chooses to play. It is a pursuit much more civilized than the games of the arena, but one played here with the same emotional violence. In this scene Maggie's friends and family show her how it is done. Amerigo sits facing his mistress, sustaining their part of the match against his eternally enigmatic father-in-law and Fanny Assingham, who knows all. Maggie moves among them for a while, "silent and discreet" and wondering at "so complete a conquest of appearances," full of the knowledge that she could, with a word, shatter forever that "high decorum," the "picture of quiet harmonies." All the while the contending players are proceeding with the business at hand: holding each his cards in secret; wondering which cards his opponents hold and what they guess about his own hand; playing card after card, faces all quiet and unrevealing, decisions only partially guided by knowledge, partially blind; and playing the carefully ordered game—quite apart from the bridge— for such high stakes. Amerigo is well suited to the contest, "as he understood and practised every art that could beguile large leisure" (II, 233). Adam Verver, as befits a self-made multimillionaire, is "a high adept, one of the greatest" in such pursuits. Charlotte too is a "good" player. But Maggie, who has never been a player and who only watches the real bridge game ("cards were as nought to her and she could follow no move"), is forced against her old inclination into the role of the novel's consummate player of cards. Shaken out of her assumptions about her family's strengths and her own inabili- ties, she beats them all with her newly discovered skill.

Thus Maggie resists the temptation that assaults her as she watches the game—the temptation to sound the doom of their common peace that jumps at her "as a beast might have leaped at her throat" (II, 235). The shunned masochistic and vindictive pleasures of self-pity, jealousy, and recrimination appear to Maggie as an attrac- tively barbarous desert apparition, "a wild eastern caravan, looming into view with crude colours in the sun, fierce pipes in the air, high spears against the sky, all a thrill, a natural joy to mingle with, but turning off short before it reached her and plunging into other defiles" (II, 237). The caravan turns off because such blatant tactics are unthinkable "for *her* husband's wife, for *her* father's daughter" (II, 236). They are not only undignified but unstrategic, unlikely to succeed. And so when Charlotte comes out onto the terrace seek- ing battle, Maggie allows herself to be thrown down in apparent humility and defeat. Later, Maggie arranges another confrontation, and accepts in apparent abjection the book's cruelest verbal barb: "I want, strange as it may seem to you," Charlotte tells her, "to *keep* the man I've married" (II, 315). Maggie accepts from her family the role of scapegoat, as Milly Theale accepts the role of dove from her predators in *The Wings of the Dove*; but Maggie uses her meekness as a means to success in this world, not transcendence of it. Outwardly, Charlotte can outshine her, but Charlotte loses the war, outmaneuvered, because—relatively speaking, and in the words of Amerigo himself—"She's stupid" (II, 348).

The cruelty in Charlotte's comment to Maggie reminds one that Maggie *is* in important ways much "better" than Charlotte. Despairing of morality's worldly success, James has not in consequence lost his sense of such moral distinctions. Maggie is about as good as she could be and still live fully and successfully in the world as James portrays it; if she were not uncommonly generous, James's exposure of her competitive behavior would not carry such power to dismay. As it is, her very goodness is largely and designedly responsible for the particular discomfort she arouses in so many readers. That is, Maggie's virtues themselves, her sensitivity and her empathy, serve as her keenest weapons; her sympathetic consciousness of the pain she is inflicting magnifies the aggressive nature of her acts. Maggie suffers for her victim, but she doesn't leave off.

Choosing to engage in living rather than withdraw, Maggie has had to abandon most of the principles symbolized by the little silver cross she wears around her neck. Her spiritual counselor, Father Mitchell, sits useless at lunch; she has "found her way without his guidance. She asked herself at times if he suspected how more than subtly, how perversely, she had dispensed with him. . . . She feared the very breath of a better wisdom, the jostle of the higher light, of heavenly help itself" (II, 298). According to life's primary moral paradox, Maggie could not be so practically good or love so much if she were ethically purer. James's heroine grows in stature as she puts on the morally ambivalent garments of personal power, just as her love grows as it becomes more demandingly passionate.[7] The

---

[7] Thus when Maggie tells Fanny Assingham that she is bearing all "for love," she refers to a love that contains both the egoistically possessive and the altruistic kinds. For readings that differ from mine on this issue, see Peter Brooks's emphasis on James's "melodrama of ethical *choice*" (emphasis mine), and J. A. Ward's emphasis on Maggie's "selflessness . . . capacity for suffering, and . . . sense of social duty." Brooks, *The Melodramatic Imagination: Balzac, Henry James, Melodrama, and the Mode of Excess* (New Haven: Yale Univ. Press, 1976); Ward, *The Imagination of Disaster: Evil in the Fiction of Henry James* (Lincoln: Univ. of Nebraska Press, 1961), p. 104.

Princess gradually acquires validity even for herself as she pits her
will against the others (II, 142): in the last scene of the book she
takes on "the very first clear majesty" her husband has ever known
her to use (II, 356). Men and women, James would seem to be
saying, accept the full strong heritage of their humanity only when
they accept their willingness to inflict as well as suffer pain, when
they can live with the truth that "Everything's terrible . . . in the
heart of man" (II, 349).

Maggie, then, does not achieve her victory on account of moral
purity, any more than she wants her husband back because she
believes in the sanctity of marriage. The Princess retains her husband
because she still has the power of her wealth, because she discovers
the powers of her own intelligence and will, and because she is
fortunate enough to have virtue—that is, the countenance of social
law—on her side. In addition, of course, though hardly incidentally,
all this power renders Maggie newly and erotically fascinating to
the Prince. Maggie wins, as creatures in a Darwinian world do,
because she is both gifted and lucky. The roles that power and luck
play in her vanquishing of Charlotte still draw the same kind of
protests from James's readers that Darwin's work drew in his day,
and for the same reason. Neither author imagines a universe where
success has much to do with moral deserts.

Thus, though he punishes adultery and finally allows his last
heroine to win, James is no closer than ever in *The Golden Bowl*
to depicting a morally just world. What happens in his fiction
resembles, rather, an artistic version of the survival of the fittest:
the strongest vision within a novel has its way in arranging that
novel's world of relationships. Ruth Bernard Yeazell describes this
clearly: The "ambivalence which so many readers have felt toward
Maggie's final victory—and less intensely, perhaps, toward Milly
Theale's—should warn us that questions of truth and morality in
these novels are to the very last oddly blurred. If we prefer Maggie's
talk to Charlotte's, it is not that Maggie speaks honestly while
Charlotte lies, but that Maggie is ultimately the superior artist—that
her language makes for the most harmonious and inclusive design
her world can sustain."[8] Maggie's reshaping of her world according

[8] *Language and Knowledge in the Late Novels of Henry James* (Chicago: Univ. of
Chicago Press, 1976), p. 86.

to her own desires is her own artist's response to the threat posed by uncivilized forces within herself and without. Moreover, her response is all the more *powerful*, not merely more pleasant, for its civility and grace.

Individuals in *The Golden Bowl* keep thinking that they have "arranged" their lives (the word appears again and again) in one fashion, only to discover that things have been quite contrarily arranged or rearranged for them by someone else, or by their own previously unapprehended needs and limitations. On one level, the existence of the book's four main characters takes the form of one superficial but quite stable structure, "a life tremendously ordered and fixed" (II, 66); but beneath the orderly surface these shifting, conflicting rearrangements bespeak a moral and emotional chaos of struggle and desire which threatens the structure's collapse. While Maggie marvels at the "miracles of arrangement" among which she has been living (II, 110), the real, the final masterpiece of restructuring is the work of her own hands.

The Princess has a "small still passion for order and symmetry," a passion quiet yet so strong that when the bowl's illusion of true moral symmetry and order has been smashed for her forever upon reality's floor, her "prompt tribute to order" is to pick up the pieces and to hold them together with her hands (II, 152, 182). Maggie sees the betrayal at last, but she despises the look of raw disarray; her husband having seen what she knows, she does not care to look at his face "till he should have had a minute to arrange it." "Arrange yourself so as to suffer least," Maggie wants to tell him, "or to be, at any rate, least distorted and disfigured" (II, 181, 183). And her Prince is the mate to oblige, for he is one of the "great people" who "always know how to re-establish a violated order" (II, 220). Maggie is learning that such an order *is* merely an "arrangement," that human motives and emotions do not easily lend themselves to any kind of moral coherence. All bowls are cracked at the very least: her own emotions and activities are teaching her this as much as the betrayal itself. But the fragile form, even the deceptive gilt that can be applied to experience are to be regarded as saving graces, not specious tricks.[9]

---

[9] See Dorothea Krook and Ruth Bernard Yeazell on the necessity and the heavy psychological price of Maggie's conscious hypocrisy. Krook, *The Ordeal of Consciousness in Henry James* (Cambridge: Cambridge Univ. Press, 1962), pp. 277–79; Yeazell, pp. 98–99.

The qualities of *harmony* and *inclusiveness* that Yeazell attributes to Maggie's design become *equilibrium* and *fullness* in the novel's own images. In *The Golden Bowl* these replace the static double-faced medal that James uses elsewhere as his metaphor for "the close connexion of bliss and bale, of the things that help with the things that hurt."[10] All of the novel's characters are "in their different ways, equally trying to save" the precious equilibrium among them, but Maggie is virtually, "in all her conscious person, the very form" of it (II, 268). The Princess "postures" and "capers" like a spangled lady balancing on horseback; trying at once to keep an equilibrium within herself and among her family members, she is the circus's "overworked little trapezist girl" (II, 71, 302).

In another, even more important series of images, Maggie holds the shards of golden glass together to retain their brimming contents, trying to preserve for her family more than mere empty form. It is too late for Charlotte personally: she and Amerigo have had, as Amerigo imagined it, "a great gold cup that [they] must somehow drain together," and she may have drunk all her happiness up (I, 359). She will probably have to be content with maintaining a high form and the "right quiet lustre" (II, 358). But Maggie can still hope for the bowl "with all our happiness in it" for herself and Amerigo, if not the impossible bowl "without the crack" (II, 217). She feels, in one of the book's most characteristic images, that through her crisis's exhausting course she has been carrying "in her weak stiffened hand a glass filled to the brim, as to which she had recorded a vow that no drop should overflow" (II, 298).

The happiness Maggie balances is really her own; her design for her family serves herself first and best. This is why she tells her father that she's "frozen stiff with selfishness" (II, 265). But, based as it is upon her understanding of their needs, her design does provide the most accommodating arrangement for the group as a whole. Maggie finds herself in the fortunate position of a superiorly gifted artist: empowered by her strong and empathetic imagination to impose a privately satisfying vision upon a world that will actually be the better for it.

There can be no relaxation of this effort, however, in a realm full of the clashing of wills. Wasn't relaxing just the mistake Maggie

---

[10] Preface to *What Maisie Knew*, p. 143.

made within her family in the first place? Amerigo's behavior during the whole of the novel's last day indicates how Maggie "has" him now; but there is no lessening of tension in the last paragraph, no resolution of the strong emotions of husband and wife. Maggie has learned that even love is not something one merits or earns, but something one has to win. Here at the end, even as she thrills at the touch of her prize, Maggie feels pity for the object of her willing and dread of the nonetheless welcome sexual force she sees lighting his eyes. Moreover, the future looms frighteningly for both of them. Maggie has been the creature she needed to be to survive the struggle just past; what capacities will be required now, by a future she cannot foresee?

As Yeazell points out, at the end of the novel "what we really witness . . . is less a closed fiction than a character struggling to will such a fiction," and the author himself conspires with Maggie to shape the ending for a story whose tensions are of the kind that have no surcease (pp. 125–26). Indeed, Maggie holding her golden fragments together is the figure of James's artistic will. His novel is a disorder of conflicting human passions and needs (his characters' and his own), held heroically together in the form of a rare and precious object. Just as social ceremonies in his fiction give polite structure to behavior at bottom merciless, so James's art of fiction gives civilizing form to a story of morally chaotic emotional violence. He values form in fiction, as in life, as literally a saving grace; but he demonstrates his awareness of its painfully provisional and compromised nature.

Maggie's lying and James's are of the same kind, then. Both know that their fictions are not fundamentally true, that Maggie can never have the ideal "golden bowl—as it *was* to have been" (II, 216), that she will have to go on holding its pieces together till the end. Nevertheless, both novelist and heroine insist upon believing that their lies do have some real power over the chaos of reality, that holding those recalcitrant pieces together can make a difference. James's and Maggie's faith in such formal "lying" is like Maggie's early faith in the Prince: divided into compartments, so that the ship will "manage not to sink" even if "most of them . . . go to smash" (I, 14). Thus when it becomes apparent that fictions cannot redeem life intrinsically, the lies still can salvage some happiness by making life tolerable in form. The connections between their fictionalizing and reality, James and Maggie know, are precarious and lamentably superficial. But neither quite gives in to the fear that there may be *no* connections, no chance for order, no sound "compartments" at all.

Such a fear did threaten James personally, threatened him so much that its magnitude becomes for us precisely the measure of his opposing determination to impose his shaping will upon experience. The Carlylean power of his insistence upon seeing or creating order places him among the last of the great Victorians, while the self-reflexive skepticism it did battle with places him among the great early modern minds.[11] He was aware of his own constant effort to mediate between what he once characterized as mid-Victorian "sincerity" and modern skepticism or, tellingly, "the new plausibility."[12] In *The American Scene*, published in 1907, three years after *The Golden Bowl*, he described such mediation between sense and senselessness as the duty of the (Arnoldian-sounding) "critic":

> From the moment the critic finds himself sighing, to save trouble in a difficult case, that the cluster of appearances can *have* no sense, from that moment he begins, and quite consciously, to go to pieces; it being the prime business and the high honour of the painter of life always to *make* a sense—and to make it most in proportion as the immediate aspects are loose or confused. The last thing decently permitted him is to recognize incoherence—to recognize it, that is, as baffling; though of course he may present and portray it, in all richness, *for* incoherence.[13]

Or, again, in a letter about how his "aged nerves can scarcely stand" the disillusionment of World War One, and how difficult the War has made it to write, James says: "And yet I keep at it—or mean to; for . . . that I hold we can still . . . *make* a little civilization, the inkpot aiding, even when vast chunks of it, around us, go down into the abyss—and that the preservation of it depends upon our going on making it in spite of everything and sitting tight and not chucking up—wherefore, after all, *vive* the old delusion and fill again the

---

[11] There is an important and complex stylistic analogue, of course, in the force of personality that James imposes upon the English language—and in that style's effect of willfully ordering chaos.

[12] In *The Middle Years* (London: Collins, 1917), pp. 24–25.

[13] Intro. Leon Edel (Bloomington: Indiana Univ. Press, 1968), p. 273. See Charles Feidelson on James's attempts "to save the very concept of 'sense'" in a modern world which more and more seemed to suffer lapses of meaning—"James and the 'Man of Imagination'," in *Literary Theory and Structure: Essays in Honor of William K. Wimsatt*, ed. Frank Brady, John Palmer, and Martin Price (New Haven: Yale Univ. Press, 1973), pp. 331–52.

flowing stylograph—."[14] "*Vive* the old delusion": the determination and the despair both are contained in this cry.

Thus James himself combats modern despair with a kind of Victorian personal heroism; yet what one must remember—what *The Golden Bowl* demonstrates—is James's understanding that even heroism is not the same as morality. His cynical, modern, post-Darwin vision of the amoral human will both concedes to it great practical power and forbids its romanticization.[15] In these respects the artistic will is the same as any other. The artist is—as James put it in another letter—a "queer monster": the use to which he puts experience is a *self*-preserving "act of life."[16] James pictures himself climbing down into *The Golden Bowl*'s bloody arena because he considers his writing as much an assertion of power as anything his characters do. Even when the "little civilization" that an artist can create is, like Maggie's, for the general good, James knew as well as Freud did that his creation of it is egoistic—a tactic in his own personal struggle to survive.

[15] This last is where my reading of *The Golden Bowl* differs crucially from Stephen Donadio's, which is in other respects rather similar. Donald David Stone agrees with me that James "repudiated" the Victorians' optimism but insists that, abandoning the world, he maintained a "reassuringly fixed belief in the sacredness of art." By contrast, Lionel Trilling's essay on *The Princess Casamassima* discusses James's understanding that the creation of art is a form of power and aggression. Donadio, *Nietzsche, Henry James, and the Artistic Will* (New York: Oxford Univ. Press, 1978), pp. 249, 247; Stone, *Novelists in a Changing World: Meredith, James, and the Transformation of English Fiction in the 1880's* (Cambridge: Harvard Univ. Press, 1972), p. 305; Trilling, in his *The Liberal Imagination: Essays on Literature and Society* (New York: Harcourt Brace Jovanovich, 1979), pp. 56–88.

[14] To Mrs. Alfred Sutro, 8 August 1914, in *The Letters of Henry James*, ed. Percy Lubbock (New York: Scribner's, 1920), II, 388.

[16] To Henry Adams, 21 March 1914, in *Letters*, II, 360–61.

The Selfish Eye:
Strether's Principles of Psychology

Susan M. Griffin

M ANY critics discuss "Jamesian perception," but few have examined what James's characters actually see. Literal and figurative "visions" are lumped together. And perception itself is either made indistinguishable from "thought" or reduced to a source of raw materials for the intellect. This failure to analyze Jamesian visual perception as a complex physical and psychological process has led to two misconceptions—that observation and experience are opposed in James, and that the Jamesian protagonist is a "passive observer," a cerebral, almost bodiless, being, completely detached from the world of experience. These notions can be traced to the beginnings of James criticism.[1]

But neither the opposition between observation and experience nor the idea of a passive observer is consistent with Henry James's fiction. Although he finally fails to distinguish between "perception" and "imagination," Paul Armstrong characterizes aptly James's position: " 'I'm not the spectator, I am involved' whenever I perceive."[2] In James, visual perception is not detached intellection. Perceptions are immediate, physical points of connection between the individual and his environment. Seeing is an active means of adapting to the world. Yet, while seeing is primary, it is not simple, crude sensation. Jamesian perception is (like Jamesian thought and the Jamesian sentence) an intricate process.

Placing James's work in the context of late nineteenth-century psychology allows us to transpose the observation-experience dichotomy into one between associationist and functionalist psychol-

---

[1] See Percy Lubbock's 1920 "The Mind of the Artist" in *The Question of Henry James: A Collection of Critical Essays*, ed. F. W. Dupee (New York: Holt, 1945), pp. 54–69, for an early example.
[2] "Knowing in James: A Phenomenological View," *Novel*, 12 (1978), 13.

American Literature, Volume 56, Number 3, October 1984. Copyright © 1984 by the Duke University Press. CCC 0002-9831/84/$1.50

ogies. And recognizing that James's perceptual psychology is functionalist rather than associationist explains why and how his characters are not passive observers. Once we understand that for the psychologists of James's time the question is whether perception is associationist or functional, we can free ourselves from the categories of observation and experience. We can study how James's characters see, without being forced to regard that seeing as detached, cerebral, and passive.

The associationist school, whose origins were Aristotelian and whose systematization is usually credited to Hartley and Hume, had dominated eighteenth and nineteenth-century studies of the mind. Associationist psychologists described a mental life composed of discrete sensations. The mind was merely a *tabula rasa*, a place where these atoms of sensation combined and recombined. Therefore, only units of sensation, not individual unified subjects, were the objects of psychological investigation. The critical commonplace that James's characters are "passive observers" is based upon this associationist model: perceivers are the passive recipients of atomistic sensations.[3]

Functionalism, while acknowledging the explanatory power of the associative mechanism, attempted to alter the study of the mind in light of Darwin's discoveries. The new evolutionary biology was a system in which "every organ and function was understood in terms of its history and its relation to the life of the creature which displayed it."[4] Psychology, it was argued, must begin to understand the mind in just this way, as "an organ which, like any other organ, has been evolved for the benefit of its possessor."[5] Mind and body were not to be the parallel objects of separate studies (metaphysics and biology), but were both to be analyzed functionally. Functionalist psychologists, like James Ward and William James, argued that psychology should study *unified subjects*, not units of sensation, that these subjects should be analyzed not in isolation but *functionally*, (that is, as engaged in adaptive interactions with their

[3] For example, J. H. Raleigh, "Henry James: The Poetics of Empiricism," in *Henry James: Modern Judgements*, ed. Tony Tanner (London: Macmillan, 1968), pp. 52–66.

[4] Gardner Murphy, *Historical Introduction to Modern Psychology*, rev. ed. (New York: Harcourt, Brace, 1949), pp. 107–08.

[5] Richard J. Herrnstein and Edwin G. Boring, "Functionalism," in *A Source Book in the History of Psychology*, ed. Richard J. Herrnstein and Edwin G. Boring (Cambridge: Harvard Univ. Press, 1965), p. 482.

environments), and, finally, that such subjects are *active*, not passive, in nature.[6]

The question of whether perception is best described by an associationist or a functionalist model is, then, a question of whether atomistic sensations impinge upon a passive subject and build into larger units of perception, or an active, unified subject selects its perceptions in the course of an interested, adaptive relation with its undifferentiated environment.

This question is answered in James's fiction: perception is functional. My argument is not that the theories of William James and others find their ways into Henry James's practice. Rather, Henry James's perceivers confront the problems and enact the solutions central to the psychology of his time. What the Jamesian eye sees is always in the interest of the Jamesian "I." To say this is not to uncover secret villainy in James's protagonists. Rather it is to place those protagonists doubly in context: to understand the historical basis for their psychologies and to recognize how those psychologies are a function of the environments that surround them. Relying on William James's *Principles of Psychology* to describe more fully how functionalists explained perception, and using Lambert Strether in *The Ambassadors* as an example of the Jamesian perceiver, I will now do just that.[7]

Strether has long been recognized as the prototypic Jamesian perceiver, and, indeed, attributes of Strether's vision are characteristic of Jamesian perception in general. Strether's perceptions take the form of a *unified* stream. The stream of perception is *functional*: it is a means of adjustment to environmental conditions. And this emphasis on the function of perception explains the *active* nature of Strether's seeing. He survives in his environment by attending actively, by selecting those perceptions which fulfill his needs.

Critics have almost universally recognized James's subjects as unified. But that unity is seen as evidence that Jamesian mental life consists of detached cerebration, a belief that, in turn, has led

[6] J. C. Flugel, *A Hundred Years of Psychology, 1833–1933: With an Additional Part on Developments 1933–1947* (London: Duckworth, 1951), p. 150.

[7] *The Principles of Psychology*, ed. Frederick Burkhardt, 3 vols. (Cambridge: Harvard Univ. Press, 1981); and Henry James, *The Ambassadors* (1903; rpt. New York: Scribner's, 1909). All quotations will be taken from these editions and noted in the text.

to the critical consensus that a Jamesian character could not experience anything so crude as a "stream of consciousness":

To a modern reader, long accustomed to the idea that much of consciousness operates below the level of language, the very look of a Jamesian
meditation on the page suggests a mind in which the intellect is very
much in control. For the unconscious does not, we suspect, obey the
rules of grammar and of syntax, and James's men and women think in
sentences which no more resemble the unpunctuated flow of words in
Molly Bloom's final monologue or the bizzare strings of neologisms in
Finnegan's Wake than their sleeping habits resemble those of Joyce's
rather drowsy characters. Though the Jamesian sentence strains, it does
not break: no stream of consciousness, the critics all agree, flows through
the pages of James's late fiction.[8]

Henry James does *not* write in what literary critics have defined
as "stream of consciousness." Yet the psychologist who originated
the phrase, William James, did not find quite so inconceivable the
idea that the "stream of consciousness" might be expressed in the
structure of a grammatically correct sentence. Indeed, he used this
structure as a way of describing the stream itself:

As we take, in fact, a general view of the wonderful stream of our
consciousness, what strikes us first is this different pace of its
parts. . . . The rhythm of language expresses this, where every thought
is expressed in a sentence, and every sentence closed by a period. . . . There is not a conjunction or a preposition, and hardly an
adverbial phrase, syntactic form, or inflection of voice, in human speech,
that does not express some shading or other of relation which we at some
moment actually feel to exist between the larger objects of our thought.
(I, 236, 238)

James proposes the analogy of the stream as a replacement for
associationism's "chain" of distinct, atomistic ideas. He explicitly
disagrees with Alexander Bain's insistence that the "stream of
thought is not a continuous current, but a series of distinct ideas"
(I, 257–38). Instead, James calls for the "re-instatement of the
vague to its proper place in our mental life" (I, 246). And he
argues that not only are most of our thoughts vague "*feelings* of

---

[8] Ruth Bernard Yeazell, *Language and Knowledge in the Late Novels of Henry
James* (Chicago: Univ. of Chicago Press, 1976), p. 17. Yeazell goes on to suggest that
such intellectual control is "more precarious—and more hard-won—than might at first
appear," p. 18.

tendency," but even the stopping-places, the nouns, are continuous with the surrounding "water of consciousness" (I, 246): "Every definite image in the mind is steeped and dyed in the free water that flows round it. With it goes the sense of its relations, near and remote, the dying echo of whence it came to us, the dawning sense of whither it is to lead" (I, 246).

William James is not arguing that all thought is verbal. His point is that all thinking takes the form of a stream: a continuous flow with stopping-places. Perception, too, is a stream, a stream which Strether's first viewing of Maria Gostrey's apartment illustrates: "It was the innermost nook of the shrine—as brown as a pirate's cave. In the brownness were glints of gold; patches of purple were in the gloom; objects all that caught, through the muslin, with their high rarity, the light of low windows. Nothing was clear about them but that they were precious. . . (I, 119–20)." What he sees is a continuous whole. There are stopping-places (the glints, the patches, the objects), but they are immersed in their surroundings (in the brownness, the gloom, the light).

Gradually, Strether begins to discriminate certain objects more clearly, and eventually he is "bent, with neared glasses, over a group of articles on a small stand" (I, 123). Strether's discriminations are perceptual here, not "cerebral." He still sees a continuous whole, yet his perception now entails analysis. The stream of perception flows towards discrimination. Associationism describes the mind as passively receiving simple units of sensation which build up into complex structures. For both William and Henry James, the procedure is exactly reversed. William James explains: "The 'simple impression' of Hume, the 'simple idea' of Locke are both abstractions, never realized in experience. Experience, from the very first, presents us with concreted objects, vaguely continuous with the rest of the world which envelops them in space and time, and potentially divisible into inward elements and parts. These objects we break asunder and reunite (I, 461)."

William James says explicitly that this discrimination is direct and perceptual. Indeed, he argues that even conceptual divisions, which result from our knowledge *about* things, can be ultimately traced to perceptual discriminations. Yet those critics who recognize that the movement, the continuity, the "vagueness," to use William James's term, in Henry's sentences are the very terms of analysis and discrimination, do not regard these complexities as perceptual.

Instead these attributes are ascribed to a rational intellect that is seeking to *control* the raw material of direct perception. Because it is assumed that perception is simple and atomistic, what the eye sees and what the mind knows are regarded as qualitatively different. Stowell, for example, who uses the image of the *tabula rasa* to characterize perception, argues that "consciousness" synthesizes discrete, raw percepts into an active, processive gestalt.[9] The failure to recognize that both Jamesian thought and Jamesian perception are streams obscures the fact that James's perceivers are unified, not despite but *in* their perception. Strether works out the correspondences between things *in* his perceptions of Maria's apartment.

What is the function of these unified perceptions? We can answer that question only by recognizing the fact that Strether is an active perceiver, not a passive observer. From the very start, he selects and arranges in the very act of seeing. To perceive in James's fiction is to compose reality into pictures. But such pictures are not proof that Strether is "blinding himself to knowledge of the material world in order to make an ideal version of that world," as Burde and others have claimed.[10] Instead, the Jamesian perceiver creates those pictures that suit his self-interest. *The Ambassadors* is hardly "Nature, red in tooth and claw." The environment that interests James is, of course, the social environment of civilized society. Nonetheless, Strether survives in his world by seeing what he needs to see. Judith Ryan misses these perceptual survival tactics when, recognizing that Jamesian consciousness is "fluid and unbounded," she goes on to argue that this fluidity is evidence that James is not interested in the self as a discrete entity.[11] Strether's perceptual pictures are always self-interested—even when they seem self-sacrificing. For example, he constructs a series of pictures of Marie de Vionnet that portray a lady in mild, romantic distress and thus in need of noble yet limited "saving." These pictures permit Strether to become safely, restrictedly, involved with her.

The fact that Strether needs to think of himself as noble does not mean he cannot act nobly. Strether's selfish eye is not the mark

[9] H. Peter Stowell, *Literary Impressionism, James and Chekhov* (Athens: Univ. of Georgia Press, 1980), pp. 24–25.

[10] Edgar J. Burde, "*The Ambassadors* and the Double Vision of Henry James," *Essays in Literature*, 4 (1977), 59.

[11] "The Vanishing Subject: Empirical Psychology and the Modern Novel," *PMLA*, 95 (1980), 861.

of a villain because it is not an organ peculiar to him. His perceptions are structured by the very conditions of seeing. In *The Sense of the Past*, James describes Ralph Pendrel as "all selfishly" asking another for help, and then goes on to say: "Immense and interesting to show him as profiting by her assistance without his being thereby mean or abject or heartless."[12] Our understanding of Strether's self-interested seeing needs to be equally "immense."

Despite this active interest, Strether does not completely determine what he sees. Understanding the activity of his perceptions means first defining the limits of that activity. Chad and Marie arrange many of the visual details that Strether uses for his compositions. Strether's environment naturally limits what he sees. And there are internal constraints as well, constraints so strong that analysis of the mechanics of Strether's perceptions must confront the possibility that such perceptions may be nothing more than mechanical.

Late nineteenth-century psychologists' insistence upon studying the mind within its environment, and, thus, the individual's necessary adaptation to his surroundings, raised the age-old question of determinism with new force. William James tries throughout *The Principles* to reconcile his belief in free will with Darwinism. Oddly enough, James finds in evolutionism itself justifications for a belief in the indeterminacy of human behavior. He argues that "chance variation" introduces the potential for spontaneity, the possibility that the cosmos is not a great clock whose motions are mechanical and determined.[13]

James also finds strong indications of indeterminacy in the mind's interested relationship with its environment. He postulates that, if free will exists, it can be located in moments of attentive perception. James explains in detail how attention is above all *interested*. He says that "what-we-attend-to and what-interests-us are synonomous terms" (II, 1164). What we perceive is thus determined functionally, by our needs. Rather than a proof of simple determinism, the biological nature of attention is the possible source of our ability to choose our perceptions.

---

[12] *The Sense of the Past* (1917; rpt. New York: Augustus M. Kelley, 1971), pp. 328, 338.

[13] John C. Greene, *The Death of Adam: Evolution and Its Impact on Western Thought* (Ames: Iowa State Univ. Press, 1959), p. 306.

According to William James, associationism, by focusing on sensations and relegating the subject to the role of passive receiver, had virtually ignored this potential source of individual power: "Locke, Hume, Hartley, the Mills, and Spencer . . . are bent on showing how the higher faculties of the mind are pure products of 'experience'; and experience is supposed to be of something simply *given*. Attention, implying a degree of reactive spontaneity, would seem to break through the circle of pure receptivity which constitutes 'experience,' and hence must not be spoken of under penalty of interfering with the smoothness of the tale (I, 380)." James finds associationism insufficient, but not irrelevant. Association takes place whether we will it or not, and attention, therefore, cannot grant complete freedom of action. We may direct our attention and thus select and compose our perceptions, but the potential objects of both attention and perception are limited. Our pasts, our bodies, and our environments work together to present us with a range of possible perceptions.

Henry James's functionalist psychology also begins with the mechanics of associationism. For example, Strether's first perception of Marie de Vionnet owes much to his Woollett past: "She was dressed in black, but in black that struck him as light and transparent; she was exceedingly fair, and, though she was as markedly slim, her face had a roundness, with eyes far apart and a little strange. Her smile was natural and dim; her hat not extravagant; he had only perhaps a sense of the clink, beneath her fine black sleeves, of more gold bracelets than he had ever seen a lady wear (I, 210)." Madame de Vionnet wears black, like Mrs. Newsome, but the European black is light and transparent. He doesn't simply perceive her hat as "modest," but rather as, in a negation of Woollett expectations, "not extravagant." She wears more bracelets than he has ever seen a lady wear. This is a delicately balanced point: Her jewelry is not that of a Woollett lady, but he cannot categorize her as "not a lady." New sights are never entirely new but are, rather, elaborations on, or reactions to, old ways of seeing.[14] Strether can never free himself of old perceptual categories; yet, new perceptions can modify old categories.[15]

---

[14] N. I. Bailey, "Pragmatism in *The Ambassadors*," *Dalhousie Review*, 53 (1973), 145.

[15] As Richard A. Hocks, *Henry James and Pragmatistic Thought* (Chapel Hill: Univ. of North Carolina Press, 1974), argues he does, p. 167.

All of these discriminations take place in the very act of perception. Strether does not see Marie de Vionnet and then try to fit this perception into his Woollett categories. He *sees her* in terms of those categories. The past organizes and intrudes upon the present. This does not mean that the past is simply a point of objective comparison for the present. When, in the opening scene of the novel, Strether sees the Chester city wall, he does not compare this present perception with his original sight of the wall. Instead, what he sees is "deeply mixed" with and "enriched" by what he saw (I, 16).

Despite perception's mechanical associationist basis, neither James brother ultimately describes seeing deterministically. Although we can only select from among those ideas which the associative machinery tends to introduce, this attentive power is far from negligible. In fact, William James calls it "*morally and historically momentous*" (II, 1180). In fixing our attention for even a second, we determine the direction of our next associations. We choose which personal interests will direct our behavior.

In Henry James's fiction, voluntary attention's direction of the associative machinery both connects his characters to, and saves them from being determined by, their environments. They survive in their environments by directing their attention towards those perceptions that interest and benefit them. When Strether returns to Paris and sees yellow books in a store window, he is inevitably affected by the fact that he saw them thirty years ago. The associative mechanism causes his past perceptions to condition his present ones. At the same time, Strether's present perception does not simply replicate his past ones. Free will is located in the perceptual nexus between past and present. In his youth the books seemed to him symbols of his plans for greatness. Now they appear as emblems of the loss of that youth, an effect which he intensifies by focusing on the glass that shields them. Strether *attends*: He forbids himself the purchase of any books, insuring that he will see them with "hungry gazes through clear plates behind which lemon-coloured volumes were as fresh as fruit on the tree" (I, 86). He sees not books but books behind a window. Strether makes sure that he sees the pleasures of Paris through a clear but clearly present barrier. His ability to freely select may be circumscribed, but it exists, and he acts upon it. Strether's characteristic turning away and his directing his vision towards safe objects (in moments of stress he repeatedly turns to look at his American letters or watch) are examples of the limited but powerful faculty that William James calls "mental spontaneity": "*My experience is what I agree to attend to.* Only those items which I *notice* shape my mind— without selective interest, experience is an utter chaos. Interest alone gives accent and emphasis, light and shade, background and foreground—intelligible perspective, in a word (I, 380–81)."

This spontaneous activity is a constant in Henry James's descriptions of visual perception. What I call picturing is the work of an active, attentive subject, who selects and arranges. James's characters do not passively receive a succession of discrete visual sensations that combine into larger structures. Rather, confronted with what William James calls "an undistinguishable, swarming *continuum*" (I, 274), James's perceivers discriminate those things that interest them, compose pictures that will serve their needs. For example, when Strether needs to be able to think of Marie de Vionnet as a romantic lady in distress, he creates a picture of her apartment that suits his purposes. Chad has prepared for this scene by praising Marie, carrying Strether off to the visit, and leaving the two alone. But Strether's own participation is evident in the description of the apartment. He works hard at what he sees: "he found himself making out, as a background of the occupant"; "he guessed"; "His attention took them all tenderly into account"; "he quite made up his mind" (I, 244–45). Although he guesses that the apartment "went further back" (I, 244), Strether sees it as belonging to the Romantic period so that he can select and arrange its details into a High Romantic picture: "He would have answered for it at the end of a quarter of an hour that the glass cases contained swords and epaulettes of ancient colonels and generals; medals and orders once pinned over hearts that had long since ceased to beat; snuff-boxes bestowed on ministers and envoys; copies of works presented with inscriptions, by authors now classic" (I, 246).

Once Strether can see Marie de Vionnet ensconced in an heroic, historic setting, he can believe that she is a lady in mild distress and he, a self-sacrificing knight. The picture he creates permits him to become involved with her in a noble, safe way. Of course, Marie has helped to make sure that this picture was available to Strether. She even seats herself on the apartment's one anomalously modern chair so that Strether can see her in the lowly position of supplicant. (Chad, on the other hand, always manages to stand above Strether.)

Thus James, like the Naturalists, analyzes the relationships between characters and their environments. Unlike the Naturalists, his work is not deterministic because he describes those relationships as active and reciprocal. A writer like Norris will catalogue a series of sights *presented to* a character. For example, after cataloguing each detail of the scene outside McTeague's window, Norris notes: "Day after day, McTeague saw the same panorama unroll itself." These are the units of sensation that build up to determine the future of the passive McTeague. Environment creates character. This technique is at work in somewhat less deterministic novels too. Dreiser begins *Sister Carrie* by listing what Carrie sees on the train to Chicago (the items of Drouet's clothing, every light and building that they pass) in order to document the way each of them *acts upon* her.

But Strether is the creator as well as the creature of his environment. Just how selective and active Jamesian seeing is will be clearer if we contrast it with perception in the work of a writer who is in many ways closer to James than Norris or Dreiser: George Eliot. Midway through *Middlemarch*, Dorothea, after a long night of watching, awakens to the realization that her crisis is shared by three others (Will, Rosamund, and Lydgate), and she is brought to a question:

What should I do—how should I act now, this very day, if I could clutch my own pain, and compel it to silence, and think of those three?

It had taken long for her to come to that question, and there was light piercing into the room. She opened her curtains, and looked out towards the bit of road that lay in view, with fields beyond, outside the entrance-gates. On the road there was a man with a bundle on his back and a woman carrying her baby; in the field she could see figures moving— perhaps the shepherd with his dog. Far off in the bending sky was the pearly light; and she felt the largeness of the world and the manifold wakings of men to labour and endurance. She was part of that involuntary, palpitating life, and could neither look out on it from her luxurious shelter as a mere spectator, nor hide her eyes in selfish complaining.

What she would resolve to do that day did not yet seem quite clear, but something that she could achieve stirred her as with an approaching murmur which would soon gather distinctness.[16]

---

[16] *Middlemarch* (1871–72; rpt. New York: Norton, 1977), p. 544.

Clearly what Dorothea sees is determined in part by what she thinks and knows. She has looked out this window many times before, but now, for the first time, she notices human figures in the scene. Similarly, James marks Strether's growing knowledge by having him return to the various Parisian apartments. But despite the selective activity implicit in Dorothea's focus on the human figures, her perception remains largely static. She has had her realization before she looks out the window, and she turns back into the room with no new knowledge. What she sees reflects but does not affect her thoughts. The three people that she sees are emphatically *not* Will, Rosamund, and Lydgate because the scene is, for her at least, a symbol for life rather than a part of it. The man bearing a bundle and the woman a child, the shepherd and the dog, are emblems for "labor and Endurance." There is no interaction between Dorothea and the world "outside the entrance-gates."

Strether perceives more actively and processively. What he sees does not merely reflect a question arrived at or even a question answered. Instead, the answering of the question, the problem-solving process, takes place *in* Strether's perceptions. As we have already seen, his first picture of Maria Gostrey's apartment is an analysis. Let us examine the nature of that analysis more closely. What Strether finds in the sight of Maria's down-to-earth entresol is a corrective to his puzzlement about Chad and Paris. This clarifying recognition takes the form of the rather blurry picture already quoted.

Strether is seeing almost with what Ruskin calls "the innocence of the eye," that is, seeing "an arrangement of patches of different colours variously shaded."[17] Of course, Strether's perceptions are *not* innocent, as phrases like "brown as a pirate's cave" make clear. Comparisons point to a past, to experience. Nonetheless, there is a sense that he is momentarily stopped by a visual perception that he does not understand. But Strether's picture of Maria's apartment is more than a reflection of his confusion. This perception is not, like Dorothea's, merely an emblem for the perceiver's state of mind. Instead it is both the statement of and the solution to his predicament. Strether works the problem out visually. He sees

---

[17] John Ruskin, *The Elements of Drawing*, ed. E. T. Cook and Alexander Wedderburn (London: George Allen, 1904), p. 27.

Maria's apartment as, like Paris and like Chad, at once confusing
and alluring. It is a dark maze in which he can discriminate only
the glint of precious objects. That is the problem. But the entresol
is neither Paris nor Chad's troisième. It is Maria's home. And
therein lies the solution. For Strether soon sees that ". . . after a
full look at his hostess he knew none the less what most concerned
him. The circle in which they stood together was warm with life,
and every question between them would live there as nowhere else
(I, 120)."

The sight of the apartment's owner transforms the scene into a
full, warm circle—still intricate but now accessible. Maria's presence in the midst of the maze brings the scene to order. That the
entresol is her home explains both her and it. Strether's growing
ability to distinguish the bibelots is, again, not simply emblematic.
Instead, his perception here is actually the next step in his understanding. What he literally sees in Maria's apartment both allows
him to understand Maria herself (her taste, her expertise, her
knowledge) and to analyze Chad. The usefulness of Strether's
seeing is made explicit when the narrator tells us that Strether
"glanced once more at a bibelot or two, and everything sent him
back"—back, that is, to the bibelots in Chad's apartment (I, 123).
Maria's furnishings remind Strether of Chad's, and her homier
setting becomes a means to understanding the owner of the "mystic
troisième."

What Strether sees continues to be both active and useful. In
perceiving Maria Gostrey's apartment for the second time, he
confronts the problem of Maria herself. Strether distinguishes the
fact that Marie de Vionnet has been there and works his way to
a realization of the guilty association between the women. "He
was sure within a minute that something had happened; it was so
in the air of the rich little room that he had scarcely to name his
thought. Softly lighted, the whole colour of the place, with its
vague values, was in a cool fusion—an effect that made the visitor
stand for a little agaze. It was as if in doing so now he had felt a
recent presence. . . (II, 295)."

The room is no longer intricate and varied. Strether now sees
it as uniformly lit and open to easy understanding. He solves the
problem of how to judge Maria Gostrey by looking at her apartment
and seeing in the "cool fusion" and "vague values" her tie to the
other woman. The two phrases are pointed allusions to Marie de

Vionnet. In descriptions of her apartment, colors are repeatedly referred to as "cool" and the painterly term "values" is used explicitly. And, of course, the complicity of the two women has effected a guilty sort of fusion between them, just as Maria's values have been, at best, "vague"—she has silently consented to Strether's deception.

Strether does not know all of these things before he arrives. His understanding comes *as* he composes his picture of the entresol. The moment of perception is a moment of engagement with the problems of life. Strether's role as a representative Jamesian perceiver marks him not as a passionless intellect who stands apart and waits for perception but as an active, interested, unified self who survives by seeing.

That James's work is detached from everyday, timely concerns is a critical maxim that has prompted both praise and blame. Combining an examination of what Strether actually sees with an understanding of the new psychology that James's contemporaries were formulating allows us to rescue James from the Ivory Tower in two ways. His characters' active perceptions tie them firmly to their environments. And James's own engagement with the problems that faced late nineteenth-century studies of the mind places him securely in his own. Basic mental and physical functions, as well as fundamental cultural questions, are the sources of Jamesian complexity.

James's Rewriting of Minny Temple's Letters
Alfred Habegger

HENRY James's orphaned cousin Mary Temple, generally called Minny, had a greater effect on his creative life than any other woman. Her early death from tuberculosis in March 1870, when she was twenty-four and James twenty-six, inspired two of the most emotional and extreme letters he is known to have written. Six years later, when he began to make plans for *The Portrait of a Lady*, Minny's image supplied the germ of his heroine Isabel Archer, and in old age, when he wrote his memoirs of youth, *Notes of a Son and Brother*, she was the subject of the last and longest chapter. James built this chapter around numerous lengthy extracts from the remarkable letters Minny wrote to a friend during her last year of life. Leon Edel has conjectured that James "doctored" these letters, but it has up to now been impossible to confirm this, as James evidently burned the originals. Exactly how James revised them, Edel predicted, "we shall never know."[1]

But we can know. Before Minny's correspondence was sent to James, it was meticulously copied in longhand by William James's widow and daughter, Alice H. James and Margaret Mary. These copies appear to be literal transcriptions of what Minny wrote, even reproducing certain accidentals. The copies were at some point deposited in the Houghton Library, where I turned them up in January 1985.[2] They not only indicate that James's omissions and alterations were far more extensive than anyone could have dreamed, but they raise some disturbing questions about his use of

---

[1] *Henry James: The Untried Years* (Philadelphia: Lippincott, 1953), p. 313.

[2] The copies are to be found in four folders numbered bMS Am 1092.12 (Mary Temple to Gray), and are reproduced here by permission of the Houghton Library. Robert C. LeClair made available Minny's three extant letters to HJ in "Henry James and Minny Temple," *American Literature*, 21 (1949), 35-48.

American Literature, Volume 58, Number 2, May 1986. Copyright © 1986 by the Duke University Press. CCC 0002-9831/86/$1.50.

historical documentation and his general accuracy and truthfulness. This article reprints the Houghton copies of Minny's first four letters in parallel columns with James's shortened version of them and discusses some of his many deletions, substitutions, and additions. (The letters herein reproduced amount to less than a fifth of the total. Although James followed the same basic procedures in editing the remaining twenty letters, the particular alterations he made in them are too numerous and striking to be commented on in the space of an article.)

Minny's correspondent was a longtime friend, John Chipman Gray. During the Civil War he had risen to the position of judge-advocate,[3] and he afterwards entered a successful law partnership in Boston; Henry James Sr. is known to have consulted him.[4] In 1869 Gray began his long teaching career at Harvard Law School. His letters to Minny have not been located. Minny's side of the correspondence consists of twenty-four letters dating from 7 January 1869 to 16 February 1870. She died three weeks after her last letter.

Gray preserved Minny's letters until shortly before his own death in 1915, when he arranged to have them sent to Henry James in England.[5] They were transferred as follows, according to a letter from James to Henrietta Pell-Clarke: "I received from J. G. through your cousin Alice [H. James] at Cambridge, that packet of Minnie's letters of long ago, which, setting his affairs in order in those days of his own very impaired health and vitality, he asked Alice to read as preliminary to sending them to *me* (to do what I would with) rather than bring himself to destroy them. She read them with intense interest and emotion and said at once 'Do, *do* let me send them to Henry!' "[6] The first sentence attributes to Gray himself the idea of sending the correspondence to James, but the

---

[3] H. W. Howard Knott, "Gray, John Chipman," in *Dictionary of American Biography*.

[4] Mary James to HJ, 21 Jan. [1873], MH. All citations to letters by date are to the holographs in the various James family collections at the Houghton Library (MH).

[5] Edel's biography gives two different versions of this transferral in *Untried Years*, p. 313, and *Henry James: The Master* (Philadelphia: Lippincott, 1972), p. 499. The latter version, claiming that the letters "were sent to him by Gray's widow," is obviously incorrect, as Gray died one year after the publication of *Notes of a Son and Brother*.

[6] Letter to Henrietta Pell-Clarke, 5 May 1914. Typewritten copy in MH. 2 pp. Hereafter "To Pell-Clarke." This and other materials in the Houghton are quoted by permission of Alexander James and the Houghton Library.

second sentence suggests that the initiative may have come from
Alice H. Perhaps it was also her own cautious foresight that
prompted her to make longhand copies of them. The Houghton
Library envelope that now contains them bears this penciled
inscription, possibly by her son Henry James 3rd: "The originals of
these letters were given by J. C. G. to A. H. J. (Alice Howe
James)—She sent them to H. J. 2nd who used them & afterwards
destroyed them without saying a word to her." At the top of the
envelope there is a penciled request, erased but still partly legible,
advising someone to compare the copies with the version in
James's memoirs. Evidently, this task was not carried out. The
copies themselves are in two hands, the large, sweeping one
belonging to Alice H. and the less slanting, more awkward one to
Margaret Mary.

The original packet reached James after he had completed
"three quarters"[7] of *Notes of a Son and Brother*. He had already
dictated a glowing but rather brief and vague account of Minny.[8]
By his own testimony no other "loose clue"—that is, no isolated
historical remains—had ever renewed in his mind an equally large
"tract of the time-smothered consciousness" (*Notes*, p. 454) as her
half-century-old letters. They enabled him to sketch a vivid
picture of a bright and lively social circle. They also gave him the
"chance to do what I had always longed in some way to do without
seeing quite how—rescue and preserve in some way from oblivion,
commemorate and a little *enshrine*, the image of our admirable and
exquisite, our noble and unique little Minnie." He was confident
he had succeeded, partly because of the praise he had received:
"dear Minnie's name is *really* now, in the most touching way, I
think, silvered over and set apart." But it had not been easy to
make just the right use of her letters: it took "the right tact and
taste."[9] James used the same phrase in writing his sister-in-law: "I
was so anxious and worried as to my really getting the effect in the
right way—with tact and taste and without overstrain."[10]

[7] To Pell-Clarke.
[8] See *Notes of a Son and Brother* (New York: Scribner's, 1914), pp. 76-79. Hereafter
called *Notes*.
[9] To Pell-Clarke.
[10] *Letters*, ed. Leon Edel (Cambridge: Harvard Univ. Press, 1984), IV, 707.

The prevailing impression one gets in comparing James's version of Minny's letters with the Houghton copies is the *thoroughness* of his editorial revision. Instead of regarding the correspondence as something unique and irreplaceable, which ought to be preserved for its own inherent value, he clearly thought of it as "my material and my occasion,"[11]—something that would require masterly redoing. There was scarcely a sentence he did not emend.

Why was James so thorough, so "anxious and worried" about "overstrain"? One possible reason is suggested by Jane P. Tompkins' essay on *Notes of a Son and Brother*: the celebratory and rose-colored quality of the memoirs was decisively undercut by Minny's tragic death.[12] Another possibility is that James sensed there was something wrong in reproducing the thoughts of a dying woman; he felt the same qualm in working up *The Wings of the Dove*.[13] Given James's extremely protective sense of privacy, one would also guess that he felt uneasy about revealing personal letters to the public. All these explanations are plausible, yet a glance at James's treatment of certain aspects of Minny's writing gives us a much more exact sense of his nervous "tact and taste."

Several of Minny's letters refer to the event that caused a flutter in the James clan in 1869—the decision of Minny's sister Ellen to marry a man twenty-eight years her senior, Temple Emmet. Like Minny's brother Bob and some of Henry James's own family, Minny had been shocked by Ellen's choice,[14] and her letters to Gray revealed her dismay. But Ellen was still alive in 1914. How did James deal with this ticklish matter? His editing, surprisingly, gave *greater* emphasis to Minny's disapproval than did the original letters. He retained this frank admission: "the irretrievableness of the step comes over my mind from time to time in such an

[11] To Pell-Clarke.

[12] "The Redemption of Time in *Notes of a Son and Brother*," *Texas Studies in Literature and Language*, 14 (1973), 688-89.

[13] *The Art of the Novel: Critical Prefaces* (New York: Scribner's, 1934), p. 289.

[14] Mary James's view was that Ellen believed she would be "safer . . . with an older man" (letter to HJ, 6 Sept. [1869], MH). Bob Temple and Minny each wrote HJ of their disapproval of Ellen's choice, and HJ voiced his own opposition in at least three separate letters home—to his father on 17 Sept. 1869, to William on 25 Sept. 1869, and to Alice on 6 Oct. 1869 (MH). Isabel Archer may have been inspired by Minny's image, but it was undoubtedly Ellen's marriage that lay behind Isabel's unpopular choice of an older husband. Minny herself disapproved of such marriages and made it clear in a letter to HJ that she would never "become the prey of a bald-headed Emmet" (quoted in LeClair, p. 45).

overwhelming way that it is very depressing—and I have to be constantly on my guard not to let Temple & Elly see it." And he omitted this one: "I am sure he will be kind and good to her always—& she is very happy, so there is no more to be said."[15] Ellen herself resented not receiving her sister's letters, and when she read them in James's memoirs she was reportedly "upset." When Alice H. informed him of this, he ridiculed the idea that anyone who lived in such "depths of illiteracy"[16] as Ellen should pretend to claim Minny's old letters. James's anxiety, then, may have been uncomfortably close to guilt: he knew, and perhaps intended, that his presentation of the letters would give offense to the surviving sister he considered unworthy of Minny.

Of course, many of James's emendations would have been standard editorial practice. Like most other letter-writers of the time,[17] including some of the Jameses themselves, Minny generally used dashes for periods or semi-colons. James did what any contemporary editor would have done and standardized her punctuation and syntax. He also trimmed wordy passages and omitted repetitions. In addition, it is clear that he sought to make her prose smoother, more regular, and more professional. He often replaced a flat or plain word with something more highly flavored: where Minny called the weather "fine," James wrote "splendid" or "grand." Where Minny wrote "the only thing that I can say," James, possibly regarding this diction as inexact or uncultured, wrote "the only advice I can give you." He consistently dropped her colloquialisms, especially those that could be seen as Americanisms. "Inside of that" (meaning *aside from that*), probably Minny's single greatest departure from approved English, became "beyond those things." Her "get very tired" got clipped to the more British-sounding "tire so." The humorous catch-phrases Minny liked to use in quotation marks—"& no mistake," "let me down easy"—were got rid of by James, who may have thought they verged on slang or were too breezy. Another reason for his anxiety, then, was the fear that Minny might be seen as vulgar.

[15] 29 Aug. 1869, MH.
[16] *Letters*, ed. Edel, IV, 707.
[17] R. W. Franklin, *The Editing of Emily Dickinson* (Madison: Univ. of Wisconsin Press, 1967), p. 124.

Some of James's alterations seem of questionable value. Minny's "raiding party" surely loses a great deal in being reduced to "raid." Her "fairly emancipated from invalidism & nursing" has a sharper causal reference than James's more witty "quite emancipated from bondage." Speaking of her hemorrhages in one letter, Minny burst out with a determined prediction: "however, *I* think they *are* going to stop *now*." James's version—"Still, they *may* be going to stop"—is acquiescent and helpless and relatively unemphatic. Where Minny complained of "the monotony of eating gruel, and thinking of the proximity of the grave," James's Minny wrote, "the monotony of gruel and of thinking of the grave." His version seems maladroit in that it makes the three "of's" more conspicuous. Why did he drop her parallel gerunds and the elegant "proximity" that briefly suspends the completion of the parallelism? Did he regard these elements as an amateur's fine writing?

James did not hesitate to alter Minny's tone and meaning as well as her words. Some of his changes are relatively minor, as when he rendered her expressed wish to dance again with someone "soon" much more urgent—"as soon as possible." But he often introduced drastic and apparently arbitrary changes. At one point Minny asked Gray about George Eliot: "Do you like her too? I don't remember ever hearing you speak of her." James's version drops the initial and very ordinary question and revises the statement: "But I don't remember ever to have heard *you* speak of her." This rewriting adds an abrupt and rather haughty or invidious note to Minny's straightforwardness and evokes a different sort of person, more cultivated and on edge.

In the four letters reproduced below, James inserted three ellipses to indicate that he was leaving something out, yet he deleted dozens of passages, long and short. His introduction to the fourth letter—"I can bring myself to abate nothing"—conceals the extent of his editing, as he silently abated five separate passages. The longest of these was a charming four-sentence segment in which Minny twitted Gray for working too hard: she accused him of harboring a wish to present himself as a more substantial and thus more attractive suitor.

It is amusing to note how consistently James pruned out Minny's bantering about courtship and marriage, and a good deal of her chaff on other subjects as well. He even dropped the passage in which Minny slyly guesses at Gray's intent in calling her "Pyramid." There is less easygoing familiarity in James's version than there is in the original, where, for instance, Minny once warns Gray that he had better not be too critical of the strict fiancées of other young men: "you may 'catch a tartar' yet." Whatever James's motives may have been for erasing all this relaxed and very personal teasing, his Minny has much more starch and propriety than the actual woman, and his editing finally gives a misleading impression of her. Among those who have been misled is Edel himself, who reports that "the letters to Gray are . . . the communications of a serious young lady."[18] But this serious young lady was to some extent James's own invention, as was his very serious fictional lady, Isabel. The real Minny, as William once wrote in a letter to Henry, tended to combine "moral" interests with a "coquettish impulse."[19]

The intensity and depth of Minny's letters as modified by James has led some readers to assume she had a romantic interest in Gray. Edel flatly calls the excerpts "love letters,"[20] thus disregarding James's admonition not to interpret them as such. The Houghton copies now prove that James had good authority for declaring them "essentially not love-letters" (*Notes*, p. 484). They indicate that Gray took a romantic interest in other women, a Miss Adams at one time and possibly a Miss Greenough at another,[21] and that Minny was the third party, a confidante. Did James omit all mention of Gray's courtship because he ended up marrying another woman, or did James consider Minny's part in the triangular situation too irregular? Elsewhere he dropped her sympathetic mention of a friend, Mrs. Clymer, who was contemplating divorce.

It is curious that James's editing of Minny's first four letters elides her four references to Lizzie Boott, the person who to some extent served as a model for Pansy Osmond. One of these passages reflected unfavorably on Lizzie by disclosing that Gray had formerly regarded her as not very "wide awake." Minny's interesting

[18] *Untried Years*, p. 317.
[19] 24 Aug. 1872, MH.
[20] *Untried Years*, p. 317.
[21] Houghton copies, 24 April 1869.

comment on this was that both he and Lizzie were "undemonstrative." Some of the James family letters offer corroboration. Lizzie
often struck others as listless, and Gray sometimes seemed priggish
or stolid. William once wrote Henry: "I have seen John Gray
several times. But what a cold blooded cuss he is."[22] As edited,
Minny's sharp view of her contemporaries has been muffled by
James's ennobling, embalming prose. Did James want us not to
guess that the "undemonstrative" aspect of Caspar Goodwood and
Pansy was drawn from John Gray and Lizzie Boott? In any case
James's deletion of Minny's references to Lizzie explains the
meaning of the rather vague sentence with which he introduced his
treatment of the Bootts—"These are great recognitions, but how
can I slight for them a mention that has again and again all but
broken through in my pages?—that of Francis Boott and his
daughter . . ." (*Notes*, p. 475). This was James's veiled allusion to
his own silent excisions.

Interestingly, James chose to retain two separate passages in
Minny's letters (*Notes*, pp. 456, 510) that cast a highly unflattering
light on his own father. Minny evidently viewed the senior James
with dislike and even contempt because of his "ignoble and
shirking" doctrines. Normally the Jameses were exceedingly cir-
cumspect in their presentation of themselves to the rest of the
world, and their caution has without a doubt introduced major
distortions in our view of them. As Edel has shown, Henry was
particularly sensitive about his father's instability. The fact that he
retained Minny's "disgusted" response is a suggestive hint about
James's attitude in old age toward his contradictory and evasive
father.

James's single most disturbing act in editing the four letters
herein reproduced was to insert a passage of his own composition in
the 3 February letter (*Notes*, p. 465). This addition implies that
one of the reasons Minny's relatives failed to accompany her to a
warmer climate was their callous unconcern. The effect of this
passage was to render Minny more isolated and victimized than she
probably was, an effect James enhanced by deleting three passages
involving the care and companionship she got from her sister

[22] 26 Aug. [1868], MH.

Katharine at Pelham. His own comments added a note of catty innuendo: "It was not at any rate to be said of her [Minny] that she didn't live surrounded, even though she had to go so far afield—very far it may at moments have appeared to her—for the freedom of talk that was her greatest need of all" (*Notes*, p. 490). In a private letter of 1914 James suggested that Minny's people lacked "presence of mind enough"[23] to care for her properly.

It appears, then, that James's elegiac protectiveness towards Minny caused him to pass off a piece of his own writing as hers. This small pious fraud tells us a great deal about the intimate pressures that helped shape some of his most important texts. In 1870, after learning of Minny's death, young James had implied in a letter home that he would now assume the care of her: "The more I think of her the more perfectly satisfied I am to have her translated from this changing realm of fact to the steady realm of thought. There she may bloom into a beauty more radiant than our dull eyes will avail to contemplate."[24] The fact that Minny's letters to Gray were actually consigned to James forty years later played directly into this old seductive dream of his. At last the energetic young woman would be safely "silvered over."

All in all, James's rewriting of Minny Temple's correspondence affords an unparalleled insight into the processes by which this nervous and resourceful wizard turned life—female life—into art. In this instance the laborious copying of two alert women has enabled us to see past James's distortions, but there are undoubtedly many other cases in which his alteration of historical fact is beyond detection. Sophia Hawthorne, Olivia Clemens, and Elinor Howells have been variously taken to task for bowdlerizing their husbands' work, but it is doubtful that any of these wives tampered with their husband's holographs as much as James did with Minny's. James has enjoyed a strange immunity from any searching inquiry into his veracity. From now on, however, the presumption must be that all the other letters in his memoirs are partly inauthentic. To what extent this long-overdue skepticism will affect our view of James's fictional transcriptions of the "American girl" remains to be seen.

[23] *Letters*, ed. Percy Lubbock (London: Macmillan, 1920), II, 417.
[24] *Letters*, ed. Edel, I, 226.

HOUGHTON COPY

JAMES'S VERSION

Pelham[25] January 7*th* 1869

Dear Mr Gray —

I will write you as nice a
letter as I know how, but I would
much rather have a nice talk with you
— As I can't have the best thing,
however, I must (contrary to my pet
theory) put-up with the second best.
But for fear you should follow in my
footsteps, let me repeat,
emphatically that this is a wicked
thing to do, on general principles —
I got your letter a few days ago, and
I hope you remark the forgiving way
in which I answer in *two* days time,
charitably ignoring the *years* that
yours took in coming. But I am
afraid my charity begins at home, in
this case — I feel as if I were in
Heaven today. And all because the
day is fine, and I have been driving
about all the morning in a little
sleigh, in the fresh air and
sunshine, until in spite of myself, I
found I had stopped asking for the
time being, the usual mental question
of why I was born — I am not going
to Canada — I know no better reason
for this, than because I said I *was*
going — I like to be out here in the
country, and Kitty likes to have me
with her. This being the case, her
husband makes such a clamor when I
propose to leave, that I am easily
persuaded, by his kindness and my own
want of energy, to stay where I am.
It is great fun living out here. The
weather you know is fine & I knock
about all day in a sleigh, & do
nothing but enjoy the sunshine, &
meditate. Then we are so near the
town, that we go in very often, for
the day, & do a little shopping,
lunch with some of our numerous

I will write you as nice a letter
as I can, but would much rather have
a good talk with you. As I can't
have the best thing I am putting up
with the second-best, contrary to
my pet theory.

I feel as if I were in
heaven to-day—all because the day is
splendid and I have been driving about
all the morning in a small sleigh in
the fresh air and sunshine, until I
found that I had in spite of myself,
for the time being, stopped asking the
usual inward question of why I was
born. I am not going to Canada—
I know no better reason for this
than because I said I *was* going.

My brother-
in-law makes such a clamour when I propose departure that I am easily overcome
by his kindness and my own want of energy.
Besides, it is great fun to live here;
the weather just now is grand, and I
knock about all day in a sleigh, and
do nothing but enjoy it and meditate.
Then we are so near town that we often
go in for the day to shop and lunch
with some of our numerous friends,
returning with a double relish for
the country. We all went in on a

[25] A New York City suburb, the residence of Minny's married sister, Katharine (Kitty) Emmet.

friends, and come out again, with a
double relish for the country. We
all went in, on a spree, the other
night, & stayed at the Everett House,
from which, as a starting point, we
poured in, in strong force, upon Mrs
Gracie King's ball — a very grand
affair, given for a very pretty Miss
King, at Del Monico's. On this
occasion the raiding party consisted
of thirteen Emmets, & a moderate
supply of Temples. The ball was a
great success — I had not been to
one before in two years, & I liked it
very much. So much that I mean to
try it again very soon, at the next
Assembly — The men in Society, in
New York, this winter, are
principally a lot of feeble-minded
boys — but I was fortunate enough to
escape them, as my partner for the
German was a man of about 35 — the
solitary *man* I believe in the room —
and curiously enough, I had danced my
last German, two years ago before, in
that very place, with the same
person. He is a Mr Lee, a man who
has spent nearly all his life abroad.
Two of his sisters have married
German princes — & he from knocking
about so much has become a thorough
man of the world, and as he is
intelligent, with nothing to do but
amuse himself, he is a very agreeable
partner for the German, & I mean to
dance another with him soon — I
don't know why I have tried your
patience by writing about an
individual that you have never seen.
This is merely to show you that I
have not retired irrevocably from the
world, the flesh & the devil. I am
conscious of a very faint Charm about
it still, when taken in small doses.
So you think Lizzie Boott more wide
awake than she used to be. It is
only that you are getting to know her
better. I do not wonder that *two*
such undemonstrative creatures as you
two are, can't make much of each

spree the other night and stayed at
the Everett House; from which, as a
starting-point we poured ourselves
in strong force upon Mrs. Gracie
King's ball—a very grand affair,
given for a very pretty Miss King,
at Delmonico's. Our raid consisted

of thirteen Emmets and a moderate
supply of Temples, and the ball was a
great success. It was two years since
I had been to one and I enjoyed it so
much that I mean very soon to repeat
the experiment—at the next Assembly
if possible. The men in society, in
New York, this winter, are principally
a lot of feeble-minded boys; but I was
fortunate enough to escape them, as
my partner for the German was a man
of thirty-five, the solitary *man*, I
believe, in the room. Curiously
enough, I had danced my last German,
two years before, in that very
place and with the same person.
He is a Mr. Lee, who has spent nearly
all his life abroad; two of his
sisters have married German
princes, and from knocking about
so much he has become a thorough
cosmopolite. As he is intelligent,
with nothing to do but amuse himself, he is a very agreeable
partner, and I mean to dance with
him again as soon as possible. I
don't know why I have tried your
patience by writing so about a person
you have never seen; unless it's to
show you that I haven't irrevocably
given up the world, the flesh and the
devil, but am conscious of a faint
charm about them still when taken in
small doses.

other. I agree with you perfectly
about Uncle Henry. I should think he
would be very irritating to the legal
mind — He is not at all satisfactory
even to mine. Have you seen much of
Willy James lately? That is a rare
creature, and one in whom my
intellect (if you will pardon the
mis-application of the word) takes
more solid satisfaction than in
almost anybody — I had begun to
think that you did n't mean to write
anymore, and that *name* which you
called me at parting, must have been
expressive of your greatest
disapprobation — "Pyramid" I think
it was, which, as far as I can make
out is a cold, hard, unsympathetic,
uninteresting body. I am sure I am
much obliged to you, Sir, for your
opinion of me — When I go in to
town, I generally meet Mrs Clymer in
the cars — She is quite a pretty
woman, I think, & I always feel very
sorry for her. There is something
pathetic to me about her. She has
had a legal divorce, I hear, so you
can marry her now, if you like, but
perhaps, being a lawyer, you had
something to do with getting her out
of it. Oh, by the way, I hope you
got something pretty for yourself
with the forty-two dollars (was n't
it?) that I saw you had received from
the public treasury, some time ago —
How gratifying and consoling it is,
when our friends don't write to us,
to have the newspaper furnish us with
these interesting items about them.
I haven't read Browning's new book —
I mean to wait till you are by to
explain it to me — which reminds me,
along with what you say about wishing
for the spring, that I mean to go to
Conway next summer. Mr. Boott says
he will take Lizzie there, if we go,
so I think it very likely that Aunt
Charlotte will go, with Elly,
Henrietta & myself. In that case,
you may as well make up your mind to
a little visit there yourself, as I
can't wait any longer than that to

I agree with you perfectly
about Uncle Henry—I should think he
would be very irritating to the legal
mind; he is not at all satisfactory
even to mine. Have you seen much of
Willy James lately? That is a rare
creature, and one in whom my
intellect, if you will pardon the
misapplication of the word, takes
more solid satisfaction than in
almost anybody.

I haven't read Browning's new
book—I mean to wait till you are
by to explain it to me—
which reminds me, along with what
you say about wishing for the
spring, that we shall go to North
Conway next summer,

and that in that case
you may as well make up your mind
to come and see us there. I can't
wait longer than that for the

have Browning read to me. Arthur Sedgwick sent me Matthew Arnold's likeness, which Harry had said was very disappointing — but I do not, on the whole, find it so — on the contrary, after having looked at it a good many times, I like it. It quite harmonizes with my notion of him, & I always had an affection for him. So Christmas has come and gone again, and we are beginning another year — I am glad it is fairly over. Anniversaries are apt to be sad things when one gets as old as I am. As for wishes and hopes for the new year you have my best. I can only say that I hope you may be happier this year than you have ever been before, (as indeed you ought to be, if you take that great step.) You must write to me and tell me something that you are *sure* is true. I don't care much what it is, & I will take your word for it. Things get into a muddle with me — How can I give you "a start on the way of righteousness"? I think you know that way better than I do. The only thing that I can say is — Don't stop saying your prayers — & God bless you. Inside (sic) of that, I hardly know what is right or what wish to give you for the new year. You told me not to write you a sheet and a half, in a big hand — Have I not obeyed you with a vengeance? If you don't like such a long letter, I give you leave to retaliate in the same manner — tit-for-tat. And now goodbye — Address to Pelham — I am here, indefinitely — and Believe me always yours

> Most sincerely
> Mary Temple.
> (Kitty took rooms at the
> Blue Blinds Conway)

Addressed to
John C. Gray jr Esq.
no 4 Pemberton Square
Boston Massachusetts.

Browning readings. (Which would have been of The Ring and the Book.) Arthur Sedgwick has sent me Matthew Arnold's photograph, which Harry had pronounced so disappointing. I don't myself, on the whole, find it so; on the contrary, after having looked at it much, I like it—it quite harmonises with my notion of him, and I have always had an affection for him.

You must tell me something that you are *sure* is true—I don't care much what it may be, I will take your word for it. Things get into a muddle with me—how can I give you "a start on the way of righteousness"? You know that way better than I do, and the only advice I can give you is not to stop saying your prayers. I hope God may bless you, and beyond those things I hardly know what is right, and therefore what to wish you. Good-bye.

Pelham, January 27*th* 1869

Dear Mr Gray,

This might be headed with that line of a hymn, "Hark: from the tombs!" &c — but perhaps it won't prove as bad as that. It looks pretty doubtful still, but I have a sort of feeling that I shall get the better of it, this one time more — by which I don't mean to brag, or I may have to pay for my proud boastings. The "it," of which I speak, is, of course, my old enemy, hemorrhage, of which I have had plenty within the last week — seven pretty big ones, & several little ones, hardly worth the name. I don't know what has come over me — I can't stop them — but as I said, I mean to try & beat them yet. Of course I am in bed, where I shall be, indefinitely — not allowed to speak one word, literally, even in a whisper — The reason I write this, is because I don't think it will hurt me at all, if I take it easy, & stop when I feel tired. It is a pleasant break in the monotony of eating gruel, and thinking of the proximity of the grave — And then too, it was so nice to get your letter this morning, that I want another — I would n't be such a baby, or such an Oliver Twist as to cry for more, if I were not ill and weak, indeed I would n't, but I think a few words from somebody who is strong and active, in the good old world, (it seems to me now,) would be very refreshing — And you'll write to me, won't you, even if it does take a little time away from the law, or from Miss Adams — and one thing I want to say before I go any further — Don't tell anybody I wrote this letter to you — because it will be sure to reach the ears of my dear relatives — & it will cause them to sniff the air, & flounce, &c. I mean, of course, only this letter, while I am ill. You will no doubt

This might be headed with that line of a hymn, "Hark, from the tombs etc.!"—but perhaps it won't prove as bad as that. It looks pretty doubtful still, but I have a sort of feeling that I shall come round this one time more; by which I don't mean to brag! The "it" of which I speak is of course my old enemy hemorrhage, of which I have had within the last week seven pretty big ones and several smaller, hardly worth mentioning. I don't know what has come over me—I can't stop them; but, as I said, I mean to try and beat them yet. Of course I am in bed, where I shall be indefinitely—not allowed to speak one word, literally, even in a whisper. The reason I write this is because I don't think it will hurt me at all —if I take it easy and stop when I feel tired. It is a pleasant break in the monotony of gruel and of thinking of the grave—and then too

a few words from somebody who is strong and active in the good old world (as it seems to me now) would be very refreshing.

But don't tell anyone I have written, because it will be sure to reach the ears of my dear relatives and will cause them to sniff the air and flounce!

hear of my illness from other
quarters, Lizzie Boott, perhaps, as I
wrote a letter to her about a week
ago, in which I told her that I had
had a very slight hemorrhage, the day
before, but I had not gone to bed, &
thought nothing of it. Of course
this was all wrong — if I had taken
care of myself, it might have stopped
there — A day or two ago, I found
that my letter had not gone, & I
added a line to say that the
hemorrhages had gone on getting worse
& worse. So she will probably tell
you, & so you won't perhaps have to
tell a lie about it. You see I *am* a ˙
good deal of a baby & don't want to
hear the reproaches of my relatives,
on this, or any other subject. Kitty
says I may write to you — & that is
enough — She takes good care of me —
& all the Emmets are so good & kind,
that I found, when it came to the
point, that there was a good deal
that made life attractive, & that if
the choice were given to me, I would
a good deal rather stay up here, on
the solid earth, in the air and
sunshine, with an occasional
sympathetic glimpse of another
person's soul, than to be put down,
under the earth, and say good bye
forever to humanity — with all its
laughter and its sadness. But you
must n't think that I am in any
special danger of dying just at
present, or that I am in low
spirits — for it is not so. The Dr.
tells me that I am not in any danger,
even if the hemorrhages should keep
on — "but you can't fool a regular
boarder" as Mr Holmes would say, & I
can't see why there is any reason to
think they will heal, a week later,
when I shall be weaker than now, if
they can't heal now — however, *I* think
they *are* going to stop *now*. I
haven't had one since yesterday at
four, & now it is three o'clock,
nearly twenty four hours. I am of a
hopeful temperament, & not easily

You see I am a good
deal of a baby—in the sense of
not wanting the reproaches of my
relatives on this or any other
subject. . . .

All the Emmets are so good
and kind that I found, when it came
to the point, that there was a good
deal to make life attractive, and
that if the choice were given me I
would much rather stay up here on
the solid earth, in the air and
sunshine, with an occasional
sympathetic glimpse of another
person's soul, than to be put down
underground and say good-bye for
ever to humanity, with all its
laughter and its sadness. Yet you
mustn't think me now in any *special*
danger of dying, or even in low
spirits, for it isn't so—the
doctor tells me I am *not* in danger,
even if the hemorrhages should keep
on. However, "you can't fool a
regular boarder," as Mr. Holmes
would say, and I can't see why
there is any reason to think they
will heal a week hence, when I
shall be still weaker, if they
can't heal now. Still, they *may* be
going to stop—I haven't had one
since yesterday at
4, and now it's 3; nearly twenty-
four hours. I am of a hopeful
temperament and not easily scared,

frightened, which is in my favor. If
this *should* prove to be the last
letter you get from me, why take it
for a good-bye — I'll keep on the
look-out for you in the spirit-world,
and shall be glad to see you when you
come there, provided it is a better
place than this — So Robert Winthrop
has got Miss Mason after all. May
they be 'appy — You had better look
out how you talk about too strict a
rule — You may "catch a tartar" yet.
My praiseworthy effort to cultivate
Society, has been snubbed by Heaven,
apparently, and the snub has been so
effectual, that I am afraid it will
be a long time before I shall make
another attempt. Elly is in town
enjoying herself immensely. I have
n't let her know how ill I have been,
because there were several parties in
the last week & I was afraid it might
spoil her fun. But Kitty wrote her a
note today — & I think she will come
to me soon. I did not mean you to
infer from my particularizing Willy
James'es *intellect*, that the rest of
him was not to my liking. He is one
of the very few people in this world
that I love — "& no mistake." He has
the largest heart as well as the
largest head — and is thoroughly
interesting to me — and he is generous
& affectionate & full of sympathy &
humanity. Don't tell him I said so,
though — or he would think I had been
telling you a lie, to serve my own
purposes. I believe I have written
enough now — but I have rested several
times, between — Good bye — Mind
what I said about not telling anybody
that I wrote to you while I was ill —
& reward me for the exertion by
writing soon to me—

Yours —
Mary Temple

which is in my favour. If this
should prove to be the last letter
you get from me, why take it for a
good-bye; I'll keep on the lookout
for you in the spirit world, and
shall be glad to see you when you
come there, provided it's a better
place than this.

Elly is in New York, enjoying
herself immensely, and I haven't
let her know how ill I have been,
as there were to be several parties
this last week and I was afraid it
might spoil her fun.

I didn't mean you to
infer from my particularising Willy
James's intellect that the rest of
him isn't to my liking—he is one
of the very few people in this
world that I love. He has the
largest heart as well as the
largest head, and is thoroughly
interesting to me. He is generous
and affectionate and full of
sympathy and humanity—though you
mustn't tell him I say so, lest he
should think I have been telling
you a lie to serve my own purposes.
Good-bye.

Pelham February 3*rd* 1869

Dear Mr. Gray

I can never tell you how much
good your letter did me. It was just

what I needed, just what I wanted —
It did comfort me, & make me happy,
and it was impossible to make me
think the world was hard to me, at
the very moment that you were making
me feel the very best thing in it. I
see now more than ever that with
every trouble there comes a
compensating happiness — for how
should I ever have known how good and
kind you are if I had not been ill?
— It is no good to talk about it,
but I don't believe you know how far
down in my heart I feel it. I wrote
a note to you yesterday, in pencil,
as I was lying down still, but this
morning I decided not to send it,
because I feel so much better today,
and I think it did not give a bright
enough view of the case. It is a
week ago today, since I wrote my last
letter, I think, & I have only had
one more hemorrhage, since — and that
was the day after I wrote you. Since
then, they have stopped entirely, and
I feel pretty sure that I shall have
no more this time. I am sitting up
in my room today, and I feel as
bright as possible. Yesterday when I
walked across the room, I felt as if
I should never be strong again, but
today it is quite different, & I feel
that, now that I am fairly out of
bed, I shall soon get over being weak
— It is so nice to be up again, that
my spirits go up, absurdly — It does
n't take much to make me forget that
I have ever been so ill. Of course
you know how much pleasure your
letters give me, but I can't help
feeling selfish in letting you write.
I know I've got no business to keep
bothering you, and perhaps, after a
while I may have strength of mind
enough to stop writing to you,
thereby, giving you a chance to stop
too. But must I be a Spartan just
yet? How can I help liking to get
your letters when they are so kind —
Perhaps if you were to snub me a
little in your next, it might "let me
down easy" — As soon as I am able, I
am to be taken to town to have my

It is a
week ago to-day, I think, since I
last wrote to you, and I have only
had one more hemorrhage—the day
after.

I feel pretty sure they have
stopped for the present, and I am
sitting up in my room, as bright as
possible. Yesterday when I walked
across it I thought I should never
be strong again, but now it's quite
different,

and so nice to be out of
bed that my spirits go up absurdly.

As soon as I am able I am to
be taken to town for another

lungs examined, and then when I know my fate, I will do the best I can.

No sentiment? And pray, sir, how do you think you are ever going to meet your fate, if this is the way you behave? Remember you are to tell me about it, when the fatal day arrives. The Conway plan has fallen through already — Aunt Charlotte is not well enough to think of taking us — My own plans all depend upon whether I get strong again — And now goodbye. I have compunctions about taking your time, *not* from Miss Adams, I confess, but from criticisms on Mrs Bradwell, & the like. I have n't seen the whole of that yet, but I shall soon have the Review.[26] You really need n't write again, if you don't want to. I shan't think it unfriendly, after your last letter. If you were to get tired & never speak to me again, I should n't mind it — because I can't thank you enough for what you have done already & moreover, sir, you may now let your moustache grow down to your toes, if you like — and I will but smile scornfully at your futile precautions. Here is the end of my paper & only room to sign myself — Yours — M. Temple.

examination, and then when I know my fate I will do the best I can.

* * * * * *

This climate is trying, to be sure, but such as it is I've got to take my chance in it, as there is no one I care enough for, or who cares enough for me, to take charge of me to Italy, or to the south anywhere. I don't believe any climate, however good, would be of the least use to me with people I don't care for. [This passage corresponds to nothing in Minny's letters to Gray (or to James) and was almost certainly composed by James himself.]

* * * * * *

You may let your moustache grow down to your toes if you like, and I shall but smile scornfully at your futile precautions.

Pelham March 4*th* 1869

Dear Mr Gray,
    I was very glad to get your letter yesterday — I supposed that you might meet Lizzie Boott often, & that she would tell you how I was, as she has been a very constant correspondent, since I have been ill, & I have sent her weekly bulletins concerning myself. And then you know that I told you that as soon as I was

---

[26] Gray had founded and at this time edited the *American Law Review*. The issue for July 1869 contains a brief anonymous notice of Myra Bradwell's *Public Laws of the State of Illinois, passed . . . 1869* (3:755). For information on Bradwell, who sought recognition by the Illinois Bar in 1870, see M[ary] A. L[ivermore], "Mrs. Myra Bradwell," *Woman's Journal*, 1 (8 Jan. 1870), 5.

well again, I would give you a little
holiday — So I kept my word — but I
might have kept my promise and still
given myself the pleasure of writing
to you, when I got ill again after
about a ten days' triumph — only I
thought that as I had no good news to
tell, I would n't write at all — I
thought that illness even was hardly
a good enough excuse for behaving
like a baby, when one had reached the
advanced age of twenty-three — and at
all events, I could not quite
reconcile it to my conscience, that
you, an unprotected man, having done
nothing to deserve such treatment at
my hands, should be the victim — fine
sentiment, wasn't it? Please give me
the credit for it. Well, "to make a
long story short" as Hannah says, I
caught a cold, & it went to the weak
spot, & I had another slight attack
of hemorrhage, but I took the
necessary steps at once, & stayed in
bed & did n't speak for five or six
days, & then it stopped, & I felt
better than I had at all, since I was
first taken ill. This last illness
did n't amount to much, and I did n't
mind it at all — but I began to get
very tired of the constant
confinement to my bedroom, and they
promised me to take me to town as
soon as I was well enough, and
perhaps to the opera. This of course
would have been a wild excitement for
me, and I had charming little plans
of music by day & by night, for a
week, which I meant to spend with Mrs
Griswold. Accordingly a cavalcade
set out from here on Monday —
consisting of myself, escorted by my
sisters and friends, who were to see
me safely installed in my new
quarters & leave me — I arrived,
bundled up, at Mrs Griswold's, & had
begun to consider myself already as
fairly emancipated from invalidism &
nursing — & I was discussing, with Mr

. . . . Well, "to make a long
story short," as Hannah (her old
nurse)[27] says, I caught a cold, and
it went to the weak spot, and I had
another slight attack of
hemorrhage; but I took the
necessary steps at once, stayed in
bed and didn't speak for six days,
and then it stopped and I felt
better than I had at all since I
was first taken ill.

But I began to tire so of
such constant confinement to my
room that they promised to take me
to town as soon as I was well
enough, and perhaps to the Opera.
This of course
would have been a wild excitement
for me, and I had charming little
plans of music by day and by night,
for a week, which I meant to spend
with Mrs. Griswold. Accordingly a
cavalcade set out from here on
Monday, consisting of myself
escorted by sisters and friends,
who were to see me safely installed
in my new quarters and leave me. I
arrived, bundled up, at Mrs.
Griswold's, and had begun to
consider myself already quite
emancipated from bondage—so that

[27] James's parenthetical explanation.

Emmet the propriety of my going that evening to hear Faust, which was but the beginning of the mad career upon which I proposed to rush headlong — when Dr Bassett arrived, who is the medical man, that I had meant to consult, *incidentally*, between the pauses in the music, during my stay there. The first thing he said was, "What are you doing here?" — Go directly back to the place you came from, & don't come to the city again till warm weather comes. And as for

music, you must n't hear it or even think of it for two months." This was pleasant, but there was nothing to be done, but obey — which I did a few hours later with my trunk which had not been unpacked, and with my immediate plan of life somewhat limited. I say my *immediate* plan because my permanent plan of life was by no means curtailed, but on the contrary expanded & varied in a manner I had not even dared to hope — This came from what the Doctor said subsequently, when he had examined my lungs, that is to say, after he had laid his head affectionately first on one of my shoulders & then on the other, and there kept it solemnly for about ten [?] minutes, in a way that was irresistibly ludicrous, especially with Kitty as spectator. This, I am aware, is a highly indecorous, not to say frivolous view to take of it, but I am proud to say that I controlled my desire to laugh, and awaited his verdict with becoming gravity. He said my lungs were *sound* — that he could not detect the slightest evidences of disease, and that the hemorrhage could not have come from the lung itself, but from the membraneous lining of the lungs and throat — whatever that may be — I know not, but I suppose he does. At all events he gave me to understand that

I was discussing with my brother-in-law the propriety of my going that evening to hear Faust, this but the beginning of a mad career on which I proposed to rush headlong—when Dr. Bassett arrived, who is the medical man that I had meant to consult during my stay *incidentally* and between the pauses in the music. The first thing he said was: "What are you doing here? Go directly back to the place you came from and don't come up again till the warm weather. As for music, you mustn't hear of it or even think of it for two months." This was pleasant, but there was nothing to be done but obey; which I did a few hours later, with my trunk still unpacked and my immediate plan of life somewhat limited.

I say my immediate plan because my permanent found itself by no means curtailed, but on the contrary expanded and varied in a manner I had not even dared to hope. This came from what Dr. B. said subsequently, when he had examined my lungs; that is to say after he had laid his head affectionately first under one of my shoulders and then the other, and there kept it solemnly for about ten minutes, in a way that was irresistibly ludicrous, especially with Kitty as spectator.

His verdict was that my lungs were *sound*, that he couldn't detect the least evidence of disease, and that hemorrhage couldn't have come from the lung itself, but from their membraneous lining, and that of the throat, whatever this may be. So he gave me to understand that I have as sound a pair of lungs at

I had as sound a pair of lungs, at present, as the next person — in fact from what he said, one would have thought them a pair that a prize-fighter might covet. At the same time he sent me flying back to the country, with orders not to get excited, nor to listen to music, nor to speak to anybody I care about, nor to do anything in short that the unregenerate nature longs for. This struck my untutored mind as somewhat inconsistent, and I ventured a gentle remonstrance, which however was not even listened to, and I was ignominiously thrust into a car and borne back to Pelham. The problem still bothers me — Either sound lungs are a very dangerous thing to possess, or there is a foul conspiracy on foot to oppress me — But I cling to the consoling thought of my matchless lungs — & this obliterates my present sufferings.

Pray *why* do you overwork yourself? Is it for the love of *drudging* for its own sake, or have you the starving wife & bare-footed children in view? — I suspect it must be the latter which imparts a magical glow to your intellect. I think it is but natural that you should wish to be able to hold out hopes to that young person to whom you talked an hour and a half the other night, that you would not eventually allow her to starve, if you could help it.   Harry came to see me before he sailed — I am very glad that he has gone, although I don't expect to see him again in a good many years. I do not think he will come back for a long time. I hope it will do him good, & that he will enjoy himself, which he has n't done for several years, I think. I have n't read all of Faust — but I think I know the scenes you call divine, at least I know some that are exquisite. But I don't know the play well enough to judge of Faust's

present as the next person; in fact from what he said one would have thought them a pair that a prize-fighter might covet. At the same time he sent me flying back to the country, with orders not to get excited, nor to listen to music, nor to speak with anybody I care for, nor to do anything in short that the unregenerate nature longs for. This struck my untutored mind as somewhat inconsistent, and I ventured a gentle remonstrance, which however was not even listened to, and I was ignominiously thrust into a car and borne back to Pelham. The problem still bothers me: either sound lungs are a very dangerous thing to have, or there is a foul conspiracy on foot to oppress me. Still, I cling to the consoling thought of my matchless lungs, and this obliterates my present sufferings.

        Harry came to see me before he sailed for Europe; I'm very glad he has gone, though I don't expect to see him again for a good many years. I don't think he will come back for a long time, and I hope it will do him good and that he will enjoy himself—which he hasn't done for several years. I haven't read all of Faust, but I think I know the scenes you call divine— at least I know some that are exquisite.

character — Why do you speak so disparagingly of King David, whom I always had a weakness for? Think how charming and loveable a person he must have been — poet, musician & so much else combined — with however their attendant imperfections. I don't think I should care to have been Mrs D. exactly. I am possessed with an overpowering admiration and affection for George Eliot. I don't know why it has so suddenly come over me, but everything I see of hers now-a-days makes me feel a deeper interest in her. I should love to see her — & I hope Harry will — I told him to give my love to her. Do you like her too? I don't remember ever hearing you speak of her. Goodbye. I wish that conventionality would invent some other way of ending a letter than "Yours truly." I am so tired of it, & as one says it to one's shoe-maker it is rather more complimentary to one's friend to dispense with it altogether & sign one's name abruptly, after the manner of Ellen Emerson & other free Boston citizens. But I am a slave to conventionality and therefore again sign myself Yours truly Mary Temple — But conceived with somewhat more of warmth than I would say it to my shoemaker!

But why do you speak so disparagingly of King David, whom I always had a weakness for? Think how charming and lovable a person he must have been, poet, musician and so much else combined—with however their attendant imperfections. I don't think I should have cared to be *Queen* David exactly. I am possessed with an overpowering admiration and affection for George Eliot. I don't know why this has so suddenly come over me, but everything I look at of hers nowadays makes me take a deeper interest in her. I should love to see her, and I hope Harry will; I asked him to give my love to her. But I don't remember ever to have heard *you* speak of her. Good-bye. I wish conventionality would invent some other way of ending a letter than "yours truly"; I am so tired of it, and as one says it to one's shoemaker it would be rather more complimentary to one's friends to dispense with it altogether and just sign one's name without anything, after the manner of Miss Emerson and other free Boston citizens. But I am a slave to conventionality, and after all *am* yours truly . . . .

Hypothetical Discourse as Ficelle in *The Golden Bowl*

Arlene Young

WHILE Henry James assessed *The Ambassadors* as "frankly, quite the best, 'all round,' of" his "productions,"[1] there can nevertheless be little doubt that in *The Golden Bowl* he achieves an unprecedented refinement of his art. In no other novel in his *oeuvre*, perhaps in all of literature, does the reader have a greater sense of intimacy both with the world and the events contained within the novel, and with the workings of the characters' minds. But at the same time, the reader is confounded, caught in the same quagmire of indeterminacy in which the characters struggle. James produces this delicate balance of comprehension and confusion largely through his use of a unique device which could best be termed *hypothetical discourse*: dialogues or monologues which are presented as quoted speech on the page, though not in fact (or fiction) ever verbalized. This device is similar to what Carren Kaston terms "imagined speech," which she identifies as an "instrument" used by Maggie to discharge her suppressed emotions. Kaston thus limits the location of "imagined speech" to Maggie's consciousness. She also limits its function to Maggie's imaginative reshaping of her world through "the expression of emotions that must be given some sort of reality in order for Maggie to reinvent herself and her fiction, but also, for success, must stop safely short of the explosive definiteness of actual speech."[2] The concept of hypothetical discourse is greater in its scope and significance, allowing

[1] "Preface to *The Ambassadors*," in *The Art of the Novel*, introd. Richard P. Blackmur (New York: Scribner's, 1934), p. 309. I wish to acknowledge the assistance of the Social Sciences and Humanities Research Council of Canada during the period in which this article was written.

[2] *Imagination and Desire in the Novels of Henry James* (New Brunswick: Rutgers Univ. Press, 1984), p. 140.

American Literature, Volume 61, Number 3, October 1989. Copyright © 1989 by the Duke University Press. CCC 0002-9831/89/$1.50.

a more comprehensive analysis of the device as James used it. For hypothetical discourse has an important place not only in the development of Maggie but also in the development of all the major characters in the novel. And hypothetical discourse proves to be provocatively elusive of analysis because, contrary to Kaston's model, specific examples cannot readily be located in any single consciousness. Hypothetical discourse is nevertheless potentially illuminating, for it also provides subtle direction for the interpretation of the world and the people of the novel, and it indeed functions in *The Golden Bowl*, in conjunction with the Assinghams, as a ficelle embedded in the narrative.

The extensive refinement of an art as complex as Jamesian narration does not produce a novel notable for its transparency. On the contrary, reading *The Golden Bowl* can be a demanding, even a daunting task. In his "Preface" to the New York edition of this novel, however, James describes his own experience of re-reading his fiction, and his response in particular to the "indirect and oblique view" of the "presented action" in his late novels:

To re-read in their order my final things, all of comparatively recent date, has been to become aware of my putting the process through, for the latter end of my series (as well as, throughout, for most of its later constituents) quite in the same terms as the apparent and actual, the contemporary terms; to become aware in other words that the march of my present attention coincides sufficiently with the march of my original expression; that my apprehension fits, more concretely stated, without an effort or a struggle, certainly without bewilderment or anguish, into the innumerable places prepared for it. As the historian of the matter sees and speaks, so my intelligence of it, as a reader, meets him halfway, passive, receptive, appreciative, often even grateful; unconscious, quite blissfully, of any bar to intercourse, any disparity of sense between us. Into his very footprints the responsive, the imaginative steps of the docile reader that I consentingly become for him all comfortably sink; his vision, superimposed on my own as an image in cut paper is applied to a sharp shadow on a wall, matches, at every point, without excess or deficiency.[3]

Surely no reader before or since has found reading *The Golden Bowl* as blissfully straightforward a process as did its author. But then James, being intelligent, attentive, and receptive, was

---

[3] "Preface to *The Golden Bowl*," in *The Art of the Novel*, pp. 327, 335–36.

undoubtedly precisely the kind of reader he desired to have
for his novels; it seems doubtful that he truly valued a passive
reader, although he does use that adjective to describe himself
as reader in the "Preface." Indeed, he rules out the possibility of
a completely passive experience with the concept of the reader
meeting the narrator halfway. The reader plays a significant role
in the creation of the fictional vision; he must be "responsive"
and "imaginative." A successful and satisfying reading of the
novel then results in a vision that coincides "at every point" with
that of the narrator.

That this process of reading is complex rather than mindless
James makes clear with the metaphor of the paper image and
the shadow. The visions of the narrator and the reader must
develop together, finally matching; the narrator does not simply
impose one. And that vision is not a precise representation, a
picture with vivid colors and explicit details. It is, rather, a paper
image superimposed on "a sharp shadow," at once as distinct and
yet indeterminate as the reality it attempts to simulate. But the
narrator, James implies, provides guidelines, a well-marked path
to follow. In *The Golden Bowl* such guidance is in part provided
by James's customary use of the ficelle, here in the person of
Fanny Assingham, and it is augmented by the treacherously
complex device of hypothetical discourse.

As Sister M. Corona Sharp notes, Fanny's role in *The Golden
Bowl* is more active and significant than that of ficelles in James's
earlier fiction.[4] Fanny plays a larger part than did Henrietta
Stackpole in *The Portrait of a Lady* or Maria Gostrey in *The Ambassadors*, not only functioning as confidante, advisor, and commentator at various places in the story, but also agonizing over
the implications and possible influence of her position within
the unfolding drama. Fanny dominates entire chapters of Book
First, including the final two, thus making her interpretation of
the relationships among the Ververs and the Prince and Princess
the last thing the reader carries with him as the narrative moves
into Maggie's consciousness in the second section of the novel.
She is given similar pride of place in chapter 31, which, though
brief, occurs almost at the center of Book Second. But while

---

[4] *The Confidante in Henry James: Evolution and Moral Value of a Fictive Character*
(Notre Dame, Ind.: Univ. of Notre Dame Press, 1963), p. 224.

Fanny is thus granted an obviously privileged position within the narrative structure, she is nevertheless presented as a distinctly limited character. Even her role as ficelle is one that is lodged less in herself than in her interactions with her husband as they indulge in *"her* favourite game": sitting up late "to discuss those situations in which her finer consciousness abounded."[5] She thus casts a somewhat oblique light on the story, rather than being, as James describes Maria Gostrey, "an enrolled, a direct, aid to lucidity."[6] Although she is frequently the agent for disclosing definite information about other characters, such as the existence of a prior relationship between Charlotte and the Prince or Maggie's discovery of the golden bowl and its implications, Fanny is most typically engaged in devising hypothetical explanations for the actions of Maggie, Adam, Amerigo, and Charlotte. Her extensive discussions with her husband allow her to create, consider, and discard endless possibilities, concurrently allowing the reader to test his own hypotheses against them.

The Assinghams' deliberations also contain both explicit and implicit warnings to the reader trying to comprehend the relationships among the four main characters, cautions regarding the efficacy or wisdom of seeking to explain the motivations of others on the basis of appearances. These signals are typically embodied in Bob Assingham's questions and comments to his wife. "What's the good of asking yourself if you know you don't know?" he, for example, demands of her (p. 49). His frustration with her confusing and often contradictory suppositions also prompts him to characterize her attempts at interpretation as a futile game. "Must you do it in three guesses," he asks, "—like forfeits on Christmas eve?" (p. 206). And while Bob's skepticism seems to be based largely on intellectual obtuseness, Fanny's will to understand the nature of Adam's and Maggie's marriages does not result in enlightenment for either the Assinghams or the reader. As Ora Segal points out, Fanny thus "contributes . . . to the effects of moral complexity and ambiguity";[7] her hy-

[5] *The Golden Bowl*, ed. Virginia Llewellyn Smith (Oxford: Oxford Univ. Press, 1983), p. 48. Subsequent references to *The Golden Bowl* are from this edition and are given in the text by page numbers.

[6] "Preface to *The Ambassadors*," in *The Art of the Novel*, p. 322.

[7] *The Lucid Reflector: The Observer in Henry James' Fiction* (New Haven: Yale Univ. Press, 1969), p. 198.

potheses can neither be espoused nor rejected out of hand, for she is neither consistently right nor consistently wrong. Fanny herself acknowledges as much to her dispirited husband: "What haven't you, love, said in your time?" he wants to know. "So many things, no doubt," she replies, "that they make a chance for my having once or twice spoken the truth" (p. 282). Accordingly, both Fanny's conclusions and her method are called into question. Her efforts to comprehend the inner meaning of the circumstances she can only observe nevertheless serve as a tentative model, complete with intrinsic cautionary signals, for the reader's attempt to interpret the novel.

Ruth Yeazell suggests that the relationship between Fanny and Bob is a parody of that between Henry James, as artist, and William James, whose literal-minded criticism so frustrated and annoyed his brother.[8] Similarly, the Assinghams can be seen as a model for the relationship between the narrator and the reader. Fanny produces fictions, hypothetical explanations of events, which Bob tests with his queries; the narrator produces fiction, the story he relates, which the reader probes for meaning. But, since the reader of James's fiction must be prepared to meet the narrator halfway, the process of interpretation does not end here. Since so much of the story of *The Golden Bowl* takes place off-stage or between the lines of the narrative, the roles of reader and narrator must at times be virtually inverted. The reader must produce the fiction, in the form of assumptions about the characters' actions or motives which remain unspecified in the narrative, assumptions which then must be tested by, or squared by, the text; the "sharp shadow" on the "wall," in other words, must be made to match the paper image. Or, to use one of the dominant metaphors of the novel, and the one used by Bob to characterize Fanny's efforts to decipher the lives of others, the narrator and the reader together play the game of deciphering the meaning of the text; a game as serious and strenuous as any of the dangerous games played out by the fictional characters within the story. Once the model is established, Fanny's hypothetical explanations gradually give way to hypothetical discourse, which usually takes place within the consciousness of one of the four main characters, and which appears to function in

---

[8] "The New 'Arithmetic' of Henry James," *Criticism*, 16 (1974), 109–19.

a way analogous to Fanny's speculations by suggesting possible motives or explanations for the characters' actions.

Almost all of the hypothetical discourse in *The Golden Bowl* occurs in Book Second, and in part functions as a means of suggesting other characters' points of view in a section of the narrative which takes place almost exclusively within Maggie's consciousness. This type of discourse is introduced in Book First, however, in conjunction with other forms of quoted speech which seem to be modulating away from true direct tagged discourse, but which are not indirect discourse because they are bracketed by quotation marks. This discourse, not part of any direct dialogue, takes place within the consciousness of one of the characters and tends to be suggestive rather than precise. The description of Charlotte's reaction to the owner of the Blooms-bury shop that houses the golden bowl, for example, includes what initially appears to be a direct statement of her assessment of him: "'He likes his things—he loves them,' she was to say" (p. 79). The sharp shift in tense in the tag, however, indicates that her words denote a later articulation of her appraisal of the shopman, which may or may not strictly coincide with her immediate response.

An even more problematic passage occurs in a section of the narrative taking place within Adam Verver's consciousness as he contemplates Mrs. Rance's attitude toward him: "his visitor said, or as good as said, 'I'm restrained, you see, because of Mr Rance, and also because I'm proud and refined; but if it *wasn't* for Mr Rance and for my refinement and my pride!'" (p. 112). This deceptively simple statement fairly bristles, as James might say, with significance. It presents many of the same problems of interpretation as do the longer and more complex examples of hypothetical discourse that occur in Book Second. The introduction of Mrs. Rance's putative remark with "his visitor said, or as good as said" implies that these are not her exact words, but there is no indication of how she communicates the impression embodied in the statement. It could be a paraphrase of an actual statement or statements made by Mrs. Rance, or it could be an interpretation of her attitudes, actions, or body language. In either case, the likelihood of subjective coloring of the perceptions by the interpreter produces an unresolvable indeterminacy, making it impossible to ascertain whether accountability for the

impression Mrs. Rance produces resides more with her than
with her observer. Indeed, even the identity of the interpreter
of her apparent communication is open to question, for while
the interpretation seems to belong to Adam, there is nothing
to indicate that it could not be assigned to the narrator or to a
combination of the narrator and Adam.

One of the effects of hypothetical discourse is an emphasis on
the high level of introspection of the characters. They appear to
do silently what Fanny does orally; they interpret other people's
reactions, formulate speeches they never utter, or consider mentally the most effective ways to express themselves when they
do speak. Adam, for example, presents his proposal of marriage
to Charlotte not in a flurry of spontaneous passion, but "quite
as he had felt he must in thinking it out in advance" (p. 161).
Moreover, as Seymour Chatman points out, the narrator's assumption of "the power to report what a character did *not* in
fact think or say" constitutes an "announcement of deeper than
ordinary plunges into the mind."[9] But for the narrator of *The
Golden Bowl*, this power does not necessarily confer the "superior knowledge" that Chatman claims for the narrators of the
passages he examines by Nathaniel Hawthorne and D. H. Lawrence. Even the relatively brief and straightforward examples
of hypothetical discourse that occur in Book First balance pre-
cariously between extraordinary insight into the workings of a
character's mind and dangerously bold but unfounded assumptions on the part of the narrator. For example, when Charlotte
attempts to assuage her conscience over her relationship with the
Prince by insisting that they had been forced "against their will
into a relation of mutual close contact that they had done everything to avoid" (p. 211), the narrator uses hypothetical discourse
to suggest a mental response in Amerigo at variance with the
acquiescence apparently indicated by his silence: "If her friend
had blurted or bungled he would have said, in his simplicity,
'Did we do "everything to avoid" it when we faced your remarkable marriage?'—quite handsomely of course using the plural,
taking his share of the case" (p. 212). Here again, it is difficult to
determine the assignability of the quoted non-statement or of the
judgments implied by the words "blurted," "bungled," and the

[9] *Story and Discourse: Narrative Structure in Fiction and Film* (Ithaca: Cornell Univ.
Press, 1978), pp. 225–26.

ironic "handsomely." To what extent is the narrator speculating about Amerigo's thoughts and to what extent simply reporting?

As the narrative moves into Book Second, the hypothetical discourse proliferates, and there is a tendency for it to become lengthy, convoluted, and increasingly difficult to assign to either a specific character or the narrator. There is also an increase in relatively straightforward examples of inner thought, such as Maggie's agonized contemplation of the effects on their lives of Adam's marriage to Charlotte: "She groaned to herself, . . . '*Why* did he marry? ah, why *did* he?'" (p. 357). This type of direct tagged discourse is easily assignable to the character, but, by providing further examples of the characters' introspective tendencies, it adds to the pervading sense of indeterminacy in the narrative. More complex are instances of hypothetical discourse which are fairly clearly speculative on the part of the narrator. These passages are similar to the one in which Amerigo does not openly question Charlotte's contention that they did "everything to avoid" their intimate relationship, but are less ambiguous about the narrator's role. Charlotte's hypothetical response to Maggie's references to Adam's "benevolence," for example, is much more clearly an instance of speculation by the narrator: "'But, my poor child,' Charlotte might under this pressure have been on the point of replying, 'that's the way nice people *are*, all round—so that why should one be surprised about it? We're all nice together—as why shouldn't we be?'" (p. 327). The narrator assumes a similar conjectural stance in assessing the responses of Amerigo, Fanny, and Adam to Charlotte and Maggie's embrace after the card party at Fawns:

They had evidently looked, the two young wives, like a pair of women "making up" effusively, as women were supposed to do, especially when approved fools, after a broil; but taking note of the reconciliation would imply, on her father's part, on Amerigo's, and on Fanny Assingham's, some proportionate vision of the grounds of their difference. There had been something, there had been but too much, in the incident, for each observer; yet there was nothing anyone could have said without seeming essentially to say: "See, see, the dear things —their quarrel's blissfully over!" "Our quarrel? What quarrel?" the dear things themselves would necessarily, in that case, have demanded; and the wits of the others would thus have been called upon for some agility of exercise. (P. 500)

In these passages, the function of the hypothetical discourse
closely resembles Fanny's earlier attempts to interpret events.
The narrator uses the discourse to suggest attitudes and feelings
in the characters, thus implicitly producing hypotheses, which,
like Fanny's, the reader must test.

This narrative speculation through hypothetical discourse does
more than present possible interpretations of the characters'
actions and responses, however; it also suggests the limitations of
the narrator's perception. He may at times be able to plumb the
depths of his characters' minds, as in Chatman's model; he may
be able to hear Maggie's inner groan. But at other times he can
only speculate about the characters' deepest feelings, he cannot
know them for certain. At the same time, hypothetical discourse
suggests the limitations of the characters' perception. These putative inner thoughts, expressed as verbal reactions, may indeed
represent the entire depth of response possible in characters who
are unable or unwilling to analyze the feelings that trigger the
words. Such an analysis would, like the articulation of their unspoken responses, have "called upon [their wits] for some agility
of exercise." These inherent problems of interpretation for the
reader are further complicated by the illusion of reality produced
by the use of the form of direct quotation rather than that of
free indirect discourse, thus giving a semblance of precision and
authenticity to what is actually vague and indeterminate. This
additional apparent barrier to an understanding of the narrative
ultimately works to illuminate its major theme: the limitations of
language and speech to express reality and the depths of human
experience.

The hermeneutic challenge to the reader climaxes in the numerous long and complex passages of hypothetical discourse that
occur in Book Second. These passages, typically occurring at
points of crisis in the story and expressing emotional turmoil
within a major character, are crucial to an understanding of the
novel. They present even greater problems of assignability than
the shorter passages of hypothetical discourse, however; some
appear to be narrative speculation about a character's feelings,
others a more complex amalgam of narrative interpretation of
one character's speculation about another character's responses.
The first of these passages occurs in the first chapter of Book
Second, as Maggie struggles to comprehend her situation *vis-
à-vis* her husband, her father, and her stepmother:

" 'Why, why' have I made this evening such a point of our not all dining together? Well, because I've all day been so wanting you alone that I finally couldn't bear it, and that there didn't seem any great reason why I should try to. *That* came to me—funny as it may at first sound, with all the things we've so wonderfully got into the way of bearing for each other. You've seemed these last days—I don't know what: more absent than ever before, too absent for us merely to go on so. It's all very well, and I perfectly see how beautiful it is, all round; but there comes a day when something snaps, when the full cup, filled to the very brim, begins to flow over. That's what has happened to my need of you—the cup, all day, has been too full to carry. So here I am with it, spilling it over you—and just for the reason that is the reason of my life. After all, I've scarcely to explain that I'm as much in love with you now as the first hour; except that there are some hours— which I know when they come, because they frighten me—that show me I'm even more so. They come of themselves—and, ah, they've been coming! After all, after all—!" Some such words as those were what *didn't* ring out, yet it was as if even the unuttered sound had been quenched here in its own quaver. It was where utterance would have broken down by its very weight if he [Amerigo] had let it get so far. Without that extremity, at the end of a moment, he had taken in what he needed to take—that his wife was *testifying*, that she adored and missed and desired him. "After all, after all," since she put it so, she was right. That was what he had to respond to; that was what, from the moment that, as has been said, he "saw," he had to treat as the most pertinent thing possible. He held her close and long, in expression of their personal reunion—this, obviously, was one way of doing so. (Pp. 310–11)

This passage initially appears to be direct speech, enclosed, as it is, in quotation marks and characterized by features of oral speech, such as emphasis on certain words (indicated by italics) and pauses or hesitations (indicated by dashes). However, as the narrator points out, these words are never spoken, and the reader is left to ponder their meaning in the text. The verisimilitude of the speech, its close approximation to spoken language, might suggest that Maggie has mentally formulated the words but does not speak them. But the narrator's statement that not necessarily *those* words but possibly similar ones, "some such words as those," were not spoken, suggests that Maggie could have formulated those words, or other words, or no words at all. There is finally no indication of who has formulated the words within the quotation marks, or words like them. It could have been Maggie, it could have been the narrator's interpretation of Maggie's unarticulated feelings, or it could be Amerigo's interpretation of Maggie's unspoken communication to him. For, speechless as she remains, Maggie does communicate and communicate powerfully with her husband in this passage.

Maggie's propensity for mute communication is also illustrated in a scene in Book First as she and others of the party visiting Fawns come upon Adam as he is being accosted by Mrs. Rance. Adam immediately observes "the look in his daughter's eyes—the look with which he *saw* her take in exactly what had occurred in her absence" (pp. 112–13). Adam and Maggie go on silently to acknowledge, while Fanny looks on and silently comprehends all, that he is now vulnerable because Maggie's marriage has left him somewhat isolated. Not only does this scene provide a slightly less complex model for the same kind of process later represented through hypothetical discourse; it is also followed by a narrative comment which expressly states the limitations and possible distortions of reality engendered by the process of narration itself: "So much mute communication was doubtless, all this time, marvellous, and we may confess to having perhaps read into the scene, prematurely, a critical character that took longer to develop" (p. 114). The even greater power of Maggie's silent message in the passage quoted above is in part indicated by the very necessity of representing it in such a long, realistic but hypothetical speech. So strong is the sense of communication that even the point at which emotion would overcome speech is evident, "where utterance would have broken down by its very weight." And the force of the message asserts itself to Amerigo almost instantly, "at the end of a moment." But at the point at which he comprehends "that his wife was *testifying*," the line between perceived communication and spoken words again breaks down: " 'After all, after all,' since she put it so, she was right." Maggie never did "put it so," at least not in words. Nevertheless, "that was what" Amerigo "had to respond to," the message more comprehensive and moving than the spoken word, appropriately answered not by speech but by an embrace.

Another crucial piece of hypothetical discourse occurs in the scene after Fanny has smashed the golden bowl. Alone together, Maggie and Amerigo must confront not just each other but all the possible implications to their relationship of the broken artifact before them:

"Yes, look, look," she seemed to see him hear her say even while her sounded words were other—"look, look, both at the truth that still survives in that smashed evidence and at the even more remarkable appearance that I'm not such a fool as you supposed me. Look at the possibility that, since I *am* different, there may still be something in it for you—if you're capable of working with me to get that out. Consider of course, as you must, the question of what you may have to surrender, on your side, what price you may have to pay, whom you may have to pay *with*, to set this advantage free; but take in, at any rate, that here *is* something for you if you don't too blindly spoil your chance for it." He went no nearer the damnatory pieces, but he eyed them, from where he stood, with a degree of recognition just visibly less to be dissimulated; all of which represented for her a certain traceable process. And her uttered words, meanwhile, were different enough from those he might have inserted between the lines of her already-spoken. (Pp. 436–37)

The convoluted tag at the beginning of this passage provides some limited guidance as to its assignability. The words seem to be a formulation within Maggie's consciousness, but a close examination of the syntax of the tag casts doubt on this assumption. For the words to be assignable to Maggie, the tag would have to read "she saw him seem to hear her say." As it reads, the tag indicates that Maggie is the object being interpreted, not the subject doing the interpreting. Accordingly, the words appear to be the narrator's formulation of Maggie's assessment of Amerigo's silent response to her. But the accuracy of her supposed assessment is further called into question by the narrator's implicit comment on Amerigo's reaction: "her uttered words, meanwhile, were different enough from those *he* might have inserted between the lines of her already-spoken" (italics mine). This statement suggests that the words that Amerigo might in fact conjecturally attribute to Maggie would be different from those that appear in the passage of hypothetical discourse. The mounting confusion of perceptions, coupled with the image of Maggie eyeing Amerigo while he eyes the broken bowl, produces a sense of sparring antagonists cautiously maneuvering while at the same time trying to anticipate each other's lines of attack and defense.

Curiously, while the unspoken words are at least tentatively assignable, the ambiguity of this passage is far greater than that of the previous one, in which the assignability is completely elusive; and the silent communication, so forceful in Maggie's unspoken "After all, after all," here seems to founder. Thus, the slight increase in the technical precision of language in the last passage paradoxically produces a significant increase in indeterminacy. Moreover, Maggie's spoken words are not preceded by a tag, but by a reference to her uttered words being different from those Amerigo might have attributed to her, which creates some uncertainty as to whether the quoted speech that follows are her "uttered words" or "those he might have inserted between the lines of her already-spoken." The tag does not appear until the final sentence of the speech: " 'In that case,' Maggie wound up, 'we can easily take the pieces [of the golden bowl] with us to Fawns' " (p. 437). The tag, "Maggie wound up," is absolutely unequivocal. And yet the ultimate effect of the entire passage is one of such perfect indeterminacy that the reader is left doubting the words he reads, unsure, finally, of what words were indeed uttered and whose words they were. Was a material Maggie winding up uttered words, or was Amerigo's image of Maggie winding up the words that he ascribed to her consciousness?

The true insignificance of words, their incapacity to express adequately the greatest depths of human experience, becomes clear in the penultimate scene at Fawns, as Charlotte conducts a group of friends on a tour of the gallery while Adam and Maggie look on. As Charlotte gives her commentary on the *objets d'art* her visitors have come to admire, Adam and Maggie hear something quite distinct from the words Charlotte speaks:

Maggie meanwhile, at the window, knew the strangest thing to be happening: she had turned suddenly to crying, or was at least on the point of it—the lighted square before her all blurred and dim. The high voice went on; its quaver was doubtless for conscious ears only, but there were verily thirty seconds during which it sounded, for our young woman, like the shriek of a soul in pain. Kept up a minute longer it would break and collapse—so that Maggie felt herself, the next thing, turn with a start to her father. "Can't she be stopped? Hasn't she done it *enough*?"—some such question as that she let herself ask him to suppose in her. Then it was that, across half the gallery—for he had not moved from where she had first seen him—he struck her as confessing, with strange tears in his own eyes, to sharp identity of emotion. "Poor thing, poor thing"—it reached straight—*"isn't* she, for one's credit, on the swagger?" After which, as, held thus together they had still another strained minute, the shame, the pity, the better knowledge, the smothered protest, the divined anguish even, so overcame him that, blushing to his eyes, he turned short away. (Pp. 511–12)

Charlotte's actual words constitute what is in effect a set speech for the house tour: "The largest of the three pieces has the rare peculiarity that the garlands, looped round it, which, as you see, are the finest possible *vieux Saxe*, are not of the same origin or period, or even, wonderful as they are, of a taste quite so perfect" (p. 511). The insignificance of this precise and articulate little speech is unmistakable, juxtaposed as it is with the supreme eloquence of Charlotte's unuttered shriek. Her mere words are overwhelmed by the poignancy of her misery and of her helplessness in her assigned and inescapable position within the Verver family and in Maggie's game (here symbolized by her physical position between her husband and stepdaughter as Adam faces Maggie "from an opposite door" across the gallery Charlotte is touring). Accordingly, what Maggie and Adam hear is not Charlotte's words but her pain.

After Charlotte's silent shriek, the exact words assigned to Adam and Maggie's mute communication have but small significance. Again, Maggie's question is presented as an example of what she might have formulated and its precision is further diluted by her mental presentation of it as something Adam will receive as a supposition. The sharpness of their communication derives not from the words in which it is couched but from its other expressive elements: Maggie's initial tears and her start, and Adam's initial immobility followed by his deep blush and subsequent abrupt withdrawal. The distinctness of Maggie's sense of her perception of Adam's response, the "sharp identity of emotion" and the unspoken message that "reached straight," also contributes to the impression of an exchange which is forceful and direct. But while the message is strong, there is finally no way to define it except through its emotional impact, the amalgam of free-floating emotions, "the shame, the pity, the better knowledge, the smothered protest, the divined anguish," which overcome Adam but which could be experienced by any or all—Adam, Maggie, and Charlotte.

The reader gains remarkable insights into the enigmatic characters of *The Golden Bowl* through the device of hypothetical discourse, which allows him to weigh the significance of what they actually say against what they avoid, resist, and are incapable of expressing or what they are afraid to hear. But the reader is also drawn into their indeterminate world and comes to understand Maggie's reluctance "to translate *all* their delicacies into the grossness of discussion" (p. 327), for words so consistently prove inadequate to express their experience. Thus Maggie's unwillingness to hear Amerigo's confession at the end of the novel is not simply the result of cowardice or of good form: "His acknowledgement hung there, too monstrously, at the expense of Charlotte, before whose mastery of the greater style she had just been standing dazzled. All she now knew, accordingly, was that she should be ashamed to listen to the uttered word; all, that is, but that she might dispose of it on the spot for ever." Maggie's shame, rather, must be at the necessarily reductive nature of the uttered word. No confession, whether of guilt or innocence, could possibly express exactly what happened between Charlotte and Amerigo, nor could it justify or explain the pain and confusion experienced by all the characters involved in the various deadly games played out within the novel. The "knowledge" conveyed by such a confession would be not only limited, but limiting, the translation of "all their delicacies into . . . grossness."

The reader is finally brought to the realization not only that words are inadequate to express reality but that reality is unknowable, both in fiction and in life. No amount of personal introspection or of carefully developed analysis can extract the ultimate truth from the experience and motivation of either ourselves or others. What is knowable is only our own imperfect perceptions, which are but partial, misguided, and misjudged. So, too, the characters in *The Golden Bowl* can understand only what they perceive from their limited angles of vision, which in the end leave Amerigo unable to see anything but Maggie, and Maggie, with her eyes buried in his breast, unwilling to see at all. Thus, while Maggie believes she "knows" how to dispose of Amerigo's confession, such knowledge is necessarily limited and fleeting, for the confession will always hang between them, unspoken. The golden bowl is broken.

Index

This index is centered on Henry James (hereinafter HJ). The titles of his writings appear as main entries, and an unqualified entry such as "aggressiveness" or "Southerner, idea of" refers directly to the content of those writings.

Notes on Contributors

Charles R. Anderson (1902–   ). Duke University, 1930–1941; Caroline Donovan Professor of American Literature, Johns Hopkins University, 1941–1969. *Melville in the South Seas* (1939); *Charles Gayarré and Paul Hayne: The Last Literary Cavaliers* (1940); *Rebirth of the Southern Literary Tradition* (1957); *Emily Dickinson's Poetry: Stairway of Surprise* (1960); *The Magic Circle of Walden* (1968); *Person, Place, and Thing in Henry James's Novels* (1977). Edited *Songs of Nothing-Certain: University of Georgia Verse, 1920–1928* (1928); *Journal of a Cruise to the Pacific Ocean, 1842–1844, in the Frigate "United States"* (1937); *Sidney Lanier: Poems and Letters* (1969); *Thoreau's World: Miniatures from His Journal* (1971); *Thoreau's Vision: The Major Essays* (1973). General Editor, *Centennial Edition of the Works of Sidney Lanier*, 10 vols. (1945).

Laurence Barrett (1915–   ). Bowdoin College, 1949–1953; Kalamazoo College, 1953–1978.

Oscar Cargill (1898–1972). New York University, 1925–1966. *Drama and Liturgy* (1930); *Intellectual America: Ideas on the March* (1941); *The Novels of Henry James* (1961); *Toward a Pluralistic Criticism* (1965); *The Publication of Academic Writing* (1966). Edited *American Literature: A Period Anthology* (1933, 1949); *The Social Revolt: American Literature from 1888 to 1914* (1933); *Contemporary Trends: American Literature since 1900* (1949); *Thomas Wolfe at Washington Square* (1954); *The Correspondence of Thomas Wolfe and Homer Andrew Watt* (1954); (with others) *Studies in the English Renaissance Drama* (1959); *O'Neill and His Plays: Four Decades of Criticism* (1961).

Sara deSaussure Davis (1943–   ). University of Alabama, 1973–   . Edited (with Philip D. Beidler) *The Mythologizing of Mark Twain* (1984).

Alfred R. Ferguson (1915–1974). Ohio Wesleyan University, 1947–1966; University of Massachusetts (Boston), 1966–1969, 1972–1974; Ohio State University, 1969–1972. *Edward Rowland Sill: The Twilight Poet* (1955); *The Merrill Checklist of Ralph Waldo Emerson* (1970). Edited *Emerson's "Nature": Origin, Growth, Meaning* (1969, 1979); *Emerson's Essays, First Series* (1979); *Emerson's Essays, Second Series* (1983).

William R. Goetz (1951–   ). University of Texas at Austin, 1977–1984; associated with the law firm of Dorsey & Whitney in Minneapolis, Minn. *Henry James and the Darkest Abyss of Romance* (1986).

Susan M. Griffin (1953–   ). University of Louisville, 1982–   . *The Art of Criticism: Henry James on the Theory and Practice of Fiction* (1986).

Alfred Habegger (1941–   ). University of Kansas, 1966–   . *Gender, Fantasy, and Realism in American Literature* (1982); *Henry James and the "Woman Business"* (1989).

Marie P. Harris

Joyce Tayloe Horrell (1926–1987). University of Maryland, 1965–1967.

Jean Kimball (1923–   ). University of Northern Iowa, 1975–   .

Annette Niemtzow. *Whittier and the Opening of Bryn Mawr College in 1885: A Letter with an Introduction* (1981).

Robert J. Reilly (1925–   ). University of Detroit, 1952–1954, 1957–1987. *Romantic Religion: A Study of Barfield, Lewis, Williams, and Tolkien* (1971); (with James T. Callow) *Guide to American Literature from Emily Dickinson to the Present* (1977).

Hisayoshi Watanabe (1934–   ). Kyoto University, 1963–   . *Henry James no Gengo* [*The Language of Henry James*] (1978); *Yeats* [in Japanese] (1982).

Catherine Cox Wessel

Arlene Young (1948–   ).

Library of Congress Cataloging-in-Publication Data

On Henry James / edited by Louis J. Budd and Edwin H. Cady.
p.   cm.—(The Best from American literature)
Includes index.
ISBN 0–8223–1064–3
1. James, Henry, 1843–1916—Criticism and interpretation.
I. Budd, Louis J.   II. Cady, Edwin Harrison.   III. Series.
PS2124.048   1990
813'.4—DC20   90-37352   CIP